THE HERITAGE OF LIBRARIANSHIP SERIES,
No. 4

THE HERITAGE OF LIBRARIANSHIP SERIES

Michael H. Harris, General Editor

Melvil Dewey
Amherst College
1874

MELVIL DEWEY

His Enduring Presence in Librarianship

edited by
Sarah K. Vann

1978

Libraries Unlimited, Inc.
Littleton, Colo.

LIBRARIES UNLIMITED, INC.
P.O. Box 263
Littleton, Colorado 80160

Library of Congress Cataloging in Publication Data

Dewey, Melvil, 1851-1931.
    Melvil Dewey, his enduring presence in librarian-
ship.

    (The Heritage of librarianship series ; no. 4)
    Bibliography: p. 231
    Includes index.
    1. Dewey, Melvil, 1851-1931. 2. Dewey, Melvil,
1851-1931--Bibliography. 3. Librarians--United
States--Biography. 4. Libraries--United States--
Collected works. 5. Library science--Collected
works. I. Vann, Sarah K., 1916-   II. Title.
III. Series.
Z720.D5A3   020'.92'4 [B]   77-21852

ISBN 0-87287-134-7

To

Godfrey Dewey (1887-1977), son of Melvil Dewey

and

Deo B. Colburn,
protege and confidant of Melvil Dewey

FOREWORD

On the afternoon of October 6, 1876, the small group of librarians who had attended what was to be marked in history as the first meeting of the American Library Association were invited to sign the official register as founding members of the ALA. In a step that was to prove prophetic of his future fame, Melvil Dewey, one of the principal organizers of the Philadelphia meeting and the youngest member present, moved quickly in front of his older and better-known colleagues, picked up the pen, and signed: "Number One, Melvil Dewey."

Today, Melvil Dewey remains the best known member of the modern librarian's pantheon of notables, though he is not well understood. While most librarians know very little about the history of the profession in America, almost all of them recognize Dewey's name and can recite a list of his major achievements: the founding of the American Library Association; the creation of the Dewey Decimal Classification; the establishment of the first library school in America; and the founding of the *Library Journal*. These contributions certainly qualify Dewey as one of the nation's most influential librarians, but contemporary librarians seem to be at least as interested in other aspects of his life: his flamboyant personality; his fondness for women; his charismatic leadership; his reputation as an anti-Semite; and his brash disdain for the library establishment.

Given Dewey's appeal to the profession (clearly evident in the fact that his face was chosen to adorn the T-shirts sold as a memento of the Association's 100th anniversary), it is at first puzzling to find that he has not yet been the subject of a full-length and scholarly biography. However, anyone who has investigated the problem in any depth can readily explain the reasons. First, Dewey was indeed an enormously influential figure, involved in a range of efforts that would overwhelm even the most active of modern librarians. Not only was he the creator of the widely used Dewey Decimal Classification, the founder of the country's first library school, a central figure in the early years of ALA, and a founder of *Library Journal*; but he was at given times in his career considered the country's leading advocate of school library services, the leading state librarian in America, one of the two or three most prominent academic librarians in the nineteenth century, and a leading library entrepreneur.

Furthermore, while involved in this amazing range of groundbreaking activities, Dewey was also a central figure in a number of other social movements that, during his years of leadership, numbered thousands of adherents. Among these activities are the American Metric Bureau, the Spelling Reform Association, and his Lake Placid Club. Simply chronicling these many activities has proven to be a formidable task for historians, which explains the emphasis to date on one or more aspects of Dewey's activities (such as the classification scheme or his efforts as a library educator) rather than any attempt at a full-length biography of the man.

But the enormous range of Dewey's activities only partly explains the absence of a full-length interpretive study. Dewey's controversial and complex nature provides another obstacle to such a study. His almost mystical influence over his followers, the unremitting hatred evidenced toward him by his enemies, the charges against him of anti-Semitism, his strange and controversial involvement with (and influence over) women, and his ruthless and often questionable entrepreneurial schemes, all contribute to his reputation as one of the most complex figures in the history of librarianship.

Finally, Dewey himself compounded the problems of biographers by keeping meticulous records of his enormous correspondence, but doing so in his peculiar shorthand notations. Although the determined historian can decipher these notes, doing so vastly increases the effort required to study Dewey's life. How much easier to study a subject who left a smaller, more compact legacy of manuscript materials and who wrote in a clear and legible hand.

Given Dewey's multitudinous activities, his widespread influence, his complex and controversial personality, and voluminous and difficult-to-decipher papers, the lack of a definitive biographical study of the man is not surprising. And yet he is clearly the central figure in the story of the evolution of the American library profession during its fledgling years. Until Dewey's complex and far-reaching contribution is interpreted, we simply will not have a clear understanding of this significant period in American library history.

This volume in the Heritage of Librarianship Series should contribute to such an understanding. Dr. Sarah Vann, who has written on the history of library education during the Dewey era and who has studied Dewey for many years, presents a concise and articulate interpretation of the man's career. While admittedly not the "definitive" study so badly needed, Dr. Vann's essay serves to point out numerous avenues needing further exploration. Equally important is her selection of Dewey's most significant and representative writings from the hundreds of contributions he made to library literature over a 50-year period. Here the reader will find Dewey's ideas fully expressed in an easily accessible format, allowing the man to speak for himself. Finally, Dr. Vann's careful and detailed bibliography of works by and about Dewey locates his manuscript collections, arranges chronologically his contributions to the literature, identifies his editorial activities, and provides a complete listing of the many specialized studies on Dewey. This bibliography provides a basic road map for future scholars interested in one of the most significant figures in American library history.

Michael H. Harris
General Editor
March 1977

TABLE OF CONTENTS

PART I. MELVIL DEWEY:
HIS ENDURING PRESENCE IN LIBRARIANSHIP

PART II. SELECTED WRITINGS OF MELVIL DEWEY

PART III. BIBLIOGRAPHY

PREFACE

Melvil Dewey is far better known for his Decimal Classification than for his other contributions to librarianship. Through its program of continuing revision the Classification has become a contentious memorial to him, overshadowing his other accomplishments. While the near universal use of the Classification accounts for this disparity, Dewey's view of the library as an educational agency and his extraordinary success in furthering concepts of service are additional notable contributions to the substance of librarianship.

The range of his interests was enormous, encompassing all aspects of professional activities. He assumed a pivotal role in the events of 1876: the founding of the American Library Association; the issuance of the first journal devoted solely to librarianship, the *American Library Journal* (later *Library Journal*); and the publication of the first edition of his Classification, which introduced subject analysis through a decimal notation for the arrangement of books on the shelves rather than through a fixed numbering of the shelves. Such involvement insured recognition of the man who had accomplished these at the *beginning* of his career. But more was yet to come: his Columbia College days, remembered more for his formalizing of the first library school program (School of Library Economy) and the problems relating thereto than for his organizational skill in unifying library services as Librarian (Director) of the Libraries; his Albany days, where as Secretary of the Regents of the University of the State of New York and Director of the New York State Library, he helped revise the laws of the state pertaining to libraries and re-directed and molded the library program of the entire state. There, too, he insured the continuity of his library school by obtaining its transfer to Albany, where it became known as the New York State Library School.

His purposeful speeches, such as "Librarianship as a Career for College-Bred Women" and "Libraries as Related to the Educational Work of the State" and his testimony at the hearings on "The Condition of the Library of Congress" were catalytic in engendering action that brought vast changes in organization and services in the library world at the state and national levels.

He was a man of, and beyond, his times. His influence extends far beyond the American scene, not because he addressed himself originally to a world audience but because many of his ideas and contributions have universal application. Yet his zealous pursuit of courses and causes to which he was committed either endeared him to or antagonized his contemporaries. Through his achievements and his writings, which vary in quality and in range from factual to futuristic, Dewey emerges as singularly complex, dynamic, influential, and, inevitably, controversial. But appraising his goals and accomplishments in perspective reveals Dewey to be, though not unblemished, ever forward-looking, a proponent of ideas and actions that permeate the library world of the twentieth century.

SKV
March 1977

ACKNOWLEDGMENTS

It is with pleasure that I acknowledge my indebtedness to the following for their contributions to my study of Melvil Dewey and his writings:

To Dr. Godfrey Dewey, who helped me in my continuing effort to learn more of his father's complex personality and achievements and who permitted me free access to his personal papers.

To Deo B. Colburn, confidant of Melvil Dewey, long associated with the Lake Placid Company and Club complex and a director, now retired, of Forest Press, Inc., publisher of the *Dewey Decimal Classification*, for background information and for use of documents in his personal papers.

To Forest Press, Inc., and to its Executive Secretary, John A. Humphry, formerly President of Forest Press and State Librarian, New York, for a sustained interest in my study and for grants made to assist in gathering data, some of which has been used as source material for this book.

To J. Richard Phillips, Special Collections Librarian and Archivist, Amherst College, for his kindness in pursuing my inquiries and for locating documents that have enlivened the account of Dewey's Amherst days.

To Columbia University, Division of Special Collections, Rare Book and Manuscript Library, for permitting me to peruse the "Melvil Dewey Papers" entrusted to its care.

To the New York State Library, Albany, and especially to Mrs. Mildred Ledden, Associate Librarian, who assisted me in my search for data on Dewey's Albany years.

To Dr. Michael H. Harris, editor of "The Heritage of Librarianship Series," for his editorial suggestions within the text and for his additions to the "Notes" which extend further the study of Dewey's involvements and relationships.

And, finally,

To my colleagues and friends who have obtained for me needed information that was available in their universities, who have relayed information concerning Dewey to me, and who, through the years, have been indulgent in recognizing my commitment—yet unfulfilled—to write a biography of Melvil Dewey.

SKV

PART I

MELVIL DEWEY:
HIS ENDURING PRESENCE IN LIBRARIANSHIP

INTRODUCTION

Visionary, quixotic, faddish, he will be
called by many, but his abounding enthusiasm
is a source of inspiration to others and his
unfailing energy carries to success many
things which to others seem impossible.

—Walter S. Biscoe, "As It Was in the Beginning,"
Public Libraries 30 (1925): 78

Melvil (originally Melville Louis Kossuth) Dewey was born on December 10, 1851, in Adams Center, near Watertown, New York.[1] He was the youngest of five children of Eliza (Green) and Joel Dewey,[2] a descendant of Thomas Dewey, who migrated from England to the Massachusetts Bay Colony where, by 1634, he had taken the Freeman's Oath. The young Dewey's parents, displaying their admiration for Louis Kossuth, the Hungarian patriot then being honored in the United States, named their son for him. Dewey later abandoned use of that part of his name and, as of 1875, he omitted the final *le* from the spelling of his first name.[3]

Despite some justifiable concern over his health, Dewey had an enviable physique and bearing.[4] Because of both his height of nearly six feet and his firm, prominent jaw line, he grew increasingly striking in appearance as he matured. His blue-grey eyes, alert and observing, seemed to reflect his inner compulsive energy. His hair and beard or mustache, when worn, were in his youth a rich chestnut in color, so dark that to some it appeared more black than brown.[5] He was quick in thought and movement and he spoke generally in "terse, vigorous, staccato phrases."[6]

The adult life of Dewey may be divided into two major phases: his early and active years in the library profession (1872-1905), and his Lake Placid Club years in the Adirondacks and later in Florida (1895-1931). This essay relates primarily to his formative years and to his contribution to the library profession. Such a limitation in scope in no way diminishes the importance of the Lake Placid Club years but rather recognizes that these years merit separate study, because the milieus and challenges of Dewey's two worlds were distinctly different.

FORMATIVE YEARS

Dewey's formative years were those spent with his family in the village of Adams Center and in Oneida before he entered Amherst College.[7] Through the two biographies, written by Fremont Rider[8] and Grosvenor Dawe,[9] and through the early pages of his "Journal,"[10] Dewey emerges as a dutiful son, a serious and occasionally emotional youth, often brooding, inventorial and self appraising, opinionated and dedicated to causes. Frequent references appear in his "Journal," which he began on his fifteenth birthday, to his attendance at school,[11] to working in his father's Boot and Shoe Store,[12] and to reading.[13]

His education was typical of that available in district schools of the time: terms of varying length, different instructors, and home study. At an early age Dewey taught briefly at Toad Hollow,[14] near his home, and he was awarded a Teaching Certificate in 1867.[15] He later attended the Oneida Seminary where his "standing was given as the best in school"[16] and, in 1869, he received a New York State Regents Certificate.

While there was a religious atmosphere in his home, there was not the "home influence & intimacy,"[18] as Dewey recalled during his Amherst days, because of the reputation of his parents as the "hardest workers in town."[19] He emulated his parents in fulfilling religious duties, however, by being active in several churches in the community. His "Journal" contains expressions of faith, of anxiety, of inner turmoil until at the age of 18 he made a decision that the ministry was not to be his calling.[20]

Dewey's boyhood years were not Spartan, viewed within the context of the times. He had friends of all ages, though he perhaps participated more intensely than they in the local lodge and other village societies such as the Young People's Lyceum.[21] He was energetic and enterprising in earning money from chores, from selling books, and from managing the circulating library which he created.[22] Even with this industry, Dewey reproached himself for idleness, feeling happiest only when "engaged in earnest labor of some kind."[23]

Among the characteristics foreshadowing his adult life was his commitment to causes; he was an activist who determinedly supported views that he considered right. One illustration of this was his early involvement with the Good Templars, a group dedicated to temperance reform.[24] So strong were his convictions that he engaged in a debate on the duty "to discountenance in all honorable [sic] ways, the manufacture, sale and use of tobacco."[25] Another was his ready recognition of the value of the metric system about which, typifying his support of current and often unpopular issues, he wrote as early as 1867.[26] Dewey's acquisitive and enumerative instincts, manifested in various ways throughout his life, were reflected in his annual appraisal, on each birthday, of himself and of his personal possessions. For example, at the age of 18, he carefully noted the titles of 85 books which he owned.[27] His concern for orderly listing is seen also in his plan to arrange and classify systematically everything in his personal collection.

After Dewey's father relinquished his business in 1868, the family moved to Oneida. While there, Dewey explored places of interest, such as the Oneida Community and its library, where he "found quite a number of books" which he wanted to see.[28] He visited also the libraries of Cornell University in Ithaca and of the University of Rochester.[29]

It was in Oneida that Dewey identified the educational world as his "destined place."[30] His wish "to inaugurate a higher education for the masses," tenuous when it was stated in 1869, was to find fulfillment in his support of public libraries.[31] A brief teaching experience at Barnhard's Bay (November 1869-March 1870) strengthened his feeling that being an educator and a reformer was to be his destiny.[32] Recognizing the need to continue his own education, Dewey was in residence at Alfred University, Alfred, New York, for 14 weeks. Though he felt that they had been some of the happiest weeks of his life, he chose to enter Amherst College.[33]

While Dewey's religious inclinations seemed to have had little influence in directing him to Amherst, he found himself in a college permeated with a heritage of religious fervor. Established in 1821, Amherst College had been conceived in controversy as the conservative Congregationalists' rejection of their liberal brethren, who were welcoming Unitarian concepts into the Church doctrine.[34] Noah Webster, one of the founders, was concerned over developments in the Harvard Divinity School and expressed his earnest hope that "This infant institution will grow up to . . . check the progress of errors which are propagated from Cambridge."[35]

Both Harvard and Amherst continued to propagate their views, and throughout the years the students Amherst admitted tended to be poor and pious, and many of them hoped to enter the ministry. Originally there was little worldliness, but eventually there were changes both in the intellectual climate and in the social life of the College. In 1872, for example, the students welcomed Ralph Waldo Emerson, a Unitarian and transcendentalist, to the village of Amherst where he addressed them despite the disapproval of the College administration.[36]

When Dewey registered in 1870 the president was William H. Stearns, who held the office from 1854 to 1876. While more "concerned with morality than creed," Stearns succeeded in selecting faculty members who had or who were to attain outstanding reputations; among these were Richard H. Mather, Julius Hawley Seelye, and Seelye's brother, Laurenus Clark Seelye, the first teacher of English literature. The president's most innovative act was to introduce physical education into the curriculum. While he was motivated more by his awareness of the precarious health of the students than by an innovative spirit, Amherst consequently became the first American college to establish a professorship of hygiene and physical education. The program was notably successful under the direction of Dr. Edward Hitchcock, appointed in 1860, who was also a pioneer in anthropometrics.[37]

Dewey was apparently attracted by the physical education program, for he had expressed his wish "to be possessed of perfect physical health" a few months before entering Amherst.[38] While he made no reference in his "Journal" to his choice, among the sources which he might have consulted was a book published in 1869, *Physical Culture in Amherst College*, written by Dr. Nathan Allen, an alumnus of the class of 1836.[39] Though determined to pursue his studies, he accepted money from his father only on condition that it would be a loan.[40] Later, while at Amherst, Dewey so impressed Professor L. C. Seelye that he negotiated another loan for his young student.[41]

Dewey's name appears in the "Freshman Class" list in *Amherst College Catalogue, 1870-71*; he was one of 71 freshmen, including George Hall Baker and Walter Stanley Biscoe, both of whom were to be associated with Dewey in the library profession.[42] The "course of study and instruction" for the freshmen emphasized Latin, Greek, and mathematics:

First Term.
- Cicero de Senectute and de Amicitia.
- Harkness's Latin Composition, Part III.
- Homer's Odyssey.
- Greek Verbs.
- Arnold's Greek Prose Composition.
- Loomis's Geometry, to the seventh book.
- Exercises in Orthography and Orthoepy.

Second Term.
- Horace: Odes and Epodes.
- Selections from Greek Historians.
- Greek History.
- Geometry continued; Loomis's Algebra.
- Exercises in Elocution and Declamation.

Third Term.
- Livy: twenty-first and twenty-second books.
- Roman History.
- Harkness's Latin Composition, Part III., completed.
- Greek Tragedy: Prometheus.
- French: Magill's Grammar and Reader.
- Geometry, finished.
- Exercises in Elocution and Declamation.

DURING THE YEAR.—Exercises in Composition. Written Translations from the Ancient Languages. Exercises in Physical Culture, four days in the week.[43]

Though not evident from the studies listed, biblical instruction was offered "during some portion of every year"; prayers were offered every morning in the Chapel, and there was public worship on Sundays. In addition, preaching or some other religious exercise, with attendance voluntary, was held every Thursday.[44]

The inadequacy of Dewey's rural educational background became evident when he was admitted to Amherst with "heavy conditions" in the areas of major study, but he quickly overcame these deficiencies.[45] In his freshman year he distinguished himself in mathematics, winning one of the

Walker prizes for excellence (second prize: fifteen dollars) and, in 1872, the same award (third prize: ten dollars).[46] His transcript of four years indicates that he maintained an acceptable, but not a superior, academic record, with a decline in his average during his senior year.[47] In that year, however, he was much involved in the creation of his classification system and may have diverted his attention to its development. His name appears in the "Second Class Orations" (Classical) in the "Appointments for the Fifty-Third Commencement, July 9th, 1874."[48]

While Dewey had determined originally, as of July 13, 1870, to "mingle in society very little during the next 4 years," he soon found himself freed from that self-imposed isolation.[49] His "Journal" records a variety of activities which must have impressed George A. Plimpton, who considered him "a natural born leader among the men of his time, both in the D K E Fraternity and in College."[50] In 1875 he lived in the home of Mrs. S. F. Pratt, widow of a missionary, who looked to him for guidance in her business affairs.[51] He seemed especially attached to Mary Eastman, though in 1875 they made a decision to call themselves "the best of friends & wait for the future to show" if they could be something else.[52] His circle of friends extended beyond the campus, particularly among the young ladies whom he visited and with whom he rode, studied, and shared many social pleasures. Dewey summarized one of his later Amherst years by saying, "I have behaved pretty wel this year—haven't girld it at all, only a little necessary gallantry."[53]

Dewey fulfilled his student obligation to exercise according to the rules, which required nothing of students which could not be undertaken safely and profitably "by any person . . . sound in body and mind."[54] So concerned was he that once when Dr. Hitchcock was away for a term, Dewey complained that his absence was "much to the detriment of our general health."[55] Outdoor exercise always occupied some of his time and, after he was able to own a horse, he found being in the saddle invigorating and relaxing.[56]

In his later years at Amherst Dewey moved toward a natural adoption of simplified spelling and the use of abbreviations in his personal writings. He finally adopted and used throughout his life Lindsley's Takigrafy, a system of shorthand, in which he became proficient in a relatively short time.[57] He also broadened his literary background during his college days, finding himself at one time absorbed in George Meredith's *Lucile*, a summary of which he faithfully recorded in his "Journal."[58]

Because of his reading interests, he found himself "making the most of the library," which, in 1872 was described as follows:

> The Libraries of the College and the Literary Societies contain about thirty-seven thousand volumes. The *College Library and Reading Room* are open every day (Sundays and holidays excepted) from nine to half-past eleven o'clock, A.M., and from half-past one to four o'clock, P.M. Books of reference may be consulted at any hour when the Reading Room is open; but books can be drawn only from eleven to half-past eleven, A.M., and from half-past one to two, P.M. The *Libraries of the two Literary Societies* are

accessible to the members of the Societies according to regulations
established by themselves, and are open for the delivery of books
on Wednesday, from half-past two to quarter-past three o'clock,
P.M., and on Saturday, from half-past one to two o'clock, P.M.
The *Social Union Reading Room* is open every day except the
Sabbath.[59]

By 1873 Dewey was employed in the library as an assistant, and here
he found an outlet for his organizational skill. Soon after joining the library
staff he identified as a major problem the system used in shelving books.
In his search for an alternate approach he began to reject the plan of shelving
by absolute or fixed location, a plan wherein the shelves were numbered and books
placed in numeric sequence after row and shelf numbers were assigned. Recognizing his need to know more about libraries and their functioning, Dewey
planned visits to several libraries of the day both in nearby Boston and in New
York. Using his own limited resources, he visited the New York State Library
in Albany in 1873 and observed that the books were "arranged alphabetically
paying no attention to subjects."[60]

Earlier in that same year he had made a memorable visit to Boston, where
he visited the Harvard College Library and later introduced himself to Charles A.
Cutter, of the Boston Athenaeum, whom he regarded as a "gentlemanly librarian,"
and to Justin Winsor of the Boston Public Library. Dewey was impressed by the
Boston Athenaeum where he observed that Cutter "put books on the horse
under 'horse' & not under zoology"; he observed too that Cutter allowed "free
access to the shelves" which he, Dewey, considered "a very neat thing but
impracticable for a public library." He shared with Winsor his views on the advantages of centralized cataloging, saying that "of necessity e bk [a book] must
be catalgd [catalogued] by some central tribunal."[61]

While at the Boston Public Library, he observed its absolute location shelving
system, which used numerals with letters as subdivision devices instead of fractions.
Reflecting his own search for a satisfactory notation, Dewey recorded in his
"Journal" that subdivisions of numerals should not be letters but rather that
"the decimal—applied with some flexibility seems to be e [the] best possible
notation."[62] His knowledge of other systems, among them "the plan of the
St. Louis Public School Library, and that of the Apprentices' Library of New
York," did not lessen his interest in a decimal notation. He studied in detail
the St. Louis plan, however, for on May 13, 1873, in response to an inquiry
from Dewey, William Torrey Harris, Superintendent of Public Schools, St.
Louis, mailed to him "some sheets containing an essay on classification & the
scheme actually in use in our library."[63]

Though Dewey was to acknowledge later his indebtedness to "the inverted
Baconian arrangement" of the St. Louis system, the letter from Harris arrived
after he had submitted to the Library Committee of Amherst College, on May 8,
1873, his own proposal for a "Library Classification System." The proposal,
emphasizing a notational pattern based on the decimal principle, began:

Select the main classes, not to exceed nine and represent each
class by one of the (ten digits) nine significant figures. Subdivide
each of these main heads into not more than nine subordinate
classes, and represent each sub class by a digit in the first, or
ten's, decimal place.[64]

While Dewey noted in the proposal that "books on the same subject are
found all together (as far as it is possible to make close classification of books),"
he did not suggest the order of the classes.

Dewey's appointment in 1874 as Assistant Librarian and later as Assistant
Librarian in Charge permitted him to complete his classification system. Convinced
of the advantages of the decimal structure in which notation would reflect content
and not fixity of location, he sought advice on the classes from faculty members
at Amherst and from librarians, among them Cutter and John Fiske, the latter
from Harvard College Library. He recorded once in his "Journal" that Prof. Seelye
"came in and worked on his heads giving me quite a lift."[65] Later, when the
classification was published, he acknowledged that "nearly every member of
the Faculty" had given him "advice from time to time."[66]

From more than anyone else, however, Dewey received valuable and continuing
assistance from Walter S. Biscoe, his classmate who had always excelled him
academically and who, like Dewey, remained after graduation on the Amherst
Campus for a one-year term as a tutor in mathematics and Latin.[67] Having had
an opportunity to experiment with the classification, Dewey assumed final responsibility for preparing and editing it for publication. He obtained copyright on it
in response to his request, dated April 2, 1876, a short time before leaving Amherst
to further his career in Boston.[68] In 1877 Dewey was awarded an A. M. degree
from Amherst.[69]

1876: ANNUS MIRABILIS

The *annus mirabilis* of the library world, 1876, was also the year which witnessed Dewey's meteoric rise to prominence. His involvement with the three major events of the year confirmed irrefutably the prediction made by *Publishers' Weekly* in 1874 that he "promises to become a valuable addition to the ranks of librarians."[70] The three events were: 1) the beginning of the *Library Journal*, 2) the founding of the American Library Association, and 3) the publication of his classification system.

While it is to "the Library Corner" of *Publishers' Weekly* that the *American Library Journal* (later *Library Journal*) traces in large part its antecedents, it is also true that Dewey had, while in Boston, initiated discussion concerning a library publication with Cutter, Winsor, and the Ginn brothers, Edwin and Fred, who were publishers.[71] However, before Dewey was able to crystalize plans for a "library monthly," he talked with Frederick Leypoldt and Richard R. Bowker, both of *Publishers' Weekly*, who not only had considered publishing a journal devoted to library affairs but were ready to assume the risks involved.

Once convinced of Leypoldt's and Bowker's interest, Dewey abandoned his earlier plans and joined them wholeheartedly in the plan for a "Library Journal."[72] As a result, Dewey was appointed Managing Editor of the new *Journal* by Leypoldt and Bowker; in addition, an array of distinguished librarians were listed as Associate Editors on the title page of the first issue of volume one, dated September 30, 1876.[73] The editors announced their intention to have the *Journal* "cover the entire field of library and bibliographical interests" and urged each reader to consider the *Journal* "in a measure his own," and to do "his part in its editing by sending every new fact as to his own library, or other library items that may otherwise escape attention." That financial difficulties were anticipated is evident from the warning also included that "it is by no means certain that the *Journal* can yet be made to cover expenses, but the experiment will be tried."[74]

The leading essay, "A Word to Starters of Libraries," was a contribution from Justin Winsor in which he advised that:

> You must not be surprised to find some diversity of views among experts. They arise from different experiences and because of the varying conditions under which a library may be administered. . . . Choose that which you naturally take to; run it, and do not decide that the other is not perfectly satisfactory to him who chose that.[75]

In contrast to the practical advice offered by Winsor, Dewey attempted to foster a sense of pride and identity in his essay on "The Profession."[76] In it he proclaimed that "the time has at last come when a librarian may, without assumption, speak of his occupation as a profession" and that "our leading educators have come to recognize the library as sharing with the school the education of the people." It was an auspicious beginning for the new *Journal*.

Simultaneous with the planning of the first issue of the *American Library Journal*, Dewey, Leypoldt, and Bowker began to discuss the need for a conference of librarians which would encourage communications and cooperation among professionals in the field.[77] The *Library Journal* description of the plans for the meeting provides a concise history of the planning stages that materialized in the meeting:

> The history of the Conference is quickly told. Taking the hint from the meeting of 1853, a few library devotees in May last proposed a like gathering in connection with the great Exhibition. Letters of inquiry called out hearty responses from prominent librarians and the Commissioner of Education, and a preliminary call was issued. It was at first proposed to hold the gathering in August, but the replies to the call generally agreed upon October as the better date, Philadelphia as the place, and Messrs. Winsor, Poole, and Smith as the proper committee to take charge of the arrangements.[78]

In reality, the fruition of plans for a national meeting of librarians required a determined and aggressive effort from those involved, especially Dewey. One of the major obstacles to be overcome was the aloof disinterest shown by the most distinguished members of the profession: men like Winsor and Poole, leaders whose support was deemed essential if the meeting were to be a success. Through flattery, determined insistence, and efficient management Dewey was able to gain the support of these leaders, and in so doing insured the success of the conference. Bowker, who occasionally refuted Dewey's claim to primacy, was quick to admit that he deserved "full credit for the Conf.";[79] and William E. Foster was more explicit when he noted that "Both by correspondence and by personal interviews and appeals he succeeded in overcoming the natural inertia of the men most influential in this connection, and in bringing together a representative gathering."[80] Even the venerable Poole, who had a reputation for hard work, was impressed by Dewey's prodigious efforts on behalf of the convention, noting "it is cruel to put so much work upon one person," even if such a "remarkable" one.[81]

Once the meeting was called the distinction between the old and the new in librarianship was clear. Among the younger members Dewey was omnipresent; confident and alert, he soon emerged as a dominant figure. Foster, one of those present at the Conference, later sketched a vivid description of the man who was in time to exert such enormous influence on librarianship:

> We have before us a young man . . . the youngest, so far as can
> be learned, of the 103 persons present . . . he is an extremely lithe,
> wiry, and 'lively' person. His mental activity is plainly as pro-
> nounced as his physical activity. . . . He appears almost smooth-
> shaven, having a moustache only, in contrast to most of the others
> present. . . . Despite his youth, he is accustomed to wear spectacles
> to help his vision. His voice is rather high-pitched than otherwise.
> His rapid method of delivery sometimes reminds one of Horace's
> description of Pindar.[82]

The meeting of librarians was held in Philadelphia, October 4-6, and resulted, unlike its 1853 predecessor, in the formation of a permanent organization.[83] When the register was passed for the enrollment of members of the new American Library Association, Dewey signed first,[84] and in a mood symbolic of his role in organizing the American Library Association wrote:

> Of the permanent results of the Conference the organization of
> the American Library Association must be put first, because this
> means the frequent repetition of the Conference; a recognized
> authority which may promote or endorse desirable improvements,
> and furnish decisions on those many points at issue in which pro-
> spective general usage is the sufficient criterion; and otherwise a
> chance to reap the benefits of organized co-operation.[85]

He became Secretary of the American Library Association, a post he held for 14 years, and as Edward Holley notes, "through his subsequent editorship of the *Library Journal* and his position as Secretary of the American Library Association, Dewey soon became known as the foremost exponent of modern librarianship."[86]

To have been among the founders of the *Library Journal* and the American Library Association, all in the same year, would appear a Herculean task for anyone. But Dewey had yet another major contribution to make to librarianship—his classification scheme, destined to be influential and enduring.

The Classification, which Dewey had been refining for three years, was published anonymously in 1876, though Dewey's name appears as copyright holder. Entitled *A Classification and Subject Index for Cataloguing and Arranging the Books and Pamphlets of a Library*, it was referred to originally as the

"Amherst Classification," even by Dewey.[87] One reason for this, in addition
to the Classification's having been developed at Amherst, was that prior to its
publication Dewey had made an agreement with Amherst that 150 copies of
it would be printed for the Library and that 50 copies would be printed for
him at the expense of the College.[88]

Wider publicity was given to the Classification when an explanation by
Dewey was included in the report on *Public Libraries in the United States of
America*, published and made available to librarians at the Conference in
Philadelphia. It was Cutter who had sought the publicity for the Classification,
for he had praised it highly and had suggested to John Eaton, Commissioner
of Education, that Dewey be invited to explain it. He wrote:

> I cannot pretend yet to fully understand the skeme in all its details
> and in all its bearings, but so far as I do comprehend it, it seems to
> me 1 of the most important contributions to library economy that
> has been made for many years. . . . How this is done by substituting
> for the succession of the letters of the alfabet known to us by the
> natural succession of numbers, Mr Dewey wil explain if you desire.[89]

Thus, a new dimension was added to Dewey's stature at the Philadelphia
Conference, for not only had he devised a classification that seemed effective
in application, but he was honored by having it instantly recognized as one of
the important systems of the time.

BOSTON: SEARCH FOR A FUTURE

Since Dewey was living in the Boston area when the events of 1876 transpired, his activities there related in large part to those events. He resided not in Boston, but in Malden, feeling that he "would not like to live in the poor places" and could not "afford to live in the best."[90]

While finishing the Classification, which had priority over his other work, Dewey explored ways of furthering his career. He conferred with the Ginn brothers about starting a library bureau, about publishing a library monthly, and about a future in publishing.[91] He pursued his interest in the metric system and discussed with Dr. F. A. P. Barnard, President of Columbia College, the possible publication of a book on the subject.[92] He talked with David Lindsley about publishing books on, and about the teaching of, Takigrafy.[93] He went to Washington to confer with John Eaton, Commissioner of Education, about the special volume on libraries and about the proposed Conference of Librarians.[94] He moved restlessly, seeking action. His days were varied, busy, stimulating.

In view of his acceptance of the position as Managing Editor of the *American Library Journal* and his involvement with the newly formed American Library Association, his time was more and more absorbed by library matters. Through the pages of the *Journal* he praised the Philadelphia meeting as having been "a success beyond all that its most sanguine friends had hoped" and he identified as the main problem of the library world:

> The education of the masses through the libraries, by securing the best reading for the largest number at the least expense.[95]

By 1879 he succeeded in having the Association incorporated under Massachusetts State law, and the incorporation date happily coincided with his own birthday: December 10. The certificate of incorporation stated that the Association was being formed for the purpose of promoting the library interest of the country, by exchanging views, reaching conclusions, and inducing co-operation in all departments of bibliothecal science and economy; by disposing the public mind to the founding and improving of libraries; and by cultivating good-will among its own members.[96]

In 1877 Dewey was one of the American librarians who participated in the Conference of Librarians held in London. With typical aggressiveness Dewey quickly assumed managerial responsibility for planning the American visitation. With the formal establishment of the Library Association of the United Kingdom, Dewey, like other delegates, was elected to honorary membership.[97]

In recognition of the importance of the *American Library Journal*, the newly formed Association voted at the London Conference (and on Dewey's suggestion) that it would be adopted as the Association's official organ, with the understanding that it would be known as the *Library Journal*. Despite this tribute, Dewey's relations with Frederick Leypoldt and R. R. Bowker were growing strained because their views differed on publication patterns and solutions to the critical financial difficulties besetting the *Journal*. Consequently, Dewey withdrew from his editorial association with the *Library Journal* as of January 1, 1881. In announcing his resignation, the publisher praised him for his "genuine enthusiasm and indefatigable labors."[98] It was a well-deserved tribute, for throughout the initial five years Dewey had contributed generously to the content of the *Journal*, a special contribution being his column, "Notes and Queries."[99] In that column Dewey's responses to questions from librarians concerning specific, technical, and routine details demonstrated the emerging profession's need for practical information.

While attempting to minimize some of these problems, Dewey also sought other ways to assist in library development, such as using standardized library supplies, forms, and equipment to simplify procedures. His first effort, The Readers and Writers Economy Company, was a financial failure; undaunted, he formed another company, the Library Bureau, which was similar to the Supply Department of the American Library Association. This venture, more successful than the first, not only introduced numerous form cards, accession records, shelf list records, and vertical files, it also fostered acceptance of the size of the catalog card (7 ½ x 12½ cm.) currently being used. The Library Bureau, involved also in publishing activities, later became a division of Remington Rand, Inc.[100]

Dewey did not endure his Boston years alone, for soon after his arrival he met Annie Roberts Godfrey to whom he was introduced at Harvard College while reviewing his Classification with John Fiske.[101] Miss Godfrey was born in Milford, Massachusetts, on February 11, 1850, the daughter of Benjamin Davenport Godfrey and Anne Roberts Godfrey. She attended Vassar for three years, then accepted a position at Wellesley College to develop a library.[102] Though Dewey's "Journal" indicates that he was not without feminine relationships, notably with Jennie Kimball, he soon found himself increasingly attracted by Miss Godfrey.[103] She attended the Conference of Librarians in Philadelphia and in

1877 was one of the librarians, along with Dewey, who attended the London Conference. Their romance flourished and in 1878 the London delegates were invited to their wedding in Milford on October 19, 1878. In her, Dewey found a complement to his personality, for she was able through their long years of marriage to counterbalance the impulsive over-extension of his activities and to moderate his often impatient and abrasive pursuit of what were generally unselfish goals.

In addition to his library-oriented activities, Dewey's interest in simpler spelling involved him in the 1876 founding of the Spelling Reform Association; he became secretary of the Association, a post he held, except for a brief period, until his death. He served also on an advisory committee for spelling and pronunciation for Funk and Wagnalls *Standard Dictionary* and later became a member of the executive board of the Simplified Spelling Board, organized in 1906 with funds contributed by Andrew Carnegie. Similarly he had sustained his early enthusiasm for metric measurement, and in 1876 he became secretary of the newly organized American Metric Bureau, the president of which was Frederick A. P. Barnard, President of Columbia College.[104]

Though Dewey's Boston years were often frustrating, chaotic, and financially precarious, he had made very substantial progress in his many-sided work. Within a decade he had established himself as an authority in library matters through his writings and his Classification, which from the beginning had evoked heated debate, and as Secretary of the American Library Association. Dewey was controversial, articulate, and seemingly remarkably successful; his reputation as an expert on library affairs grew quickly and soon eclipsed that of his fellow professionals. Thus, when Columbia College was seeking a librarian in 1883, President Barnard, knowing of Dewey's reputation in the library world as well as his interest in metric matters, informed him of the position. Dewey took action immediately and letters favorable to his appointment were soon being received in New York. Among those who endorsed him were Cutter, J. N. Larned of Buffalo, Poole, Lloyd P. Smith of Philadelphia, and Ainsworth R. Spofford, Librarian of Congress. The Rev. Julius H. Seelye of Amherst College also recommended him.[105]

NEW YORK: DEWEY'S COLUMBIA

Dewey was obviously the leading candidate for the position, and his appointment as librarian of Columbia College was confirmed on May 7, 1883. The beginning of his administration was auspicious, for both President Barnard and the Library Committee of the Trustees were impressed by his grasp of the nature of librarianship. Dewey analyzed his responsibilities and, with the initial financial support and unusually high degree of independence granted to him by the Trustees, designed a reorganization program for the library.

With the support of the College administration, Dewey was able to implement his objectives, which led to the uniting of six libraries, formerly located in nine different places, in the newly designed central library. Among his extraordinary accomplishments were: 1) integration of the collection through use of his Classification, 2) creation of a classified subject catalog, 3) design of a work flow pattern in processing which reflects aspects of scientific management, 4) formulation of selection policies which recognized the need for cooperative acquisitions among libraries in New York City, 5) extension of loan services and of interlibrary loans as of 1885, 6) strengthening of reference services with emphasis on instruction of the reader, 7) addition of a "Paid Help Department" for those requiring special or individual assistance, 8) offering of a series of bibliographical lectures to supplement user guidance already available, 9) formulation and enforcement of rules that were minutely detailed, demanding as to decorum, and restrictive, but that were drafted for the benefit of all users.[106]

He selected his staff and encouraged them to work at the pace he was setting for himself. Walter S. Biscoe, his Amherst classmate, undertook the classification of the collection and the continual refinement of Dewey's Classification as required by its application. Of the staff of twenty, thirteen were men and seven, women; all the latter were assigned to technical, not public, services. Six of the women were Wellesley graduates, one of whom later paid tribute to Dewey for his "courage and daring" not only in employing them but in accepting "six absolutely untrained women."[107]

Dewey's vast plans for reorganizing the library could not have been accomplished quietly even if he had wished for that, because the faculty were often affected by them. Thus, opposition to Dewey's rapid reorganization soon began to surface; the emergence of a central library under activist leadership and the employment of women were new approaches, and those who did not endorse these new directions were made uncomfortable.

Dewey did not confine his organizational skill to Columbia College alone, for he was soon identified with the New York library community. In 1885 he succeeded in forming the New York Library Club, the first of many similar local clubs to be formed throughout the country.[108] His sustained conviction that the library could contribute to the education of the masses extended his concern to library needs other than those for the academic student. As a result he found himself encouraging the development of library services for children in New York, with the aim of counteracting "the influence of the injurious literature so freely offered them."[109] Under his guidance the Children's Library Association adopted a new constitution, whose object was "to create and foster among children, too young to be admitted to the public libraries, a taste for wholesome reading."[110] Among the committees created by the constitution was a Reading Committee, whose membership was to consist of representatives of the "Protestant, Roman Catholic, and Hebrew faiths"; this Committee was to be responsible for the "character of the reading furnished the children."[111]

Also, in 1885, Dewey published the greatly enlarged second edition of his Classification, entitled *Decimal Classification and Relativ Index*.[112] Though he had assured the users of the 1876 edition that the Classification was "unchangeable in its call numbers," the new edition contained not only many expansions but numerous subject and notational changes and relocations.[113] Historically, then, the continuing conflict between maintaining integrity of notation and maintaining integrity of hierarchical subject relationships traces its origin to the second edition.

The second edition provoked an attack on Dewey by Fred B. Perkins and Jacob Schwartz, both creators of classification systems.[114] Not only did they claim that "there is an obvious and very large misjudgment within his foundation division of ten classes," they also questioned the accuracy of his claim to originality. Dewey refuted their charges with an equal lack of restraint, though he concluded his rebuttal with the observation that there was no time for "petty bickerings."[115]

Through the exchange of such impassioned views and through other writings, Dewey became increasingly well-known during his Columbia College days. In addition to his contributions to the pages of *Library Journal*, he began his editing of *Library Notes* (v. 1-4, 1886-1898).[116] Containing inspirational and practical articles, such as "Attractions and Opportunities of Librarianship" and "Simplified Library School Rules," his new journal served as a text for librarians who needed self-teaching aids.

Despite these accomplishments Dewey became more and more convinced of the need for formal training in librarianship. While he had experimented earlier with an apprentice training program for his staff of untrained assistants, he had regarded this as a temporary step, since the Trustees had assured him of their support for a formal program before he had accepted the position. Some two years after he had initiated his apprentice program he expressed satisfaction over the results of the training offered to promising candidates and noted that other libraries were seeking to employ his assistants at salaries higher than those offered at Columbia. Even though he could not have been unaware of the prevailing attitude toward women, many of the apprentices were women; moreover, Dewey publicly espoused the cause of women in the profession, making a singularly important address in 1886 before the Association of Collegiate Alumnae on "Librarianship as a Profession for College-Bred Women."[117]

By 1886 Dewey was making plans for a formal program in the School of Library Economy and, as announced, the official date for the initiation of the program was January 5, 1887.[118] Of his 20 students, 17 were women; yet his admission of them clearly challenged the prevailing views, if not the directives, of the Trustees. Dewey considered his action an irreversible decision and he was not willing to abandon the program. He was never able to gain official approval of his actions in regard to the School, however, and even more ominously, his relations with the faculty continued to deteriorate. Had Dewey heeded the warnings of faculty resistance to his uncompromising pursuit of his goals, the crises leading to his resignation might have been averted. Worse yet, with the retirement of President Barnard in 1888 Dewey lost his most loyal and influential defender. At the meeting of the Trustees on November 5, 1888, the members voted that Dewey be suspended from his office as chief librarian but not from his association with the School. On December 20, 1888, Dewey submitted his resignation to the Trustees; it was accepted on January 7, 1889, five and one-half years after his widely acclaimed appointment.

Library Journal recognized, more than the Columbia College faculty did, that Dewey had made a notable contribution during his years at Columbia, observing that:

> His five years' administration at Columbia has resulted in making the library of that institution an important factor in New York intellectual life, combining the functions of the university library and the public library in a remarkable degree. . . . He made the place a focus of modern library improvements, in addition to founding the Library School.[119]

More recently, scholars have recognized the pivotal role that Dewey, and Winsor at Harvard, played in placing the academic library at the very "heart" of the university and in initiating a vigorous discussion of what the library "should be and do."[120]

During their years at Columbia the Deweys had lived at the Dalhousie located near Central Park, an address that had become well known to their personal and professional friends. Not only was Mrs. Dewey a gracious hostess, but she also sustained Dewey through his difficult days filled with pressures and increasing academic opposition. She encouraged him in his professional activities and frequently attended conferences with him. One example of her unselfish nature was her willingness to have him attend the Thousand Islands Conference of the American Library Association in 1887; their son, Godfrey, was born on September 3, during Dewey's absence. The librarians attending the Conference presented to the young Dewey a silver cup with the inscription: ALA DEWI and the date of his birth. Since he was the first child born of parents both of whom were members of the Association, Godfrey became known as the "ALA baby."

ALBANY: EXTENSION OF LIBRARY SERVICES

In 1888, a particularly trying year for Dewey at Columbia College, he was invited by the Regents of the University of the State of New York to serve as a consultant on reorganizing the State Library prior to its move into new quarters in the Capitol building.[121] The invitation had been necessitated by the death of Henry A. Homes, librarian of the General Library of the State Library, and the appointment of an acting librarian, George R. Howell, who was to hold the office until the move had been completed.[122] Invited in 1888 to address the Twenty-Fifth Convocation of the University, Dewey chose as his topic "Libraries as Related to the Educational Work of the State."[123] In this stirring plea for the educational role of the library, Dewey proclaimed that "What we need now . . . is not more colleges but more libraries."[124]

Dewey's visits to Albany proved timely. With the resignation of David Murray, on December 12, 1888, as Secretary and Treasurer of the Board, the Regents, impressed by the young librarian from Columbia, identified him as the man most capable of fulfilling the responsibilities formerly performed by both Homes and Murray. By a unanimous vote Dewey, at the age of 37, was elected Secretary and Treasurer of the Board of Regents and Director of the State Library.[125]

Dewey assumed his responsibilities immediately. At the Board meeting on January 10, 1889, he reviewed his ideas on the anticipated accomplishments of the University and included the resolution of the Regents' Convocation of 1888, which had endorsed his view that "public libraries should be recognized as an essential part of the State system of higher education."[126] The Regents voted unanimously that "such libraries as may be found worthy of the distinction shall be officially recognized as a part of the University of the State of New York."[127]

At the meeting on January 10, Dewey also presented to the Regents the consent of Acting President Drisler of Columbia College to the transfer of the Library School (the School of Library Economy) to Albany.[128] The Regents quickly approved Dewey's plan for "training librarians and cataloguers in connection with the work of the library, giving them instruction and supervision instead of salary for services rendered the library."[129] At the close of the winter term on March 30, therefore, Columbia College authorities formally transferred the School and its resources to Albany, where it became known as the New York State Library School.[130] Thus, with his characteristic urge for instant action Dewey furthered two of his major concerns: 1) recognition of the public library as an educational agency and 2) continuity of his school for librarians.

Dewey continued his professional activities, assuming additional responsibilities when elected president of the American Library Association in 1890.[131] He served again as president in 1892/93, the year during which the World's Columbian Exposition was held in Chicago. He was authorized by the Regents to accept the "appointment of director of the bureau of the educational exhibit of the state of New York at the . . . Exposition." From 1889 to 1892 he was the first elected president of the Association of State Librarians, which became known as the State Library Association in 1893.

More significant for New York library development, however, was the creation of the New York Library Association in 1890, of which Dewey was the first president.[132] The purpose of the Association, as stated by Dewey, was "to give organized assistance to the University in its efforts to make the libraries of the State more useful." Among the questions discussed at the first meeting was:

> What changes in library legislation should be asked at the coming session of the legislature?[133]

Later, Dewey more specifically indicated the purposes as being:

> To organize and promote among N.Y. libraries the exchange of duplicates, inter-library loans and other forms of co-operation, specially such as concern the University of the State of New York, the Department of Public Instruction, the State Library and the New York colleges and academies, most of whose co-operation is necessarily limited to this state.
>
> To secure the passage by the legislature of needed laws in regard to the founding of libraries, exemption from taxation, subsidies, mutilation of books, distribution of state money to district libraries and all other matters affecting the relation of the state to the public libraries.[134]

The New York Library Association, like other organizations bearing Dewey's imprint, set a precedent for the founding of similar organizations throughout the country. Because of his sustained concept of the library as an educational institution, it was fitting that he be elected president of the newly created Library Department of the National Educational Association during 1896/97.

As Secretary of the Board of Regents, Dewey became embroiled in matters affecting the educational structure of the state, such as the division of responsibilities between the Board of Regents and the Department of Public Instruction. A revision enacted in 1892 of the law pertaining to higher education, whose sections on public libraries were written in large part by Dewey, strengthened rather than weakened the authority of the Regents.[135] Higher education was defined in the law as meaning:

> Education in advance of common elementary branches, and [it]
> includes the work of academies, colleges, universities, professional
> and technical schools and educational work connected with
> libraries, museums, university extension courses and similar agencies.[136]

The law clearly stated, moreover, that the State Library "shall be in charge of the regents."

According to Dewey, the law "recognized the connection of the library with education and the state with a breadth and liberality unequaled by any other state or country."[137] Coincidentally, just before the law was passed, the Superintendent of Public Instruction, Andrew Sloan Draper, who was not always in sympathy with the new directions, accepted the presidency of the University of Illinois upon the expiration of his official term in 1892.

Meanwhile, as Director of the State Library, Dewey seized the opportunity to mold it for "educating the masses" or as a "people's college."[138] He extended loans to institutions belonging to the University and encouraged its use as a reference inquiry center for the state. His fertile and imaginative genius was at its best in designing service programs, and few new ideas for such programs have developed since his day except in the use of modern technologies. Among his creations were a Medical Division (1891), a Sociology Division (1891), a Library for the Blind (1896), a Woman's Library (1893), and a Capitol Library (1892) for the use of state employees in Albany. He encouraged children's use of the library, emphasizing that use was not a matter of age but of proper behavior, and in 1898 he formed a Children's Library, which was unfortunately soon abandoned.

In 1893 Dewey instituted a program of traveling libraries to tour the state; extension or statewide library services later developed from this innovative program. His panoramic vision encompassed traveling libraries for study clubs, for reference services, for the blind, and for children, and "environment libraries" to foster systematic reading on a special topic. He expressed concern over farmers' reading and proposed the use of "book wagons" in areas without libraries.[139]

He broadened the scope of the collection by including resources other than books, which he considered "a means to an end, not a fetish."[140] As early as 1897 the Regents endorsed Dewey's view that pictures were an "essential part" of education and voted that "where the regents make rules governing the buying of books, the same rules shall also apply to pictures."[141] Thus, the State Library began to include pictures, photographs, slides, and lantern slides; Dewey anticipated including other media, for example, such as "rolls of the world's best music for the mechanical piano and organ player" and rooms wherein these could be played.[142] He sought also to "bring the general efficiency of . . . [the] staff to the highest practicable point."[143] He experimented in management techniques and with new equipment, encouraging the use of the typewriter and the telephone as time savers.

He also anticipated a move toward cooperative sharing of resources through the establishment of depository centers because of the growing cost of maintaining large numbers of great collections. He proposed as a solution that:

> A few great central libraries . . . serve the purpose of a larger
> territory for all unusual or seldom needed books.[144]

Dewey found respite from professional activities at his home at 315 Madison Avenue, where he and Mrs. Dewey welcomed their guests in a genial and cordial atmosphere. Among those especially welcomed were library school students, to whom they opened their home for festivities and receptions. As one student remembered: "the gracious cordiality of Mrs Dewey . . . gave them their first notion of social grace."[145]

His concern over library problems never abated, however, and, aware that small libraries needed assistance in organizing their collections, Dewey issued the first abridged edition of his Classification in 1894; in the same year, Edition 5 of his *Decimal Classification and Relativ Index* appeared.[146] The printing of two thousand copies, the largest number printed of any edition up to that date, promised continuing use of the Classification in libraries new and old; the printing of 7,600 copies of Edition 6, in 1899, confirmed its usefulness.

Dewey inevitably encountered suspicion and hostility because of the ever-increasing extension of his activities. Both his involvement with the educational program of the state and his personal actions prompted criticism as early as 1895.[147] A subcommittee appointed by the Regents to investigate one such matter concluded, however, that "not a single charge involving . . . [his] integrity and official conduct" had been sustained.[148]

Dewey did not heed the warning inherent in the early attacks upon him for, feeling vindicated, he proceeded with his plan to develop a retreat in the Adirondacks, an area in which he and his wife had found relief from the discomforts of the ragweed season and its pollen. The spot finally chosen was Lake Placid. In 1894, the Deweys remodeled a small boarding house, the Bonnie Blink, into a clubhouse for those invited to its opening in 1895.[149] From a modest estate the Deweys, with their charm, ingenuity, and zeal, created the Lake Placid Club, a center for summer recreation. From the beginning the Club had a policy of selective membership as well as customs reflecting "simplicity, wholesomeness, and exceptional high standards, authoritatively maintained."[150] Thus the Club was in no way similar to hotels then existing in the Adirondacks; but it was, according to Dewey, fulfillment of an "iridesent dream" of 1878.

Further professional recognition came to Dewey when he was among those invited to meet with the U.S. Congress Joint Committee on the Library "for the purpose of inquiring into the condition of the Library of Congress."[151]

Dewey expressed his hope that "with the new order will come a new name . . . the National Library," which he defined as ' a center to which the libraries of the whole country can turn for inspiration, guidance, and practical help."[152] In commenting, in 1951, on the impact made by those at the hearings, Verner Clapp concluded that "there is no doubt that Melvil Dewey's name led all the rest."[153]

Dewey was honored signally in 1898 when Governor Theodore Roosevelt, in his inaugural address, praised the accomplishments of the New York State Library through what could have been called the "Dewey Decade."[154] The Governor, who served as Chairman of the Library Committee in 1899, appointed a special commission to recommend a unification plan for the state's educational activities, thereby "doing away finally with the duplications, friction and unnecessary expense of two state departments of education" namely, the University of the State of New York and the Department of Public Instruction.

Dewey, having been appointed a member of the commission, found himself entangled politically, for it was suggested that he had fomented unification in order to encompass the elemementary schools of the state under his jurisdiction as Secretary of the Board of Regents. Dewey repudiated the charge, saying "I have profound respect and admiration for the common school work without the slightest desire to engage in it."[155] Though Dewey signed the report of the commission, he wrote to Governor Roosevelt criticizing the plan as ' needlessly extravagant" and suggesting amendments that would broaden the elective powers of the Regents.[156] Recognizing, however, that his association with the Regents contributed to the conflict, Dewey offered his resignation to the Regents feeling that:

> The fact of a vacancy in the position of secretary may be a factor
> in the solution of the much discussed question of educational
> unification, as it will leave the way clear for any reorganization
> of the work of the regents that may seem wise.[157]

The Board, while accepting his resignation, to be effective on January 1, 1900, applauded Dewey as being "an organizer of genius, an executive of great skill, [and] an educational leader of marked originality and energy."[158] The Board praised Dewey further by acknowledging that his "administration had coincided with the largely augmented usefulness and honor of the University." It was, nevertheless, a timely withdrawal because the Regents were reluctant to endorse the resolutions of the committee on unification.[159] Having removed himself from the political pressure, Dewey devoted his time to his professional interests: the Library School, the State Library, and the Home Education (Adult Education) Department. In 1902 he was awarded the honorary degree of LL.D. from two universities, Syracuse University and Alfred University.

His international reputation was enhanced during his Albany years not only by the use of his Classification in other countries but also by its use, with his permission, in 1895 by the Office International de Bibliographie, Bruxelles, associated with the Institut International de Bibliographie.[160] It was adopted after study as the basis of the Universal Decimal Classification. Dewey was an official delegate of the U.S. government to the International Library Conference held in London in 1897, where the Bodleian librarian of Oxford University praised Dewey as having "done more than all the other librarians combined in making librarianship a recognized profession."[161] Later, in 1900, as a result of the participation of the New York State Library in the Paris Exposition, Dewey received three out of nine Grands Prix awarded to the United States: one for his library exhibit, one for his home education exhibit, and one as a personal tribute.[162]

The esteem in which Dewey was held, however, had no effect on the Albany scene after 1900. The Unification Act of 1904 created the State Department of Education through consolidation of the Department of Public Instruction with the University of the State of New York. As a result of the change, Dewey was named Director of Libraries and Home Education (and of the Library School) and Andrew Sloan Draper returned to New York as the first Commissioner of Education to whom the Director of Libraries would be responsible.

Draper quickly let it be known that he had "differed much in years gone by" with Dewey and that he was "tentatively opposed to many of the projects" Dewey was undertaking. He objected further to Dewey's "unfortunate predisposition . . . to set up something different only because it is different."[163] Despite Draper's evident animosity, Dewey endured the indignities with outward equanimity, continuing his duties as Director of Libraries and Home Education, and his involvement with the Lake Placid Club, and the Lake Placid Company which operated the property for the Club.

The year 1904 was an active one for Dewey both professionally and personally. Among the events was the appearance of the *A.L.A. Catalog. 8,000 Volumes for a Popular Library, With Notes*, which, jointly edited by the New York State Library and the Library of Congress, identified New York again as a leader in the profession. The *New International Encyclopaedia* (New York: Dodd, Mead, 1904) included his concise survey of libraries, with both historical and practical data, under the heading "Libraries." More honor came to him when he was awarded a gold medal at the Louisiana Purchase Exposition, held in St. Louis, for his activities in New York State.[164]

On a personal basis, in the winter of 1904/05, the Deweys daringly experimented with a winter season for Lake Placid members, though Godfrey Dewey was the only member of his family in residence at the time. As a result of the successful season, the Club continued to experiment and became known as the pioneer in recreational winter sports in America.[165]

In 1905 a challenge to Dewey's incumbency as State Librarian created a furor that intermingled racism and politics. A petition dated December 20, 1904, addressed to the Regents, requested his removal because while serving as a "high public official," he had endorsed the anti-Semitic admission policy of the Lake Placid Club.[166] The petition was signed by eleven prominent Jewish citizens, among them Louis Marshall, Adolph Lewisohn, Isidor Straus, Nathan Bijur, Daniel Guggenheim, Cyrus L. Sulzberger, and Adolph S. Ochs. An effort was made to separate Dewey's professional reputation from his personal actions;

among those who defended him were Mary Eileen Ahern, Editor of *Public Libraries*; James H. Canfield, Librarian, Columbia University; and Herbert Putnam, Librarian of Congress.[167] Putnam, brushing aside the specific charge, praised Dewey's accomplishments in a letter dated February 9, 1905:

> My Dear Mr. Reid: The petition now before your Board of Regents, asking the removal from office of your State Librarian, rests upon incidents with which, in themselves, we other librarians have no concern, and as to which we are not entitled to speak; but from some statements in the newspapers I infer that there will be brought to the aid of the petition charges of a different nature, some of which do concern the general practice of our profession. One charge in particular is, from time to time, reiterated in connection with attempts to discredit Mr. Dewey with his Regents and with the public. It is, that he spends a considerable part of each year away from his office.
>
> Now to those of us who know Mr. Dewey professionally, and who have seen him more or less intimately, and to those of us who know what are his methods of work, such a charge is as ridiculous as its motive appears to be contemptible. Mr. Dewey eats, drinks, sleeps and talks library and library work throughout the twenty-four hours, the week, the month, and the year. His physical whereabouts at any one time is immaterial. He carries his business with him to his home; he brings it back with him in the evening and in the morning to the office. He is, in effect, as much engaged with it at Lake Placid as he is at Albany; it is as much his play as it is his work. He is the clearest example in our profession of a man who can not shake off his business.
>
> For what does the State employ such a man? Is it merely to stay at a desk during certain hours? or is it to think and plan, and promote and organize? Is he to be judged by a day? or by a year?
>
> Every one who knows Mr. Dewey knows that he is an actual and a keen sufferer from hay fever, and that during certain months existence in Albany is intolerable to him. During these months he moves his desk to Lake Placid. But is he serving the city of Albany, or the State of New York?
>
> There is no man living today to whom more than to him is due the prodigious activity of the past quarter of a century in the promotion of libraries, and in the diffusion of interest in them. There is no one who has done more to stir with enthusiasm for practical library service competent people who are needed in it. His name is more widely known abroad than that of any other living American librarian, for his contributions to library technique and to the general acceptance of public libraries as a motive force in popular education.

With the grounds of the petition itself we other librarians have nothing to do; but we should hate to see a great state estimate an administrator of large interests as though he were a thousand dollar clerk in a railroad office.

HERBERT PUTNAM[168]

Among the Jewish citizens who supported Dewey were Simon Goldman and Isidor Singer.[169]

The Regents viewed his notable attainments and reputation as inconsequential, however, when compared to the political import of the discriminatory taint widely publicized through the press, primarily *The Sun* of New York City. Consequently, within a month, the Board of Regents, of which Draper was a member, issued a "formal and severe public rebuke" to Dewey.[170] While claiming that the charges were based on a "misapprehension of facts," Dewey offered, on September 20, 1905, his resignation a "Director of the State Library, of the Home Education Department and of the Library School."[171] His resignation, to be effective January 1, 1906, was accepted. Having accepted the resignation, the Regents voted to express "grateful recognition and sincere appreciation... of the value of his services to the cause of public education and library development during the 17 years of his official labors therein."[172] They identified, as a final tribute, the years as clearly marking "an epoch in educational work in this commonwealth."

Draper immediately recommended that the State Library and Home Education Department, to be called in the future Educational Extension, each become a division of the Education Department and, further, that "supervision of school libraries be no longer allied with the State Library but made a separate division of the [Education] Department.[173] In adopting the recommendations, the Regents abrogated the concept of unity in library services which Dewey had attempted to achieve after the Unification Act of 1904.

During the critical days of 1905 Dewey attended the Portland Conference, where divisive views were being expressed concerning the value of and need for library training.[174] He later expanded the comments he made at the Conference into an appraisal of "The Future of Library Schools," wherein he surveyed the entire field of training.[175] He also sponsored the creation of the American Library Institute, whose membership would include ex-presidents of the American Library Association.[176]

Upon his resignation a feeling of "universal deep regret" permeated the profession.[177] The New York Library Association recognized his services, stating that:

His personality has been central and stimulating in the great library movement which in this and other lands has so signally characterized the last 25 years.[178]

In its conclusion, the resolution confirmed that Dewey, in his own way, had fulfilled his wish "to inaugurate a higher education for the masses" through his support of public libraries:

> To him possibly more than to any one person is due the present day intelligent appreciation of the place and value of the public library.[179]

LAKE PLACID CLUB YEARS

Dewey immediately transferred to Lake Placid the total of his organizational genius and dynamic energy. He could not have developed the Club, however, without the assistance of Annie Dewey, whose "faith, courage and . . . small private fortune" insured the continuance of the Club in its early years.[180] Dewey himself acknowledged that "their marriage and all their work had been an absolutely equal partnership."[181] Under his leadership, the Club, continuing both as a summer and a winter resort, reached a high house count of 1,500, an estate of 10,000 acres, and an annual business of two million dollars in 1930, a year before his death.[182] It was known not just for recreation; it was identified also as "a university club in the wilderness."[183] The III World Olympics, widely publicized, were held in Lake Placid in 1932, the year following his death. This event, largely a result of the untiring efforts of Godfrey Dewey, enhanced further the prestige of the Club both at home and abroad.

Among the librarians with whom he continued to share ideas and close friendships were May Seymour and Katharine L. Sharp, who, with the three Deweys, formed the "Cedars Five," the real policy makers in the formative years of the Club.[184] Following the death of Miss Sharp in 1914, Mrs. Emily (McKay) Beal of Boston was invited by the Deweys to join the administrative staff of the Club.[185] Later, after the death of Annie Dewey on August 3, 1922, Dewey was married to Mrs. Beal (on May 28, 1924) and shared with her his remaining years.

When in his seventies, Dewey fulfilled his wish of having a subtropical branch. In association with his second wife, Emily Beal, he established in 1927 the short-lived "Lake Placid Club South," located in Florida in the village of Lake Stearns, later re-named Lake Placid.[186]

In 1922, Dewey had applied for and obtained from the Regents of the University of the State of New York a provisional charter creating the Lake Placid Club Education Foundation (now the Lake Placid Education Foundation), and an absolute charter was granted in 1926. The Foundation's objectives may be summarized under three headings: restoration, schools, and seedsowing. These objectives continued Dewey's commitment to his special interests, among which were simpler spelling, the metric system, and calendar reform. Dewey considered simpler spelling the most important and requested that "this chief purpose shal not be neglected." In 1925 the Foundation took over Lake Placid Florida School, established in 1905, as the basis of the Northwood School for Boys in Lake Placid.

Dewey's Lake Placid Club years, during which a unique institution and a foundation of world-wide fame emerged, are yet to be studied. Though Grosvenor Dawe attempted "to weav a life story . . . show the man and his way . . . and his major achievements," Godfrey Dewey found his appraisal "altogether inadequate." He felt that Dawe had failed to give an "authentic or vital picture either of the man or his work . . . [a man] forever spending next year's income year before last and somehow getting away with it . . . [a man] wholly selfish in the pursuit of unselfish ideals," yet accomplishing what "no lesser genius, perhaps no other human being" could have done.[187]

While he had accomplished what "no lesser genius" could have done, Dewey's personal involvement in the library world lessened during his Club years. He continued editing his column, "Library Notes," in *Public Libraries* for several years, however, and encouraged the New York Library Association to hold their meetings at Lake Placid.

Dewey never lost interest in his Decimal Classification, though he assigned editorial responsibility for it to May Seymour, whom Godfrey Dewey characterized as a "specialist in omniscience." She devoted her time while at the Club chiefly to the Classification and was involved with Edition 11 at the time of her death in 1921.[188] Throughout the years, however, Biscoe was the chief and the most authoritative consultant on the structure and development of the Classification. Dewey's final introduction, written for Edition 12 and dated December 10, 1926, is a classic and has been included in subsequent editions (other than Edition 15) because of its historical importance.[189]

When printed Library of Congress cards were made available in 1901, librarians, individually and through the American Library Association, began to request that Decimal Classification numbers be added to the cards. While the decision to do so was 30 years in the making, Dewey supported the idea, seeing the addition of the numbers as "extending stil further . . . the [National Library's] alredy great servises to the libraries of the cuntry at larj."[190] In 1927 Dewey approved the transfer of the editorial office of the Classification to Washington, by invitation, to the Library of Congress, where it has remained since that date. In 1930, a year before Dewey's death, an office supported by the American Library Association was established in the Library of Congress for the purpose of adding DC (DDC) number to printed cards. The Library of Congress assumed the responsibility in 1933 and continues to offer the service both through its printed cards and through its book catalogs.

To insure continuity of the Classification, Dewey had conveyed earlier through a deed of gift to the Foundation in 1924 all copyrights to his *Decimal Classification and Relativ Index* with the stipulation that monies/profits derived from the sale of each edition be devoted to the editing, publishing, and dissemination of future editions. As the Classification moves into its own second century, the stipulation still holds.

Though Dewey had withdrawn from active participation in the American Library Association, he was invited to the Fiftieth Anniversary Conference in 1926. It is reported that in his address, "Our Next Half-Century," the "clear, far-seeing vision of the dreamer was in full cry" and that he was received with great applause.[191] At the Seventy-Fifth Anniversary of the American Library Association in 1951, Dewey was among the distinguished personalities honored by inclusion in "A Library Hall of Fame."[192] The Association honored his memory further in 1952, with the establishment of the Melvil Dewey Medal, to be given annually to "an individual or a group for recent creative professional achievement of a high order." In describing the award, the Association acknowledged Dewey's far-ranging interests, noting that the award was to be made to those working in "fields in which Melvil Dewey was actively interested: notably, library management, library training, cataloging and classification, and the tools and techniques of librarianship"–in short, every aspect of librarianship.

His imprint endures. His influence on librarianship has been perhaps greater and more enduring than that of any other librarian. His Classification, his innovative ideas on library services, his clearly articulated conception of library education, the work of the graduates of Columbia College and the New York State Library School, and his involvement in associational activities at the national, state, and local levels, remain impressive and influential.

The enormous popularity of his Classification and the growing significance of his other innovations of 1876–the *Library Journal* and the American Library Association– must have been a constant source of encouragement to the aging Dewey. The most heartening development of all, certainly, was when his Albany Library School returned, in 1926, to Columbia University, where it was merged with the Library School of the New York Public Library and became known as the School of Library Service. This act belatedly acknowledged the wisdom of his youth. In 1938, some seven years after his death, a Melvil Dewey Professorship of Library Service, endowed by the Carnegie Corporation of New York, was established at Columbia University as an enduring tribute to his pioneering contributions to librarianship.

On December 10, 1931, Dewey wrote his "80th birthday letr" to his many friends and disciples, and it reflected his never-failing optimism and commitment to work, as he wrote: "Melvil Dewey is not a watch that wears out to be discarded but lyk a sun dial wher no wheels get rusti or slip a cog or get tired & long for rest." But time had run out, he died a short time later on December 26 of a cerebral hemorrhage at "Lake Placid Club South." His ashes now lie in a family vault in the North Elba Cemetery near his beloved Lake Placid Club in the Adirondacks.

NOTES

1. Melvil Dewey, "3/4 of a Century," February 1926. Original in "Melvil Dewey Papers," Columbia University Libraries, Division of Special Collections, Rare Book and Manuscript Library, p. 2. (Location of a manuscript is noted only in the first entry in which it is cited. Location hereinafter cited as In "Melvil Dewey Papers."). Melvil Dewey, perhaps the most influential and in many ways the most controversial American librarian, has not been the subject of a full-length and historically sound biography. Much of the problem lies in his enormous energy and endless activity in every aspect of librarianship. His pivotal roles in such developments as the founding of the American Library Association, the founding of the *Library Journal*, the authorship of the *Decimal Classification*, and the founding of the first library school in America, all contribute to the overwhelming complexity of his life. Furthermore, the sheer bulk of his correspondence and other manuscripts, combined with the difficulty of deciphering his shorthand, prove enormous obstacles to even the most determined of his would-be biographers. Perhaps this explains why Dewey has been so often studied "in part"—as educator, or cataloger, or library association activist. Such special studies abound, and they will be cited where pertinent throughout this essay. A few comprehensive attempts at Dewey biography have been made. The most useful of these are: Grosvenor Dawe, *Melvil Dewey: Seer; Inspirer; Doer, 1851-1931* (Lake Placid Club, N.Y., 1932), an idiosyncratic work which does, nevertheless, cover aspects neglected elsewhere; Winifred B. Linderman, "Melvil Dewey," *Encyclopedia of Library and Information Science* 7 (1972): 142-60, an assessment based on years of research; and Fremont Rider, *Melvil Dewey* (Chicago: American Library Association, 1944). The present essay on Dewey's enduring presence in librarianship is based not only on the printed sources identified in the bibliography but, more rewardingly, on the author's personal study of the Dewey papers at Columbia University, at the Lake Placid Club, and at the New York State Library, and on interviews with the few remaining who knew Melvil Dewey, notably Dr. Godfrey Dewey and Deo B. Colburn, to whom this book is dedicated.

2. Adelbert M. Dewey, *Life of George Dewey . . . and Dewey Family History. Being an Authentic Historical and Genealogical Record . . .* (Westfield, Mass.: Dewey Publishing Co., 1898). Entry 4775: "Melvil Dewey."

3. Dewey, "3/4 of a Century," p.5. Dewey shortened his family name to Dui for a brief time. See title pages of volume 5 of *Library Journal* (1880). See also Dawe, Melvil Dewey, p. 29.

4. Dewey, "Journal," 10 February 1868; 21 August 1868. In "Melvil Dewey Papers." Though there is little information about Dewey's youthful days, some insight into his growth and development can be gained through a study of his journal or diary which he began on his fifteenth birthday (December 10, 1866) and continued, with sporadic entries, through part of 1877, the last entry being dated August 27, 1877. The entries are tantalizingly uninformative at times—for example, about his deep involvement in the creation of his Classification and in the founding of the American Library Association.

5. Dawe, *Melvil Dewey,* pp. 104;105. Also based on recollection of Godfrey Dewey and study of Dewey portrait at Lake Placid Club, New York.

6. Isabel Ely Lord, "New York State Library School, 1895-97," In New York (State) Library School, Albany, *The First Quarter Century of the New York State Library School, 1887-1912* (Albany: New York State Library School, State of New York, Education Department, 1912), p. 50.

7. Dewey's family moved to Oneida after his father sold his Boot and Shoe Store. The family had moved there by May 1869. See his "Journal," 22 May 1869.

8. Rider, *Melvil Dewey*, passim.

9. Dawe, *Melvil Dewey*, passim.

10. Dewey, "Journal," 10 December 1866–10 December 1870.

11. Ibid., 18 December 1866; 2 January 1867; 16 February 1867.

12. Ibid., 14 December 1866; 12 January 1867; 11 April 1868.

13. Ibid., 18 January 1867; 1 April 1867; 11 May 1867; 11 August 1867; 13 August 1869; 13 July 1870. There are frequent references to study throughout the "Journal."

14. Ibid., 10 December 1868.

15. Ibid., 12 October 1867.

16. Ibid., 10 July 1869.

17. Ibid., 26 October 1869.

18. Ibid., 30 August 1872. Dewey expressed a similar feeling in a letter to "My dear Bro," 74/11/1 (November 1, 1874), In "Melvil Dewey Papers." Dewey wrote: "I often regret exceedingly that there was never much affection manifested in our immediate family."

19. Dewey, "3/4 of a Century,' p. 8.

20. Dewey, "Journal," 9 December 1869.

21. Ibid., 23 April 1867. Dewey was joint editor, with E. E. Hall, of "The Literary Star," published weekly by the Young People's Lyceum, according to data on v. 1, no. 5 (n.d.)

22. Dewey, "3/4 of a Century."

23. Dewey, "Journal," 13 July 1870.

24. Ibid., 22 January 1867; 21 February 1867; 5 May 1867; 4 September 1867.

25. Dawe, *Melvil Dewey*, p. 32.

26. Dewey, "Journal," 12 October 1867.

27. Ibid., 9 December 1869.

28. Ibid., 28 August 1869.

29. Ibid., 11 August 1869; 14 April 1870.

30. Ibid., 18 November 1869.

31. Ibid., 15 November 1869.

32. Ibid., 26 November 1869.

33. Ibid., 18 June 1870.

34. For information on the founding and later years of Amherst College, consult the following: Claude M. Fuess, *Amherst, the Story of a New England College* (Boston: Little, Brown, 1935); Thomas Le Duc, *Piety and Intellect at Amherst College, 1865-1912* (New York: Columbia University Press, 1945); William S. Tyler, *History of Amherst College During Its First Half Century, 1821-1871* (Springfield, Mass.: C. W. Bryan, 1873); and George F. Whicher, *Mornings at 8:50; Brief Evocations of the Past for a College Audience* (Northampton, Mass.: Published by the Hampshire Bookshop for the Trustees of Amherst College, 1950).

35. Quoted in Le Duc, *Piety and Intellect at Amherst College*, p. 4.

36. Ibid., p. 120.

37. Ibid., pp. 129-34.

38. Dewey, "Journal," 9 December 1869.

39. Nathan Allen, *Physical Culture in Amherst College* (Lowell, Mass.: Stone and House, 1869).

40. Dewey, "Journal," 10 December 1870; 15 July 1871.

41. Ibid., 15 July 1871.

42. Amherst College, *Catalogue of the Officers and Students of Amherst College for the Academical Year, 1870-71* (Amherst, Mass., 1870), pp. 15-16. One of Dewey's boyhood friends from Adams Center, Charles Harris Phalen, entered Amherst in the same year as Dewey. They lived in the same places during their residency and were graduated in the same class. Phalen was drowned in the year following their graduation. Dewey, grief-stricken, attended the funeral in Camden, New York, on June 26, 1875.

43. Ibid., p. 20.

44. Ibid., p. 23.

45. David Addison Harsha, *Noted Living Albanians* (Albany: Weed, Parsons, 1891), p. 83.

46. Amherst College, *Catalogue of the Officers and Students of Amherst College for the Academical Year, 1871-72* (Amherst, Mass., 1871), pp. 32, 34; and *Catalogue of the Officers and Students of Amherst College for the Academical Year, 1872-73* (Amherst, Mass., 1872), pp. 31-32, 34.

47. Dewey's transcript is in the archives of Amherst College. Copy obtained for this study with the permission of Dr. Godfrey Dewey. Melvil Dewey made the following observation in his "Journal" on his academic rank on May 15, 1874:

> My last rank given out was first term sophomore year 93. For freshman year it had been 87, 90 & 88. . . . I find that my rank since has been 87, 87, 89 ofer 2 years. In Junior year 76, 86, 70 ofer 3 years 85. . . . If I get 65 for senior year it gives first index of a man's true position. I hope I may get 65.

His final average noted on his transcript is 75.

48. Amherst College, *Catalogue of the Officers and Students of Amherst College for the Academical Year, 1874-75* (Amherst, Mass., 1874), p. 38.

49. Dewey, "Journal," 13 July 1870.

50. Dawe, *Melvil Dewey*, p. 98.

51. Dewey, "Journal," 10, 11, 13, 14, 15, 16, 19, and 21 April 1875.

52. Ibid., 3 March 1875.

53. Letter to "My dear fellows," from Dewey, May 1, 1875. In the James I. Wyer Autograph Collection, 1855-1951, American Library Association Archives, University of Illinois. Written at the request of Biscoe, Dewey began beguilingly: "I undertake a brief autobiografy of a very worthles character."

54. Amherst College, *Catalogue of the Officers and Students of Amherst College for the Academical Year, 1870-71* (Amherst, Mass., 1870), p. 28.

55. Dewey, "Journal," 10 December 1872.

56. Dewey made frequent references to his horse, Florie, in 1875. He referred to his joy of riding on February 13, 1875, in his "Journal."

57. Dewey, "Journal," 10 December 1873. Dewey's enthusiasm for Takigrafy became known on the campus, and in 1875 the freshman class petitioned that Takigrafy be given twice a week as required study instead of some studies they were taking ("Journal," 23 January 1875). The faculty agreed to the request and Dewey held twice-weekly classes for the rest of the term ("Journal," 27 January 1875). The text used by Dewey was probably David Philip Lindsley, *The Elements of Tachygraphy* (Boston: O. Clapp, 1869), or a later edition.

58. Dewey, "Journal," 6 May 1872. Dewey's growing interest in literature indicated a broadening view when contrasted to his earlier objection to the reading of fiction ("Journal," 18 November 1869).

59. Dewey, "Journal," 1 August 1872. For the description see Amherst College, *Catalogue of the Officers and Students of Amherst College for the Academical Year, 1872-73* (Amherst, Mass., 1872), p. 25. A history of the Amherst library will be found in Donald B. Engley, "The Emergence of the Amherst College Library, 1821-1911," Master's thesis, University of Chicago, 1947.

60. Dewey, "Journal," 1 April 1873.

61. Ibid., 15 February 1873.

62. Ibid.

63. William T. Harris to Dewey, May 13, 1873.

64. Dewey, "Library Classification System," at head of title: "Original idea of May 8, 1873, Submitted to Library Com. of Amherst College." Copy in files of Dr. Godfrey Dewey and of Deo B. Colburn, Lake Placid Club, New York. Reproduced in Dawe, *Melvil Dewey*, pp. 319-21.

65. Dewey made several brief references to his classification in his "Journal" in 1875, but they offer little insight into the problems relating to the design and development of his system. References may be found on the following dates: 26 April 1875; 15 May 1875; 2 June 1875. It was on June 2, 1875, that Prof. Julius H. Seelye offered his services.

66. Dewey, *A Classification and Subject Index for Cataloguing and Arranging the Books and Pamphlets of a Library* (Amherst, Mass., 1876), p. 9.

67. Dewey frequently acknowledged his indebtedness to Biscoe. See his "Introduction," dated December 10, 1926, which is included in *Decimal Classification and Relative Index*, Devised by Melvil Dewey, Ed. 16. (Lake Placid Club, Essex Co., N.Y.: Forest Press, 1958), v. 1, p. 72.

68. Letter to copyright Office, April 2, 1876, accompanied by title page which differs from the title as it appeared in the 1876 edition. On march 22, 1876, Dewey had sought "to enter for copyright a little work just passing thro' the press" but he had not included evidence of actual publication.

69. A letter from J. Richard Phillips, Special Collections Librarian and Archivist, Amherst College, to Vann, dated March 15, 1976, states:

> An issue of the *Springfield Daily Republican* (6/29/1877), p. 5, states that 'Melville [sic] Dewey of Boston' received the degree along with several others. Nowhere did I find an indication for what area of study the degree was awarded.

70. "The Library Corner," *Publishers' Weekly* 5 (10 January 1874): 34.

71. "The Library Corner" appeared for the first time in *Publishers' Weekly* 5 (10 January 1874). For Dewey's early plans, see his "Journal," 19 April 1876; 20 April 1876; 22 April 1876.

72. An announcement of the appearance of the first issue of the *American Library Journal* and of Dewey's association with it appeared in *Publishers' Weekly* 10 (7 October 1876): 601-602.

73. Among the names were those of Chas. A. Cutter, Chas. Evans, Reuben A. Guild, H. A. Homes, Wm. F. Poole, and A. R. Spofford. Also included were the names of J. Eaton, Bureau of Education, and W. T. Harris, St. Louis.

74. *American Library Journal* 1 (1876): 12-13.

75. Justin Winsor, "A Word to Starters of Libraries," *American Library Journal* 1 (1876): 2-3.

76. Dewey, "The Profession," *American Library Journal* 1 (1876): 5-6.

77. Edward Holley has presented a remarkably perceptive analysis of the events leading up to the 1876 conference in his introduction to the edited version of the "A.L.A. Scrapbook of 1876." See Edward Holley, *Raking the Historic Coals: The A.L.A. Scrapbook of 1876* ([Urbana, Ill.]: Beta Phi Mu, 1967). Two other recent works provide additional detail on the meeting: Sister M. A. J. O'Loughlin, "Emergence of American Librarianship: A Study of Influence Evident in 1876," Doctoral dissertation, Columbia University, 1971, and Dennis

Thomison, "The History and Development of the American Library Association, 1876-1957," Doctoral dissertation, University of Southern California, 1973. For a study of the major issues faced by A.L.A. during the first ten years of its existence see Lucy Jane Maddox, "Trends and Issues in American Librarianship as Reflected in the Papers and Proceedings of the American Library Association, 1876-1885," Doctoral dissertation, University of Michigan, 1958.

 78. *American Library Journal* 1 (1876): 13.

 79. Bowker to Charles Ammi Cutter, 3 January 1878, quoted in Holley, *Raking the Historic Coals*, p. 9. Bowker is the subject of a substantive biography: Fleming E. McClurg, *R. R. Bowker: Militant Liberal* (Norman: University of Oklahoma Press, 1952).

 80. William E. Foster, "Five Men of '76," *ALA Bulletin* 20 (1926): 319.

 81. William Frederick Poole to R. R. Bowker, 14 November 1876, quoted in Holley, *Raking the Historic Coals*, p. 16. Poole, who frequently opposed Dewey's aggressive innovations, is the subject of a notable biography: William L. Williamson, *William Frederick Poole and the Modern Library Movement* (New York: Columbia University Press, 1963).

 82. Foster, "Five Men of '76," p. 318.

 83. Donald Krummel, contrasting the failure of the 1853 meeting with the success of the 1876 gathering, concluded that the difference was Dewey— "restless and outspoken, but who was strengthened by a perseverance" that the organizers of the 1853 meeting lacked. See "The Library World of *Nortons Library Gazette*," In David Kaser, ed., *Books in America's Past: Essays in Honor of Rudolph H. Gjelsness*. (Charlottesville: Published for the Bibliographical Society of the University of Virginia [by] University Press of Virginia, [1966], p. 263.

 84. Holley, *Raking the Historic Coals*, p. 18.

 85. ["Editorial"], *American Library Journal* 1 (1876): 90-91.

 86. Holley, *Raking the Historic Coals*, p. 15.

 87. Dewey, *A Classification and Subject Index for Cataloguing and Arranging the Books and Pamphlets of a Library* (Amherst, Mass., 1876), also his "The Amherst Classification," *Library Journal* 3 (1878): 231. The history of Dewey's scheme is covered in John Phillip Comaromi, "A History of the Dewey Decimal Classification: Editions One Through Fifteen, 1876-1951," Doctoral dissertation, University of Michigan, 1969. See also his *The Eighteen Editions of the Dewey Decimal Classification* (Albany: Forest Press, 1976).

 88. Dewey, "Journal," 28 March 1876.

 89. Dewey, "A Decimal Classification and Subject Index." In U. S. Bureau of Education, *Public Libraries in the United States of America, Their History, Condition, and Management*, Special Report, Part I (Washington: Government Printing Office, 1876), pp. 623-48, and Cutter to John Eaton, Commissioner of Education, April 20, 1876. Dewey made a copy of the letter from Cutter to Eaton, which Cutter had forwarded to him, in his "Journal," 27 April 1876. Cutter's early advocacy of Dewey and his later disenchantment are analyzed in Francis Miksa, ed., *Charles Ammi Cutter: Library Systematizer* (Littleton, Colo.: Libraries Unlimited, 1977).

90. Dewey, "Journal," 24 April 1876.

91. There are frequent references to his association with the Ginn brothers, Edwin and Fred, in his "Journal" during the month of April 1876 (for example, on 13, 19, 27, and 30 April 1876).

92. Ibid., 20 May 1876.

93. Ibid., 14 April 1876.

94. Ibid., 19 May 1876.

95. Dewey, "The American Library Association," *American Library Journal* 1 (1877): 247.

96. Melvil Dui, "Incorporation of the A.L.A." *Library Journal* 5 (1880): 308.

97. For an account of the London Conference, see Budd L. Gambee, "The Great Junket: American Participation in the Conference of Librarians, London, 1877," *Journal of Library History* 2 (1967): 9-44.

98. ["Editorial"], *Library Journal* 5 (1880): 303.

99. Dewey edited the column while serving as Managing Editor from 1876 through 1880.

100. Much mystery surrounds Dewey's complex business dealings, and, unfortunately, little has been done to explore fully his commercial involvements. Some of Dewey's colleagues were highly critical of his entrepreneurial side, while others applauded his efforts. A final assessment cannot be made until there has been a thorough study of this aspect of his multi-faceted library activities. A short but useful study of the Bureau will be found in Harry R. Datz, "A Pioneer: The Library Bureau," *Library Journal* 51 (1926): 669-70. See also Dewey's own brief account of his years between 1874 and 1884 in Jesse F. Forbes, *1874-1884: The Chronicles of '74 Since Graduation from Amherst College* (Warren, Mass.: H. M. Converse, Printer, 1885), pp. 15-18.

101. Dewey, "Journal," 18 April 1876.

102. Emma H. Gunther, "Annie Godfrey Dewey, February 11, 1850–August 3, 1922," *Journal of Home Economics* 15 (1923): 357.

103. References to Jennie Kimball appear in Dewey's "Journal," for example, on the following dates: 29, 30, 31 [sic] April; 4, 28 May 1876.

104. Dawe, *Melvil Dewey*, pp. 112; 119; 272-73; 287. Dewey's business card identified his relationship with each of the three organizations:

General Offices 6, 7 & 8, No. 32 Hawley Street, Boston.

Besides the ECONOMY Co., (a commercial corporation, manufacturing labor-saving devices for readers and writers,) three missionary educational societies have these offices as headquarters for the U. S. The collections illustrating each work are the largest known and are free to all. Each society desires as members all friends of education and progress, and many belong to all three. Otherwise they have no connection except the economy and convenience of offices in common.

"The best reading for the largest number, at the least expense."

AMERICAN LIBRARY ASSOCIATION.

President, Justin Winsor, Librarian Harvard University.   Secretary, Melvil Dewey.

"The exclusive use of the International Decimal Weights and Measures."

AMERICAN METRIC BUREAU.

President, F. A. P. Barnard, S.T.D., LL.D., Pres't Columbia College.   Secretary, Melvil Dewey.

"The simplification of English Orthografy."

SPELLING REFORM ASSOCIATION.

President, F. A. March, LL.D., Lafayette College.   Secretary, Melvil Dewey.

Each society has a SUPPLY DEPARTMENT, furnishing at low prices, often at half former rates, everything it recommends pertaining to the Library, Metric or Spelling Reform movements. Supported entirely by gifts and members' fees, the smallest sums are gratefully received.

105. Winifred B. Linderman, "History of the Columbia University Libraries," Doctoral dissertation, Columbia University, 1959, pp. 87-88.

106. Ibid., Chapter 3: "Dewey the Organizer," pp. 87-183. Dewey's meteoric success and decline during his Columbia years are authoritatively portrayed by Dr. Linderman. His contributions to reference services are less known than his other achievements; yet his concept of a "Paid Help Department" is similar to developments of the 1970s: the fee dilemma or service charges and information brokerage service.

107. Letter from Martha T. Buckham, quoted in Rider, *Melvil Dewey*, p. 79. See also "More Reminiscences of the 'Wellesley Half-Dozen'," *Columbia Library Columns* 3 (1954): 14-17; Ray L. Trautman, "Melvil Dewey and the 'Wellesley Half-Dozen'," *Columbia Library Columns* 3 (1954): 9-13.

108. "New York Library Club," *Library Journal* 10 (1885): 148.

109. "Children's Library Association," *Library Notes* 1 (1887): 261.

110. Ibid., p. 262.

111. Ibid., p. 265. Dewey was also instrumental in organizing children's libraries within the NEA. See Budd L. Gambee, "An 'Alien Body': Relationships Between the Public Library and the Public Schools, 1876-1920," *Ball State University Library Science Lectures*, First Series (1973): 1-23.

112. Dewey, *Decimal Classification and Relativ Index for Arranging, Cataloging and Indexing Public and Private Libraries and for Pamflets, Clippings, Notes, Scrapbooks, Index Rerums, etc.*, 2nd ed., rev. and greatly enl. (Boston: Library Bureau, 1885).

113. U. S. Bureau of Education, *Public Libraries in the United States of America: Their History, Condition, and Management*, Special Report, Part I, p. 641.

114. Fred Perkins and Jacob Schwartz, "The Dui-Decimal Classification and the 'Relativ' Index: A Duet," *Library Journal* 11 (1886): 37-43; 68-74.

115. Dewey, "The Decimal Classification: A Reply to the 'Duet'," *Library Journal* 11 (1886): 100-106; 132-139.

116. *Library Notes: Improved Methods and Labor-Savers for Librarians, Readers and Writers*, edited by Melvil Dewey, v. 1-4, June 1886-Sept. 1898 (Boston: Library Bureau, 1887-1898).

117. Dewey, *Librarianship as a Profession for College-Bred Women: An Address Delivered before the Association of Collegiate Alumnae on March 13, 1886* (Boston: Library Bureau, 1886). Dewey's championship of women in librarianship was probably stimulated by practical as well as idealistic motives. For a highly critical assessment, which would appear to blame Dewey beyond the evidence, see Dee Garrison, "Tender Technicians: The Feminization of Public Librarianship, 1876-1905," *Journal of Social History* 6 (1973): 131-59.

118. Dewey's activities as a library educator have been more thoroughly studied than any other aspect of his library involvement. Five works of particular value are: Columbia University School of Library Service, *The School of Library Economy of Columbia College, 1887-1889: Documents for a History* (New York: Columbia University, 1937); W. Boyd Rayward, "Melvil Dewey and Education

for Librarianship," *Journal of Library History* 3 (1968): 297-312; Ray L.
Trautman, *A History of the School of Library Service, Columbia University*
(New York: Columbia University, 1954); Sarah K. Vann, *Training for Librarianship
Before 1923...* (Chicago: American Library Association, 1961); and Carl L.
White, *A Historical Introduction to Library Education: Problems and Progress
to 1951* (Metuchen, N.J.: Scarecrow Press, 1976).

119. ["Editorial"], *Library Journal* 18 (1888): 364.

120. Kenneth J. Brough, *Scholar's Workshop: Evolving Conceptions of
Library Service* (Urbana: University of Illinois Press, 1953).

121. Cecil R. Roseberry, *A History of the New York State Library* (Albany:
New York State Library, State Education Department, University of the State
of New York, 1970), p. 51. A letter from Dewey to Whitelaw Reid, a Regent
of the University of the State of New York and a friend of Dewey, dated November
25, 1888, indicates that Dewey had given serious attention to a reappraisal of
the Regents' responsibilities and to an extension of the State Library services.
Three paragraphs in the letter relating to 1) "People's University," 2) "Peripatetic
Libraries," and 3) "State Guidance & Supervision of Public Libraries" proved to
be prophetic. The letter, written before Dewey was elected Secretary and
Treasurer of the Board of Regents and Director of the State Library, seems in
retrospect to be a blueprint of Dewey's course of action after he assumed his
position in Albany. Reproduced in Dawe, *Melvil Dewey*, pp. 336-44.

122. Ibid., Dewey had known Homes through the years, since Homes had
served as an associate editor of the *American Library Journal* (later *Library
Journal*) during the years 1876-1880, when Dewey was Managing Editor. Homes
was also a member of the American Library Association, having joined by the
end of 1877. He was member #84.

123. Dewey, *Libraries as Related to the Educational Work of the State*
(Albany, N.Y., 1888).

124. Ibid., p. 14.

125. New York (State) University, *Official Minutes of the Regents of
the University During the Secretaryship of Melvil Dewey, 1889-99* (Albany,
1900), p. 486.

126. Ibid., p. 525.

127. Ibid.

128. Ibid., pp. 522-23.

129. Ibid., p. 523.

130. Ibid., pp. 542-43. For detailed reports on the activities of the New
York State Library School, consult the annual reports for 1889-1905. Reports
of the School before 1900 appear in the annual reports of the New York State
Library within the text or as an appendix. From 1900 to 1905 the reports were
published separately.

131. ["Editorial"], *Library Journal* 15 (1890): 227. See also official
proceedings of the Conference of the American Library Association held in
St. Louis in *Library Journal* 15 (1890). Dewey resigned before serving a full
term because of illness. See "Special Meeting of the Executive Committee,"
Library Journal 16 (1891): 200.

132. Dewey, "New York Library Association."*Library Journal* 15 (1890): 267-68.

133. New York (State) Library, Albany, *Seventy-Third Annual Report . . . 1890* (Albany: James B. Lyon, 1891), p. 15.

134. Dewey, "New York Library Association," p. 267.

135. Dewey reminded the Regents on December 22, 1899, that on the date on which he had assumed his position, January 1, 1889, Governor Hill had sent his fourth and last message "recommending the complete abolition of the regents as a body no longer active or useful."

136. New York (State) Laws, Statutes, etc. *Laws of the State of New York . . . Passed at the One Hundred and Fiftieth Session of the Legislature . . .* (Albany: Banks & Brothers, 1892), Chapter 378: "An Act to revise and consolidate the laws relating to the university of the state of New York. Approved by the Governor April 27, 1892." Paragraph 2: Definitions.

137. New York (State) Library, Albany, *77th Annual Report, 1894* (Albany: University of the State of New York, 1897), p. 31.

138. For information on Dewey's reorganization and extension of services of the New York State Library, see the minutes of the meetings of the Regents, his annual reports of the Library, and Roseberry, *History of the New York State Library*.

139. Dewey, *Traveling Libraries: Field and Future of Traveling Libraries* (Albany, 1901). (University of the State of New York, Home Education Department, Bulletin 40, Traveling Libraries and Collections, 2).

140. New York State Library, Albany, *87th Annual Report Including Home Education and the Library School, 1904* (Albany: New York State Education Department, 1906), p. 17.

141. New York (State) University, *Official Minutes of the Regents . . . 1889-99* (Albany, 1900), p. 456.

142. New York (State) Library, Albany, *87th Annual Report . . .* , p. 17.

143. New York (State) Library, Albany, *81st Annual Report, 1898* (Albany: University of the State of New York, 1899), p. 6.

144. New York (State) Library, Albany, *83d Annual Report, 1900* (Albany: University of the State of New York, 1901), p. 55.

145. W. S. Biscoe, "As It Was in the Beginning," *Public Libraries* 30 (1925): 78. The author, who signed his name as "Albany Student," was identified as E. D. Tweedell in "Responsibility for Sketch of Dr Dewey," *Public Libraries* 30 (1925): 236.

146. Dewey, "Abridged Decimal Classification and Relativ Index," *Library Notes* 4 (January-April 1895): 3-192. The advertisement for Edition 5 appeared in the same issue of *Library Notes*, p. 2.

147. See Roseberry, *History of the New York State Library*, p. 61, for one accusation concerning bicycles.

148. Ibid.

149. Godfrey Dewey, "Sixty Years of Lake Placid Club," [1955?], p. 2. Reprint of a talk given at Agora Auditorium, August 4, 1955.

150. Ibid., p. 4.

151. U.S. Congress, Joint Committee on the Library, *Condition of the Library of Congress* [Washington: Government Printing Office, 1897]. (54th Congress, 2d Sess. Senate Report No. 1573). For a discussion of this episode in the light of the evolution of the Library of Congress see John Y. Cole, ed., *Ainsworth Rand Spofford: Bookman and Librarian* (Littleton, Colo.: Libraries Unlimited, 1975).

152. U.S. Congress, Joint Committee on the Library, *Condition of the Library of Congress*, pp. 142-43.

153. Verner Clapp, ["Tribute to Dewey"], transcript of remarks made by Clapp at the "Melvil Dewey Centennial Saturday Evening, December 8, 1951." Copy in files of Dr. Godfrey Dewey and of Deo B. Colburn, Lake Placid Club, New York.

154. Theodore Roosevelt, *State Papers as Governor and President, 1899-1909* (New York: Scribners, 1925), p. 26.

155. New York (State) Library, Albany, *83d Annual Report, 1900* (Albany, 1901), p. 11.

156. Letter from Dewey "To his Excellency Theodore Roosevelt, Gov. of the state of New York, 2 Jan. '00." Reproduced in Dawe, *Melvil Dewey*, pp. 349-53.

157. New York (State) University, *Official Minutes of the Regents. . . 1899-99* (Albany, 1900), p. 561.

158. Ibid., p. 565.

159. Ibid., pp. 561, 563-65. One of the defeated resolutions stated that the Regents "deprecate any legislation consolidating these two departments as dangerously experimental, and opposed to the true interests of education in this state."

160. Letter from Paul Otlet to Dewey, June 8, 1895; letter from Dewey to Paul Otlet, June 29, 1895. Copy in files of Dr. Godfrey Dewey and of Deo B. Colburn, Lake Placid Club, New York.

161. Quotation from Walter S. Biscoe, "Melvil Dewey, 1851-1931," *New York Libraries* 13 (February 1932): 40. For background on the conference see Budd L. Gambee, "The Role of American Librarians at the Second International Library Conference, London 1897," In Harold Goldstein and John Goudeau, eds., *Library History Seminar, Number 4* (Tallahassee: Florida State University School of Library Science, 1972), pp. 52-85.

162. New York (State) Library, Albany, *83d Annual Report, 1900* (Albany, 1901), p. 22; Godfrey Dewey, "Melvil Dewey, 1851-1951," *Library Journal* 76 (1951): 1964.

163. New York (State) University, *Journal of Meetings of the Board of Regents . . . 1904-1908* (Albany: University of the State of New York, 1908), pp. 2-3; 21-31; 70-72.

164. Ibid., p. 109.

165. Godfrey Dewey, "Sixty Years of Lake Placid Club," pp. 6-7.

166. Text of petition included in Melvil Dewey, *[Answer to] Petition to the Regents of the State of New York [For the Removal from Office of Melvil Dewey, the Present State Librarian]* (Lake Placid Club, N.Y., 1905), pp. 1-5.

167. See, for instance, Mary E. Ahern, "The Charges Against Mr Dewey," *Public Libraries* 10 (1905): 127-28.

168. Dewey, [*Answer to*] *Petition*, pp. 49-50.

169. Ibid., pp. 21-24; 41-45.

170. New York (State) University, *Journal of Meetings of the Board of Regents . . . 1904-1908*, p. 134.

171. Ibid., pp. 159-60. Note that Dewey used the titles he held before the implementation of the Unification Act of 1904.

172. Ibid., p. 160.

173. Ibid., pp. 160-61.

174. American Library Association, "Proceedings, 1905," *Library Journal* 30 (1905): C164-C176.

175. Dewey, "The Future of Library Schools," *Public Libraries* 10 (1905): 435-38.

176. American Library Association, "Proceedings, 1905," *Library Journal* 30 (1905): C179.

177. Mary E. Ahern, "The Resignation of Mr Dewey," *Public Libraries* 10 (1905): 471.

178. "Library Week at Lake Placid Club, N.Y.," *Public Libraries* 10 (1905): 485.

179. Ibid.

180. Gunther, "Annie Godfrey Dewey," p. 359.

181. Ibid.

182. Godfrey Dewey, "Sixty Years of Lake Placid Club," p. 3.

183. Reginald T. Townsend, "A University Club in the Wilderness," *Country Life* 38 (1920): 50-53.

184. Interviews with Godfrey Dewey about the early days of the Club. Letter from Godfrey Dewey to Rose E. Phelps, January 4, 1963. Copy in files of Dr. Godfrey Dewey, Lake Placid Club, New York.

185. Katharine Sharp was one of Dewey's many "disciples" in American librarianship. She graduated from his Albany school and later became Director of the University of Illinois Library and founder of the Library School there. She constantly looked to Dewey for guidance, which he readily and unselfishly rendered. See Laurel A. Grotzinger, *The Power and the Dignity: Librarianship and Katharine Sharp* (Metuchen, N.J.: Scarecrow Press, 1966). Miss Sharp died following a tragic touring car accident in Keene Valley, near Lake Placid Club, in 1914.

186. Lake Placid Club in Florida, Sub-tropic Branch of Adirondack Placid Club, *Bulletin* 1 (Dec. 1, 1931); see also Satoru Takeuchi, "Dewey in Florida," *Journal of Library History* 1 (1966): 127-32.

187. Letter from Godfrey Dewey to Grosvenor Dawe, 6 December 1932. Copy in files of Dr. Godfrey Dewey and Deo B. Colburn, Lake Placid Club, New York.

188. "Memorial Service for May Seymour. Full Report of Meeting at the Club on Anniversary of her Birth," 1921, 4 p. Reprinted from the *Lake Placid News* of September 16, 1921.

189. "Melvil Dewey's Introduction to Edition 12,"*Decimal Classification and Relative Index*, Edition 18 (Lake Placid Club, N.Y.: Forest Press, 1971), pp. 67-112.

190. Ibid., p. 111.

191. Dewey, "Our Next Half-Century," *ALA Bulletin* 20 (1926): 309-313. [Comment on Melvil Dewey's address, "Our Next Half-Century"], *Libraries* 31 (1926): 463.

192. "A Library Hall of Fame for the 75th Anniversary [of the American Library Association]," *Library Journal* 76 (1951): 466-72.

PART II

SELECTED WRITINGS OF MELVIL DEWEY

Note: Dewey's simplified spelling, as used originally, is retained in these reprints of his writings.

A. LIBRARIANSHIP AS A PROFESSION

Dewey's experience in the library at Amherst College, his inquiring visits to libraries, his classification, and, significantly, his concern for the "education of the masses," add authority to his assumption, confidently stated in 1876, that librarianship deserved to be known as a profession. While the tone is somewhat hortatory, Dewey synthesized his basic belief in the library as an educational institution, claiming that "the free library ranks with the free school," and that librarians were "in the front rank of the educators of their communities." No immediate rebuttal was offered, but the challenge implicit in Dewey's proposition has provoked debate and questioning since 1876.

1. THE PROFESSION

The time has at last come when a librarian may, without assumption, speak of his occupation as a profession. And, more, a better time has come—perhaps we should say is coming, for it still has many fields to conquer. The best librarians are no longer men of merely negative virtues. They are positive, aggressive characters, standing in the front rank of the educators of their communities, side by side with the preachers and the teachers. The people are more and more getting their incentives and ideas from the printed page. There are more readers and fewer listeners, and men who move and lead the world are using the press more and the platform less. It needs no argument to prove that reading matter can be distributed better and more cheaply through lending libraries than in any other way, and we shall assume, what few will presume to dispute, that the largest influence over the people is the printed page, and that this influence may be wielded most surely and strongly through our libraries.

From the first, libraries have commanded great respect, and much has been written of their priceless worth; but the opinion has been largely prevalent that a librarian was a keeper only, and had done his full duty if he preserved the books from loss, and to a reasonable extent from the worms. There have been noble exceptions to this rule, but still it is a modern idea that librarians should do more than this. It is not now enough that the books are cared for properly, are well arranged, are never lost. It is not enough if the librarian can readily produce any book asked for. It is not enough that he can, when asked, give advice as to the best books in his collection on any given subject. All these things are indispensable, but all these are not enough for our ideal. He must see that his library contains, as far as possible, the best books on the best subjects, regarding carefully the wants of his special community. Then, having the best books, he must create among his people, his pupils, a desire to read those books. He must put every facility in the way of readers, so that they shall be led on from good to better. He must teach them how, after studying their own wants, they may themselves select their reading wisely. Such a librarian will find enough who are ready to put themselves under his influence and direction, and, if competent and enthusiastic, he may soon largely shape the reading, and through it the thought, of his whole community.

The time is come when we are not astonished to find the ablest business talents engaged in the management of a public library. Not that we have less scholarship, but that we have more life. The passive has become active, and we look for a throng of people going in and out of library doors as in the markets and the stores. There was a time when libraries were opened only at intervals, and visitors came occasionally, as they come sometimes to a deserted castle or to a haunted house. Now many of our libraries are as accessible as our post-offices, and the number of new libraries founded has been so great that in an ordinary town we no longer ask, "Have you a library?" but "Where is your library?" as we might ask where is your school-house, or your post-office, or your church?

And so our leading educators have come to recognize the library as sharing with the school the education of the people. The most that the schools can hope to do for the masses more than the schools are doing for them in many sections, is to teach them to read intelligently, to get ideas readily from the printed page. It may seem a strong statement, but many children leave the schools without this ability. They can repeat the words of the book, but this is simply pronunciation, as a beginner pronounces another language without getting any clear idea of the meaning. Could the schools really teach the masses to *read*, they would be doing a great work. The children of the lower classes have to commence work at a very early age, and it is impossible to keep them in the schools long enough to educate them to any degree. The school teaches them to read; the library must supply them with reading which shall serve to educate, and so it is that we are forced to divide popular education into two parts of almost equal importance and deserving equal attention: the free school and the free library.

Source: Melvil Dewey, "The Profession," *American Library Journal* 1 (1876): 5-6.

It is in the interest of the modern library, and of those desiring to make its influence wider and greater, that this journal has been established. Its founders have an intense faith in the future of our libraries and believe that if the best methods can be applied by the best librarians, the public may soon be brought to recognize our claim that the free library ranks with the free school. We hold that there is no work reaching farther in its influence and deserving more honor than the work which a competent and earnest librarian can do for his community.

The time *was* when a library was very like a museum, and a librarian was a mouser in musty books, and visitors looked with curious eyes at ancient tomes and manuscripts. The time *is* when a library is a school, and the librarian is in the highest sense a teacher, and the visitor is a reader among the books as a workman among his tools. Will any man deny to the high calling of such a librarianship the title of profession?

B. THE AMERICAN LIBRARY ASSOCIATION

From his early youth Dewey found himself involved in formal organizations such as societies and lyceums, and he served frequently in an official capacity. He was quite observant of details of organizational structure and goals—for example, of the Good Templars, of which he was a charter member. It was not unusual, therefore, once he had identified himself with the library world, that he fostered and agitated for an association of librarians.

His idea was not original, as Edward G. Holley chronicles skillfully in his book, *Raking the Historic Coals*. Nor, indeed, was he the only one expressing an interest in such a meeting in 1876. He was in the right place at the right time, however, and the continuity of the 1876 Conference is due in large part to his zeal and conviction. It was due even more to his willing assumption of the duties of secretary for the fledgling American Library Association, created by a resolution endorsed by those attending the Conference in Philadelphia.

Dewey's own feeling that he had initiated the move for the Conference of Librarians was somewhat exaggerated; nevertheless, he could never have exaggerated his contributions to insuring the permanency of the Association. Three years after the founding of the Association, Charles A. Cutter presumably reflected a commonly held view when he paid the following tribute to Dewey:

> It is not too much to say that more contrivances have been devised, more improvements have been suggested in the three years since Melvil Dewey conceived the happy idea of founding the American Library Association, than in the previous three decades.

The following, extracted from Dewey's many writings on the Association, represent his involvement in and concern for it. The selections are preceded by the text of the first printed "Call for a Library Conference," which identifies Dewey as a key figure in the planning.

2. CALL FOR A LIBRARY CONFERENCE (FIRST PRINTED CALL)

The undersigned, connected with the library interest of this country, believing that efficiency and economy in library work would be promoted by a conference of librarians, which should afford opportunity for mutual consultation and practical co-operation, issue this preliminary call, inviting librarians and all interested in library and bibliographical work, to meet at Philadelphia, on the 15th of August next, or otherwise as may be found more generally acceptable.

Lack of time forbidding more general consultation by direct correspondence, the present method is used as the most available for soliciting further signatures and suggestions for the preparation of the formal and general call to be issued at a later date. Those approving of the plan and willing to indorse such a call, whether they may be able to be present or not, are requested to send their names, with suggestions as to topics to be presented, etc., to MELVIL DEWEY, care of the PUBLISHERS' WEEKLY, 37 Park Row, New-York.

The place and date suggested are named in view of the usual library vacation about that time, when a large number of librarians would be likely to visit the Centennial Exhibition, with its book and library displays. Those preferring another date or place are requested to signify their choice.

Justin Winsor, Boston Public Library.

J. L. Whitney, Boston Public Library.

Fred. B. Perkins, Boston Public Library.

C. A. Cutter, Boston Athenaeum.

John Langdon Sibley, Harvard Univ. Libr.

John Fiske, Harvard University Library.

Ezra Abbot, Harvard University.

S. F. Haven, Am. Antiquarian Soc., Worcester.

J. Garson Brevoort, Astor Library.

F. Saunders, Astor Library.

W. S. Butler, New-York Society Library.

W. T. Peoples, New-York Mercantile Library.

Jacob Schwartz, Apprentices' Library, N.Y.

S. B. Noyes, Brooklyn Mercantile Library.

H. A. Homes, New-York State Library.

Lloyd P. Smith, Philadelphia Library Co.

Reuben A. Guild, Brown University Library.

J. D. Hedge, Providence Athenaeum.

Addison Van Name, Yale College Library.

Franklin B. Dexter, Yale College Library.

A. S. Packard, Bowdoin College Library.

Melvil Dewey, Amherst College Library.

Jas. G. Barnwell, Philadelphia Merc. Library.

John Eaton, Bureau of Education, Washington.

Wm. F. Poole, Chicago Public Library.

Chas. Evans, Indianapolis Public Library.

Thos. Vickers, Cincinnati Public Library.

Jno. N. Dyer, St. Louis Mercantile Library.

Source: "Librarians' Conference, October 1876," as reproduced in Edward G. Holley's *Raking the Historic Coals: The A.L.A. Scrapbook of 1876.* [Urbana, Ill.]: Beta Phi Mu, 1967. (Chapbook no. 8). pp. 54-55.

3. THE AMERICAN LIBRARY ASSOCIATION

"If such an organization [of Librarians] could be created upon a solid basis without ostentation, and without attempting to achieve too much, some, at all events, of the difficulties which beset appointments, under circumstances such as have been glanced at, would be put in a way of removal. In proportion as the number of Public Libraries shall increase and as the public concern in them shall be broadened, both the means and the desirableness of creating a Librarians' Association will, in all probability, evince themselves. . . . But unless an association bring with it increased means of systematic study, and of public evidence of the fruits of study, no result of much worth can be looked for."–Edward Edwards.

The interest manifested in the proposed library co-operation is sufficient to satisfy the most sanguine. Evidence from all sides proves that the time is fully come for something to be done. An editorial note on page 178 of the *Journal* called attention to this subject, and the Constitution reported by the Board is simply another step in the same direction. The satisfactory organization of the Association should take precedence of every thing else, for individuals are backward in urging their plans when there is no authority to which they can be submitted for consideration. Even when brought forward, they amount to little, whatever may be their real excellence, because of the need of official approval. An equally important service will be rendered by this tribunal in pointing out worthless propositions before time and labor are wasted in trying what has been repeatedly found without value. Here again individuals hesitate to come forward and demonstrate the folly of the crude ideas submitted and zealously supported by those of little actual experience. There are scores of matters already broached, all of them worthy the examination and attention of the Library Association. But until the organization is perfected, and some one has the authority to appoint committees and divide the work, each waits for the other, and while all are anxious to have something done, comparatively few feel at liberty to do any thing. We have had the Conference, and it was a success beyond all that its most sanguine friends had hoped. If there were those who doubted the necessity of a library organization, their doubts vanished after those three days of earnest and profitable labor, and there was established the *American Library Association*. The next thing of importance is agreement on a constitution under which to work, and after due consultation that is now adopted.

The interest had to be developed–of the profession and of the public. The Government Report, the establishment of the *Journal*, the Conference, the permanent organization, the preparation and adoption of a constitution–all these things have taken time and deserved it, are done and well done. The necessary preliminaries are finished, and we are ready for actual work.

One of the oldest living librarians recently said, in reviewing the year, "Through all coming time 1876 will be looked upon as the most eventful year in the history of libraries– the year in which the librarian fairly claimed and received at the hands of the public his place among the recognized professions." Something of this feeling has spread, not through this country alone, but in nearly all countries a new interest and activity in library matters is noted. It has been the proud fortune of America to lead in this movement, and the best informed of other countries are frank to say that they have much to learn on this side the Atlantic.

The result of this interest is naturally a large number of new ideas and suggestions from those experienced, and from those little versed, in the technicalities of library work. It is no small part of the work of the Association to control this interest and to guide it into profitable channels. For a time much attention must be given to details, and only a librarian appreciates the importance of library details. Most of these, once fairly settled, will require little, if any, more attention, and, when fairly out of the way, the Association will have opportunity to attempt that work which to the public will seem more important

Source: Melvil Dewey, "The American Library Association,"*American Library Journal* 1 (1877): 245-47.

and profitable. But we cannot build the house until we have made the bricks, for they are not ready to our hands. The problem before us is briefly this: to make the libraries better— their expenses less. If the average voter cannot be made to understand the importance of improvement, he is very susceptible to arguments in favor of economy, and the proposed work receives the most cordial endorsement of practical men.

As much uniformity as is consistent among the differently constituted libraries is a necessity for the full measure of economy; the present extravagance is almost entirely in doing things by ones, instead of by thousands, and the possibility of labor-saving in cataloguing and money-saving in supplies is conditional upon the degree of uniformity in methods and appliances. If no two libraries use the same size catalogue card, it will be difficult to devise any system of co-operative cataloguing applicable to all alike, and it will be wholly impossible to make the cards by the hundred thousand, and thus reduce their cost one half. There are several hundred different blanks and appliances already sent in as contributions to the Bibliothecal Museum. Many of these are of exceeding convenience, and help materially in the satisfactory and economical administration of both large and small libraries. If they could be obtained of the most approved patterns and at the lowest possible cost, it would be desirable to use them in many places where it is *not* desirable for the librarian to spend the amount of money and time necessary to devise and superintend the making of the few that he himself needs. A competent committee on supplies could do some exceedingly valuable work for the Association by carefully comparing the great variety in use, selecting the best models for all needed purposes, reporting them as standards, and then securing, as could easily be done, their manufacture in large quantities, so that they could be distributed to all libraries desiring, at a much lower price than they could otherwise be obtained. The advertising value of such supplies to any book house competing for library trade would induce it to furnish them at a trifling advance on the wholesale cost of manufacture; or should there be objections to this plan, offers have already been made by prominent and responsible parties to make needed library supplies under direction of a committee of the Association, and to hold them in stock subject to the orders of the committee, who may pay for them as fast as distributed to participating libraries. It would thus be possible for a Supply Committee to carry on this work without drawing on the Association for capital or support, and still the whole matter would be under the control of the Association. Without discussing details, it is evident that there is opportunity for a material saving in one considerable item of library expense. The catalogue cards, call slips, special blank books, notices, borrowers' cards, placards (many apply equally to all libraries), ledgers, slip boxes, devices for holding books upright, library trundles, steps, indicators, check boxes, etc., etc., while costing comparatively little to any one, amount to a very large sum when many libraries or a number of years are considered, for many of the supplies named from their nature require constant replenishing.

The proposed saving should not be confounded with Co-operation in the ordinary sense, which is simply a device for reducing the cost of getting articles from producer to consumer, without paying too much to middlemen. Library supplies are hardly any of them in the ordinary market, but are things made to special order. Such co-operation will conflict little with any established business. In each town some stationer, carpenter, and jack-of-all-trades may miss an occasional job of "puttering up something for the library;" but heretofore it has been about as practicable to make the supplies in quantity for all the libraries as it would have been to make the false teeth for an entire commonwealth from a single mould. Every thing had to be fitted to its special destination. While the field is not large enough to bring in capital and competition so that what is wanted can be secured, like the necessities of life, at a simple living profit above cost, the field is altogether too large to continue the wasteful and unsatisfactory system of each entirely for himself. In addition to the direct saving in money, such a series of standard supplies would assist a young librarian very materially in adopting the best methods, besides tending largely to secure uniformity in other matters. The Supply Committee, if it do vigorous work, can effect a substantial saving in money and patience to all the profession. At the first it will be no little labor, but, once done, the standing committee will have simply to consider actual improvements worthy adoption, and to keep the plan in repair.

Similar foundation work must be done by other competent committees, so that uniformity of some kind may be established in regard to a code of library abbreviations, capitals in cataloguing, preparation of titles; in fact, the foundation will only be laid when the Association has given suitable attention to all these matters, and recommended to its members for uniform use what seems to be the best. Then we can intelligently and with some hope of success enter upon measures for co-operative cataloguing and indexing, and important bibliographical or bibliothecal works. At present the diversity in details is so great, that it is a serious impediment to progress in these more important matters. Then with these details properly disposed of, we shall be ready to grapple directly with the main problem—the education of the masses through the libraries, by securing the best reading for the largest number at the least expense.

4. ORIGIN OF A.L.A. MOTTO

"The best reading for the largest number at the least cost," before the eye so constantly as our official motto, often prompts questions as to its origin. From the founding of the A.L.A. at Philadelphia in 1876, till my marriage, Oct. 19, 1878, I lived in Auburndale and Newton, and went back and forth 10 miles to my office in the saddle. Twenty miles a day on horseback gave nearly three hours to "think things over." One blustery winter morning I tried all the way to Boston to formulate for my own guidance a brief statement of what it was to which I was giving my life. Its use as a motto did not occur to me. I had refused what seemed to my family a most desirable position and salary in order to keep up this work for the A.L.A. In trying to get at the root of the matter it seemed that back of all our technical discussions and study for improved methods the supreme thing was to approximate at least the best reading, to make it reach as many people, young and old, as possible, and as a corollary and necessity for efficiency with the limits we should always find in everything, to utilize the principle of coöperation to make our money go farther, first by combining to supply books for common use in public libraries, since cost made it impracticable for each person to buy all the books he ought to read, and in the next step to increase efficiency of such libraries by adopting every labor-saving method or device that would enable us to do more with the time and money at our disposal. "The best reading for the largest number at the least cost" seemed to imply these essentials, for the best reading covered not alone what was read, but the methods of reading. I used this to explain my position, began to put it on corners of envelops as a suggestion, and others followd the example. It was in wide use and recognized as our slogan before it could be said to have been formally adopted as the official motto of the A.L.A.

Source: Melvil Dewey, "Origin of A.L.A. Motto,"*Public Libraries* 11 (1906): 55.

5. [INCORPORATION OF THE A.L.A.]

Prof. Justin Winsor, Pres. A.L.A.—Dear Sir: I propose to incorporate the A.L.A. under Massachusetts State law, the same as the Bible Society and other educational or missionary associations are incorporated. This involves some trouble and expense, of course; but I have faith enough in the wisdom of my plan to remove this only possible objection by offering to assume all the trouble and expense personally, so that it shall cost neither the A.L.A. nor any of its members a cent. Having done this, there are absolutely no objections to my plan. It imposes no added responsibilities or liabilities, and as an educational corporation we are free by law from taxation. I speak advisedly after careful examination and legal consultation, for which I have already paid all the fees. There are not even annual reports to the State to be made in the form in which we shall incorporate, *i.e.*, without capital stock. It involves no changes in our constitution, by-laws, officers, titles, or duties. In short, we could incorporate and gain the advantages without any of our members discovering the fact from any changes, except the new and valuable privileges which we acquire. We gain the following advantages without losing anything:

It gives us a permanence and dignity not to be secured under our present organization. We have a long and great work before us, and need all the help that comes from official recognition by the State.

We can then hold property legally and without taxation, and I hope we shall secure some large gifts which, as we are now situated, we have no legal authority to receive or own.

The A. L. A. becomes an individual and assumes its own responsibilities. Whatever complications might arise out of the various enterprises with which we are or may become connected, *e.g.*, the A. L. A. catalog, there cannot possibly be any liabilities to members, while, as it is at present, some very cautious people are a little afraid that any mistake *might* impose a liability on our members.

As a corporation, we can do many things which we cannot now do. In short, we gain much and lose only the trouble and expense for which I provide personally.

I wish to complete this work at once, because of an interest in a wealthy quarter which I am hoping, soon after this incorporation, will give us a handsome sum to help on our work. Till the matter is entirely completed, it will not do to call names, nor is it necessary. If I fail, no harm whatever has been done. We are ready to try somewhere else, and have the authority of the State to receive and hold as large a gift or legacy as we can get.

I know your approval will be prompt and hearty, and with it I shall go through the necessary formalities at once. If it involved new responsibilities or expense of any kind, the matter should be submitted to our next year's meeting, but it is unwise to wait for that, and the most hypercritical member would not object to the incorporation, if I take all the trouble and pay the bills. I should still advise it, even if such a thing as objection were possible, because, under the impossible supposition that the Association did not ratify the action, it would cost nothing to surrender our charter and go back to the old order of things. But of course this is useless talk. The possibility of getting a handsome sum to help our work counterbalances a thousand-fold these imaginary objections.

Any seven members in this vicinity can go through the necessary formalities, and the entire membership will profit by the advantages gained.

I shall look for your early and cordial approval.

Very truly,
MELVIL DUI.

Source: Melvil Dui, "[Incorporation of the A. L. A.]," *Library Journal* 5 (1880): 307.

6. [CERTIFICATE OF INCORPORATION OF THE ASSOCIATION]

No. 997. COMMONWEALTH OF MASSACHUSETTS.

Be it known that, whereas Justin Winsor, C. A. Cutter, Samuel S. Green, James L. Whitney, Melvil Dui, Fred B. Perkins, and Thomas W. Bicknell have associated themselves with the intention of forming a corporation under the name of the "American Library Association," for the purpose of promoting the library interest of the country, by exchanging views, reaching conclusions, and inducing co-operation in all departments of bibliothecal science and economy; by disposing the public mind to the founding and improving of libraries; and by cultivating good-will among its own members; and have complied with the provisions of the statutes of this Commonwealth, in such case made and provided, as appears from the certificate of the president, treasurer, and executive board of said corporation, duly approved by the Commissioner of Corporations, and recorded in this office.

Now, therefore, I, Henry B. Peirce, Secretary of the Commonwealth of Massachusetts, do hereby certify that said Justin Winsor, C. A. Cutter, Samuel S. Green, James L. Whitney, Melvil Dui, Fred. B. Perkins, and Thomas W. Bicknell, their associates and successors, are legally organized and established, and are hereby made an existing corporation under the name of the "American Library Association," with the powers, rights, and privileges, and subject to the limitations, duties, and restrictions which by law appertain thereto. Witness my official signature hereunto subscribed and the seal of the Commonwealth of Massachusetts hereunto affixed, this tenth day of December, in the year of our Lord one thousand eight hundred and seventy-nine.

HENRY B. PEIRCE,
Secretary of the Commonwealth.

Source: Melvil Dui, "[Incorporation of the A. L. A.]," *Library Journal* 5 (1880): 308.

7. PAST, PRESENT, AND FUTURE OF THE A.L.A.

The share of the writer in the library work of the last four years will excuse, in part, at least, the personal character of this summary.

When I commenced, in the early summer of 1876, to agitate for a *Library Journal* and Association, most of the leading librarians were doubtful of the possibility of accomplishing much. A few were more hopeful, most prominent among them Mr. Cutter, of the Boston Atheneum. In spite of discouragements I went forward. The four years have past, and every one acknowledges that a great deal has been done. The public has awakened to an interest in libraries never before known. Librarianship has been elevated to the rank of a profession, and there are more and better aspirants for places in libraries than ever before. Those who had been doubtful became enthusiastic, and worked side by side with the more hopeful. True, the time had come for all this, but without our efforts little would have been done. The thousands of letters scattered through the country, conferences, circulars, Journals, etc., have stimulated to activity and caused the delivery of addresses, publication of articles, and, in many cases, the better management or equipment of old libraries, or the opening of new. While so much has been done, vastly more might have been done, and may still be done, if we heed the lesson of the past four years. Read the Secretary's report to the Boston conference, then add to it the list of the things we ought and want to do as an Association. Without exception, it will be found that for any satisfactory work two things are absolutely necessary: An office as head-quarters, and a man or woman giving exclusive time and thought to library interests. Hosts of letters must be written and answered; circulars with suggestions for better work must be distributed; visitors, librarians, and committees must be seen. An office-secretary devoted to the task would have every minute crowded with solid work. This has never been done. The A. L. A. has never paid a cent for either office or work, although my own office was apparently looked upon as head-quarters.

In 1879, the Readers and Writers Economy Company, just started, offered office accommodations for that year without charge. Any gain from this, however, was neutralized because there was no one there to do the work, and both Mr. Jackson and myself were at once plunged so deeply into the cares of the rapidly growing Economy Company, that neither of us could give any proper attention to library work, so we have really had no office except through 1879, and that lost most of its value for want of the right man in it.

As to work, our officers, committees, and members from the first have shown the best disposition, but the pressure of their regular duties was too great, and it was and always will be quite impracticable for more than one or two persons to do our work. Done in twenty different places by twenty different people, it has not over 1-20th the value that it would have focalized in one office, done by one person who gave each duty the benefit of all the rest, and thus practically carried out the idea of co-operation. No one, on second thought, will see any possibility of getting our work done by scattered volunteers. Much help may be secured in this way, but even that requires the central office to lay out and utilize this work. Mr. Cutter, Mr. Jackson, and Mr. Perkins have given a great deal of time in the past to the work of the Co-operation Committee, and Mr. Jackson has often given time to visitors; but for the most part the work has been left undone, except such as I have myself been able to do by stealing time from vacation, sleep, or from pressing duties. This is the past—much done of which we may all feel proud; much more undone for lack of time and facilities.

Now the present. In January last, I thought the future was assured when I induced Mr. Fred. B. Perkins to join me in the office, resigning his long connection with the Boston Public Library. We planned, after getting other work in order, to build up the library interest under his direct charge. He was the right man to have done this. No one without practical library experience, without executive force and no little tact, could succeed. But, with only a few days' warning, there came in June the urgent offers of the San Francisco Public Library. The opportunity to do work he had long desired to do made it seem necessary to Mr. Perkins to take the position, and we accepted his resignation with great regret, but in hopes that in some way we might divide up the work among those left, and carry it

Source: Melvil Dui, "Past, Present, and Future of the A.L.A.," *Library Journal* 5 (1880): 274-76.

forward. The same week came an equally heavy blow in the sudden offer to Mr. R. R. Bowker of the position in London which he now holds. Again the opportunity to do desired work made it seem best, and Mr. Bowker, who had more and more assumed the heaviest work on the *Journal,* and who was the most active and efficient of all our members and workers, sailed for London as Mr. Perkins started for San Francisco. At about the same time, ill-health and proposed long absences from home compelled Mr. Jackson to resign. Both Mr. Leypoldt, the publisher of the *Journal,* and myself were before all this so overworked as to fear a complete break-down. It seemed impossible to carry another straw. All coming as if by fatality at once, seemed to make the suspension of the *Journal* necessary, and it was hastily announced as the June number went to press. After further reflection, and in spite of his heavy losses, Mr. Leypoldt has determined to complete the volume, with a noble generosity and devotion to the library interests which only those who know him personally will appreciate fully. I wish to thus publicly bear witness, in behalf of many prominent librarians with whom I have talked, to our appreciation. The five volumes of the *Journal* will be complete and indexed.

By resigning all business connection with the Readers and Writers Economy Co., and by transferring to Mr. T. R. Vickroy, of St. Louis, the newly elected Treasurer and Corresponding Secretary of the Spelling Reform Association, most of the detail work that has heretofore fallen to my lot as Secretary, I am released from the pressure that made it impossible for me to do any part of my various duties as they should be done. I am still very busy, and, like most of our old guard, overworked. I can hereafter perform the regular duties of Secretary, records of meetings, certificates of membership, collection of fees, etc., for all these things can be done at odd moments and evenings, giving them needed time and attention. But this is simply like committee work, and even a busy man can contrive to do it, but it is not enough. It is necessary that there be one whose business and duty it is to work constantly for the library interest. Officers who do what they can with pleasure cannot and will not accomplish what we want done.

This is our present. What shall the future be?

We are well started. We have over 400 members. We have the sympathy of the press and of every one who knows us. We have learned valuable lessons as to our work and how to do it. The A. L. A. Catalog, the best fruit of co-operation, is nearly complete and can be shortly sent to press. We have many enthusiastic members, ready to work and give. We have a large constituency looking to us and depending on us for aid and guidance. The expression of opinion thus far indicates that the *Journal,* in a more condensed and economical form, at about half the present price, can pay expenses and continue its good work, and do still better. Finally, experience justifies me in saying that the necessary money to go forward can readily be raised if our need of it is properly made known. For the first three years we were always behind, and I paid necessary bills on faith that the money would some day come. Last year a little special effort was made for two or three months, and the debt was paid, and we have over $400 in the treasury to-day with which to start our work.

It seems as if there could be but one answer, and that in favor of a vigorous forward movement, in which each shall try to do his part in awakening new interest, securing new members, and contributing to the common fund the result of his own experiments and experience. Let us have a general and prompt expression of opinion which will practically decide the question. All letters sent to the Secretary will be submitted to the Executive Board and summarized for the next *Journal.* The office and the worker is the main thing to be decided upon. The right woman for the place could render efficient service, and suggestions of names, with salary expected, etc., will be specially welcome. The question is all important, and every reader of the *Journal* interested should send something, if only a postal card, to say "go ahead." But every one must have something to say, and I hope to receive during November a letter or card from every reader of this paper.

MELVIL DUI.

8. [DEWEY'S ADDRESS AT THE TWENTY-FIRST ANNIVERSARY OF THE ASSOCIATION, 1897]

LADIES AND GENTLEMEN: I cannot help looking back 21 years to the time when we came to Philadelphia to organize the American Library Association. Since then, year by year, and by little groups of years, we have taken up one work after another, but none of them have been finished. Yet we have had distinct periods when the library associations and library journals and state and local associations dotted the country all over. We have had meetings of state associations and city associations where the attendance was larger than at our national meetings. There was in the very beginning, in 1876, a movement for library extension. It was a society of propaganda; we all went out with the idea of spreading the library movement. The old idea of the library as a reservoir was giving way to that of the fountain; we were to have a fountain where each one might go. And then it was a question of piping the water from the fountain to almost every house and every room in a city. And step by step we had the different kinds of libraries: the reference library, and the branches, and the travelling library carrying books to all who wished to use them. Then there was a development from the very first library methods—the development of the science of library economy. And some said we were threshing over old straw and learning the lessons that older men had already learned. But that was not true, for we were laying the foundations for the new science.

If we study the proceedings of the American Library Association in those early years it will be seen that we were laying foundations. That work has been largely done. We shall improve upon it from time to time, but when the history of the Association is written it will read that from 1876 for nearly 10 years was the time when most was done for the development of library methods and toward making it possible to do a larger amount of good work with the time and money at disposal. Then came the work with the library in the schools. And we only understand the a, b, c, of that at the present time. For 20 years different branches of that work have been going on, but it was not until the organization last year of the Library Department of the National Educational Association that the library was recognized as an essential part of education. I say essential, for the library is now looked upon as a useful adjunct of the school. We have been compelled to do like a man who puts a building on an insufficient foundation and when it begins to settle down repairs it and makes it a little stronger; and still it sinks, and he repairs it again and again until it gets down to bed rock. That is what we are doing in this 19th century; we are finding bed rock on which our educational fabric will stand.

Mr. Seeds said that if only the boys and girls of Philadelphia had the settling of this question of whether Philadelphia should have a central library, that the question would be settled beyond peradventure, but he said the boys and girls have not the settling of the question. I contend the boys and girls of Philadelphia are going to settle this question in a very few years. The boys in a very few years are going to be the voters who will decide this question. A prominent politician in one of our great cities said to me he had the power and the votes to overturn the work that was done in our free libraries. I said: "You have the votes perhaps, and if you dared you might do this thing, but let me tell you, you will be surprised how many men in the city of New York favor free libraries and, if need be, will carry a gun before they will give up this part of their educational system." And I say to you here that the boys and girls of Philadelphia will settle this question, and their fathers and mothers will settle it in the same way when they come to realize the benefit of the free library system.

Following the period of specific co-operation in library work, came the relation of the library to the state and nation. That was the hitching of the wagon to the star. It is no more possible to build up a satisfactory system of libraries for supplying reading-matter to the people without aid, both state and national, than it would be to carry on our schools in that way.

Source: Melvil Dewey, "[Address at the Twenty-First Anniversary of the Association]," *Library Journal* 22 (1897): C117-C119.

Then most important of all comes this period upon which we are just entering, which I like to call the filtration period. We had the reservoir and we changed it to the fountain. We not only went on from that and piped the books to every house and every room, but that was not enough and we must go farther. I remember a few years ago there was an appropriation of five or six hundred thousand dollars made in the city of Albany to get a greater water supply for the city, and the money was spent in bringing the water of the Hudson and distributing it by pipes throughout the city, and it was piped into every room. But we discovered the faster the water was piped to the city the faster our citizens went to the cemetery, so we appropriated another million of dollars to take up the subject of filtration. No city expects to send poisoned water to its citizens; neither does a library desire to furnish bad reading, but the public library is at fault, in my judgment, in not doing more for quality in all it is doing for quantity. It is a necessary work to get books to the people, but we should constantly endeavor to improve the quality of the books, for the library must be the library militant before it can become the library triumphant.

The "yellow journalism" of to-day is the most serious problem that confronts us. We would do well in dealing with it if we followed out the plan of the little girl who complained that her brother had set a trap to catch the pretty birds. She said she had prayed real hard that the birds would not get caught in the trap. She was asked what else she did. She said: "I went out and kicked that trap all to pieces." Possibly there is a lesson for us here, because some of our libraries have been content with a great circulation of books to record, but they have thoroughly seized upon the idea of having the books used without having before them this problem that comes under the head of filtration, and this is a work that can be done only through the public library system and not through book-stores. The idea in my mind is that by and by the library is to take almost entirely the place of the book-store; it will be a place where the reader will be shown a book and be interested in it and will buy it. . . .

* * * * * *

9. MAN-A-MONTH VOLUNTEERS

Every intelligent member has a distinct duty to the A. L. A. for 1907. Mr Lane in our last number urged all to read our *Bulletin* and thus keep informed of what the A. L. A. has done, is doing and is going to do. That will give you faith, but faith without works is dead. We have lived, worked and hoped for thirty years, or a full generation. Now, larger and better things are just ahead. In 1876 librarians were, like the conies, feeble folk. Our first conference was a bibliothecal John the Baptist crying in Philadelphia, and our field was in Locust street and Wissahickon. Some of us dreamed dreams and saw visions, and the wisest thought us prophets and the foolish called us cranks, but with an eye single to the highest public good, we faithfully pressed on. At the close of thirty years we should inventory results.

The small beginnings based on mustard seed faith have grown from the little shrub to a great tree and now certain fowls of the air incline to roost in its branches. Some are useful birds, but some will bear watching and a vigorous "shoo." But the best ship accumulates some barnacles and the noblest trees some fungous growths which should be lopped off.

No one questions that modern librarianship has become a world movement. It has won its place as a profession. Its national, state and local associations, training schools, state departments and commissions, liberal appropriations favoring legislation, unparalled gifts and universal public commendation have placed it side by side with the public school system. In this wonderful work among all civilized nations America is the unquestioned leader, and her work has been mostly done by the A. L. A. Its record should command heartiest support not only of its members but of the public. When we dreamed great things and those of limited vision called us crazy, we have comforted ourselves with Longfellow's Keramos, "Divine insanity of noble minds that never falters or abates, but labors and endures and waits, till all that it foresees it finds, and what it can not find, creates." We have been guided by the Fabians [sic] society's wise motto, "For the right moment you must wait most patiently as Fabius did when warring against Hannibal, though many censured his delays. But when the right moment comes you must strike hard, else your waiting will have been in vain and fruitless." We have been patient and persistent. We have worked and waited. With 1907 the right moment has come when we must strike hard. Few of those who have lived and shared in it fully realize what this quiet and steady growth has brought us. Some one farther away in time will get a better perspective. Who hath eyes so keen and strong that he has seen *when* the acorn became an oak? Thus the library movement has won its high place by slow, steady, constant growth, till we stand in awe before its almost limitless possibilities for good. Those who look deepest see more in the future than in the past. We are proud of what has been done, but we are responsible for what is to be. To whom much is given, of him much will be required. When we add new power and labor-saving machinery, our factories must turn out greater products, unless some one neglects plain duty and opportunity.

We have waited thirty years for our official *Bulletin* and for our own official home in national library headquarters. Our membership has grown twenty-fold, and yet includes not more than one in a hundred who would be keenly interested in our work, could he see it with our eyes and understand its infinite usefulness. The present duty is to enroll as many as possible of this ninety and nine, for this is the field of largest promise.

Each member will hereafter receive our bulletins, with frequent messages of progress and encouragement. They will keep his interest alive instead of letting it die down for lack of fuel or be crowded out by causes with more active promoters. Could we inspire every member with one-tenth the zeal of the men who build up commercial, industrial, political, financial or social successes, 1907 would be a red-letter year in library history.

Have we in our two thousand members one who could not with a little effort and time enlist one new member each month from now till the Asheville meeting? That would mean ten thousand members, each a center to be influenced and to influence. This is not an irridescent dream. We can attain it if each will try. For one who fails to make his quota,

Source: Reprinted by permission of the American Library Association from "Man-a-Month Volunteers," by Melvil Dewey, *ALA Bulletin* 1 (1907): 1-3.

others will make up, if all canvass the circle of acquaintance thoroughly. We have no right to rest on our laurels or to stop our vigorous growth. The A. L. A. is like a tree, when it ceases to grow it begins to rot. Can any member claim to have the real library spirit and yet be unwilling to make this effort for a cause without a peer in educational and philanthropic promise?

Let us have an honor roll of those who really give this much-needed support in bringing to the highest efficiency these new great agencies which we have started on a small scale, but with large faith. Encourage Headquarters by sending a card saying, "Enroll me in the man-a-month volunteers." If half the men you secure are women, so much the better for the cause to which woman has contributed much more than her half. Then at Asheville let the secretary read the names for honorable discharge of those who have found at least one each month willing to join in the splendid work which has made the A. L. A. famous and is destined to carry its banner to still higher peaks of achievement.

10. [DEWEY'S FIFTIETH ANNIVERSARY STATEMENT TO THE ASSOCIATION, 1926]

To A L A

We compute the orbit of a planet by studying its past speed and direction. This summer completes ALA's first half century. This is an arc of its orbit long enuf so its study shud indicate speed and direction for the years before us.

In 1876 W F Poole, Nestor of librarians, said, "We hav had a wonderful library conference. I attended the first conference held in N Y 1/4 century ago. In another 25 years we shud hold a 3d meeting".

Rushing in where angels feard to tread, I insisted that the work before us was so vast and urjent that annual meetings wer necessary and agreed to call a meeting *every* year if 5 or more wud come. One year we had only about 30, but step by step A L A has grown to world-wide recognition for the work it has done for popular education. I used to tel Andrew Carnegie that he cud accomplish 10 to 100 fold more by endowing A L A, whose influence reaches 10,000 centers, than by giving the same money for a beautiful granit building in a single place. A L A would stimulate interest til *local* money wud provide the building. The greatly needed inspirational work cud be done only by a national body thoroly organized and with central executiv offices from which experts wud radiate continual inspiration and guidance. The most optimistic of 1876 did not dare vision 1/2 what we hav today and a few of us wer very good seers.

Most of the leaders hav gone into the silence. We who ar left owe it to them and to the public good to carry on the torch.

1926 shud be another red letter year in library history. Our semicentennial wil attract attention thruout the cuntry and some 1000s of people who hav money to be given for the public good wil hav lojd in their minds the thot that A L A offers perhaps the biggest dividend on their investment.

Let us look back in pride on the magnificent work done in the past 50 years. Let us look forward with supreme faith in the future. And chiefly let us all 'lend a hand.'

Melvil Dewey
Sr. ex-president A L A

Source: Reprinted by permission of the American Library Association from "To ALA," by Melvil Dewey, *ALA Bulletin* 20 (1926): 102.

C. QUALIFICATIONS OF A LIBRARIAN

As formerly unavailable channels of communication opened in 1876, librarians began to express concern over qualifications for the profession. Through the new *American Library Journal*, Dewey's own proclamation that librarianship deserved the "high calling" of a profession depicted the impact of his unstated qualifications. These would identify the librarian as "in the highest sense a teacher," and he contrasted skillfully the "new" librarian with the old, whom he regarded as a "mouser in musty books."

At the 1876 Conference of Librarians Lloyd P. Smith, of the Library Company of Philadelphia, magnified this concern by using as his theme, "The Qualifications of a Librarian," in a carefully prepared address.

In the report on *Public Libraries in the United States of America*, also released in 1876, no entry appears in the index under "qualifications"; however, William F. Poole, based on his own experience, presented his somewhat disillusioned opinion of applicants for the position of librarian. His deprecating appraisal was a rebuke then, and is now, to those seeking to enter the profession unprepared for its demands. His frank observations follow:

> Even before the lists of books to be purchased are made and a place
> is provided for their reception, the board will have received a score
> of applications for the position of librarian. Every one of these
> applicants is abundantly qualified (in his or her own opinion)
> for the duties, and will furnish many testimonials to sustain this
> claim; and yet probably not one of them has had any experience
> in the work. The directors, if they use the same good judgment which
> they apply to their own private business, will appoint a person who
> has had experience; and such a person can be obtained at a moderate
> salary if inquiries be made at some of the large libraries where young
> persons of both sexes have been regularly trained. The local prejudice
> that the librarian must be a resident is absurd, and one which the
> individual members of the board do not observe in conducting their
> own affairs. The business of a librarian is a profession, and practical
> knowledge of the subject is never so much needed as in starting a
> new enterprise. If a person of experience cannot be found, the best
> material that offers, resident or otherwise, must be taken. Persons
> who have failed in everything else are usually the local applicants
> for the position. Broken down ministers, briefless lawyers, unsuccess-
> ful school teachers, and physicians without patients, especially,
> are desirous to distinguish themselves as librarians. The same energy,
> industry, and tact, to say nothing of experience, which insure
> success in other avocations are quite as requisite in a librarian as
> book knowledge. A mere bookworm in charge of a public library,
> who has not the qualities just named, is an incubus and a nuisance.

In 1886, after becoming Librarian of Columbia College, Dewey made an address before the Association of Collegiate Alumnae on "Librarianship as a Profession for College-Bred Women," in which he identified an academic degree as a desirable qualification. He shared his view with a wider audience by reprinting a section of his address on the "Librarians' Qualifications, Hours, and Salary" in an issue of *Library Notes* for the same year.

The subject of qualifications continued to be of searching interest both in library schools and in training programs. Though the search continues to the present time, Dewey codified, tersely but exuberantly, the qualifications that he deemed essential. Designed primarily for the use of New York State Library School students, the qualifications related to character, scholarship, bibliographic knowledge, and library economy; they are reprinted here as a summation of Dewey's views on the matter.

Since admission policies of library schools should be designed to identify those with desirable qualifications, the "Application for Admission to the New York State Library School" (1902) is also included to demonstrate how Dewey attempted to obtain appropriate information.

11. QUALIFICATIONS OF A LIBRARIAN

A   As a man. Character

1   Fiber, inborn qualities

"Every man is as God made him and ofttimes a good deal worse."

You can polish an agate, but not a pumpkin.

2   Spirit of work

    a Aspiration for excellence, for higher things, not mere ambition ("going round for votes") but constant struggle against tendency to sag. Every soul like every drop of water, is pulled steadily toward the lowest point by gravity. No boat ever drifts upstream when the oars stop. He who aspires to the best must never wholly relax earnest effort.

> Heaven is not reached by a single bound;
> But we build the ladder by which we rise
> From the lowly earth to the vaulted skies,
> And we climb to its summit,
> Round by round.   *J. G. Holland*

    b Courage (active) is brave to do, e.g. to lead cavalry charge; "heart in." Fortitude (passive) is brave to suffer and endure.

    c Enthusiasm; love; zeal; "soul in," "God in"; earnestness; inspiration.

    d Energy; force; "work in."

    e Patient persistence; steadfast purpose. Too great haste will make an ugly scar from a seal suddenly struck on wax, when patient pressure will give an impression as clear cut as a cameo. The world is afloat and lazy and can be moved by patient pushing. A heavy blow on a loaded canal boat will cause only a tremor. Half the force patiently applied will move it to the other shore. Illustrations: Kipling; "crabs don't let go"; mushrooms v. oaks.

"Time is of the essence of the contract."

"For the right moment you must wait most patiently as Fabius did when warring against Hannibal, though many censured his delays. But when the right moment comes you must strike hard, else your waiting will have been in vain and fruitless."

                           Motto of Fabian Society

    f Faith; optimism. Self-confidence, but not overconfidence. Believe in yourself and your work. "Hitch your wagon to a star."

                           Emerson

    g Unselfishness. The ideal rule of life is to do anything, anywhere, at any time, that sober judgment says will do the greatest good to one's fellows.

Care more for your work than for personal reputation, salary, power, etc. Resign if it is the best way to help a cause. You may be right and yet it may be duty to resign for general good. Don't do it on impulse, but ask honest, competent judges and convince them that you want truth, not flattery. Square person in round hole; 22 caliber cartridge when Flobert cap is better.

    h Loyalty; to library, trustees and official head. Follow your leader. Resign if you can't be loyal. A useful soldier must support his captain in action, even if he is taking wrong course. Convince him of error at some other time, but in action work as for your own plan.

    i Cooperation. Utilize others; team work.

With feet on the firm rock of high character, educated intelligence and steadfast purpose you are sure to win. Some are called unbalanced when it is the

Source: Melvil Dewey, "Qualifications of a Librarian," New York (State) Library, *Bulletin* 75, Library School 12 (October 1902): 91-96. (University of the State of New York, Bulletin 268).

> Divine insanity of noble minds
> That never falters nor abates,
> But labors and endures and waits
> Till all that it foresees it finds,
> And what it can not find, creates.

3   Plane of work

     a   Physical. Mere faithful doing of task; treadmill, like horse, machine or hitching post. Virtues all negative; no fault or vice.

     b   Mental. Intellectual ambition: the "thirst delirious yet divine, to know." Chemist's researches.

     c   Moral. Altruism; missionary spirit; highest good of others. The spirit of the deed, not the thing done, determines its plane. A pestilent marsh may be reclaimed either to protect neighbors from disease or merely as land speculation.

4   Social qualities

     a   Personal appearance; presentableness; dress; neatness.

     b   Good habits. A librarian, like a minister or teacher, is an educator and stands on a pedestal. His standards must be higher than is necessary for other professional or business men. He must not be addicted to alcohol, drugs, tobacco, gambling, profanity or vulgarity.

     c   Good manners essential to highest success. Inward spirit vastly more than outward form marks the truest gentleman. "Good form" which assumes that time and money are of no account, and all fashionable extremes are wholly out of place in a library.

     d   Ease. Shyness and awkwardness are fences that keep people away and limit usefulness in all positions in contact with the public.

     e   Tact. Two to one more important than mere talent.

        The ideal of these essential qualities is like the best literary style and the best window glass: i. e. that which is not noticed and causes no remark. Overdressing, affectation or undue "ease of manner" is as objectionable as the opposite fault.

5   Physical qualities. Health; strength; endurance; trained powers. See 7. Body is machine through which work must be done. Unless it is properly cared for the best work is as impossible as to win a race with an overtired horse.

Health modifies (helps or harms) temper, tact and most other qualities. It is a vehicle for them like water for giving medicine. Greatest dangers are overwork, too long hours, too short vacations, too little sleep. Greatest needs are regular habits, intelligent diet, and exercise by walking, cycling, dumb-bells, movements, rubbing, flexing, etc.

6   Mental qualities

     a   Orderly habit. A misplaced book or pamphlet is a needle lost in a haystack. Some professions admit lack of order, but not the librarian's. A ditch-digger may smoke, but not an employee of a fireworks factory.

     b   Memory. Less essential but very important. Library memory may be largely cultivated.

     c   Accuracy. Invaluable but must not be at sacrifice of speed.

     d   Speed; dispatch; prompt decision; readiness. Expert riflemen and billiard players take quickest aim. Fastest stenographers are often most accurate. Quickness may be cultivated. Tennis is admirable discipline in prompt decision. Preparing copy for daily paper trains to completion of work at specified time. After dinner speeches without previous warning train quick wits. "Reading maketh a full man, writing an exact man, and conference a ready man." Accuracy and speed must be equally developed to get best results. Quality and quantity must be multiplied together like length and breadth to get efficiency or area. A perimeter gives the maximum area only when evenly divided. If perimeter is 40, each side may be 10 and the area 100. If sides are unequally divided 15 x 1 equals 75, 19 x 1 equals 19. Efficiency depends on product of accuracy and speed, or quantity and quality, as much as momentum or impact depends on mass multiplied by velocity.

Conciseness helps speed. Telegram written like polite note shows a frank or folly. Gotten (got 10) seats.

   e Executive ability; power to organize and delegate work, to marshal and use
four m's which produce results: i. e. materials, machinery (tools, labor-saving
devices), methods, men. Without this can get only maximum wages for
individual. With it you get pay for what others do. This is unjust no more than
to take pay for utilizing forces of nature, horses or mere labor. Architect takes
ugly pile of stone, makes a temple and gets pay for brains put into it. Must make
work go smoothly. If there is creaking of the machinery there is usually waste
of power. A good executive does not inflict his troubles on others but burns
his own smoke. He makes stepping-stones of stumbling blocks rather than go
round them or sit down and wait for road commissioner to remove them.

B   As a scholar

7   Education. All powers disciplined and ready for use with precision, force, speed
and continuity. Life's problems must be bombarded with mental batteries. Victory
requires all these four factors. The man behind the gun who aims and pulls the
trigger decides the issue. Therefore the training of that man is the chief concern.
Needle gun in Franco-Prussian war. The boy is like ore fresh from mines. The
elementary school modifies and makes from the ore pig iron. The high school and
college modify further and make steel, which may be used equally well for any
use demanding good steel. The professional or technical school takes the steel and
makes springs and levers and wheels for special uses. Experience in life demonstrates
fitness for any good work as the complete machine must prove its fitness before it
commands a market. A librarian commands salary as a machine commands price,
according to improvement in practical value made by education. The same steel
sold in a bar for $1, modified into the parts of a typewriter sells for $100.

8   Languages. Chief tools for work. Every language learned adds to the librarian's
opportunity for usefulness more than equal study of other subjects, for language
is a key which readers often wish to borrow for opening foreign books.

   a German and French most used; with English the three great world languages.
A good equipment needed in all library work. These three are expected in all
cases. Other languages are much less valuable and need not be mastered by those
with no special aptitude.

   b Italian and Spanish. Since Cuban war Spanish has become of commercial importance
and is more likely to be useful in a library.

   c Latin. Less used; valuable as introduction to French, Italian, Spanish.

   d Scandinavian and Russian, Dutch, Greek, Sanskrit, Hebrew, etc. are of trifling
use except in rare libraries or for unusual investigations, or where there is
some colony from these nations.

9   Knowledge. Any possible information may be useful. All librarians are expected to
read German and French and to know general history and literature. As library
covers entire field of knowledge which no man could master, the librarian's training
should be not to accumulate facts, but to know where and how to get any facts
promptly when wanted. Don't buy fish which will soon cease to be fresh, but poles,
lines, hooks and bait and learn holes where they may be quickly caught when
wanted. Librarian like guidepost is always pointing the way for others instead of
going himself.

   a Sociology. Public press and university are all making sociology prominent.
This is sociologic century. 19th was scientific, 18th was theologic. After German
and French, which are working tools, no subject is more useful to a librarian
than sociology.

   b Useful arts. Some general knowledge is valuable in the growing work of helping
mechanics and artisans in their own field.

C   As a bibliographer

10   Knowledge of books. Appreciation, not creation
Physical (outside)

   a Printers' and publishers' work. In print the great aim should be to convey
the author's meaning to the reader's mind clearly, in the quickest and easiest
way. Omit everything not needed for this end.

(1)   Paper. Color, thickness, durability, cost.
(2)   Printing. Size and face of type, leading, spacing, length of line, margins, ink, presswork, mechanical proof reading, cost.
(3)   Binding. Materials, methods, cost, durability, color, convenience in handling.

Intellectual (inside)

b   Editor's work. Contents, indexes, footnotes, editorial proof reading and verification.
c   Author's work. Style, facts, accuracy; i. e. subject-matter.
d   Bibliographer's work. Organized and comparative bibliography; knowledge of editions, publishers, prices and comparative merits and faults of *a*, *b* and *c*. Catalogues, selections, annotations, evaluations, "filtrations." Object to select for reader the book that then, there and to him is most useful.

D   As a library economist
11   Knowledge of library systems and methods
a   Scope and founding of libraries.
b   Legislation, local, state, national.
c   How to raise money.
d   Connection with schools.
e   Reading of the young, children's libraries.
f   Buildings and equipment.
g   Library assistants.
h   Salaries, hours, vacations, etc.
i   Accession department (all methods of getting books).
j   Preservation of books.
k   Use of books, for reference and in lending. Get, keep, use – the greatest of these is use.
l   Cataloguing and classification.
12   Library experience. For best results, must combine knowledge and experience (like quantity and quality or speed and accuracy). Physician must add hospital work to graduation and M.D. before he is fully trusted.
13   Knowledge and experience
a   in business principles and methods.
b   of the world at large (travel).
c   in special accomplishments; mechanical ability. Value not intrinsic, but for convenience in trifling needs; desirable but not essential. Some great mathematicians can't add or multiply accurately, but must use machine or clerk.
    (1)   Book repairing ⎫ Of greatest practical value in saving time and
    (2)   Book gilding   ⎬ cost of sending away to bindery.
    (3)   Handwriting, lettering. Very useful for bulletins, notices, etc. Easily learned.
    (4)   Notehand. Learned in an hour and saves quarter of labor without appreciably affecting legibility for one's own use. Also readily learned and used by regular correspondents. Should be used by all who do not learn shorthand.
    (5)   Shorthand. Invaluable labor-saver, but useless unless well learned. To begin and stop for a time is like taking long rests when rowing boat up strong current; you may float back farther than you have rowed. Most systems too complicated for anyone except professional stenographer. Tachygraphy is easily learned and best for librarian's use.
    (6)   Typewriting. More legible, quicker, cheaper and easier, so should be used personally as well as by assistants and copyists.
    (7)   Duplicating processes. Stencil, carbon, roller copier, composition and aniline.
    (8)   Labor-saving methods and appliances.

14   Efficiency. Total or resultant of all foregoing factors. World wants results, not explanations (however good) of failure. The best men compel success and remove obstacles. Cheaper men explain clearly why success was impossible. They may be clever, clear-headed, honest, industrious, but not efficient in high sense that compels success.

12. APPLICATION FOR ADMISSION TO THE NEW YORK STATE LIBRARY SCHOOL

I have read carefully the handbook explaining the aims, methods and requirements of the library school.

I wish to enter the school . . . 190 to remain for . . . Below I give as accurately as I can the information required to decide my claim for admission.

1 Full name

2 Address

[Answer accurately, in your own handwriting. Where more space is needed, complete the answer on the last page, prefixing the proper number. The arbitrary scale in questions 5, 10 and 28 conveys a clearer idea than words, and care should be taken to assign the numbers accurately. The opinion of judicious friends will help greatly. The faculty needs these details in deciding which of the numerous candidates have the best claims on the strictly limited facilities of the school]

3 Age   4 Married   5 Health

[Give here the figure fairly estimating your place in this scale: 4=very delicate; 5=delicate, but able to work; 6= fair; 7= good; 8=very good; 9=perfect]

6 How many days have you lost in the past year because of ill health?

7 Have you any noticeable physical defect of any kind; e. g. in sight, hearing or speech?

8 Addresses of references who can speak positively of your character, abilities and experience.

9 Education. Give schools and years; if a graduate, degrees and dates of graduation.

[Forward with your application, if practicable, catalogues for years when you were in attendance]

10 With what languages are you familiar?

[Mark against each the figure showing the degree of familiarity, thus: 2=slight acquaintance, can pick out common titles; 4=read with dictionary; 6=read fluently; 8=read, write and speak fluently. Use the odd figures for closer approximation; e. g. 5= read with slight use of dictionary. Use 9 for mother tongue only]

Language	Familiarity	Where acquired?	How much used? Where and how?
English			
German			
French			
Italian			
Spanish			
Latin			
Greek			

Source: "Application for Admission to the New York State Library School," In New York (State) Library School, "Handbook . . . Including Summer Course and Library Handwriting," New York (State) Library *Bulletin 66, Library School 9* (September 1901): 383-84.

11 To what extent have you pursued special studies or courses of reading?

12 What has been the character and extent of your general reading since leaving school?

13 If you use shorthand or the typewriter, note how many words a minute you can write, system or machine used, and extent of experience.

14 Library experience. What work?

15 Where?

16 How long?

17 When and why terminated?

18 Experience in other occupations, business, teaching, etc.

19 Do you take or read *Library Journal*?   20 *Public libraries*?

[If the answers to no. 19, 20 or 21 be "Yes," add length of time or extent of reading]

21 Of what library associations or clubs are you a member?

22 Do you wish to prepare for general library work or for some special department; e. g. executive, cataloguing, reference or loan department?

23 Have you a library position now in view?

24 Do you wish to secure one on leaving the school?

25 What is your motive in engaging in library work?

26 How long do you intend to continue in library work?

27 How low a salary would you accept for the first three years after leaving the library school?

[This question has no bearing on any engagement. Its answer enables us to advise candidates who hope for too high salaries at first not to enter on a course which will probably disappoint them pecuniarily]

28 Add any farther facts as to personal abilities, habits, tastes or experience that occur to you as likely to influence your success in library work; e. g. as to

order	quickness	tact
methodical habits	memory	earnestness
accuracy	executive ability	enthusiasm

[The most compact answer can be given by marking opposite each word 2, 4, 6 or 8 as in question 10, languages. Call 5 the average. If your memory, in your own judgment or by common repute among friends, is something better than the average, mark 6 under that word; if decidedly above the average, mark it 8]

When filled, mail to N. Y. State Library School, Albany N. Y.

D. WOMEN IN LIBRARIANSHIP

The presence of women in the profession was not considered a novelty among librarians of the nineteenth century. At the 1876 Conference of Librarians in Philadelphia, thirteen of the one hundred registrants were women though it must be noted that women were not represented on any of the committees created as a result of the Conference.

In the following year two women were among the first official delegates of the newly formed American Library Association who attended the Conference of Librarians in London: Annie R. Godfrey (later Mrs. Melvil Dewey), of Wellesley College Library, and Mrs. Cornelia B. Olmsted, Wadsworth Library, Geneseo Village, New York. Both women held administrative positions in their respective libraries. While in London, some of the American delegates commented on the absence of women from the library scene and Lloyd P. Smith of the Library Company of Philadelphia expressed surprise that "in England a lady-librarian was scarcely ever heard of, while in America the great majority of librarians were women." Justin Winsor, President of the American Library Association, added that two-thirds of the Boston Public Library staff were women.

F. B. Perkins in "How to Make Town Libraries Successful," published as part of the *1876 Report*, recommended that "Women should be employed as librarians and assistants as far as possible, as the nature of the duties is, to a great extent, and in many cases, suited to them." A bit chauvinistically he added that "Precautions will sometimes be needed against curious troubles arising from the fact that women in such places often do not get along with other women as well as men do."

Despite some criticism, women were to become more and more involved in educational activities throughout the nineteenth century. In 1839 the first State Normal School "exclusively for women" was established in Lexington, Massachusetts, and, by 1872, there were 101 such normal schools. Though there was some debate over the scholarly ability of women, female colleges were also being established; among these were Mount Holyoke Female Seminary (now Mount Holyoke College), chartered in 1836; Wellesley Female Seminary (now Wellesley College), incorporated in 1870; Smith College, chartered in 1871; and, in the South, the Georgia Female College (now Wesleyan College), chartered in 1836.

While career opportunities for the graduates were primarily in teaching, Justin Winsor had observed at the 1877 London Conference that "We can command our pick of the educated young women whom our Colleges for Women are launching forth upon our country." Dewey demonstrated that such a selection could be made when, as Chief Librarian (later Professor of Library Economy) at Columbia College, he employed six graduates of Wellesley College. Having done this, he became increasingly committed to preparing women for the library profession.

Dewey's personal view, his reputation at Wellesley, and his acquaintance with graduates of women's colleges probably contributed to his receiving an invitation to address the Association of Collegiate Alumnae in 1886 on the subject of "Librarianship as a Profession for College-Bred Women." In his address he surveyed the educational field, expressing his concern over the quality of books being read, referred to reading as "a mighty engine," appraised the new library as "active, an aggressive, educating force in the community," chronicled the developments of the preceding ten years, and spoke frankly of the inequality in salaries paid to men and women. Among the opportunities which he identified for women were those in the "Scholars' and People's Libraries" and in "promoting the founding of new libraries, [or] infusing new life into old ones." In the address Dewey invited those interested in the profession to write for a pamphlet containing information on the proposed School of Library Economy.

Despite the crisis that ensued at Columbia College when he admitted women to the School of Library Economy, there is little doubt the women admitted were largely responsible for the continuation of the first formal training program begun in the United States. Of the twenty students admitted, seventeen were women; only five, all women, were college graduates.

13. LIBRARIANSHIP AS A PROFESSION FOR COLLEGE-BRED WOMEN

Librarianship means to-day quite a different thing from what it meant twenty years ago. Only the few who have given the subject special attention are aware of its present status. If I were to speak at once of library work as a profession for college women, most of you would be thinking of something quite different from what I have in mind. We shall progress faster, therefore, if you will follow me in finding out what librarianship means to-day and more exactly what this work is, before we discuss its special adaptability.

I might tell you at once, without taking time to get to a common standpoint, about the clerical work of large and small libraries and about many technical details, but as college women, considering so important a question as a life work, you will certainly prefer to get a broader view of the field.

You must think of the library, whether popular or scholarly, circulating or reference, as an essential part of our system of education. Whatever it has been in the past, this is what it is to be in the future and, while it will still do a great work in furnishing innocent recreation, even this feature will be utilized to develop the taste for better books, thus making the main work of educating and elevating the more practicable.

Let us look first at the present machinery for general education. Their most enthusiastic admirer does not claim that the public schools can do more than teach the masses how to read intelligently and the mere rudiments of arithmetic and writing, with possibly a little geography, hygiene and training of hand and eye. Most children must become bread winners before they are really taught to take the author's meaning readily from the printed page; not merely to pronounce the words like a parrot or as a bright child may be taught in an afternoon to pronounce a phonetically spelled language like Italian. In fact, with all the millions we are spending on our public schools and all the pride we take in them, we seem to be losing ground. In 1870 less than 15 per cent were unable to write, but in 1880 this ugly item had grown to 17 per cent. Some reply that this illiteracy is caused by the great tide of immigration; but explaining the cause still leaves the fact that we are each year falling behind. The man with an income of $1,000 and living expenses of $1,100 is sure to find breakers ahead, unless he can somehow reverse the relations. In a country where suffrage is universal and where it is conceded that the ballot cannot be taken away from those who already have it, this problem is the gravest, and thoughtful men familiar with its details have studied it deeply.

There are two great obstacles in the way of elementary education, to the removal of which earnest men and women are giving time and strength and money. Those best qualified to judge tell us that at least a year of the school-life of every child who passes through our public schools is worse than wasted on compound numbers, our so-called "system" of weights and measures, and that this year would be saved by the complete adoption of the international or metric system, which is merely our ordinary arithmetic applied to all other measures as it now is to our currency. While there are the widest international, commercial and economic reasons for this reform, the members of the American Metric Bureau are chiefly interested in the question from this educational side.

The second great obstacle is our absurd spelling, which scholars agree is the worst on the planet. In trying to learn this, two or three years more are worse than wasted. A few years ago it required some hardihood for an educated man to declare himself in favor of simplified spelling, but since the founding of the Spelling Reform Association in 1876 every prominent student of English living, both American and foreign, has conceded that scholarship, as well as common sense, requires the change which is quietly but steadily going forward. Each year the Philological Society of England and the American Philological Association, the two fully representing the English scholarship of the world, commit themselves anew to the reform and agree on a gradually growing list of changes which they

Source: Melvil Dewey, *Librarianship As a Profession for College-Bred Women*. An Address Delivered Before the Association of Collegiate Alumnae on March 13, 1886 (Boston: Library Bureau, 1886).

recommend for immediate adoption.* Here, as in metric work, while there are other weighty reasons for the reform, it is really carried on by those chiefly interested in the welfare of the masses, freedmen, Indians, Chinese, immigrants, criminals, and all the unfortunates, who by the present system are shut out from the priceless privilege of reading.

With these two great obstacles removed, we shall easily gain something each year on illiteracy and, like the man who has reduced his expenses below his fixed income, we can look forward to a brightening future.

But even then the masses can get from the public schools not much information or culture, but only the simplest tools which if rightly used will enable them to educate themselves by reading.

Of old it was only the learned few who could read; most of the world were limited to conversation. Now, we are told this is an art more rare than music, and only the educated few are able to converse; but, except the illiterates, everybody reads. Less and less from the living voice, from pulpit or rostrum, and more and more from the printed page are people getting their ideas and ideals, their motives and inspiration. As we study the question, it becomes clear that the difficulty and expense of reaching the people by the voice, and the cheapness and permanence of print make it necessary, if we are to educate and elevate the masses and make their lives better worth living, that we should in some way put in their hands the *best* reading. I say the best, for reading is not necessarily good or elevating, although it will certainly average much higher than conversation, for much greater care is taken in preparing matter for print. The labor and cost bring into activity the law of the survival of the fittest. But if good books average much higher than good conversation, the same rule makes bad books more powerful for evil; i. e. when ideas good or bad get into book form they are apt to become vastly more potent and we have thus a double reason for our missionary work: to give the good reading for its own sake and also as the best means to drive out and keep out the bad. To teach the masses to read and then turn them out in early youth with this power and no guiding influence, is only to invite the catastrophe. Human fashion they are quite as likely to get the bad as the good and the down hill road is ever easiest to travel.

The world agrees that it is unwise to give sharp tools or powerful weapons to the masses without some assurance of how they are to be used. Even George Washington got into mischief with his first hatchet. You remember the strong words of Carlyle:—

"Readers are not aware of the fact but a fact it is of daily increasing magnitude, and already of terrible importance to readers, that their first, grand necessity in reading is to be vigilantly, conscientiously select; and to know everywhere that books, like human souls, are actually divided into what we may call sheep and goats—the latter put inexorably on the left hand of the judge; and tending, every goat of them, at all moments, whither we know, and much to be avoided, and if possible, ignored by all sane creatures."

And this need of guidance is emphasized by the thoughtful words of Frederick Harrison:—

"Every book that we take up without a purpose is an opportunity lost of taking up a book with a purpose—every bit of stray information that we cram into our head without any sense of its importance, is for the most part a bit of the most useful information driven out of our heads and choked off from our minds. It is so certain that information, that is, the knowledge, the stored thoughts and observations of mankind, is now grown to proportions so utterly incalculable and prodigious, that even the learned whose lives are given to study can but pick up some crumbs that fall from the table of truth. They delve and tend but a plot in that vast and teeming kingdom, whilst those whom active life leaves with but a few cramped hours of study can hardly come to know the very vastness of the field before them, or how infinitesimally small is the corner they can traverse at the best. We know all is not of equal value. We know that books differ in value as much as diamonds differ from sand on the sea shore, as much as our living friend differs from a dead rat. We know that much in the myriad-peopled world of books—very much in all kinds—is trivial, enervating, inane, even noxious. And thus, where we have infinite opportunities of wasting our efforts to no end, of fatiguing our minds without enriching them,

*To those interested full information will be sent on application to the Secretary of the Spelling Reform Association, Melvil Dewey, Columbia College, New York.

of *clogging* the spirit without *satisfying* it, there, I cannot but think, that the very infinity of opportunities is robbing us of the actual power of using them. And thus I come often, in my less hopeful moods, to watch the remorseless cataract of daily literature which thunders over the remnants of the past, as if it were a fresh impediment to the men of our day in the way of systematic knowledge and consistent powers of thought: as if it were destined one day to overwhelm the great inheritance of mankind in prose and verse."

The children of another generation will see nothing specially wonderful about the telephone or electric light. So we, born to the constant sight and use of books, seldom stop to think what a miracle they are. As distinguished from the brute the savage has the divine gift of speech. And when we think that the vibrations of the air started by the vocal chords, convey to another the workings of the human soul, we no longer wonder that speech has been looked upon as the direct gift of the Almighty, a power too wonderful to have been invented by man. And when a step higher the image of his Maker learned to make the spoken word permanent on wood or stone or clay, that is, had discovered the art of writing, we do not wonder that the savage was ready to worship the chip that could talk or the bit of paper that unaided made a complete communication. To one who had never known of writing, has there been anything in the history of the world so wonderful as a modern book?

To communicate our ideas we use the voice; to send them farther than the voice will reach or to preserve them for future reference, we write; to multiply them so that we may speak to many people in different places at the same time, we print. But mere printed matter is not a book in the best sense, any more than mere talk is an address. The name book seems to imply that its contents were worthy of communication and multiplication and of carrying to a distance and above all, of preservation. You recall how well Ruskin says this:—

"But a book is written, not to multiply the voice merely, not to carry it merely, but to preserve it. The author has something to say which he perceives to be true and useful, or helpfully beautiful. So far as he knows, no one has yet said it; so far as he knows, no one else can say it; he is bound to say it, clearly and melodiously if he may, clearly, at all events. In the sum of his life he finds this to be the thing, or group of things, manifest to him; this piece of true knowledge, or sight which his share of sunshine and earth has permitted him to seize. He would fain set it down forever; engrave it on rock, if he could; saying, 'this is the best of me; for the rest, I ate and drank, and slept, loved, and hated, like another; my life was as the vapor and is not; but this I saw and knew: this if anything of mine is worth your memory.' That is his 'writing;' it is, in his small human way, and with whatever degree of true inspiration is in him, his inscription, or scripture. That is a 'book.'"

And remember that of late years the printing press has called to its aid graphic methods, color, form, the curves and coördinates of geometry and the many photographic processes, so that in many cases the book makes the author's meaning clearer and more easily understood than would be possible for a score of authors with the living voice. In proof of this consult some recent statistical atlas or the profusely illustrated volumes in science. Or take this very point of illiteracy:—here is a map of the country in which is indicated by the darkness of the shading the amount of illiteracy in each section. Or to be more exact, here is a page with the list of all the states at the left, followed by columns representing each decade of this century, with the dates at the top of the page. Running across this page, opposite each state, is a curved line indicating by its height above the ruling, the per centage in that state that cannot write; for each year the rise and fall of the lines show the fluctuations geometrically. A similar line in red opposite the same state in the same way shows the percentage that cannot read. Thus on this single page, at a glance, is told with geometrical accuracy, conveying to the mind a clearer idea than would figures (in some such charts, indeed the figures are also inserted), the amount of illiteracy for the whole country; or for any given year, by reading down the proper column; or by reading across, the condition of any given state during the whole century; or, by consulting the intersections of these columns as on a railroad time table, the condition of any place, at any time. No amount of oral statement could begin to give so clear an idea as a few minutes' study of these two pages. Similar methods are being applied to almost every subject of human interest. Similarly the recent photographic processes have made exact pictures and all kinds of illustrations so cheap that a modern book, as compared with those of the last century, is like a modern lecture on science in which every point is illustrated by experiments performed before the listener or by pictures thrown upon the screen with a lantern, when compared with a mere oral statement which, however skillful the word painting itself and however clearly defined in the mind of the speaker were all the ideas of objects referred to, simply could not reproduce them as clearly in the mind of the listener.

Let me add a few brief sentences from men whose opinion of the value of books will have infinitely more weight than any words of mine: Emerson says:

"Consider what you have in the smallest chosen library. A company of the wisest and wittiest men that could be picked out of all civil countries, in a thousand years, have set in best order the results of their learning and wisdom. The men themselves were hid and inaccessible, solitary, impatient of interruption, fenced by etiquette; but the thought which they did not uncover to their bosom friend is here written out to us, the strangers of another age."

And his friend Carlyle adds:

"Of the things which man can do or make here below, by far the most momentous, wonderful, and worthy, are the things we call books."

Cicero says:—"Books are the food of youth, the delight of old age; the ornament of prosperity; the refuge and comfort of adversity; a delight at home, and no hindrance abroad; companions by night, in traveling, in the country."

Let me also quote from Lord Macaulay's review of Montagu's Bacon:—"The great minds of former ages. The debt which he owes to them is incalculable. They have guided him to truth. They have filled his mind with noble and graceful images. They have stood by him in all vicissitudes; comforters in sorrow, nurses in sickness, companions in solitude. Their friendships are exposed to no danger from the occurrences by which other attachments are weakened or dissolved; time glides on; fortune is inconstant; tempers are soured; bonds which seemed indissoluble are daily sundered by interest, by emulation, or by caprice. But no such cause can affect the silent converse which we hold with the highest of human intellects. That placid intercourse is disturbed by no jealousies or resentments. There are the old friends who are never seen with new faces, who are the same in wealth and poverty, in glory and in obscurity. With the dead there is no rivalry. In the dead there is no change. Plato is never sullen. Cervantes is never petulant. Demosthenes never comes unseasonably. Dante never stays too long. No difference of political opinion can alienate Cicero. No heresy can excite the horror of Bossuet."

To this testimony of orator and historian I add that of science in the words of Sir John Herschel: "If I were to pray for a taste which should stand me in stead under every variety of circumstances, and be a source of happiness and cheerfulness to me through life, and a shield against its ills, however things might go amiss, and the world frown upon me, it would be a taste for reading. Give a man this taste, and the means of gratifying it, and you can hardly fail of making a happy man, unless, indeed, you put into his hands a most perverse selection of books. You place him in contact with the best society in every period of history—with the wisest, the tenderest, the bravest, and the purest characters who have adorned humanity. You make him a denizen of all nations, a cotemporary [sic] of all ages."

And how happily does William Ellery Channing express his appreciation: "In the best books, great men talk to us, with us, and give us their most precious thoughts. Books are the voices of the distant and the dead. Books are the true levelers. They give to all who will faithfully use them, the society and the presence of the best and greatest of our race. No matter how poor I am; no matter though the prosperous of my own time will not enter my obscure dwelling, if learned men and poets will enter and take up their abode under my roof,—if Milton will cross my threshold to sing to me of paradise; and Shakspere open to me the world of imagination and the workings of the human heart, and Franklin enrich me with his practical wisdom,—I shall not pine for want of intellectual companionship, and I may become a cultivated man, though excluded from what is called the best society in the place where I live. . . . Nothing can supply the place of books.

They are cheering and soothing companions in solitude, illness, or affliction. The wealth of both continents could not compensate for the good they impart. Let every man if possible, gather some good books under his roof, and obtain access for himself and family to some social library. Almost any luxury should be sacrificed to this."

And so I might go on quoting these pregnant paragraphs till all our time was gone, but these few suggestive words will be to you as good as many. We shall not get our estimate of the value of good reading too high.

Reading is a mighty engine, beside which steam and electricity sink into insignificance. Four words of the five are written: "it will do infinite": It remains for us to add "good" or "ill." What can we do? Good advice and example, encouragement of the best, addresses, all these help, but no one questions that the main work is possible only through the organization and economy of the free public library. Many have practically accepted this fact without clearly seeing the steps that have led to it. It is our high privilege to live when the public is beginning to see more than the desirability, the absolute necessity, of this modern, missionary, library work. With the founding of New England it was recognized, though opposed to the traditions of great powers in church and state, that the church alone, however great its pre-eminence, could not do all that was necessary for the safety and uplifting of the people. So side by side they built the meeting-house and the school-house. The plan has had a long and thorough trial. None of us are likely to question the wisdom of bringing the school into this prominence, but thoughtful men are to-day, more than ever before, pointing out that a great something is wanting and that the church and the school together have not succeeded in doing all that was hoped or all that is necessary for the common safety and the common good. The school STARTS the education in childhood; we have come to a point where in some way we MUST carry it on. The simplest figure cannot be bounded by less than three lines; the lightest table cannot be firmly supported by less than a tripod. No more can the triangle of great educational work now well begun be complete without the church as a basis, the school as one side, the library the other. The pulpit, the press, and wide-awake educators everywhere are accepting this doctrine. There is a general awakening all along the line. The nation is just providing in the congressional library a magnificent home for our greatest collection of books; the states are passing new and more liberal laws to encourage the founding and proper support of free libraries; individuals are giving their means for the stablishment of these great educational forces, as never before; as witness Walter Newberry's three millions to Chicago, Mrs. Fiske's million and a half to Cornell University, Enoch Pratt's million and a half to Baltimore, Judge Packer's half million for the library of Lehigh, Andrew Carnegie's proffered quarter million to Pittsburg, not to mention the hundreds of smaller gifts which have marked the last few years. New and beautiful buildings are being rapidly provided; new libraries are being started at the rate of one to three each week; old ones are taking on new life and zeal, the Sunday school and church libraries are organizing to enlarge and make their work more effective, and a great field of usefulness at present hardly realized is opening in this special direction; the schools are being brought into direct and active relations with the local public libraries. To one studying this great problem, the air is full of the signs of the time. As with the free school, so again, New England is leading in adopting the free library and thus completing the triangle, but her example is being followed with constantly increasing rapidity.

It is settled that this work is to go on. The problem is how to make the money and effort given to it productive of the best results.

To the success of any library various elements contribute:–location; building, with its furniture, fittings, conveniences and attractions for readers; regulations; the books themselves. But the great element of success is the earnest, moving spirit which supplies to the institution its life. This should be the librarian, though often the one who bears that name is little more than a clerk and the real librarian will be found as the active member of the trustees or the committee, or possibly not officially connected with the library. Such a librarian will shape the other factors very largely. Without him it is unlikely that they will be all they ought to be.

It has been proved so often that it is an axiom among us, that under the best management a given amount of money or number of volumes can be made to do double the good that can be done by the same amount under the old conditions and poorer methods. The old library had two things in common with this ideal library of which I am speaking. It was a collection of books and it bore the name "library." Otherwise the two are as different as daylight and darkness, but as these shade into each other at dawn so of course there are libraries representing all the intermediate steps. But let us take a type of the old and the new.

The old was located in an out-of-the-way street, specially inconvenient to the majority who might want it; the building was unattractive, dark, damp, cold, unventilated and ingeniously inconvenient; many of the books were on shelves so high as to require a ladder, were covered with dust, in shabby bindings, protected often with shabbier paper covers, soiled, torn and in general discouraged in appearance; unused public documents, old school-books, etc., nearest the door; the more attractive works in the attic or cellar; the shelves unlabeled; the books without numbers on the back and possibly with none inside, and put on the shelves haphazard as they had come in, or in a classification so coarse that a reader seeking matter on a minute topic might require a week to look over the disorganized mass of literature in which he may, or may not find something that he wishes; its catalogues and indexes were chiefly conspicuous by their absence, or were so meager, unreliable, and so destitute of clear grouping that the only way to find what was wanted was to read the whole catalogue. The library was open an hour or two now and then, and closed evenings, holidays and vacations, for annual cleaning or for almost any excuse—on busy days, because no one had time to come; on holidays, because the librarians also wanted those days for rest; finally and most important the old type of librarian was a crabbed and unsympathetic fossil who did what he was forced to do with an air that said plainly he wished you hadn't come, and a reader among his books was as unwelcome as the proverbial poor relation on a long visit. It is a sorry picture, but by no means wholly fanciful. In many places those who knew would pronounce it a study from life.

Contrast all this with the library as it should be and in many cases will be. Placed centrally where it is most accessible to its readers; the building and rooms attractive, bright and thoroughly ventilated, lighted and warmed, and finished and fitted to meet as fully as possible all reasonable demands of its readers; the books all within reach, clean and in repair; those oftenest needed nearest the delivery desk, labeled and numbered; arranged on the shelves so that each reader may see together the resources of the library on the topic which he wishes to examine kept constantly ready for inspection; with simple and complete indexes and catalogues to tell almost instantly if any book or pamphlet wished is in the building; open day and evening throughout the year and in charge of librarians as pleased to see a reader come to ask for books or assistance as a merchant to welcome a new customer; anxious to give as far as possible to each applicant at each visit that book which will then, and to him, be most helpful.

These are the facts. The old library was passive, asleep, a reservoir or cistern, getting in but not giving out, an arsenal in time of peace; the librarian a sentinel before the doors, a jailer to guard against the escape of the unfortunates under his care. The new library is active, an aggressive, educating force in the community, a living fountain of good influences, an army in the field with all guns limbered; and the librarian occupies a field of active usefulness second to none.

Is all this possible, practical, probable? Or is it a day dream of an enthusiast? Review with me very briefly the past ten years.

In every great movement there is a long, slow growth till the idea ripens and some special step is taken which marks an epoch. We date the new library movement from August, 1876, when, taking advantage of the Centennial, a hundred leading librarians were called together in a four days convention where it was found that the time was ripe and the American Library Association was founded to carry on that important part of the movement which demanded national organization of librarians. Its work has been successful beyond our expectations and we begin the second decade with the avowed determination to double its great usefulness. Similar conventions followed in New York, London, Boston and

Cambridge, Washington and Baltimore, Cincinnati, Buffalo, Lake George, and July 7, 8, 9, and 10, 1886 we meet again at Milwaukee. This Association, or as the busy librarian always names it, the A. L. A., has acquired a marked reputation for the large amount of hard work done at its sessions, the profitable discussions and the admirable spirit and earnestness which characterize its officers, members and working committees.

In summing up a long editorial on one of our meetings, the *Christian Union* gave the following deserved compliment, which encourages us to cultivate at each meeting the rare art of doing a great deal of profitable work in a short time: "The discussions of the American Library Association are notably pointed and often lively. There is less formality and much less garrulity than is commonly found in conventions. The librarians well understand the value of moments, and many of them cultivate the art of expressing in two minutes what it commonly takes ten to get uttered."

At the Philadelphia meeting was received the first copy of the "Public libraries in the U. S. A., their history, condition and management, special report, Department of the Interior, Bureau of Education." This was a cyclopedia of library information, the best available at that time and the 1187 pages of the first volume included the list of 5000 public libraries in the United States, containing 300 volumes and upward. This was another evidence of the growing interest which had led the National Bureau of Education to recognize their importance and to make libraries one of the most important sections of the Bureau, which each year includes library statistics in its report and has already published or has in hand, a number of valuable pamphlets concerning libraries. It has been proposed to create at Washington a special Bureau in charge of library interests under a competent officer, who shall devote himself wholly to promoting and guiding the founding of libraries and increasing the usefulness of those already started. Without doubt, this work will soon be done by the government or by an association employing a permanent, paid secretary.

The third significant beginning was the Library Journal, the first number of which also came from the printers during the sessions of our first convention. This was to give the means of monthly communication between those most interested in library progress, or, as it has been sometimes called, "a monthly conference in print." Twenty leading librarians made up its editorial board and it was made the official organ of the American Library Association and, at the London meeting a year later, of the British libraries as well. The Journal has been, like the Association, pre-eminently practical. Ten volumes have been completed and minutely indexed and a set is the essential foundation of every collection on libraries, and a work that even a poor library finds it true economy to buy at the outset.

Thus in the Association and Journal two great library wants were at once supplied. But some of the most important work was impracticable for either a learned society or a magazine. The corner stone of all this modern library movement has been coöperation, thus securing vastly better results at greatly reduced cost. This work included the examination of the multitude of blanks, records, and technical appliances and devices connected with books, cataloguing, indexing, etc. The A. L. A. Coöperation committee gave much time and labor in consolidating the general experience into tangible results, so that each might stand on the shoulders of all his predecessors, utilizing every valuable experiment and experience. To make all these practical, it was necessary that these improved devices should be manufactured and distributed in large enough quantity to secure low prices. Of some articles, perhaps a hundred were made and sent out as called for to a hundred different libraries, each understanding that it was to report to the makers any points in which it seemed possible to improve it. These criticisms and suggestions were kept together in numbered envelopes and as the time approached for making a second supply the committee carefully considered them, making such changes as this added experience had shown to be wise. In this way year by year closer approximation has been made to perfecting all the technical machinery which is vastly more extensive than any one unfamiliar with the subject would dream. As a result a new library starting to-day, may send a postal card to this Library Bureau in Boston asking for whatever it needs, e. g., for a complete card catalogue outfit for their library, and secure at a great saving of time and expense a more perfect set of appliances than would have been possible ten years ago had they given six months to the preparation of specifications and supervision of the work by mechanics who had never done the same before. It was also necessary that there should be published many things valuable to libraries but which no regular publisher would undertake; that there should be a headquarters or exchange where libraries and cataloguers, assistants or librarians could be brought together to their mutual advantage. All this work was started in the same offices with the Library Association and Library Journal and is constantly increasing its field of activity and usefulness.

In the same offices in Boston were the headquarters of the American Metric Bureau and the Spelling Reform Association and after the mere hint I have given, you will understand that it was no accident that brought these five interests into the same suite of rooms but that each was an essential part in a clearly defined scheme for meeting the demands of popular education.

Thus the Association, the Journal and the Bureau divide the work; but for the fourth important factor we had to wait ten years, i.e. for the School for the training of librarians.

If you consider the circumstances you will see how grave a difficulty will be removed after the Library School to be opened next year is in complete operation. At present, though recognizing fully the importance of librarianship and its rank as a profession and the fact that with the best methods and profiting by the sum of previous experience at least double the good may be accomplished, and that it is possible to secure this advantage only by a technical training, one is confronted by the fact that there is absolutely no provision for such training or instruction in either the science or art of librarianship. The demand is only for experienced librarians and the candidate is met by exactly the old and famous condition of keeping out of the water till he is an expert swimmer. If he tries to secure his training by joining the staff of some library, a series of lions are in the way.

1. No library sufficiently combines in itself the many things the learner needs. To get any breadth of views and to avoid the ruts to which an apprenticeship in a single library is so subject he must manage to spend his time in a series of the best institutions.

2. Being untrained, he has to begin at the bottom of the ladder at little or no salary. If he is able and willing to make such a beginning, when he learns this department well it is impossible to advance him till some one above him dies, resigns, or is discharged and while deserving promotion it may be years before the most appreciative trustees can grant it. Again, it is directly against the interests of the library itself to change the work just when the learner has mastered one subject and made himself specially valuable. As a result, the learner absorbs not a little about librarianship but receives real training in only one of the many departments. In all libraries of sufficient life to make their teachings of value, the librarian and experienced assistants and cataloguers are too crowded with their regular work to give time to improving the education of their help and training assistants for other libraries.

If one stays long enough and carefully observes everything that goes on about him and improves every opportunity to see something of other departments, he comes in time to quite a familiarity with most of them, but is exactly in the position of a man who has worked about a single engine for years and has come to know it well but has never had opportunity for comparative study nor has received systematic instruction in mechanical engineering. A librarian who should attempt not only to explain but to give the reasons for all his methods would require much more than twenty-four hours per day to answer the applicants that continually come to all prominent librarians for help. The most courteous librarian can not find time for more than a trip through his departments with a running commentary on his methods. To an experienced fellow worker this has great value, for he has the necessary technical knowledge to understand what he sees and profit by it, but to a beginner is like educating an engineer by walking through machine shops. Even if one can command the time and money to make extensive travels, visiting all the better libraries here and broad, he still finds the great want of technical training unsupplied.

We have looked these grave difficulties in the face for ten years and the one solution possible is about to become a fact.

At the Buffalo meeting of the American Library Association it was announced that Columbia College had directed a Committee of seven Trustees to consider the establishment of such a school. From the ensuing discussion I will read a few extracts which will make clearer the views of leading librarians as to the need of such training and may suggest some other means of getting started in the profession to those who cannot attend this school.

Dr. Wm. F. Poole of Chicago, whom you all know as the author of the famous Poole's Index to Periodical Literature and who has probably helped start more libraries large and small than any other American, opened the discussion. I quote only part of the summary.

"New libraries are springing up all over the Western states, and librarians are appointed from the local candidates, who have had no library experience of any sort. Scarcely a day passes in which one or more of these tyros does not come to my library for information; and I am always glad to give them such help as I can–but how little they can take! They have the impression that they can learn in one day all they need to know. I have spent an hour in explaining the simplest details of library management, and then found, by putting some test question, that the person I had been trying to instruct had understood little or nothing of what I had been talking about. I usually tell these people frankly, at the start, that they will not understand the explanations I should make until they have some practical experience in library work. If they will come to the library and work for a month, reading up in the meantime the theory of the subject, they will be in a condition to receive some oral instruction. Several persons have accepted this proposal, and have worked without pay in our regular corps of attendants. At the end of a month they have begun to appreciate how much there is to learn in order to be a competent librarian, and are put in a way of making some progress by themselves. There is no training school for educating librarians like a well managed library. There is a dearth at present of trained librarians, who, at moderate salaries, are willing to take charge of small libraries, and grow up with them. Of trained cataloguers there is a still greater dearth. I am constantly receiving applications for them, and they are not to be found. The few persons in the country who follow this work as a specialty are constantly engaged. It is a duty, I think, which the larger libraries owe to the profession, to attach to their cataloguing departments a corps of competent young persons to learn the art of cataloguing; for the work can be learned no where else than in a large library. The service they would render would be sufficient to pay for their instruction. We can scarcely blame the managers of libraries for appointing as their librarians persons who have had no experience in library work, when there are not trained librarians enough to supply the demand. We cannot blame them for not having their libraries catalogued, when there are not cataloguers enough to do the work."

Mr. B. Pickman Mann said of present facilities:–"I have lived in Cambridge and Boston fourteen years and have tried to learn all the details of library work in vain."

Mr. J. L. Whitney, assistant librarian of the Boston Public Library and for many years in charge of its great catalogue department, said:–"It is an endless trouble to instruct volunteers one at a time. I have found it a weariness and a loss."

Mr. C. A. Cutter, author of the famous "Rules for a Dictionary Catalogue," now editor of the Library Journal, said:–"Undoubtedly it is well that a librarian should have worked in a library; there are some things which he will never understand unless he has. But any one merely employed as assistant in a large library is likely to be assigned to one particular department, and to understand that only. And, even if his chief takes care that he shall have variety of work, he only learns the methods of one establishment; and as those are probably all determined upon before he goes there, he only learns them by rote, and, unless he is unusually philosophic, never thinks of the reasons for them. No one is thoroughly fit to have charge of a library who has not pursued some comparative study and learned to reason about what he does. This discussion reminds me of something that occurred lately in our town.

"A young man in Winchester wished to become a civil engineer. When he left the High School he was advised by his uncle, who was himself a civil engineer in Buffalo, to come here and begin at the bottom of the profession, that is, as chainman, and gradually work up, if he could. He did so. At the end of a year his uncle said to him, 'You know now what engineering is; you have become familiar with the practical details, and you have begun to find out how little you know and what you need to know. Now go to a professional school and study the theory. There are men of both sorts among us,–those who have learned only by practicing the profession, and those who have been taught in the schools; and I have always noticed that the regularly educated men get the best positions and the best salaries.' "

Mr. C. W. Merrill, librarian of the great Cincinnati Public Library, said:—"I should have been glad to have been told things I have had to learn by experience. Our teachers are taught in Normal schools; let us have librarians taught in a Library school." To this Mr. S. S. Green of Worcester one of the best known and most successful librarians added:—"I remember that the matter of trying to have facilities provided for training and educating persons wishing to become librarians was talked over at length by the gentlemen and ladies who went to the conference of librarians in London in 1877. They held long conversations on shipboard regarding the subject, and it was generally considered very important that such facilities should be somewhere provided. On our return I wrote to Professor Winsor, urging him to try to make use of the opportunities afforded by his connection with Harvard College to interest that great institution in undertaking such a work, and his connection with librarians to interest in the scheme the managers of libraries in Boston and its neighborhood, thus securing the means to seekers after information of getting at the experiences of librarians through lectures, etc., and practical training in libraries.

The matter now under consideration has been frequently discussed at meetings of this Association; if not publicly, certainly in the conversation of librarians attending them, and by librarians when they have met on other occasions than these meetings. It is very desirable that there should be some such school as that the establishment of which is contemplated by Columbia College. There certainly can be no doubt that it would be of solid advantage to persons wishing to become librarians to have the opportunity of listening to the experiences of the best librarians, speaking on their specialties. It is better that their instruction should come from several rather than from one librarian, and that they should be protected from narrow views which would follow instruction in a single library.

Columbia College, one of the greatest universities of the country, can certainly be trusted if it undertakes to give instruction, to give good instruction."

In 1884 Columbia College, at a full meeting of its Trustees, and after considering the subject a year, voted to establish as one of the regular courses of the University, a School of Library Economy. I will not take time to give you the details of the plan which has been worked out in consultation with many of our ablest librarians who are deeply interested in the success of the new school. It aims to give to its pupils, during either its short three months course of active instruction or the full two years which includes actual library work under the daily supervision of the teachers, whatever will do most to fit them for successful librarians, cataloguers or assistants. It is wholly practical and includes no more of the historical and antiquarian than is necessary to illustrate modern methods. The school is also technical and duplicates no part of the college course and attempts no instruction in languages, literatures, science or art except as its bibliographical lectures discuss the side of each subject that the librarian most needs to know. Those who are interested can get a pamphlet with full information by sending their address to the School of Library Economy, Columbia College, N. Y., and I will not attempt even to summarize the matter so easily obtainable in print.

I have spoken thus far of the missionary and popular side of libraries, but there is another side as distinct as is the university from the common school. To some of you this scholarly work will be more attractive than the popular. The library is the real university of the future, not simply for the people but for scholars. Paul sat at the feet of Gamaliel; and in the Academy, the Lyceum and the Porch, the pupil was continually with the master; but the printing press has changed all this and to-day many an earnest disciple has never seen the face nor heard the voice of his master, but has received his teachings entirely through the printed page.

Of late years the college library has been taking an entirely new position. Of old it was attached to the chair of some overworked professor or put in charge of the janitor and opened four or five hours per week in term time only. Now it is being raised to the rank of a distinct university department; there are professors of bibliography, of books and reading, and at Columbia we have for the first time a chair of Library Economy. The libraries are being made as accessible as the traditional college well, some of them opening from 8 A. M. to 10 P. M., including all holidays and vacations; they are receiving endowments, e. g., the million and more to Cornell University, Prof. Horsford's great gift to Wellesley,

Judge Packer's half million to Lehigh, and the long list of funds given to Harvard, the Phoenix gift to Columbia, and so I might go on with hundreds of illustrations; new and beautiful buildings, some fire-proof, all vast improvements over what was thought sufficient in the last generation, are going up, e. g., Harvard, Amherst, Dartmouth, University of Vermont, Oberlin, University of Michigan and so on. In New York City alone three splendid collegiate library buildings have just been finished; for the General Theological Seminary, Union Theological Seminary, and our own at Columbia which has cost over $400,000 and already we plan for an enlargement. The colleges are waking to the fact that the work of every professor and every department is necessarily based on the library; text books are constantly yielding their exalted places to wiser and broader methods; professor after professor sends his classes, or goes with them, to the library and teaches them to investigate for themselves and to *use* books, getting beyond the method of the primary school with its parrot-like recitations from a single text. With the reference librarians to counsel and guide readers; with the greatly improved catalogues and indexes, cross-references, notes and printed guides, it is quite possible to make a great university of a great library without professors. Valuable as they are in giving personal inspiration, they can do little in making a university without the library. Just as truly as we found in popular education that the real school for the mass of people and for all their lives except early childhood, was the library, so in the higher education the real university is a great library, thoroughly organized and liberally administered.

So library work offers to you two fields analogous to the work of the public school teacher and the college professor. Many libraries largely combine these functions. The types would however be, for the one the college library or the reference library for the use of scholars; for the other the popular circulating library among the people where the librarian is in hourly contact with her constituency of readers, advising, helping and elevating their lives and exerting a far-reaching influence for good not to be exceeded in any profession open to women or to men.

Both the Scholars' and the People's Libraries offer to women both employment and a profession. Whether what is done in the library is called merely employment or a "profession," depends less on the work than the spirit in which it is done. The janitor does "library work," yet I can conceive of his doing it with so much intelligent interest in the results that he would better deserve to rank as a member of the profession than some librarians. No one questions that the best work, e. g. of the great libraries of Boston and Cambridge, has already attained to the rank of a profession, and no one claims that all the library work now being done deserves so dignified a name. We will use the words "work" and "profession" to indicate the types, though there is so large a middle ground where they merge into each other. The professional work is also on two planes which I will call, for want of better names, mental and moral, these again being combined in various proportions in different persons. On the mental plane I put all those who do the work from a personal ambition to make a reputation or to gain a higher salary. It is the plane of most business men, lawyers, etc. On it librarianship is the *business* conducted primarily for the comfort and advancement of the librarian. These motives are those of the great masses of laborers in all fields and ambition and mere intellectual industry often secure much excellent work of a high grade, but never of the highest. Very often they build better than they know and do greater good than was intended, just as a man may drain a tract of low land from purely selfish motives in making it available for cultivation, but without having once thought or cared for it, he may by so doing have improved the sanitary condition of a hundred neighboring cottages. His credit is only for what he aimed to do.

In the library profession, the best work will always be done on the moral plane, where the librarian puts his heart and life into his work with as distinct a consecration as a minister or missionary and enters the profession and does the work because it is his duty or privilege. It is his "vocation." The selfish considerations of reputation, or personal comfort, or emolument are all secondary.

In every library there is a class of mere routine work, physical and clerical, copying, covering books, pasting in labels, giving out and taking in books, replacing on the shelves and a hundred details that may be well done by any intelligent and faithful clerk. This employment commands only the very small pay of overcrowded clerkdom, or even less, as there are always those looking to the higher positions who are willing to do this work temporarily at a merely nominal salary in order to get the needed experience and as a stepping-stone to something better. In this side of the work we are not specially interested except as it serves as a screen by which the best material is sifted out for the real work. Yet in itself it is one of the pleasantest avocations for a woman fond of books. As a result the supply of this grade of help at low prices will always exceed the demand.

This great work is only fairly started. Its rapid growth needs to be guided in the best channels. Leaders are wanted. Certainly in this profession there is most room at the top, but good privates are wanted as well as officers, for if they have the natural ability and earnestness they may grow into leaders; if not, they are perhaps as well off here as anywhere in the rank for which nature has fitted them.

There is a large field of work for college-bred women in promoting the founding of new libraries, infusing new life into old ones, or serving on committees or boards of trustees where their education and training will tell powerfully for the common good. Active interest of this kind may fairly be expected of every college graduate.

In the more direct work for which salaries are paid there is an unusually promising field for college girls and in few lines of work have women so nearly an equal chance with men. There is almost nothing in the higher branches which she cannot do quite as well as a man of equal training and experience; and in much of library work woman's quick mind and deft fingers do many things with a neatness and despatch seldom equaled by her brothers.

My experience is that an increasing number of libraries are willing to pay for given work the same price, whether done by men or women. Yet why are the salaries of women lower? In all my business and professional life I have tried to give woman more than a fair chance at all work which I had to offer. Experience has taught me why the fairest employers, in simple justice, usually pay men more for what seems at first sight the same work. Perhaps these reasons may help you to avoid some of the difficulties.

1. Women have usually poorer health and as a result lose more time from illness and are more crippled by physical weakness when on duty. The difficulty is most common to women, as are bright ribbons and thin shoes and long hair, but it is a question of health, not of sex. A strong, healthy woman is worth more than a feeble man for the same reason that a strong man gets more than a weak woman.

2. Usually women lack business and executive training. Her brothers have been about the shops and stores and in the streets or on the farm hearing business matters discussed and seeing business transacted from earliest childhood. The boys have been trading jack knives and developing the business bumps while the girls were absorbed with their dolls. It would be a miracle at present if girls were not greatly inferior in this respect and it is this fact which accounts for so few prominent chief librarianships being held by women. But this is the fault of circumstances, not necessarily of sex, and women who have somehow got the business ideas and training and have executive force are getting the salaries that such work commands. When girls have as good a chance to learn these things, I doubt not that they will quite equal their brothers and will keep cash and bank accounts and double entry books for their private affairs. A man brought up girl-fashion, as not a few are, proves just as helpless on trial and as a result gets only a "woman's salary."

3. Lack of permanence in her plans is one of the gravest difficulties with women. A young man who enters library work and later thinks of a home of his own, is stimulated to fresh endeavors to make his services more valuable. Many a young man's success in life dates from the new earnestness which took possession of him on his engagement. But with women the probability or even the possibility that her position is only temporary and that she will soon leave it for home life does more than anything else to keep her value down. Neither man or woman can do the best work except when it is felt to be the life work. This lack of permanence in the plans of women is more serious than you are apt to realize. If woman wishes to be as valuable as man she must contrive to feel that she has chosen a profession for life and work accordingly. Then she will do the best that is in her to do as long as she is in the service and if at any time it seems best to change her state, the work already done has not been crippled by this "temporary" evil.

4. With equal health, business training and permanence of plans, women will still usually have to accept something less than men because of the consideration which she exacts and deserves on account of her sex. If a man can do all the other work just as well as the woman and in addition can in an emergency lift a heavy case, or climb a ladder to the roof or in case of accident or disorder can act as fireman or do police duty, he adds

something to his direct value just as a saddle horse that is safe in harness and not afraid of the cars will bring more in nine markets out of ten than the equally good horse that can be used only in the saddle. So in justice to those who wish to be fair to women, remember that she almost always receives, whether she exacts it or not, much more waiting on and minor assistance than a man in the same place and therefore, with sentiment aside, hard business judgment cannot award her quite as much salary. There are many uses for which a stout corduroy is really worth more than the finest silk.

The natural qualities most important in a library are accuracy, order (or what we call the housekeeping instinct), executive ability, and above all earnestness and enthusiasm.

Library work is of two kinds, though both are often done by the same person in smaller libraries. The Reference and Loan work requires chiefly skill in meeting people, finding out exactly what they wish (or often better what they need) and tact and skill in answering their infinite variety of questions. Some do admirable work of this kind and lack the qualities essential to a good cataloguer, while some quiet, shy women who would be simply worthless in meeting the public are invaluable in the accession and catalogue departments where patient, scholarly accuracy and rapid, steady work are more important than tact and affability. In the smaller libraries the successful candidate must combine the qualities needed in the reference and catalogue departments, but in the larger organizations there is room for those strong on either side though lacking on the other.

The education needed is the best attainable; a college training to begin with if possible; the wider reading and study in addition the better, for absolutely every item of information comes in play. It is specially important in most reference libraries to know German and French. Italian, Spanish, Latin and Greek are valuable but in most cases much less important than German. A general acquaintance with history and literature, specially English and American, and with literary history, is essential and at least a smattering of the sciences is important. Trifling as it may seem, a very legible handwriting, free from flourishes, shading and fashionable "individualities" is practically more important to most applicants for library positions than a half dozen sciences; but in most cases the library hand has to be acquired as a part of the technical library education which includes bibliography and library economy. I have already given you a hint as to this technical field in speaking of our Library School.

We greatly prefer college-bred women in selecting new librarians: 1. Because they are a picked class selected from the best material throughout the country. 2. Because the college training has given them a wider culture and broader view with a considerable fund of information all of which will be valuable working material in a library as almost nowhere else. 3. Because a four years' course successfully completed is the strongest voucher for persistent purpose and mental and physical capacity for protracted intellectual work. 4. Chiefly because we find that the training of the course enables the mind to work with a quick precision and steady application rarely found in one who has not had this thorough college drill. Therefore we find it pays to give higher salaries for college women.

I said that this great work is in its infancy; that our great need is workers. At the same time one of our constant trials is the number of applicants to whom we can wisely give no position. Shall I mention some of the people we do not want? There is no room for those who wish to take up library work simply because they fancy it to be easier and more agreeable to one who is fond of books and cultivated society; because it will give such a good chance to read; or because there seems to be nothing else to do and so they try to get in a library. In fact, the work is not easy except in some small libraries where the pay is still easier, and though surrounded constantly by thousands of books which are handled during all the working hours there is hardly any occupation which gives so little opportunity to read. Our traditional motto is: "The librarian who reads is lost." Of course I am speaking now of working hours. The librarian who does not read at other times is certainly lost to growth. There is no place for those who are seeking chiefly for good salaries. The average pay of librarians is much too small, though happily it is increasing year by year as the importance of the work is more generally recognized and as workers *deserving* more pay are increasing. But the people who command the highest salaries are exactly the ones who do that higher grade of work which is done for its own sake and not for pecuniary reward. So fortunately the better pay is attainable only after one has done the better work and there is absolutely no attraction for salary-hunters.

While there is great difference among libraries the average hours of service are about eight per day. Our own rule is that 2,000 hours of actual library work or ten months of 200 hours each make the year, leaving two months vacation. Many small libraries are open only part of the day but the salary is usually cut down even more than the hours. Libraries that are open on holidays and evenings usually close all the routine departments so that only a part of the staff need be on duty.

The salary to women for the first year is seldom more than $500 and at present few have grown to over $1,000, though here and there $1,200 to $1,500 are paid to women of experience. But there is no reason why a woman cannot do the same work for which our leading librarians receive $3,000 to $5,000 and I have no doubt that as women of education, thorough technical training and experience come forward the salaries will rapidly increase. For this highest grade work the demand exceeds the supply and will grow steadily with the new development of the library system. If one finds many more well paid positions for teachers, there are vastly more competitors for each of these places than for that of the trained librarian. After careful study it seems to me that to an earnest woman of superior ability the library field already offers in its present period of rapid growth as good an opening financially as teaching.

While library work is no sinecure it is peculiarly fascinating to almost every person of culture that undertakes it, and it is common to hear of the refusal of much higher pay for other work. The constant contact with the best minds of the world as represented by their books, is at once a keen pleasure and a direct profit as shown in the wide general culture which results. While the hours of actual service seem longer and the vacations shorter, I believe in something like a hundred cases where I have inquired, every teacher who has also tried library work agrees that it avoids much of the nervous strain and the wear and tear of the class room and of the direct responsibility for pupils and that physically the library is less exacting than the shorter hours of the school. The librarian has no lessons to prepare out of hours; she escapes the bad air of crowded rooms and the anxiety for pupils sent to school because unmanageable at home. In the library all the courses are elective, for only those come to whom it is a pleasure. As many of you know by experience, the strain of teaching is not in imparting information to those eager to learn but in trying to force it into the minds of those who would gladly escape it. As compared with the work of the physician, the librarian avoids the night work and contact with suffering and misery which often exhausts the vital forces more than the direct professional duties. In fact there is hardly any occupation that is so free from annoying surroundings or that has so much in the character of the work and of the people which is grateful to a refined and educated woman.

Compare this work with that of the clergyman or teacher whose fields of usefulness are universally put in the first rank: The clergyman has before him for one or two hours per week perhaps one-tenth or one-twentieth of the people in his parish. Not so many indeed when we remember how there are often little struggling churches of a half dozen denominations where one strong church could do all the work much better. Beyond this very limited number for this very limited time the clergyman is dependent on the slow process of personal, parochial calls. I yield to none in my appreciation of the great work which he does and do not forget the constant stream of good influences coming from his daily life and the many direct efforts he puts forth; but I am speaking now of his work as a preacher and of the limits which circumstances seem to set to it.

The teacher has a larger proportion of her constituency in the earlier years, but only for a few hours a day and only in the months when schools are in session. It constantly happens that just as the teacher becomes deeply interested in a bright, promising boy or girl and feels that here is an opportunity to develop a strong character by patient work, the child comes and says: "Teacher, I am not coming to school any more. I am going to work in the factory," or, "I am going to help mother at home." For the great majority the work of education is hardly begun before the necessities of life take them away from the teacher's influence.

But the earnest librarian may have for a congregation almost the entire community, regardless of denomination or political party. Her services are continuous and in the wide reaching influences of the library there is no vacation. When a bright boy or girl has been once found and interested and started, he is almost sure to continue under these influences all his life. It has been found entirely practicable for a skillful librarian thus to reach and interest people who have never been in the habit of reading; to lead readers into new and more profitable fields, and to create a thirst for better books. In fact the number of ways in which people can be helped is only equaled by the power and lasting character of this influence which comes from good books. Recognizing these facts there are preachers who are looking to the adoption of the library profession as a way to spread the Master's word even more effectively than in the pulpit; and there are teachers, whose whole hearts have been given to the cause of popular education, who are eager to enter this newer field, because they recognize in it a still wider opportunity.

Is it not true that the ideal librarian fills a pulpit where there is service every day during all the waking hours, with a large proportion of the community frequently in the congregation? Has she not a school in which the classes graduate only with death?

E. EDUCATION FOR LIBRARIANSHIP

In the first issue of the *American Library Journal*, Justin Winsor's essay, "A Word to Starters of Libraries," is preceded by this statement:

> We have no schools of bibliographical and bibliothecal training
> whose graduates can guide the formation of, and assume management
> within, the fast increasing libraries of our country; and the demand
> may perhaps never warrant their establishment . . .

This observation might have been the stimulus for Dewey's sustained effort to establish a formal training program for librarians. While still associated with the *Library Journal*, he identified as a need "a training school for preparation for the special work" of a librarian and urged that such a school "be attached to some considerable library." In an essay published in 1879 and reprinted here, Dewey submitted no definite plan but he did predict that

> Perhaps by and by we may have one central library school . . . but
> the first step to be taken is to arrange systematic instruction and
> apprenticeship in connection with some of our best managed
> libraries.

Dewey's appointment on May 7, 1833, as librarian of Columbia College associated him with a "considerable library" and he submitted to the Trustees, through President F. A. P. Barnard, his proposal to open a school for the training of librarians. Dewey presented the plans for his School to the readers of the *Library Journal* in July 1884, though the School was not opened officially until January 5, 1887. The tone of the program was identified by Dewey as follows:

> Its aim is entirely practical—to give the best obtainable advice,
> with specific suggestions on each of the hundreds of questions
> that rise from the time a library is decided to be desirable, till
> it is in perfect working order, including the administration.

The School was close to failure from the beginning, not because of any particular weaknesses but because of Dewey's insistence on the admission of women. The administrative crisis thus created was solved only by Dewey's departure from Columbia College and his success in transferring the School to the New York State Library. The transfer was achieved when the Regents of the University of the State of New York resolved that they should accept Dewey's plan

> For training librarians and cataloguers in connection with the work
> of the library, giving them instruction and supervision instead of
> salary for services rendered to the library.

On April 10, 1889, the New York State Library School, regarded by Dewey and the Trustees as a continuation of his School of Library Economy, held its first class.

In 1905, the final year of Dewey's association with the New York State Library and Library School, he meditated on the future of library schools. Among the trends noted, some of which have been implemented in intent though not as envisioned by Dewey, was that graduate library schools be located in a university atmosphere. He thus anticipated C. C. Williamson's major recommendation by almost two decades.

14. APPRENTICESHIP OF LIBRARIANS

We hear a great deal of the importance of having trained librarians; of the folly of employing those unqualified for their special work, and similar talk, such as would fit the employment of physicians without medical education. Some of us forget how few fill these requirements, and the reasons why the many are so deficient. In any case the fact cannot be gainsaid that the number of librarians who approximate to the standard we set is exceedingly small. Some are very learned, but are so lacking in practical business qualities, in administration, that they could not earn their board in the business world. Others have enterprise and business capacity, but are lacking in culture or mental training, and labor under constant disadvantages. As in all professions, there is an almost infinite variety of unfitness for the position. This article is concerned only with those who are naturally endowed with the qualities that make our ideal librarian, and who have received the necessary general education. We ask and demand that the positions should be given to men and women thus fitted, but this is not all. We need a training school for preparation for the special work. The village school-mistress is provided with normal schools by the hundred, where the best methods of teaching are taught. Physicians, lawyers, preachers, yes even our cooks have special schools for special training. But the librarian, whose profession has been so much exalted, must learn his trade by his own experiments and experience.

There has not been even a system of apprenticeship. Assistants picked up what they could and sometimes were promoted as vacancies occurred, but no regular plan of training to all the varied work has been attempted. The result has been as good as could be expected. Here and there an invincible determination to master the subject has surmounted all obstacles, but the majority have plodded on largely in the ways that they inherited from their predecessors, without much care as to their improvement.

Of late, much has been done in print. Edwards' works, to those who have had access to them, were a mine of needed information, but there was little else. The Bureau of Education made a great step in advance in bringing out the Government Report on libraries in 1876, but like Edwards' much of that was historical. Then came the *Library Journal*, which has brought forward scores of plans and suggestions of value. All this is something to be grateful for, and the opportunity for the aspirant of to-day is infinitely better than it was five years ago. But we need more than has been done in print and more than the much greater helps that are to be put in print, during this and succeeding years.

Successful training requires that the student have personal intercourse with men full of the library spirit, and thoroly qualified for their work. His enthusiasm must be roused, till with the guidance furnished, he will press forward to a complete mastery of the subject. Probably no one man would unite in himself all the qualities desired in the faculty of our librarians' college. The man who would give the best lecture and guidance in bibliografy might be quite unfit to take the class thru the practical details of library economy and administration. As in all training schools, different men must take in charge different branches. If such persons are not to be had, we must do the best we can with those we have, which plan is, I believe, pursued by all other schools.

Another thing that seems clear is that this librarians' normal school must be attached to some considerable library. It would require an unhoped for patronage to support it independently, and even if this were possible, it is not desirable unless a large library can be at the service of the school. A large variety of books are needed in the work; the pupils must see all the work doing from day to day in all its details; they must have practice in doing each part of it under careful supervision.

My design is to submit no definite plan, but to provoke thought and discussion. The form that seems most probable is that certain librarians will take assistants for the special purpose of training them to take charge of other institutions. These assistants will give their services as far as they can be made available in doing the work of the library without other compensation than the instruction given, and the opportunities for practice under trained supervision. There are many aspirants who would be glad to give their time and best efforts in this way, and a librarian with any enthusiasm for this part of our work

Source: Melvil Dewey, "Apprenticeship of Librarians," *Library Journal* 4 (1879): [147]-48.

could plan to get assistance enough to avoid loss to the library. Any other than the enthusiastic librarian would not undertake the training department, and if he did would not succeed in it. While it would be better if all students could be centered in the best library, there are two reasons why I fear it will not be possible. The main one, that only a limited number can be made of service in any one library, and few would be willing to give their time, pay their own expenses and tuition beside. If training departments can be founded in various parts of the country, it will draw some students who would not go to a distant state.

Perhaps by and by we may have one central library school, where all will want to "finish off," but the first step to be taken is to arrange systematic instruction and apprenticeship in connection with some of our best managed libraries under the charge of our most enterprising librarians.

I am well aware that some have given more attention to this matter than others. Mr. Poole has sent out not a few "graduates" who have done much better work because of the years they spent with him. The Boston Athenaeum has the reputation of being as much as any a kind of training-school. But at the best, the half has not been done. Let me illustrate. Suppose Mr. Cutter or Mr. Winsor took five new assistants, who came for training rather than for salary. Let them meet each day for a lecture or talk which shall begin at the foundation, and day by day progress towards a complete view of the whole field. These talks should serve to rouse interest and enthusiasm; to guide very closely the reading and study of the pupils, and to give the facts, methods and inspiration which is not to be found in print. Such a plan would take an hour of valuable time that neither Mr. Winsor nor Mr. Cutter can well spare, but is it possible to get such results in training for librarianship with any less effort?

15. [THE NEED FOR FORMAL TRAINING IN LIBRARIANSHIP]

In the past few years the work of a librarian has come to be regarded as a distinct profession, affording opportunities of usefulness in the educational field inferior to no other, and requiring superior abilities to discharge its duties well. The librarian is ceasing to be a mere jailer of books, and is becoming an aggressive force in his community. There is a growing call for *trained* librarians animated by the modern library spirit. A rapidly increasing number of competent men and women are taking up the librarian's occupation as a life work. Thoughtful observers say that public opinion and individual motives and actions are influenced not so much by what is uttered from the rostrum or the pulpit as by what is read, that this reading can be shaped and influenced chiefly and cheaply only through the library, and therefore that the librarian who is master of his profession is a most potent factor for good.

In our colleges every professor and every student, in whatever department, necessarily bases most of his work on books and is therefore largely dependent on the library.

Recognizing the importance of this new profession and the increasing number of those who wish to enter it, we are confronted by the fact that there is absolutely nowhere any provision for instruction in either the art or science of the librarian's business. Prominent library officials tell us that it is not uncommon for young men and women of good parts, from whom the best work might fairly be expected, to seek in vain for any opportunity to fit themselves for this work. It is simply impossible for the large libraries to give special attention to training help for other institutions. Each employee must devote himself to the one part of the work that falls to his share, so that he can know little of the rest, except what he may learn by accidental and partial absorption of methods. There is a constantly increasing demand for trained librarians and cataloguers, and there is no place where such can be trained. A limited number may here and there be found who have had experience in certain parts of library work, but few who have been systematically trained in any one thing, and fewer still who have had such training in all. The few really great librarians have been mainly selfmade, and have attained their eminence by literally feeling their way through long years of darkness.

Such a school is called for, not only by the inexperienced who wish to enter on library work, but by a growing number of those already engaged in it. Of the 5,000 public librarians in the United States, not a few would gladly embrace such an opportunity to bring themselves abreast of modern library thought and methods; and their employers would find it economy to grant the necessary leave of absence. If it be true, as is so often stated, that 10,000 volumes catalogued and administered in the best way are more practically useful than 30,000 treated in an unintelligent or inefficient manner, then it is of the greatest importance to advance by every possible means the general standard of library work throughout the country.*

---

*This justification appeared originally in Columbia College Library, School of Library Economy. *Circular of Information, 1884,* pp. 21, 22. The "Original Plan," as it is referred to in the *Circular,* was presented on May 7, 1883.

Source: New York (State) Library School, "Handbook . . . Including Summer Course and Library Handwriting," New York (State) Library *Bulletin 66, Library School 9* (September 1901): 373-74.

16. SCHOOL OF LIBRARY ECONOMY AT COLUMBIA COLLEGE

On May 7, 1883, there was laid before the Board of Trustees a plan for a School of Library Economy. The Board referred the proposition to the Library Committee of seven trustees, who gave it mature consideration, and May 5, 1884, reported unanimously in favor of establishing the school. The trustees thereupon

Resolved, That there be established, in connection with the college, a school in which instruction may be given in the principles of library management, and in which learners may qualify themselves to discharge the duties of professional librarians; such school to be called the Columbia College School of Library Economy.

Resolved, That the school established by the foregoing resolution shall be under the superintendence and control of the Library Committee, who shall prescribe the course of instruction to be pursued in it, fix the amount of the tuition fees to be paid by its students, and enact all necessary rules for its government, subject to the approval of the Board of Trustees.

Resolved, That the Chief Librarian under the Committee, and with the advice and approval of the President, shall have the general direction of the school and of the course of instruction so established, with the style and title of Professor of Library Economy.

Resolved, That the Library Committee be authorized to make arrangements with experienced librarians or experts whose co-operation in the conduct of the school may be desirable; and that any expenses incurred may be defrayed out of the fees received for tuition in said school.

Resolved, That instruction in the school shall commence on the first Monday of October, 1886, or at such other date as the Library Committee may fix.

GENERAL PLAN.

The Board have intentionally avoided deciding details, hoping that the suggestions of the large number of experienced librarians who have professed interest in the school, and the expression of the needs of those hoping to attend it, together with the practical experience gained from teaching meanwhile two preliminary classes, will make clear what is really needed. Such expressions of what those interested think will be most valuable to the library profession, will be cordially received, and have due attention, if sent to the Chief Librarian, who has been made Director of the school.

While the two years' preparation will doubtless result in minor changes, the general plan of the school will be substantially as outlined below.

There will be only one session each year, beginning probably immediately after the Christmas holidays, 1886.

The amount of fees and the nature of certificates or degrees to be given will be decided and announced during the preceding year. The expenses will be made as moderate as possible, in order to permit the attendance of students of limited means.

PRIVILEGES, PARTIAL COURSES.

Members of the school will be entitled to all university privileges, the use of libraries, reading-rooms, scientific collections, etc., and admission to the various courses of evening lectures. It is desirable that as many as possible take the entire course; but to provide for those whose limited time will not allow this, but who wish instruction on the subjects of special personal interest, the study will be taken up by topics, completing one before beginning another, so that one interested in any special topic may attend while the school is engaged on his subject without taking the full course *e. g.*, a private book-owner may attend the lectures on Cataloging, Binding, and Buying, without studying the details of the management of public circulating libraries, in which he may have no special interest.

Source: Melvil Dewey, "School of Library Economy at Columbia College," *Library Journal* 9 (1884): 117-20.

The hours of class exercises in the Library School will allow those wishing it to arrange for instruction in other college departments if their time is not fully occupied. The opportunities are so great for study and investigation in other subjects that all time can be used to the best advantage, and it is expected that many library students will utilize their university residence for special studies, and that members of the various other schools will often elect a part at least of the course in Library Economy.

GENERAL SCOPE.

While no time, study, nor cost has been spared in perfecting the methods, fittings, etc., adopted for the College Library, the School of Library Economy is not to teach these methods, nor those of any individual or class of libraries or librarians.

It interprets Library Economy in its broadest sense, as including all the special training needed to select, buy, arrange, catalogue, index, and administer in the best and most economical way any collection of books, pamphlets, or serials.

METHODS OF INSTRUCTION.

As the school aims to give not only information, but practical training, something more than the ordinary scholastic method is essential, and any means that promise to make more efficient librarians will be tried.

Thus far it has been decided to give the training and instruction by Lectures, Reading, The Seminar, Visiting Libraries, Problems, and Work.

As mere lectures and text-books, however good, will not give the best preparation for the law without practice in office work and moot courts, and observations of the methods of the ablest members of the bar; nor the best training to the physician without clinics and experience in the hospitals; and as no good working chemist was ever made without the laboratory, so lectures and reading alone will not achieve the best results in training for librarianship without the conference, problems, study of various libraries in successful operation, and actual work in a library. The aim of the school is wholly practical, and therefore it will use all these methods in such proportion as experience proves will give the best results.

OBJECT TEACHING.—Throughout the course object teaching will be used wherever possible.

Every book, blank, or other article referred to in the lectures will if practicable be on the desk for inspection, and of all blanks, forms, blank books, etc., extra sheets will be provided, so that each member of the school may not only see, but have a sample to retain, attached to his notes of the use, merits, faults, and modifications desirable for various special uses. A similar distribution will be made of many other inexpensive articles, *e. g.* improved shelf-support pins, card-catalog guides, etc., which no description or notes can make as clear or useful as a sample. Each subject will be summed up in concise but explicit rules or directions, embodying what the preceding discussion indicates to be the best, *e. g.* after explaining the necessity and uses of the shelf catalog and the various forms in use, with references to discussions in the *Library Journal* and other sources, a model form in an actual sheet from a shelf list with sample entries filled in will be given each student. This will show paper, size, rulings, and headings, and will be accompanied by explicit rules for entry of all kinds of books, pamphlets, periodicals, maps, etc. The various forms of binders, cases, or books to use for the shelf sheets, etc., will be shown, their practical working described, and their merits and faults for various uses pointed out.

In discussing the CARD CATALOGS, model cards filled out in the most approved form, and in the standard "library hand" writing, will be given each student, illustrating all the many rules, with footnotes and references wherever the point can thus be made plainer. The cataloging rules themselves will be given separately so far as differing for various kinds of catalogs, so that the novice may not be compelled to study out how much of each rule may apply to the special style of catalog he is making.

Under BUYING, with the warnings and suggestions how to get the most for the money, will be given various tables to show net cost to the library of books at the usual price per franc, mark, shilling, etc., after adding commissions, fees, freight, insurance, brokerage, etc., tables of various discounts to enable bills to be checked up more accurately and rapidly, and specimen sheets with directions for library book-keeping on the most improved and simplified plans. These few random illustrations will show the general scope of the work.

Whenever any article is described, which cannot be placed before the class, its size, best material, maker, cost, etc., will be given, with an engraving to accompany the notes wherever desirable and possible, the purpose being to omit nothing that the inexperienced may need to know, in order to get the most practical good from these suggestions.

THE BLACK-BOARD will be freely used, and the more valuable illustrations, tables, and figures will be printed or otherwise duplicated, in order to supply each student with copies for his notes. During and at the close of each lecture opportunity will be given for questions, and a box for anonymous queries will be always available for those preferring to suggest difficulties in this way.

As the study will be by topics, when any subject is under consideration all these methods will be used, *e. g.*, the Accession Catalogue will be treated in a LECTURE pointing out its importance, illustrating its various uses, and explaining the best forms. References will be made to articles worth READING on this topic; in the SEMINAR, or round table conference, the discussion will be on the Accession Book; in the PROBLEM class, various peculiar cases, all connected with the Accession department, will be given out for solution; in the WORKROOM or laboratory the practice under supervision will be in writing up a model Accession Book; and in VISITING other libraries, attention will be given specially to this feature. By thus approaching each subject on all sides at once, it will be more thoroughly mastered and in shorter time.

THE LECTURES are designed to develop interest in the work, give needed inspiration, and such information as is not more effectively given by one of the other methods below. Here as everywhere, object lessons, samples for each student, black-board illustrations, questions and answers will give the most practical character possible to the work.

THE READING method aims to put in the hands of students such matter as must be read in connection with their studies and practice, and to direct to such other matter as should be read later, if not during the course. Critical estimates of the books, pamphlets, and articles will be given, with cautions where allowance must be made for the peculiar circumstances or prejudices of the writers, and reports and summaries of the matter read will be required of the students.

THE SEMINAR, Conference, or Round Table, will bring together teachers and students for familiar discussion and examination of the subject before the school.

Short original papers, summaries of books and articles read, new theories or stricture on old ones, and withal the greatest freedom of inquiry and criticism, will make these frequent conferences of the greatest interest and practical utility.

THE PROBLEM method, closely connected with the Seminar, will test the proficiency of the students and specially will cultivate self-reliance. After each topic is studied in the school, each student will be given problems taken from experience, or oftener prepared to better illustrate the point, the solution of which will require thorough knowledge of the subject.

Toward the end of the course these subjects will include a large portion of the topics treated, *e. g.*, a student is given a memorandum such as might be prepared by a competent library trustee and sent to a newly elected librarian, who had no knowledge of the peculiar circumstances of the institution over which he was to preside.

Such notes would include size of town, character of inhabitants, extent of manufacturing element, etc., other libraries or reading-rooms, amount of property and annual income, nature of governing board, tenure of office, number of volumes, annual increase heretofore, and specially the number and exact state of the catalogues and indexes, the regulations in force, the system of issuing and charging books, selecting, buying, binding, etc. With such data the student after study of the case states before the class what he would do as librarian, being prepared to defend his decisions against the criticisms of his associates.

As problems can readily be made to fit any special requirements, the variety available is limitless, and the careful solution, discussion and final criticisms and suggestions of the teachers will serve the same purpose as a well conducted moot court for a student of law.

The repeated study of definite cases will give self-reliance, a quality without which many able men fail in new undertakings, from an unwillingness to trust their own powers.

These practical problems will include difficulties such as librarians are liable to meet and advise upon in all departments, cataloging, indexing, aids to readers, hunting down hard questions involving the skilful use of a large bibliographical apparatus, etc.

VISITING other libraries, either individually or in classes, will be a regular feature of the school. In the Seminar each student will report what he has seen in the last library visited, with his criticisms. The other students who have visited the same library will first be heard, and the teacher will supply the points, pro or con, which none of the others have noted. In this way not only will practical knowledge of value be gained from the visits, but the students will have learned how to get most good from such opportunities in after experience.

The public and private libraries of New York and vicinity which will be open for such visits afford a very large field for this method of work.

WORK.—Provision has been made to give each student daily library work, carefully supervised by trained teachers, who will supplement the instruction of the lecturers. Those taking the full course will thus have had some actual experience in all the varied duties of a great library, the option being given any student of omitting certain departments.

Here as elsewhere it will be arranged as far as practicable that the student shall carry away with him tangible results of his work, e. g., in practising the rules for cataloging he might prepare a card-catalogue of select works on bibliography and library economy. These cards, corrected by the teachers, would be retained as the student's property, and would be of double value as a list of books in which he was specially interested, and as illustrating the errors he had made and against which he needed specially to guard.

To the more advanced will be given work including many and special difficulties. Librarians are invited to send to the school for such practice, cases that are specially misleading to catalogers. Dealing in a few days with as many such cases as may arise in several years of actual work will concentrate experience and act as a safeguard to the young librarian.

For practice in the use of reference books specially in bibliography, problems will be frequently given out, and several literary papers in New York, that receive many suitable questions for such practice, have offered to furnish them for the use of the school. After the student has looked up and prepared the answer, the teacher will point out how and where fuller or more reliable information might have been found, or the same result obtained with less labor.

SUBJECTS OF STUDY.

Beside the Professor of Library Economy, and the teachers now being trained for their special work, specialists in various departments will be engaged for lectures and instruction. The list of teachers and lecturers with their subjects will be printed as soon as decided.

The course will include the antiquarian or historical only when necessary to illustrate or enforce modern methods. Its aim is entirely practical—to give the best obtainable advice, with specific suggestions on each of the hundreds of questions that rise from the time a library is decided to be desirable, till it is in perfect working order, including the administration. A few topics will illustrate, until the schedule is ready for publication. Developing interest, press, pulpit, school, personal effort; raising funds by taxes, private bequests, membership fees, lectures, fairs, etc.; location; building; heating, lighting and ventilating book- and reading-rooms, shelving, furniture and fittings; labor-saving devices; trustees and committees; qualifications necessary in librarian and assistants; duties, titles, salaries and vacations; selection of books and periodicals; buying, prices, auctions, old book catalogues;

gifts, judicious begging; official and society publications; order slips, sheets and book; reception and collation; accession catalogues; shelf lists; printed *vs.* MS. catalogues; card *vs.* book catalogues; author *vs.* subject catalogues; dictionary *vs.* classed catalogues; classification on the shelves; systems of notation; charging systems; regulations, delinquents and fines; access to shelves; special privileges; evening opening; Sunday and holiday opening; closing for vacation or examination; aids to readers; practical bibliography; books, choice of editions; methods of reading; literary methods; binding, leathers, sewing, lettering, significant colors; repairs, etc., etc.

For those who wish direct information of the plans and progress of the new school an address register of the "Interested" is kept. To those who send their addresses for this register fuller details of the course, teachers, subjects and other matters pertaining to the School of Library Economy will be mailed promptly when issued. The address is Melvil Dewey, Columbia College, New York.

17. THE FUTURE OF LIBRARY SCHOOLS

Twenty-one years ago the Columbia university trustees, after considering the question during my first year, voted to establish the first training school for librarians. The usual doubts and fears were expressed by those who never think the time ripe for any new movement, but the period of experiment is now long past. Librarianship has won its place as a profession and the library school its place among institutions for professional training. Need of such training is now so fully recognized that no sane man would propose giving up the library school any more than he would normal schools for teachers or training schools for law, medicine and engineering.

But near the close of our second decade we have to face new questions, not as to existence but as to number, scope, location and cost. At the risk of seeming dogmatic I set down what seems to me the probable future of library training. Beginning with the simplest, we should have wherever practicable by means of traveling librarians, visitors or inspectors (as different states may call them) round tables, where for a day or two the librarians and assistants of a single locality meet a recognized authority for information and inspiration, to submit difficulties, ask questions, and get any help that an expert studying many libraries can give so well to a novice spending all his time in one.

For larger sections there should be a library institute lasting a week instead of two days and taught not by volunteers, many of whom have no special gift for teaching, but by those who have shown extraordinary qualities for this peculiar work. Leaders with these gifts should abandon all routine work and be available for institutes in different sections of their own states and if needed in adjoining states so that each might give his time and strength wholly to the highest work for which he was specially fitted.

Our summer schools will be maintained, increased in number and steadily improved. As for institutes, there should be traveling collections of books and appliances most needed for instruction and the faculty should be chosen with greatest care. The great majority of the thousands of librarians simply can not attend library school for one or more full years. Training and instruction given to them must be in institutes or in summer schools for about six weeks each year, for which it is easy to get leave of absence. As in the older summer schools in other subjects, the spasmodic and unattached schools, many of them started with the most unselfish motives, will die out when their work is better done by established institutions with faculty, equipment, endowment and experience which enables them to give students much more in the short six weeks of the course.

These summer schools, institutes and round tables, with the national, city and local library meetings and our professional journals, will do most of the work for the mass of librarians, and it is idle to decry these agencies because their standards are lower and their courses shorter than the schools for the few who are able to give one or two full years. Of these we need two types. Our oldest school has moved steadily for 20 years toward an ideal but is still far from its attainment. We need in English-speaking America three thoroly equipped graduate schools for the highest training. To cover the country satisfactorily one should be on the Atlantic seaboard, in Boston, Washington or preferably New York. One should be in Chicago as perhaps the best library center of all because within 1,000 miles on all four sides are to be found the greatest number of new, rapidly developing, aggressive libraries. The third is needed on the Pacific coast to care for the immense territory west of the Rockies, and for this no location is so good as at the University of California, with all the libraries of San Francisco at its doors for study, and standing on the very shore of the Golden Gate, which will inevitably, for centuries to come, be the great center point for an immense portion of the earth's surface. No recent news has been more gratifying than the enthusiastic assurance of Pres. Wheeler, Gov. Pardee, and several of the regents that a school creditable to the Golden state will be opened within a year or two at Berkeley. These three graduate schools should have equipment, faculty and endowment or support so complete that each will be easily recognized as the leader in its own great territory. Great as is modern development, and strong as is my faith that the next decade will show even greater progress than the past, I can not believe that there is room for more than these three schools in this first class. But between these and the summer schools there is a

Source: Melvil Dewey, "The Future of Library Schools," *Public Libraries* 10 (1905): 435-38.

large field to which most American library schools will belong. The three graduate schools requiring a college degree for admission and at least two full years of hard work in the university will provide for qualified candidates time, money and purpose to fit themselves for the highest positions. But their graduates can man but a small percentage of American libraries. Even if their number were large enough the great majority of libraries could not pay salaries sufficient to secure their services. Either nine tenths of our libraries will be conducted by the untrained or there must be courses, open to well-qualified graduates of high schools who will give one year of earnest study to the best preparation for librarianship to be had in so short a time. These schools will develop in different sections of the country to meet the demand, the less satisfactory giving way to the stronger and better just as an inferior machine gradually drops out of the market as the public find they can get for the same money one that will do better work. We are paying the penalty of success. The earliest school, when its record showed calls for its graduates beyond any previous experience of professional schools, was a temptation to many to offer training without adequate facilities. Most of these proposals were abandoned because librarians have been so outspoken in asking for proper standards.

I do not forget that many of the larger libraries have training schools of their own. These are usually local in purpose and result, training simply for that one institution. If work grows broader and their students go out to other positions such classes might be included with the smaller library schools.

We are often asked as to the cost of a satisfactory training school. Not unfrequently we have found that some visionary librarian had tried to impress on some institution the idea that such a school would be not only self-supporting but a source of profit. It is not difficult to disabuse intelligent minds of so absurd a notion. Not a few have taken the initial steps for library training on the theory that the service of students in a local library would be a decided gain to the institution. As a fact these services are of no more value than the time required for competent supervision. The item of profit should be left wholly out of the question. Our minimum estimate for a creditable school is an endowment of $200,000 to $500,000, which at 5 per cent would yield $10,000 to $25,000 a year. This sum is trifling compared with that required to open a department of engineering or electricity, as an expensive plant is not required. Lecture and study rooms and a collection of models and appliances needed for instruction make the problem of equipment comparatively simple. A separate building is neither necessary nor desirable, for the most successful school must have its home in a well administered and growing library, the atmosphere of which is one great element of the course. The cost is salaries of a competent faculty. It is equally important that the library itself should have the right environment. So much of library training is practical and dependent on constant observation and study of other libraries that a school should be where it has ready access to many large and small libraries within a short distance. It is a poor substitute to be compelled as the oldest school has been for many years to make long journeys which because of their expense must be made all too brief for the best results. It would be a great advantage if these visits could be made a few at a time instead of being massed in a single fortnight of the course.

A university atmosphere is highly desirable for the graduate schools and desirable also for the others, tho for them the right city and library are more important than a university. A school supported by the state should be in connection with the state university or in the metropolis and not at the state capital, except in rare instances like Boston where capital and metropolis coincide. Above all it should not be in the capitol building. Recent developments in all states are in the direction of multiplying offices, boards and commissions with inevitable pressure for rooms in the state house. Sooner or later the school will be a target for those impatient to inherit the space it occupies. Its opponents' question 'why a school is kept in the capitol any more for one profession than for another' sounds very plausible. The atmosphere of the capitol is quite the reverse of what would be chosen for a school. Finally, and most serious, the danger that the school may sooner or later be involved in politics makes it most unwise to locate it in the capitol. The state ought to support the training of professional librarians just as surely as it does that of professional teachers, but what school man would consent to have his normal school carried on in the office of the superintendent of public instruction in the capitol building? For five or six years it has been clear that the advantages of our own location were small compared with its disadvantages, and I have repeatedly expressed my willingness to see the original school transferred to a satisfactory university connection, much as I should dislike to part company with the work which has seemed to me the most important of all the library enterprises with which I have been associated. When asked by other states about establishing state library schools I have strongly advised against locating in the capitol building and usually against the capital city. Many of these objections would disappear or be minimized if a state library had a wholly independent building. Of late years it has often been suggested that the school ought to go with the proposed national headquarters. Obviously there would be many practical advantages to both sides if one of the three graduates schools were very near the headquarters offices, but I feel more and more strongly that a graduate school should be in a university atmosphere, that its students should be mingling with other university graduates and should have all the facilities of a great university just as the professional and technical schools are usually best carried on as departments of a university and not as independent institutions. As in the other cases, large endowment or peculiar conditions might make it clear to the best judges that it was wise to have the school independent of a university, but the chances are ten to one that its natural home with other schools in the university atmosphere would prove best.

Library courses in schools and colleges are so closely allied to this professional training that they must be reckoned with. The tendency grows in normal schools, colleges and universities to offer courses in bibliography, books and reading, library science or some other form of our general subject. These must not be looked on as professional training. The courses in music in our best universities are not to make great performers or artists, but to give a broad and clearer comprehension of what music and art really are and to qualify people to enjoy and profit from it in future life. School library courses have three functions-to teach the students to use and care for their own private libraries to best advantage; to use and understand the methods of the school and other public libraries; to understand the modern library movement, and to be so sympathetically informed as to its objects and methods that each graduate of the school may be better prepared to serve if necessary on library boards or committees or to coöperate actively with the library authorities in their community. In normal schools each teacher should have enough library training to qualify him to work effectively with the local librarian and to select books, care for them or supervise them in his own library.

This, briefly, is the future of library training which every earnest librarian should have in mind so that if opportunity offers he may help to establish or to encourage and develop every desirable agency whether it be round table, institute, summer school, library courses in other institutions, one-year course for high school graduates, or graduate school for the most thoro training of those fitted by nature and previous education to qualify for the highest positions.

Sept. 1, 1905.

F. LIBRARIES AND EDUCATION

Dewey's youthful goal of 1869, when he was in his eighteenth year, of devoting his life to education—"to inaugurate a higher education for the masses"—had a decisive influence on his actions and his career. As early as 1872 he was referring to his keen interest in "books and reading specially Public Libraries," and it appears that he was beginning to identify the public library as an instrument in fulfilling his goal.

Though Dewey's early career advanced in areas other than in the public library, he crystallized his view and propagated it at every opportunity. When interviewed by the *Boston Herald* in 1886, he envisioned public library development as follows:

> The public library is an institution whose importance is not recognized by the mass of people. It is our purpose to show it to be of equal value with the public school and the church, these three forming a grand trinity as means of public education and advancement. Most people now look upon the library as a good thing to have in a community, but by no means an essential. This idea is to be done away with. In the small town of the future, the library will be recognized as one of the prime necessities. There's no way of reaching the public so effectively as by the printed pages. It far exceeds the pulpit or the rostrum in force and power of extension. Here, then, is the trinity. The public school makes the base, giving the foundation for education; the church forms one of the sides by its moral teachings and its care for the spiritual man; and the public library makes the other side by its broad and general training of all classes and sects. It will not be many years before the public library will be recognized for its full value, and the little libraries will be found wherever churches and schoolhouses are. Every small town will have its library. That this change is surely coming is proved by the communications which our association is constantly receiving from cities and towns all over the country, where public libraries are contemplated. In most of the cases somebody has left an endowment, large or small, as a public library fund, or the nucleus for one, and the people want information about how to begin. One aim of our organization is to give just this information, for we have learned that experience and wisdom directed toward the proper starting of a public library yield splendid returns, and are a source of perpetual satisfaction in the later career of the library. A small but wise expenditure at the beginning is equal to a much larger outlay in later years.

Within two years, Dewey was given an opportunity to present his challenging concept to the Regents of the University of the State of New York. Feeling the need for expert advice on library matters, and especially about moving into new quarters, the Regents invited Dewey, who was well known at the time, to act as consulting librarian on a temporary basis in 1888.

While acting as a consultant, Dewey addressed the University Convocation of the State in 1888. It was a unique opportunity for him to further his long-held belief that the library should be an effective agency in the education of the masses. Consequently, choosing the title "Libraries as Related to the Educational Work of the State," he identified the functions of the library as being those of a "people's university." Dewey argued persuasively that:

> Higher education . . . demands new libraries at accessible points throughout the state and their wise and economical establishment requires guidance and supervision such as the Regents of the University can best supply.

Having urged the Regents to assume leadership, he offered as the alternative that, "If New York will not now lead as is her wont, at no distant day the greatest of the states will have to follow." The text of his address, which has become a landmark in the history of the State Library, is included here. Dewey's address was convincing and inspiring; its dynamic appeal is reflected in the following preamble and resolution, which were endorsed at the Convocation and transmitted to the Regents for action:

> WHEREAS, This Convocation believes that the time has come when certain of our public libraries should be recognized as an essential part of the State system of higher education and as properly a factor with the academies and colleges in the composition of the University of the State of New York; and,

> WHEREAS, To secure to the State the full advantages of such recognition, it is necessary that proper provision should be made by the State for advisory supervision and guidance of existing institutions and for stimulating the formation of new libraries; therefore,

> *Resolved*, That this Convocation requests the Regents of the University to take such action as may seem to them expedient for giving to such libraries as their official inspection shall show to be worthy the distinction, their proper place as a part of our State system of higher education.

So compelling had been Dewey's impact on the Regents that, upon the resignation of David Murray as Secretary and Treasurer of the Board, he was elected unanimously by the Regents to fill the position. At the same meeting, the following resolution was adopted before his election as if in anticipation of the vote:

> *Resolved*, That hereafter the Secretary and Treasurer of the Board
> be given general charge and direction of the State Library with the
> title of Secretary, and Director of the State Library, and that Mr.
> George R. Howell be continued as Librarian in immediate charge
> of the general library, and Mr. S. B. Griswold be continued as
> Librarian in immediate charge of the law library, each to act under
> the supervision and direction of the Secretary and Director as
> aforesaid.

Dewey accepted the appointment and assumed his responsibilities
immediately. He attended the meetings of January 9 and 10, 1889, during
which time the following action was taken in response to the resolution of the
Convocation of 1888:

> *Resolved*, That the Regents heartily approve the request of the
> University Convocation of 1888 that such libraries as may be found
> worthy the distinction shall be officially recognized as a part of the
> University of the State of New York, and given a seat in the University
> Convocation.

> *Resolved*, That the officers of this Board be directed to submit to
> the Regents at their next meeting plans for determining what libraries
> are entitled to the proposed recognition and for carrying into effect
> the proposition of the Convocation so far as existing laws permit.

> *Resolved*, That the Chancellor and the Committee on Legislation
> be requested to procure any needed legislation to enable the Regents
> to comply fully with the request of the Convocation for the official
> recognition of certain libraries as a part of the University of the
> State of New York.

The momentum engendered by Dewey's address continued unabated. On
June 15, 1889, the new University bill enlarging the powers of the Regents and
broadening the scope of the University became law. Soon after that, Dewey
delivered his second Convocation address, in which he identified himself as
"the mouthpiece of the time, which, at last, has fully come." In it he offered
definite proposals for action through a remarkably detailed analysis of goals and
procedures. The address in full reveals the enormous scope of Dewey's organizational skill and imagination in planning a statewide program for the University.
Only those sections relating to libraries are reprinted here.

Dewey was not content with speechmaking, however gratifying the
responses were. In addition to his reorganization of the State Library, his most
notable achievement during his early years as Secretary to the Regents was his
part in drafting the revisions of the law of New York State pertaining to higher
education. The law became effective in 1892 and was regarded by many as one
of the most comprehensive and far-reaching state library laws ever penned.

Throughout his life, the library's role as an educational force in society remained foremost in his mind. Nearly everything he wrote touched in some way on this role and how it might be achieved. From his many writings on this subject three specific selections—"Libraries as Book Stores," "The Function of the Trustee," and "Field Libraries"—are included here as illustrations of his continuing emphasis on this theme.

18. LIBRARIES AS RELATED TO THE EDUCATIONAL WORK OF THE STATE

There runs a tradition of our craft "The librarian who reads is lost." Who writes is indeed without hope. How grave his case who tries to make a speech! The modern librarian is too crowded with daily work to bring you carefully rounded periods or polished sentences. He is content if able to make his meaning clear and lodge the thought of his mind in yours.

You listen from year to year to special pleaders. Each man, as a rule, tries to magnify his office, and demonstrate that the topic in which he feels special interest is clearly first in importance. He pleads for vocal music, elementary science, hygiene, gymnastics, ethics, manual training, civil government, drawing. We are convinced of the value of every one, but alas, the list of necessary studies is like art, long, and school life for most of us pathetically short. We are forced mentally to brace against the carefully prepared points of the advocate. For three reasons I ask you to-day to follow me without this customary bracing against extreme views.

1. I do not magnify my office because it is mine, but rather have chosen it as a life-work because unable to escape the conviction of its superlative importance to education.

2. I come to you without carefully prepared arguments, and ask you simply to answer to your own minds my plain but vital questions.

3. Most important, the action to which I seek to lead you, instead of taking more time, means relief to your overcrowded curriculums.

What I propose, you will see is no entangling alliance, but rather is annexing a continent. Were there time, I should speak of the admirable work that has been going on in both east and west for the last five years between the schools and libraries. This has met with hearty recognition, has been often described in print, and is making its way rapidly through the country. But this is only the introduction to that deeper relation and recognition which is in the immediate future.

And let me remind you before we begin that the library for which I speak is one which few of us have seen, except in promise. It is a library at present in its infancy. Remember your own history. "Schools" were old when Paul sat at the feet of Gamaliel and the quick-witted Greeks hung on the words of their teachers in the Academy, Lyceum, and the Porch. But schools like those of which this Convocation is the crown are *young*. When in this discussion we speak of schools, we mean that ideal for which we strive, which ought and is to be. Observe the golden rule, and when we speak of libraries, picture that ideal which I will briefly sketch. Go back neither to the storied bricks and slabs of Nineveh and Babylon, nor to the myriad mss. of mighty Alexandria, nor, coming to our own time, to those institutions which in our library evolution correspond to Squeers and Dotheboys Hall.

We have many libraries still which have naught in common with our ideal, except books and the name; many that seem still carefully administered for the least good to the smallest possible number. Our evolution comes after yours. We are not so far advanced. Barely a generation ago the harmless incompetent, fit for nothing else, was set to teach school. But in their dignity and strength most schools have now crowded out the incompetents. The libraries are following, and already the idea is giving way that men and women, who fail in everything else, and can get neither church nor school, patients nor clients, are just the ones for librarians. Glance with me a moment at a sample of the old library and the new.

The old was located in an out-of-the-way street, specially inconvenient to the majority who might want it; the building was unattractive, dark, damp, cold, unventilated and ingeniously inconvenient; many of the books were on shelves so high as to require a ladder, were covered with dust, in shabby bindings, protected often with shabbier paper covers, soiled, torn and generally discouraged in appearance; unused public documents, old school-books, etc., nearest the door, the more attractive works in the attic or cellar; the shelves unlabeled; the books without numbers on the back, and possibly with none inside, and put on the shelves haphazard as they had come in, or in a classification so coarse that a reader seeking matter on a minute topic might require a week to look over the disorganized mass of literature in

Source: Melvil Dewey, *Libraries as Related to the Educational Work of the State* [Albany, N.Y., 1888].

which he might or might not find something that he wished; its catalogues and indexes were chiefly conspicuous by their absence, or were so meager, unreliable and so destitute of clear grouping that the only way to find what was wanted was to read the whole catalogue. The library was open an hour or two now and then, and closed evenings, holidays and vacations, for annual cleaning or for almost any excuse – on busy days, because no one had time to come; on holidays, because the librarians also wanted those days for rest. Finally, and most important, the old type of librarian was a crabbed and unsympathetic fossil who did what he was forced to do with an air that said plainly he wished you had not come, and a reader among his books was as unwelcome as the proverbial poor relation on a long visit. It is a sorry picture, but by no means wholly fanciful. In many places those who knew would pronounce it a study from life.

Contrast all this with the library as it should be, and in many cases will be. Placed centrally, where it is most accessible to its readers; the building and rooms attractive, bright and thoroughly ventilated, lighted and warmed, and finished and fitted to meet, as fully as possible, all reasonable demands of its readers; the books all within reach, clean and in repair; those oftenest needed nearest the delivery desk, labeled and numbered; arranged on the shelves so that each reader may see together the resources of the library on the topic which he wishes to examine, kept constantly ready for inspection; with simple and complete indexes and catalogues to tell almost instantly if any book or pamphlet wished is in the building; open day and evening throughout the year, and in charge of librarians as pleased to see a reader come to ask for books or assistance as a merchant to welcome a new customer; anxious to give, as far as possible, to each applicant at each visit that book which will *then*, and to *him*, be most helpful.

These are the facts. The old library was passive, asleep, a reservoir or cistern, *getting in* but not giving out, an arsenal in time of peace; the librarian a sentinel before the doors, a jailer to guard against the escape of the unfortunates under his care. The new library is active, an aggressive, educating force in the community, a living fountain of good influences, an army in the field with all guns limbered; and the librarian occupies a field of active usefulness second to none.

We will speak then of the relation of schools and libraries as they ought to be, and not of the failures of the past.

It takes the world a great while to learn what seem afterward very simple lessons. A happy thought sometimes revolutionizes the common practices of centuries. It comes out as clear as lightning in the darkness and the world recognizes and accepts it, as witness the telegraph and telephone and other modern miracles. Sometimes the new idea crystallizes so slowly that it seems like a geological formation. But whether with swiftness of light or slowness of granite the world moves steadily forward.

I suppose the man who first proposed attaching a wagon to the horse and making him draw that as well as his load, was voted as great a visionary as the modern flying machinist. But when on a smooth road he proved that the same horse could draw ten times as much as he had carried, why the wise old world said "the man is right. Go to, now, let us build ourselves wagons." Then the obstructionist (for the dear, dreadful, omnipresent old fossil was surely there) said, "In spite of his proof, the wagons are useless for they can not run on our bridle paths." And there was truth, as there often is, in the obstructor's position. But the world that built the wagons has built the roads. And when we remember that the builders have gone on to cross the continent with roads of iron and were not dismayed at the great span of the Hudson at our feet, or at the huge Hoosac bulk which we can almost see beyond the other shore, you will hardly think the task too great to build the road of which I am to give you a bird's-eye view to-day.

If you will follow me you will recognize that without the libraries our schools can do but a fraction of their work. They are horses without wagons, engines without cars, canals without boats, except such skiffs and scows and rafts as chance may throw upon their waters. We must have proper carriages as well as motive power, and then must make suitable provision for broad and straight and level roads.

We are spending our time and money with a freedom of which all the world is proud, to give our youth in our public schools not much information or culture, but only the simplest tools which, if rightly used, will enable them to educate themselves by reading.

Of old it was only the learned few who could read; most of the world were limited to conversation. Now, we are told this is an art more rare than music, and only the educated few are able to converse; but, except illiterates, everybody reads. Less and less from living voice, from pulpit or rostrum, and more and more from printed page, are people getting their ideas and ideals, their motives and inspiration. The mass of knowledge credited to nature and observation comes most of it, not directly, but through print. The eye, not the ear, is the great gate to the soul. The town-crier no longer rings his bell and shouts his message through the streets. Even if told orally, most readers wish to see "how it looks in print," as an average reader of French wishes to see rather than hear the words. All that is worth knowing soon gets into type. What a boon if such only were printed!

As we study the question, it becomes clearer that the difficulty and expense of reaching the people by the voice, and the cheapness and permanence of print make it necessary, if we are to educate and elevate the masses and make their lives better worth living, that we should, in some way, put in their hands the *best* reading. I say best, for reading is not necessarily good or elevating, though it certainly averages much higher than conversation because much greater care is taken in its preparation. Labor and cost bring into activity the law of survival of the fittest. But if good books average higher than good conversation, bad books are more powerful for evil; for when ideas good or bad get into book form, they are apt to become vastly more potent. We have thus a double reason for our missionary work; to give good reading for its own sake and also as the best means to drive out and keep out bad. To teach the masses to read and then turn them out in early youth with this power and no guiding influence, is only to invite the catastrophe. Human fashion, they are quite as likely to get bad as good. The down hill road is ever easiest to travel. The world agrees that it is unwise to give sharp tools or powerful weapons to the masses without some assurance of how they are to be used. Even George Washington got into mischief with his first hatchet.

The children of another generation will see nothing specially wonderful about the telephone or electric light. So we, born to constant sight and use of books, seldom stop to think what a miracle they are. As distinguished from the brute the savage has the divine gift of speech. And when we think that the vibrations of the air started by the vocal chords convey to another the workings of the human soul, we no longer wonder that speech has been looked on as the direct gift of the Almighty, a power too wonderful to have been invented by man. And when, a step higher, the image of his Maker discovered the art of writing, and learned to make spoken words permanent on wood or stone or clay, we do not wonder that the savage worshipped the chip that could talk or the bit of paper that unaided made a complete communication. Has there been anything in the world's history so wonderful as a modern book?

And remember that of late years the printing press has called to its aid graphic methods, color, form, the curves and coördinates of geometry and the many photographic processes, so that in many cases the book makes the author's meaning clearer and more easily understood than would be possible for a score of authors with the living voice. In proof of this consult some recent statistical atlas or the profusely illustrated volumes in science. Or take this very point of illiteracy:—here is a map on which is indicated by darkness of shading the amount of illiteracy in each section. Or to be more exact, here is a page with the list of all the states at the left, followed by columns representing each decade of this century, with the dates at the top of the page. Running across this page, opposite each state, is a curved line indicating by its height above the ruling, the percentage in that state that can not write; for each year the rise and fall of the lines show the fluctuations graphically. A similar line in red opposite the same state in the same way shows the percentage that can not read. Thus on this single page, at a glance, is told with geometrical accuracy the amount of illiteracy for the whole country; or for any given year, by reading down the proper column; or by reading across, the conditions of any given state during the whole century; or, by consulting the intersections of these columns as on a railroad time-table, the conditions of any place, at any time. No amount of oral statement could begin to give so clear an idea as a few minutes study of these two pages. Similar methods are being applied to almost every subject of human interest. Recent photographic processes have made exact pictures and all kinds of

illustrations so cheap that a modern book, as compared with those of last century, is like
a modern lecture on science in which every point is illustrated by experiments performed
before the listener or by pictures thrown on the screen by a lantern, when compared with
a mere oral statement which, however skillful the word painting itself and however clearly
defined in the mind of the speaker were all the ideas of objects referred to, simply *could*
not reproduce them as clearly in the minds of the listener.

Emerson says:

"Consider what you have in the smallest chosen library. A company of the wisest
and wittiest men that could be picked out of all civil countries, in a thousand years, have
set in best order the results of their learning and wisdom. The men themselves were hid and
inaccessible, solitary, impatient of interruption, fenced by etiquette; but the thought
which they did not uncover to their bosom friend is here written out to us, the strangers of
another age."

And his friend Carlyle adds:

"Of the things which man can do or make here below, by far the most momentous,
wonderful and worthy are the things we call books."

Reading is a mighty engine, beside which steam and electricity sink into insignificance.
Four words of five are written: "It will do infinite _____." It remains for us to add "good"
or "ill." What can we do? Good advice and example, encouragement of the best, addresses,
all these help, but no one questions that the main work is possible only through the organization
and economy of free public libraries. Many have practically accepted this fact without clearly
seeing the steps that have led to it. It is our high privilege to live when the public is beginning
to see more than the desirability, the absolute necessity, of this modern, missionary,
library work.

With the founding of New England it was recognized, though opposed to the traditions
of great powers in church and state, that the church alone, however great its preëminence,
could not do all that was necessary for the safety and uplifting of the people. So side by
side they built meeting-house and school-house. The plan has had a long and thorough
trial. None of us are likely to question the wisdom of bringing the school into this prominence,
but thoughtful men are to-day, more than ever before, pointing out that a great something
is wanting and that church and school together have not succeeded in doing all that was
hoped or all that is necessary for the common safety and the common good. The school
starts the education in childhood; we have come to a point where in some way we *must*
carry it on. The simplest figure can not be bounded by less than three lines; the lightest
table can not be firmly supported by less than a tripod. No more can the triangle of great
educational work now well begun, be complete without the church as a basis, the school
as one side, the library the other. The pulpit, the press, and wide-awake educators everywhere
are accepting this doctrine. There is a general awakening all along the line. The nation is
just providing in the congressional library a magnificent home for our greatest collection of
books; the states are passing new and more liberal laws to encourage the founding and proper
support of free libraries; individuals are giving means for establishing these great educational
forces, as never before. Witness Walter Newberry's three millions to Chicago, Mrs. Fiske's
million and a half to Cornell University, Enoch Pratt's million and a half to Baltimore,
Judge Packer's half-million for the library of Lehigh, Andrew Carnegie's proffered quarter-
million to Pittsburg, and proudly at the head, greatest of all library gifts, Governor Tilden's
five to ten millions left to New York, not to mention the hundreds of smaller gifts which
mark the last few years. New, large and beautiful buildings are being rapidly provided; new
libraries are being started at the rate of one to three each week; old ones are taking on new
life and zeal; Sunday school and church libraries are organizing to enlarge and make their
work more effective, and a great field of usefulness, at present hardly realized, is opening
in this special direction; schools are being brought into direct and active relations with local
public libraries. To one studying this great problem, the air is full of the signs of the times.
As with the free school, so again, New England leads in free libraries, but her example is
being followed with constantly increasing rapidity.

Our fathers had to revise their ideas and introduce the free schools as an essential factor. The time has come when we must revise our conceptions of education, or refuse to recognize very significant facts.

Education is a matter of a lifetime. We provide in the schools for the first ten or fifteen years and are only come to the threshold of seeing our duty to the rest of life. We begin to see that the utmost that we can hope for the masses is schooling till they can take the author's meaning from the printed page. I do not mean merely to pronounce the words or pass the tests for illiteracy, but to *understand*. Observation has convinced me that the reason why so many people are not habitual readers is, in most cases, that they have never really learned to read; and, startling as this may seem, tests will show that many a man who would resent the charge of illiteracy is wholly unable to reproduce the author's thoughts by looking at the printed page. And even with this tremendous modifier of the real number of readers we lose ground. I am no pessimist. I have no sympathy with croakers. I am proud to the last degree of the great work that is being done. But we can not shut our eyes to the census. In 1870 fifteen per cent of illiterates seemed an ugly item, but it had grown to seventeen per cent in 1880, in spite of all our millions and all our boasts. Of the children of school age in this great state, how pitifully few get beyond the grammar school? And of those who become academic pupils, how many enter college? And to the saving remnant that graduates from college, how much of the knowledge of after life came from schools and how much from reading? We must face the facts. We must *struggle* to teach our masses to read in our schools. Then they must become breadwinners; and if we carry on their education we must do it by providing free libraries which shall serve as high schools and colleges for the people. Our schools, at best, will only furnish the tools (how rudimentary those tools for most people now); but in the ideal libraries, towards which we are looking to-day, will be found the materials which, with these tools, may be worked up into good citizenship and higher living. The schools give the chisel; the libraries the marble; there can be no statues without both. As this fact becomes more generally recognized, the time draws nearer when the traveler will no longer ask *have* you a library, but *where* is the library, assuming its existence as much as he now assumes that there must be a church and school and post-office.

But if the library is to do the ideal work that we have in mind it must have some of the ideal qualities on which such work depends. This means a library differing materially from both the types most familiar in the past, which we may call storage and recreation libraries. The first is a storehouse, a cistern, an arsenal, mediaeval in its spirit, a literary miser, always getting in, seldom giving out. It was for holding and preserving, and not for use, and is best illustrated by the miser who gets gold not to spend, but merely for the satisfaction of possession. The European libraries are largely of this character, as are most state and government collections.

The recreation type is a mental candy shop, and at the other extreme in every feature. It is wholly for use, but the use is wholly for amusement. It could be illustrated by a school that taught only games, or a hotel that in its dining-room served only sweetmeats. It has, to be sure, some excellent books, but supplied to meet the taste of its pleasure-seekers, as the confectioner gives those who wish it a bit of good bread to eat with their ice cream.

Surely every library ought to have an ambition to get and preserve books, and surely some place should be found in every general collection for fiction and humor. These ought, however, to be the embroidery and not the web. A circulating library run as a business will, of course, take on the latter character and supply whatever will be most readily taken by its customers. But the library in which we are interested to-day combines the good features of both these with others of its own, and is the institution that deserves the name of people's university. It might well copy that broad legend from the seal of Cornell, "An institution where any person may find instruction in any study." Perhaps we should more clearly recognize its proper functions and be in less danger of confusing it with old ideas, if we called it not a "library" but a "people's university."

To the making of such a library many elements contribute. A building will not do it, though it be as beautiful as the Taj and as great as the Coliseum. Money and books, though essential, will not of themselves make such a library. I recall visiting a magnificent building on which about a million dollars had been spent. In it were many valuable books. It was in a great city, and a thousand readers daily ought to have found their way through its open doors. When I looked with surprise at the four or five readers who seemed lost in its superb rooms, my witty friend, the chief librarian, said, "Why, there is hardly a day passes that some one does not come into this library."

And I recall a similar illustration which came under my personal knowledge. The detective force of a great city were in hot pursuit of a man who thought it impossible to hide from them. A literary man, to whom he had done a favor, undertook successfully to secrete him through the entire day, and after dark he escaped. The place chosen, where he would be least exposed to recognition from chance observers, was in the public reading-room of a great library, which, like the one before mentioned, was famous for the number of people who did not go there.

We have no time to-day to go into the questions that determine a library's measure of success. Mere mention of heads must suffice. Its location should be central and accessible to all. Its building should be comfortable and convenient. Grandeur plays no part in usefulness. Its hours of opening should be long, for the people's university, like the town pump, should seldom be closed to those needing it. The regulations should be liberal, with as little red tape as is consistent with the safety of the books. It goes without saying that books, pamphlets and serials, should be well selected and as liberally provided as means allow. It would be hard to find a library in which from ten to fifty per cent of its books could not be replaced with others more valuable for its use. In fact it is common to find collections where, if the very best could be chosen from the open market, one-quarter the number of books would have more value than the whole miscellaneous assemblage. After the books, comes the little-understood catalogues, classification and analysis which vastly increase their practical value.

Only those with special experience can understand how essential to any high success are such appliances. Working in a library without them is like trying to find a score of men in a great city without a directory. You may chance on some one who knows the man you seek and can direct you to him, but the chances are that you will have a long disheartening search and perhaps fail entirely to find him.

Finally and perhaps more important than all the rest is the librarian. If he can furnish inspiration and guidance to the readers who seek his help then may we indeed look for a true university whether large or small, for the small library should have all the high ideals of the large with the best of their books.

And such a library is the real university for the scholar as well as for the people. Of old the pupil was continually with the teacher, and from his lips learned the sought-for wisdom; but the printing press has revolutionized all this, and to-day many an earnest disciple has never seen the face nor heard the voice of his master, but has received all his teachings through the printed page. The "new education" is chiefly distinguished by substituting the library for the text book and dogmatic lecture. Seminaries are springing up in the best colleges in all departments. Students are taught to work in the library as the main object of their course, and when one is able to use skillfully a large bibliographical apparatus and to get quickly and accurately from a great library what he needs, he may indeed claim to have a good education.

Of late years the college library has been taking an entirely new position. Of old it was attached to the chair of some over-worked professor or put in charge of the janitor and opened four or five hours per week in term time only. Now it is being raised to the rank of a distinct university department; there are professors of bibliography, of books and reading, and at Columbia we have for the first time a chair of Library Economy. The libraries are being made as accessible as the traditional college well, some of them opening from 8 A. M. to 10 P. M., including all holidays and vacations; they are receiving endowments, *e. g.*, the million and more to Cornell University, Prof. Horsford's great gift to Wellesley, Judge Packer's half million to Lehigh, and the long list of funds given to Harvard, the Phoenix gift to Columbia, and so I might go on with hundreds of illustrations. New and beautiful buildings, some fire-proof, all vast improvements over what was thought sufficient in the last generation, multiply; Harvard, Brown, Amherst, Dartmouth, Oberlin, Yale, the Universities of Michigan, Vermont and Pennsylvania; in this state, Cornell, Syracuse and Madison Universities, and so on. In New York city alone three splendid collegiate library buildings have just been finished; for the General Theological Seminary, Union Theological Seminary, and our own at Columbia, which has cost over $400,000, and already we plan an enlargement. The colleges are waking to the fact that the work of every professor and every department is necessarily based on the library; text books constantly yield their exalted places to wiser and broader methods; professor after professor sends his classes, or goes with them, to the library and teaches them to investigate for themselves, and to *use* books, getting beyond the method of the primary school with its parrot-like recitations from a single text. With the reference librarians to counsel and guide readers; with the greatly improved catalogues and indexes, cross-references, notes and printed guides, it is quite possible to make a great university of a great library without professors. Valuable as they are in giving personal inspiration, they can do little in making a university without the library. Just as truly as we found in popular education that the real school for the mass of people, and for all their lives except early childhood, was the library, so in the higher education the real university is a great library thoroughly organized and liberally administered.

What we need now in higher education is not more colleges but more libraries. Railroads have largely annihilated space and for the preliminary training it is easy to send our boys and girls a few hundred miles to college; but for the training that must be carried on all through life they need the people's university, close at hand where it may be reached without serious interruptions of regular pursuits. It is like the post-office and market compared to the registry of deeds. One does not object when he buys an estate to go a long distance to record his title but when he wishes to mail a letter he insists on having a post-office at hand. Higher education therefore demands new libraries at accessible points throughout the state and their wise and economical establishment requires guidance and supervision such as the Regents of the University can best supply. State after state has partially recognized the claim of the library by passing laws allowing communities to tax themselves for its maintenance and the time has come when the recognition of its true place must be made complete. If New York will not now lead as is her wont, at no distant day the greatest of the states will have to follow.

If time allowed I should like to sketch to you the recent development of the modern library idea. I merely mention the great steps, referring you for fuller information to the *Library Journal, Library Notes*, and the circulars to be had on application at the Columbia Library School. We date active progress from 1876 when, after a four day successful conference in Philadelphia, the American Library association was organized. It holds annual meetings, marked among conventions by their practical work and enthusiasm. The same year we started an official monthly organ, the *Library Journal*, now in its thirteenth volume. Shortly after followed that most important practical factor in the library work, the Library Bureau of Boston, which undertakes to do for libraries such work as is not practical for the association or magazine. It equips large or small libraries with everything needed (except books and periodicals) of the best patterns devised by or known to the officers and committees of the association, of which it is the tangible representative for manufacturing and distributing improved appliances and supplies. It secures trained cataloguers and assistants or finds positions for those out of employment, gives technical advice in its consultation department, and in all practicable ways fosters library interests. Ten years after the *Journal* which, because of its limited circulation, barely pays expenses at five dollars a year, came its colaborer, *Library Notes*, a quarterly magazine of librarianship, especially devoted to the modern methods and spirit, and circulated widely because of its low price. Last of the great steps came the school for training librarians and cataloguers which two years ago was opened at Columbia College through the same influence which had before started the association, *Journal*, Bureau and *Notes*. You who appreciate what normal schools are doing to improve our teaching will remember that librarians need a training school more than teachers who have had the experience of their own school-life as a pattern; for librarians till two years ago never had opportunity for training, and came to their work like teachers who had been self-taught, and not only had no normal school advantages but had never been in a school or class-room even as pupils. As evidence of the growth of the idea we may note that this Library School which began two years ago with a twelve week's course and provision for five to ten pupils has in two years developed to a course of two full years with four times as many students at work, and in spite of the rapidly increased requirements for admission is to-day embarrassed by five times as many candidates as it can receive. This means a recognition of the high calling of the modern librarian who works in the modern spirit with the high ideals which the school holds before its pupils. Of this work I said recently to the collegiate alumnae:

"Compare this work with that of the clergyman or teacher, whose fields of usefulness are universally put in the first rank. The clergyman has before him for one or two hours per week, perhaps one-tenth or one-twentieth of the people in his parish. Not so many, indeed, when we remember how there are often little struggling churches of a half-dozen denominations, where one strong church could do all the work much better. Beyond this very limited number for this very limited time the clergyman is dependent on the slow process of personal, parochial calls. I yield to none in my appreciation of the great work which he does, and do not forget the constant stream of good influences coming from his daily life, and the many direct efforts he puts forth; but I am speaking now of his work as a preacher, and of the limits which circumstances seem to set to it.

"The teacher has a larger proportion of her constituency in the earlier years, but only for a few hours a day, and only in the months when schools are in session. It constantly happens that just as she becomes deeply interested in a bright, promising boy or girl, and felt that here is an opportunity to develop a strong character by patient work, the child comes and says: 'I am not coming to school any more; I am going to work in the factory,' or, 'I am going to help mother at home.' For the great majority the work of education is hardly begun before the necessities of life take them away from the teacher's influence.

"But the earnest librarian may have for a congregation almost the entire community, regardless of denomination or political party. His services are continuous and in the wide-reaching influences of the library there is no vacation. When a bright boy or girl has been once found and interested and *started*, he is almost sure to continue under these influences all his life. It has been found entirely practicable for a skillful librarian thus to reach and interest people who have never been in the habit of reading; to lead readers into new and more profitable fields and to create a thirst for better books. In fact the number of ways in which people can be helped is only equaled by the power and lasting character of this influence which comes from good books. Recognizing these facts there are preachers who are looking on the highest work of the library profession as a way to spread the Master's word not less truly than is the pulpit; and there are teachers whose whole hearts have been given to the cause of popular education, who are eager to enter this newer field because they recognize in it a still wider opportunity."*

Is it not true that the ideal librarian fills a pulpit where there is service every day during all the waking hours, with a large proportion of the community frequently in the congregation? Has he not a school in which the classes graduate only at death?

Much is already done, and while the work is in its infancy it is an infant so vigorous as to leave no fears of its manhood. A last great step remains to be taken and to-day and here it ought to be begun. The state long ago recognized its school system as one of its bulwarks and fosters it with yearly increasing expenditure. Now it must recognize educational libraries as necessary companions of the most successful schools. This eminent body represents the higher education of the Empire State, which the Regents of the University are charged with fostering. Tell me if you think they can, without taking action, face our facts that the best reading more than the schools gives education to our people; that the colleges provide for only the trifling minority who can afford time and money to share in their great advantages; that the influence conceded to be the most potent is left without guidance, supervision, stimulus or support. When inspection shows that a school has attained a certain standard, it is honored by being made a "Regents' academy." Can we do less than

---

*The quoted section was extracted from his address to the Association of Collegiate Alumnae on March 13, 1886, entitled "Librarianship as a Profession for College-Bred Women."

give similar inspections to libraries, and when one is found doing the high work at which we have glanced to-day, honor it by making it a "Regents' library," and by virtue of success in its high calling, a member of this Convocation which represents the institutions that give New York its higher education? What greater stimulus can we place before our growing libraries than such certain and official recognition of superior work?

Many advantages are sure to spring from entering wisely on this course. I do not advocate undue haste. The essential thing is to recognize the principle and then meet year by year the growing demand for advice and inspiration. There need be no obligatory supervision. A library secretary would soon have more requests for advice and help than he could well answer. New communities are constantly waking to the need of libraries, and would be deeply grateful for wise advice as to the best means of developing interest, raising money, selecting, cataloguing and circulating books, and the thousand details which make or mar success. It is well known to the experienced that the same money can be made to do double good under wise administration, and yet for lack of just such help as could be afforded, at a cost to the state too trifling to be worth mentioning, many a community either fails to secure its library or fails to get from it all the good that the time and money could be made to yield.

There are few topics where technical knowledge and experience are so important as in establishing and administering successfully a library of the highest grade in its ideals, even though its income be small and its books comparatively few. It requires no vivid imagi-nation to picture the practical value to the state if any town about to found a new library or improve an old one could come to the Regents and have, without charge, the best guidance for its case that the combined experience of the library world had yet worked out. Time allows me only to lodge the thought in your minds. No expensive machinery is required. A single salary with hearty recognition of the work would start it creditably.

Such an officer would soon find money and books placed in his hands by those wishing to give them where they would do most good, and recognizing his superior facilities for wisest distribution. The excellent results that have become notable from the Regents' school examinations would be duplicated in good effects on library interests by competent inspections, reports and suggestions to such libraries as wished them. New York's splendid collection, the best owned by any state library, is about being moved into these adjoining rooms which are admirably adapted for the focus of state library interests and the central people's university. The Regents' office is ideally fitted to be the center of a system of university extension, such as is marking an era in the great English universities, and carrying to all parts of the kingdom the learning of Oxford and Cambridge and the other great schools, and for the first time giving them a practical connection with the lives of the masses, and making them a new and mighty force in working out higher standards of good citizenship. This work naturally centers at local libraries. Fellows and teachers from the colleges, for a trifling fee, go out to distant towns, to give courses of ten to twenty lectures on political economy, history, literature, science or art; indeed the whole range of the university curriculum is open. With the lectures are given references to the best books to be found in the local libraries. And the common people hear them gladly. Interest is aroused. Many are led to read and learn more than has been told them in the lecture. Those most interested meet for discussion and further instruction, and the practical results have been so much beyond expecta-tion that the universities are allowing work of this kind to be credited as a part of a university course leading to a degree. This means that many a man who would otherwise spend his time idling about saloons, secures instead a higher education worthy the name. Cambridge alone, I am told, has carried on over 600 of these admirable university extension courses in the past ten years.

Do I hear some one say that New York has tried the scheme of libraries for the state and that it has failed? With that story I am familiar. We have learned by experience what not to do. Every great movement is apt to succeed only through repetitions and failures. The district school system failed because too widely dissipated and because it had no supervision such as I have merely hinted at to-day. Who could expect 12,000 libraries to be administered successfully in a state where there were not twelve men that could be fairly said to be thoroughly trained for the work?

The great state of New York led all the rest in recognizing, many years ago, the importance of good reading and in trying to meet the want. Seventeen other states followed its example and we were proud of our leadership. To-day state after state has left New York behind. More than once in our national library conventions have we of New York been forced to hear her slightingly spoken of because she was doing so little modern library work. But no state has yet given recognition to all that this new work implies. If New York will again rise to the occasion and officially recognize the library as part of its system of higher education and give to libraries of the highest type, as fast as they reach the standards, a seat in this Convocation as being in fact as well as in resolution co-workers with the colleges and the universities, then again shall she wear her crown of leadership. If she fails, before many more meetings some other state will have seized the opportunity that now is hers.

Gentlemen of the Convocation, it is to-day your high privilege to lead. To-morrow it may be your bounden duty to follow.

19. THE EXTENSION OF THE UNIVERSITY OF THE STATE OF NEW YORK

Libraries. — We now come to the most important part of university extension;—libraries, museums and lectures, those great elements in the university which are only just beginning to be fairly recognized, and which are destined to play so great a part in the university of the future. Still we will merely glance at their part in our own University extension. Our State Library and State Museum are now made integral parts of the University and as such should be developed and made as perfect as possible. The colleges and academies in the different villages and cities of our State have a claim on them and can make them of more practical use than heretofore.

We can barely mention the steps in this extension of usefulness:

1. The library and museum* should be developed here as central institutions.

2. The Legislature—it is hardly possible that there would be any opposition—should pass a satisfactory working law for the formation of libraries throughout the State. It is discreditable and mortifying to see how far behind is the great State of New York in this matter of public libraries.

3. All through the State there should be an organized effort to stimulate, under the new law, the judicious formation of practical libraries.

4. The University should give its advice in the starting, reorganization and administration of these libraries and museums in any part of the State. Just as the government sends lieutenants of artillery to certain schools to give instruction in military tactics, we should send competent persons to give information in regard to libraries and museums. The people who raise money for these institutions, are usually very anxious to use that money in the best way and it can be made to do double good if it is used in exactly the right way instead of taking its chance with inexperienced people, meaning well, but without sufficient technical knowledge. They ought to apply to the University, saying "We are about to start a library in this town. It will apply for admission to the University as a part of the educational machinery of the State for higher culture and education. Will you send some one to show us the right way?"

The State Library ought to have a specially trained assistant, paid by the State, who should go for a day or a week, or even a month, if necessary, to the town and give the result of his experience and instruct the local librarian how to make a right start. And this would pay. The State now gives $50,000 annually towards the support of district libraries. If it is worth while to buy books, how much wiser it would be to spend a little of the money in making the books bought doubly useful. As secretary of the American Library Association I get constant calls for help in these matters, and have at least weekly instances where such practical assistance would prove of great value, for most new libraries wish to do the very best thing if they can only find out just what that is.

Reports and supervision. — Another useful feature would be annual reports from the different libraries, similar to those from our colleges and high schools. These should be not simply dry statistics, but reports of such things as can clearly be made of practical use in affording assistance to those who report, in studying the many problems of library organization and administration, and in supplying to local institutions which ask it, reliable information of the experience of others. We stand ready to meet more than half-way anyone who comes to ask assistance, and shall have plenty of work without intruding our services, for though this department is not yet started, we have had three applications for help of this kind within a week. All these we welcome, and it would be a very good dinner which the best members of my staff, or myself, would not leave at any time if we could help any community in this State to better library facilities.

---

*Nearly all the following points apply as well to museums as to libraries, and I use the word libraries as covering both, since one building so often and so properly houses both.

Source: Melvil Dewey, "The Extension of the University of the State of New York." *In* New York (State) University, *Proceedings of the Twenty-Seventh Annual Convocation . . .* (Albany: James B. Lyon, 1889), pp. 91-99.

As I pointed out last year, the experiment of district libraries in New York has been little better than a failure, for lack of just such library supervision as would naturally go with a thorough system of annual reports. The $50,000 a year given by the State can not accomplish one-fifth the good of which it is capable if its expenditure and administration must be trusted, without supervision, to inexperienced local officials, most of whom lack not only technical library knowledge, but any proper interest in the work. They not only do not know how to do it, but few of them have any comprehension what it is that ought to be done.

As under the new law the State Library is the university for the whole State, it owes to the public the discharge of certain functions, very important and desirable in themselves, but impracticable to any other institution, because they are in their nature as broad as the State, and should be supported from the general treasury to which all the State contributes. If the Regents will accept this view of their duty towards the scattered institutions of the University, they can at small cost do a wonderful service. Important departments of this work are: duplicates, university loans, traveling libraries and paid help.

Duplicates.—Probably every New York library of any extent has more or less valuable works in duplicate. Except in special cases where two copies may be needed in different rooms, or for other peculiar reasons, the second copy is worse than useless. It takes room, and in any proper system must be cleaned, inventoried and reported safe from year to year. Certainly every library in this State, without exception, feels the need of more books, and nearly every one feels the need of more space. However much any one of you may prize his Webster's Unabridged, he would doubtless vote a second copy on his study table to be a positive nuisance. If one man has two Websters and no dictionary of biography, and another, a hundred miles away, has two biographies and no Webster, you can understand the service if exchange could be made practicable. Some library may have two sets of the *North American* and none of the *Edinburgh Review*, while another will reverse the difficulty. It is much as if a college had two professors of Greek and none of Latin, or two college halls and no gymnasium, except that in such cases the difficulty is so prominent that it leads to prompt correction, but to even the best librarian there is no more puzzling question than that of duplicates. While it is easy to know the value of books just published, it requires long training and constant study to be able to give anything like a fair judgment of the present worth of miscellaneous books. It constantly happens that only an expert can tell whether a certain old volume is worth $100, or one dollar, or perhaps only its price for old paper. The librarian fears to accept the always low offers of book dealers, feeling sure that he is not getting half the real value, while possibly the trustees hesitate to sell their property at any price. The result is, in most cases, that the duplicates continue to cumber the shelves and are worse than useless, while their owners go on fearing to send them to the paper mill, or to accept a speculative offer. Both the difficulties would be removed if the Regents should authorize such institutions to send all their needless duplicates by cheap freight to Albany. This would involve no labor or cost except boxing. One expert could readily appraise for the whole State, keeping himself well posted as to values by study of old book catalogues and auction sales. Having no possible pecuniary interest he could be trusted to mark a fair price on each volume, and could report promptly to senders the total worth of books received, and return in books for which there was use, an equivalent at prices marked when they were sent in by others. In the hands of such an expert, the occasional rarity of enhanced value would count for its full worth, while a great mass would find its way to the paper mill without danger of including any treasures. A library that sends in $100 in duplicates, and receives an equal value in useful books, is more profited than by the gift of $100, for it not only receives the value, but relieves itself of a useless burden. Not only has a flower been planted but at the same time a weed has been removed. You will find in section 18 of the new University law, direction for the establishment of a State Library Duplicate Department, which will insure libraries complete sets of any State publications which they wish to keep. Ample and admirable quarters have already been provided in the great pavilion, in which can be stored, if necessary, 250,000 volumes. The small cost of freight both ways would be borne by the library sending, and, if thought necessary that the department be wholly self-supporting, a trifling fee would pay the cost of appraisal and handling.

University loans.—If the great collection owned by the State is to do anything like its full work, it must adopt the principle of itineracy, for single books as well as for small working libraries. When a professor at the other end of the State wishes to see one of our books for an hour, he must now spend a day or two and several dollars in traveling to it. Even if he has abundant means he may have no alternative, for it constantly happens that books are wanted of which no copy can for some time be found for sale, and for foreign books before they can be imported his time of need may have passed. Is not this another clear case of bringing Mamohet to the mountain? Where the distant reader is an officer of some department of the University, and so known to be responsible, and is willing to pay the express or postage both ways, is it not more reasonable to send the book to him instead of compelling him to come to the book? Modern devices for mailing have removed the objection that the book would be injured in transit. The reader's official position is a full safeguard against irresponsibility, and the quickness, cheapness and ease with which our books could be made available to all sections of the State would add enormously to the practical value of its great collection as the real University library of a real University of the State.

Traveling Libraries.—The same principle applies to sending small working collections to communities which feel the need and ask such help for intellectual advancement. The history of the little libraries sent out under the district library law was exactly what we should expect. Perhaps 200 volumes were bought by some village and for the first year were constantly in demand. After they had become an old story they ceased to attract even those who had not read them but only knew their familiar backs and titles. The books were little worn and yet had ended their usefulness. If, as soon as interest waned, they could have been boxed and returned here and replaced promptly by another case which in turn had come back from some other village, both communities would have renewed their interest and both libraries would have renewed their usefulness. At trifling cost this constant exchange could be carried out till the volumes were literally worn out in the service of the State, thus supplying the best reading, to the largest number, at the lowest possible cost. This peripatetic principle would also allow a much closer supervision and better organization. Printed catalogues could accompany each selection, and at each return losses could be made good and the books put in thorough repair. While it is desirable that every community should have its own permanent library, there can hardly be a better means to stimulate interest and create a demand for that than by sending carefully selected traveling libraries to teach the people how much pleasure and profit they could derive from the best books. Even with permanent local collections it seems highly probable that the principle can always be used to great advantage, except where means are so unlimited that every desirable book can be added to the permanent collection. It is really the same plan which experience has proved to be best for even wealthy readers in England, where the great circulating libraries like Mudie's and Smith's take most of the edition of many books. These cases of carefully selected books, constantly traveling back and forth throughout the State, would be active missionaries in the cause of higher education, and would keep those interested in such work in constant touch with the central office, and it, in turn, in closer and warmer sympathy with its immense constituency.

Paid help.—It often happens that a teacher or student, in order to continue his work, must secure some isolated fact, verify some quotation, or get an extract from some book, pamphlet or serial, or the transactions of some society. Often he makes a long journey to do only a few hours work which might have been done quite as well by cheap proxy had he only known where to find a competent clerk, near the distant library. Indeed for many library investigations a trained assistant can do more and better work in a given time than the principal himself. Students who know the value of time hesitate to ask such favors from others, and prefer to lose a day themselves rather than interrupt another for thirty minutes. It ought therefore to be understood throughout the University that all are perfectly free to send to the State Library for verifications, translations from the more common languages, or any similar literary work within the capacity of a competent librarian who is not a specialist. For this service a fee, barely covering actual cost to the State, would prevent all criticism and abuse of the privilege, and also remove any hesitation on the part of those whom we wish to feel entirely free to ask as much and as frequent service as they may need. To illustrate, if some one wished a dozen pages type-written from some book he could ask it on the blank provided, and if simple work, an operator, receiving at the rate of thirty cents an hour, could copy it, and, if desired, have its accuracy verified and attested before one of the librarians who is a notary public. If the clerk spent four hours on this outside work, and so lost four hours in the service of the State, the fee paid would be four times thirty cents an hour, or one dollar and twenty cents. As a result the State would have lost nothing, while the applicant might have been greatly helped. I have proved in other libraries that such a system can be worked with simple machinery and regulations. Many a scholar will accomplish much more work each year if he can thus command help for any routine work in the great University library, without cost beyond the trifling charge for actual time employed. As this most useful system involves no expense to the State beyond the inappreciable wear of its books, it ought to extend, the privilege to scholars in other States or broad who may wish anything which can be found here to better advantage than elsewhere.

. . . . . .

If all these improvements and extensions of the University were already accomplished, if in incorporations, supervision, educational headquarters, publications, examinations, degrees, scholarships and fellowships, libraries and museums, we had already attained all that we have so briefly noted under these heads, there would still be lacking what seems to me the most vital factor in University extension. One year ago I made before you an earnest plea for the recognition of the modern library as a "people's college" and as properly an integral part in our University. You voted unanimously to ask the Regents to make such recognition. At their next meeting the question was considered and they voted to ask from the Legislature the necessary powers. The question went before the Legislature and its committees, and from first to last has commanded the unanimous and warm approval of our best men and as a result to-day we are working under a law which provides for all the recognition for which I argued one year ago. But more than all this is needed, and for that I ask to-day. The library alone, even the best is not enough. Suppose you have an ideal school-house and grounds, with perfect apparatus and equipment, but no teacher, what kind of education would the pupils get? Suppose you have the best steam fire-engine ever made, but no engineer. Suppose you have the finest building and the best library that can be selected, but no library teacher or librarian.

A library without *life* is like faith without works, of no avail. You will find to-morrow in visiting the new State Library rooms, elaborate electric lamps, and fixtures and wires, but they are cold, dark and useless, because not yet connected with the dynamo. The wires are, in fact and in name, dead. The same substance, whether we call it ice, or water or vapor or steam, freezes or burns according as it has life or heat. In the work of the past year, in the recognition of the library, in the new and broadened law, it is as if we had put in radiators and engines and in a good sense laid our pipes. Now, it remains to put fire in our engine, turn steam into our apparatus, and give it life. We must man our engine. A library may be the best educational machine known, but can not do its work unless it has brain and heart behind it. Man without tools or weapons can do little, but the tools without man can do nothing. Our last and greatest problem therefore in university extension is to put men of the right type in contact with our machinery, men who shall act like moral dynamos and send along every cold dark wire a glow of warmth and life.

The mistake of not appreciating how much greater is the man than the machine is perhaps oftenest made with libraries, and I venture to say there are a score of presidents and principals present who are making it. They think they have libraries when they have only a collection of books. A pile of bricks or stones is not a house till the brain of the architect has planned and the hand of the mason has put them in their places. Mere books are not a library, but simply the material out of which one may be made. Some of you think your libraries are doing their full work. It is as if you had a fine pipe organ, which experts assure you is unsurpassed, but your organist is capable only of pumping out a few popular hymns. Some day a master of every stop and pedal will sit down to this same organ, and the divine music will seem a miracle to the old listeners.

* * * * * *

20. LIBRARIES AS BOOK STORES

The *Library Journal* recently remarkt that some years ago I advocated this radical change. Insted of dying out, this idea hs grown stedily stronger. I hav red every number of the 97 volumes of the *Publishers' Weekly* since its foundation and hav studied this problem for nearly half a century. The conviction grows stedily stronger that the only satisfactory solution is for tax supported public libraries to perform the vitally important functions of the ideal book store, which, with few exceptions existing book stores not only fail to perform but, becauz of economic conditions, must more and more fail. The whole trend of the world is to provide the essentials of public education at public expense. The high school, with rare exceptions, displaces the oldtime private and select school, to our infinit advantage. The public library has in equal degree servd general interests by displacing commercial circulating libraries and increasing almost beyond belief the amount of good reading.

But a book ownd is better than a book loand. We must encourage buying books. The best results ar possible only if there is either an ideal book store or a library where a prospectiv book buyer may hav expert guidance in selecting what wil best meet his needs. It is simply impossible to hav a competent staff for doing this unless book stores ar hevily subsidized. The *Atlantic Monthly* rendered a valuable servis in publishing Mr. Arnold's article on the "Welfare of the Bookstore" and Mr. Newton's "Decay of the Book Shop." Its Contributor's Club is following this up. An extract shows the spirit:

"I am not condemning the bookseller; I am only explaining the trubles of the customer. I know how difficult it must be to get a salesman or saleswoman who knows anything of books, or is willing and able to lern about them; and I take pains to say that I hav found some who ar more than polite, who ar cordial and frendly, and 2 or 3 who, within their special provinces, ar competent also.

"As a rule, however, the attendant, as wel as the shop itself, is a weariness to the body and soul. Far better may one go to the public library if he wants information about books."

The public needs this servis and has made a long stride toward it in supporting public libraries. The bildings, books, attractiv rooms and a staf vastly more competent than any book store can afford is alredy paid for. It wud be as silly to duplicate these facilities at enormus cost as to bild a second trolley line thru a crowded street. Those financially interested wil get excited as they did when I first propounded this doctrin and wil use the same arguments put forward by private schools and academies; "destroying vested rights," "taking bred out of mouths," etc. etc. *ad nauseam*. Hundreds of times we hav gone thru this process. Hotels last year flooded the cuntry with statements that their vast interest wud be entirely ruind when the dry law took effect, and millions believed it. But alredy reports from all sides agree that the hotels never made as much money in the same time, not becauz of no bars, but in spite of it. We always adjust ourselvs to new conditions and all history teaches us to do the ryt thing and not worry over the imaginary evils that ar always predicted before any important change. The space, capital and employes of the retail book trade wud adjust themselvs satisfactorily if their most important function was hereafter turnd over to the tax supported libraries.

One interested in any subject wud go to the library for much better expert advice than can ever be had in a self-supporting bookstore. He cud borrow the best books for his use and if he wisht, cud hav a copy to own come in the next of the frequent packages received from the great publishers' clearing house which wud evolv as a necessary part of the plan. At les cost we shud hav vastly better servis and the ownership of good books wud be mitily increast.

The department and other stores cud as now handle gift books and popular best sellers, which can be past over the counter like fancy goods by any salesman.

The modern magazine, supported by advertising, givs so much for so little that it has made it utterly hopeless for the bookstores needed in every community to be self supporting. The *Publishers' Weekly* for April 17 gave statistics of the Curtis plant showing

Source: Melvil Dewey, "Libraries as Book Stores," *Library Journal* 45 (1920): 493-94.

that the *Saturday Evening Post* sold yearly 110 million copies or more than the entire book production of the whole cuntry, duble all the school books sold, and 4 times all the trade books sold by all publishers in a year. The paper for the *Post* wud supply all our book-making twice over. Each number, almost given away, is equivalent to 2 averaje books of 400 pajes or, dropping advertising, reading matter equals a good size book. In the face of wel known facts, one can not hope to hav the immensely valuable servis of an ideal book store in any other way than by combining it with the public library where it can be done better at a small fraction of the cost.

21. THE FUNCTION OF THE TRUSTEE

MELVIL DEWEY: I take it the supreme function of the trustee is to administer the funds which are in his hands so they will do the most good. It seems to me they are to settle the sort of books to be bought, whether it is more feasible to keep the money for books that are most useful or to spend it for something that will be useful only to the few. I think Mr. Rosengarten put very generously what the relations should be between the librarian and the trustee, from the trustee's standpoint.

From the librarian's standpoint, I can never forget that the trustees are a board, not private owners, on which rests the responsibility for the wise use of library property. If they have a competent librarian let them advise with him about matters pertaining to the library; I believe in that thoroughly. But, if they have a man or woman in charge of the library who is entirely incompetent, then it becomes their duty to get some one who is competent. A man in my office a few days ago, talking about a prominent library at the head of which is a very prominent man, said the librarian was simply an employee and asked what business he had representing the library; "the president of the board of trustees represents this library." He was an earnest, sincere man, but he actually believed that the librarian was rather impertinent to speak for the library. I said to him frankly that his attitude would be sure to ruin his library; that he was like a man with a spirited pair of horses and a coachman. If the coachman is good for anything, of course, he will not sit still and let the man take the reins; if he is not competent and the horses are good for anything, they will run away with him, and that is what is apt to occur in a library. But, if you were out driving, as I have been in the last few days, with my little boy, and the horses became frightened, you would take hold of the reins and help him; I might do the same thing if a competent driver were on the box, but he might then get off and leave the whole thing to me.

It is not the function of the librarian to invest the funds and attend to financing, but in my conception it is a trustee's function to see that the library work is properly done, and if he does not do this it is an oversight on his part. We librarians would do well to put ourselves in the attitude of having accepted a trust, and if the trustees would meet with us and put themselves in our place, we should work together more and more in sympathy. It is not my experience that trustees who make trouble do it from any ill-will to the librarian; it is because they have not thought or studied their mutual relations; but of that enough has been said.

Two or three things occur to me as specially important. The modern church, you will find very often, has fifty or sixty distinct agencies in operation, social rooms, libraries, clubs, etc. The old high school was a place to hear a few recitations. Our modern school, in library facilities and educational methods, is far in advance of the college of a generation ago. There has been the same development in these as in our modern railways, wireless telegraphy, etc., and the library is going along with the rest. It is an age of electricity and of libraries. Libraries are as old as Hindu records, and there were books in those early days just as much as now. There were also electricity and steam; but the difference is that we have learned to use these forces, and the public is coming to understand them; and following it back we find that the printed page, which means the work of the library, is the thing which will influence men from the cradle to the grave. The world has come to understand that the whole system of education is in two distinct parts; school education, from kindergarten to university, is part; but there is another part, just as important, just as deserving, that is not for the young only, but for adults also, that is not in an institution but in the home. This, which we call "home education,"—a library,—is the second part, and those two things have to travel on together from this time on. That is the first fact for the library trustee to understand. The librarian or trustee who looks upon a library from the point of view of a generation ago, as simply a collection of books, isn't going to do the best kind of work till he gets a broader view.

As to the library staff, the trustees ought to come themselves and send their assistants to these meetings. That is what we have done in Albany. We find it pays to give our assistants

Source: Melvil Dewey, "The Function of the Trustee," *Library Journal* 27 (1902): C217-C219.

the time to attend library meetings. Our observation proves it the best investment we can make. If I were running a library as a private institution, I would send my staff to this meeting every year. They do better work and it pays for the assistants all along the line. Dr. Canfield's last words to me were, "Emphasize that fact; that men won't do team work unless they have instruction," and if you can't make them do team work they are not good for much in this world. That is the kind of man that doesn't want a telephone, or any modern invention, he wants to go along in the same old way. Library work isn't done that way. We must get into full touch with all the world, and we want our trustees to come to all our meetings.

A great thing is to keep in mind all the modern demands on a library. In every community we have the school board, that is an established custom. We cannot get the best results unless the library business is kept distinct from the school business. A man that is in any kind of business and thinks some other business is better doesn't make much of a success, and the people we want on the library boards are the people that believe the library is more important than the school, more important, with a more lasting and longer influence over the whole community, therefore the public library should be the center of the educational life of the community, and the museum, art, history, and sciences naturally cluster around the library. It is the best place for them—not in the same room perhaps, but in the same building or adjoining, so that when people are working in the museum and want to refer to books they are at hand. Secondly for students, colleges, meetings on scientific subjects and other subjects they ought to go to the library as naturally as a home pigeon will fly back to its home. The library is the cornerstone of all this and trustees ought to recognize that. But libraries have other functions. Information is exceedingly important in an economic sense for reasons which can be demonstrated; it pays; but most important of all is inspiration. The public library should also be a source of amusement. We can give the public no amusement so wholesome as books. What can be a more legitimate expenditure of public money than to give to people so burdened down that they can hardly stagger another step, a book that takes them into another world? We librarians and you trustees together ought to see our work in the broadest way, and we ought to look forward, not back, and above all things lend a hand.

22. FIELD LIBRARIES

Every civilized nation has learned that education pays on the material side as well as on the higher plane. No wise statesman dares neglect it. Our free schools reach the remotest hamlet. Indeed, distribution of schools has been overdone, and like other states New York finds that many of its 11,000 school districts could wisely be consolidated; for it would often be cheaper to transport the children from two or more of the weakest districts to a better school, than to attempt to support so many different buildings and teachers. What-ever the method, no intelligent man denies that every home must be reached with educational facilities.

This education is for the young, in school, and for a limited course. It is of priceless importance, and well worth the many millions paid for it yearly. But there is another means of education quite as important, not for the young alone but for all, to be had at home instead of in school, and lasting not for a short course but through life. For this the term "home education" has wisely been chosen to differentiate it from school education, which is obtained not at home but in regular teaching institutions. The problems of home education are comparatively new. There is great lack both of men and money for its work. We must choose from many possible plans those that will give the best practical results from limited resources. In a comprehensive view of home education we find five distinct factors: libraries, museums, clubs, extension teaching, and tests and credentials. Of these any competent student is sure to find libraries easily the most important, efficient, and economical, and the natural centre for the other four agencies. The growing recognition of this fact is shown by more than a hundred new laws concerning libraries passed in America, and 402 gifts, made from private resources, aggregating $16,000,000, in a single recent year. There has been nothing in educational history equal to this modern library movement. It has the most support and the least opposition, the most liberal grants by taxpayers, the most generous gifts from philanthropists. We are astounded to find how much has been done for this side of education, but more astounded when we study deeper to see how little of what is needed has as yet been accomplished. We spend fabulous sums each year and are proud of our statistics, but we reach only a small proportion of those who most need help. Any observer who looks below the surface finds many houses in both city and country where no good books are bought or read. Some people read nothing; some only newspapers, and these often the poorest rather than the best; some read magazines, good, poor, or indifferent; but the number of book readers is pathetically small. There are some whole villages where not half a dozen of the best books find their way. There are colleges where the amount of the best reading outside the prescribed text-books is startlingly restricted. Students are too busy with required studies and other duties, and as a result are graduated and sent out to swell the army of non-readers, though the reading habit would have been worth to them more than all the learning of their college text-books.

We have learned that in education as in farming new soil gives the largest crops. A given amount of effort does double good when spent on the young rather than on adults. Profiting by this knowledge, we give more attention than ever before to the needs of children. Special rooms, and librarians naturally fitted and trained for assisting children, are being added to the best libraries. Home libraries reaching little groups "with books and a friend" are sowing good seed, but there is not more than one where a thousand are needed. The wise farmer who has more land than he can work properly looks over his territory and selects for first attention that which promises best returns. As we look over the library field ripe for the harvest on every side, we find the greatest need at present in the rural sections. A little over half of our people live in the country. They have a larger margin of leisure, fewer distractions, and fewer opportunities to get the best reading. They read more slowly and carefully, and get more good from books than their high-pressure city cousins, whose crowded lives leave little time for intellectual digestion. These facts are unquestioned, and one would think that philanthropists wishing to do the greatest good with a given sum of money would look to the country, rather than to the town where large numbers in a small territory make it easy to support public libraries. One might fairly expect that more than half the gifts for books and libraries would go to that half of the people who by common consent

Source: Melvil Dewey, "Field Libraries," *Dial* 40 (1906): 75-77.

have most leisure for reading and fewest opportunities to get books; but instead of having their *pro rata* share, which would have been about 52 per cent., an analysis for the 402 gifts of a recent year aggregating $16,000,000 shows less than one per cent. devoted to this rural reading. The explanation is doubtlesss that attention has never been properly called to the facts, and that the solution is not obvious. A rich man who wishes to improve the reading of his fellows can build a library or stock it with books in a city, but he hardly knows how to reach rural homes even if he understands their pressing needs.

As a partial solution of the problem, we started our New York State system of travelling books, pictures, and collections, in 1892. Remarkable results have been secured, and the system, still growing rapidly, has been gradually but generally accepted as a permanent factor in education. A community which is too small, or which thinks itself too small, to own and support a public library may thus feel free to accept, for a small fee for transportation, a hundred of the choicest books for six months. Novelty has then worn off. A library, like a reservoir, becomes stagnant, and the interest of readers can be maintained only by adding new books at frequent intervals, or by changing the entire libraries in the travelling system. Thus the same books move on from point to point till they are actually worn out in service, giving larger returns for each dollar invested than has ever been found possible in any other field. This method, one of the most valuable in modern librarianship, does the greatest good at moderate cost.

It is easy to devise ways of doing good, but most of them cost too much to be practicable. It is easy to devise inexpensive plans, but most of them are not effective. To secure efficiency at low cost is the great problem in all educational, religious, or philanthropic work. You may compel your horse to go to the water, but he will drink only if he wishes it. The best library, either permanent or travelling is of little use to the man who will not read. It is well worth all its costs to supply books to those who are hungry for them, but we must not neglect the underlying problem of creating the appetite. Our system is not a complete success until it reaches most of the people for whom it was planned. The inexorable law of circulation, which applies to a community as much as to the blood, has taught us that we cannot safely ignore the submerged tenth. Five Points filth may beget Fifth Avenue fever. Their folly may cause our funeral. If there is a cancer in the foot the poison will circulate to the heart and brain. A town is not safe because it has sewer mains through every street if the residents fail to connect their houses with them. Schoolhouses and teachers do not educate if the children stay away. Boards of health may compel reckless citizens to connect their houses with the sewer system, truant officers may enforce compulsory education laws, but statutes cannot help us in our equally pressing need of inducing people to read the best books.

As in war and manufacturing, it is the man behind the machine or method that determines its efficiency. Much good is done by making books readily available. The taste of readers improves by reading even without guidance, but the best results demand that behind the library's books there shall be an earnest human soul, whose chief concern is to make other lives better and more useful, through the influence best exerted by good reading. The visitor in our little home libraries who meets once a week with the children, to give needed help; the reference librarian, now so prominent a factor in the best libraries; and the children's librarian, one of the best of the new special workers,—these are all practical recognitions of the fact that no magnificence of buildings, wealth of resourses and endowments, excellence of catalogues and indexes, or liberality of hours and rules, can ever take the place of the trained expert who is at heart the reader's sympathetic friend. Such a helper may change the whole course of a life by giving the experimental reader confidence and stimulating interest at the first short interview. The man or boy who has been spending his evenings lounging about the country store or saloon and doubtfully tries the experiment of going to the library instead, should be handled with as much skill as the trout that approaches the bait, for he is as easily frightened away. He needs a sympathetic helping hand across the stepping-stones of an untried stream. The range of books is vast. The new reader needs not only books, but a friend. A country boy, who has never seen the city, dropped at night in the Grand Central station of New York may have skill and self-reliance enough to find his way safely, but he is infinitely better off if a friend meets him. In our best large libraries the reference and children's librarians perform these functions, for the constituency is large enough to justify the expense. How are we to give at practical cost similar help to these scattered readers in rural homes who need it even more? Obviously no one small community can afford to pay for the whole time of a competent guide to books and reading.

The itinerant principle offers a solution. The travelling book must be supplemented by the travelling librarian, who can give a day or two each week or month to the locality too small to afford his entire time. The economic principle is sound. Hundreds of thousands of commercial travellers prove that business men find the itinerant principle the cheapest and best way to get their wares into communities too small to support a permanent store or agent. The missionary who has seven stations to each of which he gives one day a week, the judge who moves from point to point to hold his court, the orchestra or company who give only one or more entertainments in places too small to support a permanent organization, illustrate the universal application of the principle which we must adopt in order to get best results at least cost.

The commercial traveller does his best work only when he can carry his samples with him. People need object lessons. The travelling librarian must have with him a considerable collection of books for his house-to-house and individual work. He can do much good by gathering those interested in schoolhouses or churches for an evening talk, stimulating interest and good resolutions and giving helpful suggestions; but when he sits down with the family or an individual to talk about personal reading he must have open before him some of the books for which he is trying to create an appetite. As these are too heavy to carry about by hand, we must have a book wagon with horses or motor, holding perhaps a thousand volumes carefully selected for this peculiar work. With this equipment the man or woman with a genius for the work has a rare opportunity for usefulness. If it suggests the religious colporteur distributing books and tracts, we must remember that only religious and educational work has ever moved deeply the human heart to missionary effort, and the work of which we are talking belongs clearly to this class. The book wagon would have its regular route, repeating its visit at intervals of perhaps two or more weeks. This book missionary would come to know his constituency as a pastor knows his people. He would learn natural abilities and tastes, and would become skilful in developing latent interests and leading promising readers steadily on to higher and better things. If on any trip he did not have in his wagon just the book wanted, he could record the need and bring the book next time from the central library from which his routes would radiate. He would invite his readers to visit the central library whenever they went to town and to feel free to ask for help in person or by letter.

All would know that there was no commercial interest behind the work, and would feel confidence in asking guidance when they wished to buy books of their own. A book owned is much better than a book loaned. If the travelling librarian can induce his readers to apply their money to buying good books he will have done an educational work of incalculable value. To assist in this, endowments or gifts should pay necessary expenses of administration, so that any reader may have brought to him at wholesale cost any book among those it is especially desirable to distribute. It is pathetic to see how books manufactured simply to sell are scattered through rural homes. People impressed with the value of good reading give their hard-earned money to clever agents who charge them high prices for books which ought to go to the paper-mill and not on the book shelf. The best way to cure this evil is not by declaiming against it, but by giving people the best books at cost instead of these poor books at high prices. The distribution of trash will stop as soon as it is unprofitable, for it is done only from pecuniary motives.

No one who fully appreciates the great influence of books and reading can doubt that the money required to equip such a book wagon and to pay the salary of such a travelling librarian would yield very large educational dividends. The wagon, horses, and harness would cost about $1000, and the thousand suitable volumes would cost as much more. If as many books were in the hands of readers as in the wagon, so that while changing the books from house to house the wagon continued substantially full, the stock would be perhaps two thousand volumes. This investment would mean about $3000, besides the salary and travelling expenses. This latter item would be small, for farmhouses would compete with each other for the privilege of keeping the wagon over night and having extra opportunity to examine its resources. A man worth $3000 a year could use his time to good advantage in this way. There are men of real ability so deeply interested in the work that they would do it for much less if necessary. Age, experience, and other elements would determine the necessary salary, but it would be perhaps a moderate estimate to allow $3000 for the equipment of the wagon and $2000 a year for salary and expenses. When I first proposed this new work some five years ago the term "field libraries" seemed well suited to designate the idea. Admirable opportunities, with coöperation and needed supervision, await the first gifts for launching this very practical enlargement of the itinerant principle.

G. COOPERATION AND CATALOGING

Dewey recognized early that cooperation would lessen some of the repetitive and duplicative activities that were performed in library after library throughout the country. In 1873, soon after becoming associated with the Amherst College Library, Dewey visited libraries in Boston and New York and viewed them more critically than he had on previous visits because of his increased awareness of management problems.

The summary of his observations and some of his conclusions with which Justin Winsor of the Boston Public Library seemingly agreed are recorded in Dewey's "Journal." In it he not only identified the need for cooperation but also offered as a possible solution a plan remarkably similar in intent to the "Cataloging-in-Source" project of the twentieth century.

Illustrative of his concern is the following extract from Dewey's "Journal" for 15 February 1873:

> He [Winsor] agreed with me that it was wholly impossible to secure competent cataloguers with the multitude of libraries springing up (thank God) all through the world. They secure competent help only by taking promising persons and training them to the work.

> The catalog [sic] having so very great influence on all workings of a library it becomes a prime consideration to decide how each library shall be supplied with a perfect catalogue. Of necessity the book must be catalogued by some central tribunal where the most perfect aids shall supplement the efforts of the most skillful catalogers [sic]. One copy of an edition being thus treated the whole (1000) edition is . . . perfectly catalogued.

> The final catalogue tribunal being established the only thing remaining is to furnish a copy of this work to any library having a copy of this edition.

> My plan is that the Congressional Library (if for any reason that failed, some other—the Boston Public—would be glad to do the cataloguing [which they would have to do anyway for themselves] if they could have it printed for them) . . . make a perfect catalog of each volume copyrighted, and then have the publishers . . . strike off slips with this prepared title, ready to paste on cards . . . as desirable, and send a slip with each volume and . . . furnish extra slips to libraries keeping up cross references. [slightly edited]

Dewey thus became a proponent of cooperative cataloging, seeing it as an escape from the repetition which occupied so much of the librarians' time. Three years later, speaking at the Conference of Librarians in 1876, he made his view known while observing critically that:

> People on all sides are continually urging the great desirability of doing something [about co-operative cataloguing]. About once in so long articles appear in different countries rehearsing the follies of the present system of doing the same thing over a thousand

times, as we librarians do in cataloguing books that reach so many
libraries. But right here they stop. . . . Now, I believe, after giving
this question considerable attention, that it [co-operative cataloguing]
is perfectly practicable.

Dewey's fervent endorsement of centralized cataloging, with its consequent
emphasis on standardization, made him less than sympathetic, indeed quite
reactionary, when the question of changing cataloging rules was being discussed
in 1902. His opposition to "continual change" in cataloging rules was expressed
at the meeting of the Catalog Section of the American Library Association and
revealed a conservative and practical attitude.

The formal establishment of the American Library Association also set
up two committees, the Finance Committee and the Co-operation Committee,
to which references have been made. The Constitution of 1877 (Article IV,
Section 6) identified the duties of the Co-operation Committee as follows:

The Co-operation Committee shall consider and report upon plans
designed to secure uniformity and economy in methods of administration; and the Association, Board or Committee shall have power
to refer subjects to special committees.

Dewey, though not a member of the Committee, was kept informed of its
activities in his position as Secretary of the Association and he contributed
to its success.

He continued his campaign for the acceptance of a cooperative plan,
noting in his article on "Co-operative Cataloguing" that

There has been no subject oftener in the minds of thoughtful librarians
who desire to accomplish more than the time and means at their
disposal will allow them to accomplish, than the vast economy of
labor and patience and money which would be brought about if
the cataloguing of libraries could be done on some good plan of
co-operation.

He proposed that "when the title is once properly examined, copied, and
revised, and the note prepared and added, the result should be made easily accessible to [other libraries]." His proposal is accompanied by a preliminary report
on the rules of descriptive cataloging submitted earlier to the American Library
Association. Omitted from the report, however, were the "signatures of the half
dozen prominent librarians and cataloguers who had shared in its preparation"
in the hope that criticism would be made more freely. The report represents
the first tentative code, incomplete though it may be, designed by members
of the newly formed Association. Further study by the Committee on Co-operative
Cataloguing led to the preparation of "Condensed Catalog Rules for an Author
and Title Catalog," published in 1883. Dewey's catalog rules in his *Library
School Rules*, first published in 1890, were based on these.

Another "happy idea" conceived by Dewey was the preparation of a
"Manual" including a list of "10,000 volumes, the best that they [the Committee
members] are able to select, for a general library in an average community."
His proposal for such a manual clearly shows his extraordinary skill at detailing

the procedures for implementing an idea. The proposal, endorsed by the Co-operative Committee, is the genesis of what was later published in 1904 as the *A.L.A. Catalog. 8,000 Volumes for a Popular Library*. To bring the project to fruition Dewey agreed in 1884, long before the *Catalog* was published, to serve as editorial director without pay. He fulfilled his obligation in part by permitting the staff of the New York State Library, under the direction of May Seymour, to allocate time to its completion. "The Coming Catalogue," written in 1877, discusses his ambitious plan.

Dewey adhered to his self-determined goal of reducing libraries' cataloging costs through cooperative efforts, and in 1901 he was urging the use of cards printed by a central agency. As he had done in 1873, Dewey identified the preferred agency for implementing his plan as the "National Library in Washington," and he expressed that view in his essay, "Printed Catalogue Cards from a Central Bureau."

The Portland Conference of the American Library Association, held in 1905, was the last Dewey attended before his resignation as New York State Librarian. His speech, entitled "Unity and Cooperation in Library Work," reiterated, as Dewey acknowledged, what he had "been harping . . . for thirty years." In it he rhetorically posed the question:

> Do you forget what librarianship means—that civilization itself
> is simply the accumulation of the wisdom and the experience of
> all the world as preserved in books, that the book is the most
> wonderful thing that has been evolved in all the history of the
> race?

He revealed also his sustained faith in seed sowing, a faith which was incorporated into the objectives of the Lake Placid Club Education Foundation, which he established in 1922.

His 1905 speech, while a fitting recapitulation of developments during his long involvement with the profession, concludes with Dewey's urging librarians to "look forward and not back" even though great things had been accomplished in the past. It continues to be a message of enduring relevancy.

23. CO-OPERATIVE CATALOGUING

There has been no subject oftener in the minds of thoughtful librarians who desire to accomplish more than the time and means at their disposal will allow them to accomplish, than the vast economy of labor and patience and money which would be brought about if the cataloguing of libraries could be done on some good plan of co-operation.

The public and the press have time and again questioned why this obvious means of saving was not put in operation. Probably the difficulty lay largely in the lack of any means of communication such as is now afforded by the *Library Journal* and the Library Association. How was it possible to get the libraries at work on any plan? No individual had either time or money to travel throughout the country laboring with each other individual interested; and had such a person been found, his efforts would have been looked on with curiosity by some, laughed at by others as hopeless, and seconded and co-operated in by too few to make the movement a success. But no sooner are our interests organized than this subject is brought forward and ably advocated from a dozen different stand-points. Even the wealthiest are compelled to do something to decrease the cost of their cataloguing, and the public is clamoring at the large appropriations asked to carry on the catalogue department. When the cataloguing costs more than the books themselves, there is certainly some ground for inquiry. But this same public that clamors at the cost of good catalogues, clamors even more if it is not furnished with them. So the problem is how to make these catalogues at a less cost, and to stop making them will be no solution.

At the present time, if a specially valuable book is published it finds its way to at least a thousand different libraries, in all of which it must be catalogued. One of the highest salaried officers of each of these thousand libraries must take this book and examine it for the scores of points that only a cataloguer can appreciate the necessity of looking up. Then the title must be copied and revised. Perhaps a half day is spent in preparing a satisfactory note to append for the benefit of the readers, etc., etc. And all this work is repeated to a certain extent in each of the thousand libraries! Can librarians complain if practical business men call this sheer extravagance?

When the title is once properly examined, copied, and revised, and the note prepared and added, the result should be made easily accessible to the other nine hundred and ninely [sic] nine librarians. They would thus secure at slight trouble and cost a fuller and better catalogue than any one of them would be able to make for himself, even if he had plenty of time and money at his disposal; for the chief of the general cataloguing bureau should be a leader in his profession, and should have greater facilities and take greater pains than would be possible for any individual.

But we purpose to repeat none of the arguments. The feeling evinced at the late Conference surprised even the friends of the project, and convinced, as far as we have learned at least, those doubtful of its expediency. The ablest librarians and cataloguers of the country gave in their testimony in favor of the attempt, and the letters addressed to the secretary since the meetings are very largely tinged with this all-important matter of co-operative cataloguing.

It is evident that something must be done and will be done. Our present problem is to devise the best possible beginning. Every one having ideas on this subject not yet made public should put them in compact form and furnish them to the *Journal* for early publication. By the combined efforts of the thousands directly interested we shall probably be able to agree upon something that will improve our present condition. Shall we try to establish a central cataloguing bureau supported by the Association? Can the publishers be induced to prepare suitable titles and furnish them with books? Is it practicable for the Library of Congress to catalogue for the whole country? There will be a score of plans, all having more or less merit, and from them the committee appointed at Philadelphia will be able to select something satisfactory.

The first step in any plan is to know how the separate titles are to be prepared. Every possible catalogue is made up of individual titles. This question has already received considerable attention, and the plan submitted to the Association is given below. Its adoption in preparing the titles for the *Library Journal*, the *Publishers' Weekly*, and, as

Source: Melvil Dewey, "Co-operative Cataloguing," *American Library Journal* 1 (1877): 170-75.

far as possible, in the trade lists of the various publishers, will greatly help in giving it currency, and the design and desire of the committee is to make the plan so satisfactory that it will be recognized and adopted as the standard. The preliminary report is submitted herewith without the signatures of the half dozen prominent librarians and cataloguers who shared in its preparation. It has seemed better to present the plan in this informal manner, in order that the formal report signed by the committee may be made after the matter has been completely canvassed, and all suggestions have been carefully considered. It is desired that criticism be made with absolute freedom, and all suggestions sent to the office of the *Journal* will be submitted to the committee before their final report is made up. To the various sections of the plan as submitted are appended explanatory remarks.

It should be borne in mind in reading the proposed rules that they are for *printed titles* to be made in quantity and distributed to many different libraries. This fact modifies certain questions not a little. The greater compactness and legibility justify greater fulness and more information on the printed title, while the duplication in large numbers will so much reduce the cost that another serious obstacle will be removed. In the preparation of the rules, the growing feeling that full titles cannot be afforded, has been constantly in mind, and considerations of economy have decided several minor points.

> The title is an exact transcription of the title-page, neither amended, translated, nor in any way altered, except that mottoes, titles of authors, repetitions, or matter of any kind not essential to a clear titular description, are *omitted*. Where great accuracy is desirable, omissions are indicated by three dots (. . .). The phraseology and spelling of the title are exactly copied; but capitals are given only to proper names and adjectives, and to initial words of sentences. Any additions needed to make the title clear are supplied and enclosed by brackets.

It should be noted that this rule admits omissions of all matter not essential to a clear titular description of the book. The rule requires the omission of the author's name in the body of the title, where it is identical with the form used as a heading, and where its repetition is not essential to the wording of the title. If the title contained a ,eudonym or any other form of the name, the omission would not be made. This change to a less degree of fulness has been recently made in the Boston Public Library and in the Library of Congress, and many other prominent cataloguers deem it unwise to incur the expense of absolutely full titles in all cases. A further object is gained because the shorter titles are more easily consulted. As the plan contemplates the distribution of printed titles for the common use of libraries, a greater degree of fulness is allowable than in making titles for only a single library. Still the omission of useless matter is desirable in almost any catalogue, and the space thus saved is much more valuably used in giving additional facts in regard to the book, or in brief notes as to its literary character.

A second change from the common rule, as given by Prof. Jewett, is the omission of stars and dots except where great accuracy is desired. These take space, disfigure the titles, and of course cost as much as solid matter in printing the titles. Still there are cases where the exact place of omissions should be indicated, and here three dots are proposed as the more convenient symbol.

No mention of punctuation is made, it being understood that the cataloguer will introduce the proper marks in unpunctuated titles.

The rule for capitals leans towards their sparing use, still is sufficiently broad to admit wherever really needed. This is a point on which a general expression of opinion is specially desirable. Mr. Cutter's able review of Mr. Fiske's Harvard "Rules for the Use of Capitals," which fortunately appears in this number of the *Journal*, will represent one side of the question. On the other it is urged that the uniform omission of capitals is very much the simpler rule to understand and follow; that there is a growing tendency to write only one form for each letter, and that the lower case; and that eminent authority justifies and recommends the change. Probably most will admit that there is a prejudice in favor of capitalizing certain classes of words, but special students of these subjects are more and more coming to the opinion that two forms for each letter are useless, and that the language will outgrow the older and less convenient capitals. If this be, as it seems to be, true, then the case against the capitals is stronger. Too many on a page certainly give it something the appearance of the common advertisement. There are some cogent reasons on both sides, and still uniformity in our catalogues is more important than either omission or retention.

After the title, are given in order: the edition; the place of publication; the publisher's name, in italics; the year; the year of copyright, if different, in brackets; the number of volumes, or of pages if in only one volume; the illustrations, maps, plates, or portraits; and the approximate size from actual measurement regardless of the fold of the sheet, in accordance with the report of the committee of the American Library Association.

In books having more than one pagination the number of pages is indicated by giving the last number of each pagination connected by a +, an added + indicating additional matter unpaged.

These imprint entries give the facts regardless of the title-page, and are left blank only when they can be ascertained neither from the book itself nor from other sources.

The edition, if specified, is considered as more closely allied to the title than is the imprint, and so is given as the last item of the former, or between title and imprint. It is proposed to use 2d ed., 4th ed., etc., instead of *second edition, fourth edition*, etc., because of the greater economy and legibility of the abbreviated form.

The preparation of a full table of library abbreviations for the common use of the Association is an early duty of the Committee on Co-operation. These abbreviations should include all the more important places of publication, and perhaps the names of leading publishers. The list might also include standard abbreviations for the more common Christian names, and thus effect a large saving both in the preparation and in the use of titles. The publisher's name should doubtless be introduced in a printed slip for general distribution, though it might be a questionable matter for an individual library. The italics are thought desirable in bringing out the name more distinctly from the other entries.

The year of copyright, when differing from the year of publication, is introduced, and special attention is called to its desirability. It indicates whether the book is really a new one or simply a newly-dated copy of an old work. The Italian scheme of co-operative cataloguing mentioned at the Conference, sometimes at least, gives the exact date—year, month, and day—of first publication. It is suggested by some that this date be given only when there is a difference of five or more years. Others propose to give it only in cataloguing books whose value would be affected, omitting it in fiction, poetry, etc. When used, the century figures can be omitted, *e. g.*, 1876 [63].

Attention was called to the fact that many publishers would greatly prefer this date of copyright to be omitted, as it would expose the common trick of issuing old books as new, sometimes with new titles. The librarian should be protected as far as possible against this deception, so that he will not buy unneeded duplicates. The date of the actual issue of the book is of interest to all concerned. Every intelligent reader would be glad to know the time of the first appearance of even a novel or poem, and when works of science, or politics, or history are considered, the value of this item is greatly magnified. The introduction of the year of copyright is something of an innovation, but it is thought that it will be endorsed as one of the most useful items in the imprint entries.

Pages are proposed, in books of only one volume, since this item is so easily given, and is so valuable for collation and even more for getting a close idea of the size of the book.

The old rule of specifying pages only when less than a hundred, was defended on the ground that the item was given simply to determine whether the work were a pamphlet or a book. It is claimed that it is quite as important to know whether a book be of 103 or of 1803 pages, and the numerals occupy so little space that the fact should be given. Certainly it is vastly more useful than to repeat the author's name in the midst of a title, after having given it in the same form as a heading; or to use space in giving dots and stars to indicate omissions; or, worse still, to print mere repetitions that add nothing to the titular description of the book.

Maps, plates, etc, are arranged alphabetically, and it is proposed to give the number of plates, counting them if necessary, and the number of illustrations, in case it is specified. By plates are meant illustrations or other matter printed on separate sheets pasted or sewed into the book. Such plates are not paged and form no part of the original signature. If abstracted, it might be next to impossible to detect their loss; hence the exact number is of importance. By illustrations are meant such engravings, etc., as are printed on the same paper and at the same time with the letterpress. Thus, whether full page or not, they are an integral part of the book, and if removed, the remainder of the mutilated signature gives ample evidence of the fact; besides being a part of the original "form," they are paged. It is therefore much less important to know the number of illustrations, and the rule is to give it only when, being already counted, it can be done without extra labor.

These items are introduced before the indication of size instead of after, because the size of the plates, etc., is often larger than the corresponding text (373 p. 8°, 7 maps 4°), and so the size should be indicated. By writing 373 p., 7 maps, 8°, it is clearly indicated that both text and maps are 8°, and it is also more logical in describing the contents of the covers than to say 373 p. 8°, 4 maps.

As the size follows the report of the Committee on Sizes, no special comment is needed in this place, unless it be on the small space occupied by the designation of size. The Committee on Sizes recommend for general use only the single letters which indicate approximately the size by actual measurement. Thus a single character does the work for which half a dozen have often been used, *e. g.*, superroyal 8°, medium 32°, etc. For special cases the committee have provided simple and efficient methods of exact designation, but it would seem that for ordinary purposes the size-letter was sufficient.

The point is one for special consideration, and it is not at all improbable that a majority of the cataloguers will desire the exact measurement of the book, and possibly of the letterpress, in a printed descriptive title, where the compactness and cheapness so largely remove the ordinary objections.

The + is used instead of the comma to connect the various paginations, because of the danger of reading 3, 147 p. as three thousand one hundred and forty-seven instead of 3 + 147 p. By the use of the small + no more space is required than when the comma is used, and the meaning would be plain to any one not versed in cataloguing; for 3 + 147 + 8 + p. indicates clearly that there is a preface of 3 p., a body of 147 p., an appendix of 8 p., and some additional matter.

It is much better to give the pages as proposed rather than to add the numbers and give the entry as 158 p., because the labor of adding and the danger of mistakes are avoided, the fact of the length of preface and appendix is brought out, and it is much easier to collate the book.

In giving the title, the title-page was followed closely, but in giving the place, dates, etc., the facts should be given, whether on the book itself or not. Sometimes they may be incorrectly given on the title-page, sometimes they may be omitted. The facts are given in the order named above, whether that be the order of the book itself or not, and any needed corrections or additions are put in place in brackets. These entries are made to tell in the briefest and most convenient manner possible *where* and *when* the book was published, how large it is, etc. This rule would seem to require that the place should be given in the common English form, though on the book itself it may be given differently. This is another point on which criticism is especially invited. Should the imprint give the English or the vernacular— *Vienna* or *Wien? Milan* or *Milano? Florence* or *Firenze?*

If the title-page is followed, we shall have a large variety in the names of some places where books are published in many different languages. The rule as it stands, to tell in plain English *where the book was printed*, is certainly as simple as any. There is much to be said on both sides, but again uniformity is of greater importance than any particular method.

The contents of volumes are given when on title-pages, or when necessary to properly describe the volume, but no analysis is attempted. Necessary notes are given after the imprint entries.

A history of New England might treat the subject territorially, and, though not on the title-page, it would be desirable to specify the section covered by each volume—*e.g.*, v. 1, Maine; v. 2, New Hampshire; v. 3, Vermont, etc. Or it might be chronological, in which case the dates included in each volume should be given. This enables the reader to call for the volume he wants directly from the catalogue, while otherwise he may be compelled to call for the whole set and examine it to find the one volume which he wishes. Still no effort is made to analyze the different volumes pointing out the various topics or their method of treatment.

Books are entered under the *surnames* of authors when known; under the *initials* of authors' names when these only appear, the last initial being put first; under the *pseudonyms* of the writers when the real names are not ascertained; under the names of *editors* of collections; under the names of *countries, cities, societies,* or other *bodies* which are responsible for their publication; under the *first word* not an article of the titles of periodicals and of anonymous books the names of whose authors are not ascertained. *Commentaries* with the text, and *translations*, are entered under the heading of the original work, but commentaries without the text are entered under the name of the *commentator*. The Bible or any part of it in any language is entered under the word *Bible*. Books having more than one author are entered under the first named in the title.

The fixed rule of omitting only initial *a, an,* and *the,* and then entering under the first word, though it may be a preposition, seems the only safe one. The rule for *Bible* is given for want of a better. But as yet no one has been able to give the better one.

In the headings of titles, the names of authors are given in full and in their vernacular form. In English and French surnames beginning with a prefix (except the French de and d'), the name is recorded under the prefix. In other languages and in French names beginning with de and d', the name is recorded under the word following the prefix. Compound surnames are entered under the first part of the name. Noblemen and ecclesiastical dignitaries are entered under their family names, but *sovereigns, princes, oriental writers, friars, persons canonized*, and all other persons known *only* by their first name, are entered under this first name.

In the headings, it is thought in the end most economical to give the full names of the authors. The rule calls for the vernacular form, and is probably the best rule; still many cataloguers would make exceptions, and enter names as familiar as household words under the familiar form, though it be not the family name—*e. g.*, Vecellio under Titian. An expression of opinion on this point is specially desired.

It is thought the ordinary rule for prefixes is stated much more concisely than is common, without sacrificing any thing of distinctness.

Compound names require special attention. It seems impossible to have a satisfactory rule, but the one given appears to be the best, and is certainly the simplest.

A single dash indicates the omission of the preceding heading; a subsequent dash indicates the omission of a subordinate heading or of a title. A dash connecting numbers signifies *to and including;* following a number it signifies *continuation*. A ? following a word or entry signifies *probably*. Brackets enclose words added to titles or changed in form.

The German diphthongs ä, ö, ü are written ae, oe, ue.

This is in accordance with the common practice of cataloguers, because of the difficulty in alphabetizing the *umlauts*. Some German scholars urge that this should not be done, but from philological rather than bibliographical reasons.

Dates are all given in years of the common calendar, and Arabic numerals are uniformly used for all numbers.

The desirability of reducing the O. S. dates to the common calendar will hardly be questioned. The rejection of Roman numerals in cataloguing may not be so clear a case. In favor of such rejection is the economy of the more compact symbol and the much less danger of mistakes. It seems folly to fill a catalogue with MDCCCLXXXVIII and similar relics of barbarism, when 1888 is written so much more quickly, read so much more easily, printed so much more cheaply. There is nothing to be said in favor of retaining these old characters except that some publishers of good taste in other things persist in using them. Actual trial proves that A, B, C, etc., can be used with much less danger of confusion, or Arabic figures of different sizes are just as good for distinguishing chapter and section.

24. THE COMING CATALOGUE

Co-operation has become among librarians a household word during the past year. Under this name much valuable work has been done already, and there is abundant promise of much more. The Co-operation Committee, in their supply department, now fairly started, have furnished better models at greatly reduced prices, and the libraries have accepted heartily the proffered assistance. This department of library co-operation is an assured success, and much vexation and money are to be saved.

An equal measure of success seems probable for Poole's Index and its annual supplements, and in a number of directions new life and efficiency have resulted from the work of the year so happily begun by the conference of '76. While we have so much with which to be satisfied, there has been less progress in what seemed the main question – co-operative cataloguing. Here the greatest need was felt, and to this most of the profession look for the greatest benefit. The September meeting will probably remove the first difficulties, by agreeing upon a code of rules by which the titles in any system shall be made. This decided, we are ready for the question, Who shall prepare the titles of new books as published? The Library of Congress or its copyright department? The publishers themselves? A cataloguing bureau, established and maintained by the libraries of the country? An individual or firm, as a commercial venture? There are arguments for and against each one of them, but these will appear when the discussion of the plan is opened. "What shall be done with the old books?" takes precedence of all this, and the best plan for new titles cannot be of very great service till we agree upon something for the old.

A universal catalogue has received thought, and its desirability for certain purposes has been clearly pointed out, but there are very few of us who feel that the time is near when we can profitably discuss plans for making such a catalogue. In a word, common consent leaves the universal catalogue among the impracticables for a considerable time at least, and it is an open question whether a list of all the books, good, bad, and indifferent, would be of as much value, except in very rare cases, as a list from which 90 per cent of the poorest had been omitted. However this may be decided, it is clear that only a select list is possible to us now, and the plan proposed aims to give in the possible selection a much more valuable work than the impossible, or at least impracticable, universal catalogue.

While lists of book-titles serve many excellent purposes, something more than the mere title is imperatively demanded. The ordinary bibliography of a subject to which readers are referred is likely to consist of an alphabetical or perhaps chronological list of titles, in number anywhere from a dozen to several thousands, and without any indication as to which are the best and which are the poorest, except as one may infer from the dates of issue, the number of editions, chance knowledge of the reputation of the author, and such information (often misleading) as the title-page affords. If the reader knows in advance which the best books are, he has, except in special cases, no need to consult the bibliography. If he knows nothing about it, as is so often the case, he puts down the book overwhelmed by the multitude of the titles. He was unable to select from the half-dozen books of which he knew, because he was not sure which was the best. He went to the bibliography to help him, and must now choose from the six hundred volumes instead of six, and has not an added hint as to which is the best for his purposes. And yet with all these deficiencies, bibliography has been of service so great as to call forth the eulogies of scholars. Even as it is, it has been of priceless worth. If the difficulties pointed out can be removed, who can measure its usefulness?

A serious difficulty in bibliographies, as in all other books of reference of limited sale, is the infrequency of revision and bringing up to date. If sufficient means were provided by publisher, public, or Association, there would be no difficulty in keeping up bibliographies (book-titles only) of all the prominent subjects; and if nothing better could be done, it would be well worth the attention of the Library Association to devise a system of bibliographies of special subjects in the same way that class-lists are issued by our best libraries, instead of attempting a full catalogue. But the titles are not enough; they should be followed by notes, giving, in the fewest possible words, a clear idea of the merits and

Source: Melvil Dewey, "The Coming Catalogue," *American Library Journal* 1 (1877): 423-27.

faults of the book, its reliability, form of treatment, etc. The reception accorded to these notes in some of the best of our recent catalogues proves clearly how valuable they are to the general reader. Theory and experience agree that when from a trustworthy source, they are of more service to a community than anything else, except the library itself. The better class of librarians are anxious to include such notes in their own catalogues and class-lists, and there seems to be only one opinion as to their pre-eminent importance.

Here is then one of the ripest fields for co-operation, for the value of the notes depends entirely on the ability of the maker, and no one person living unites in himself the wisdom necessary to make the best notes on all the books of the library. The aid of specialists must be called in, and not one but many minds must contribute to the work; for the writer of the best note on the last geology may not be a suitable person to prepare the note on the latest edition of Shakspere or the newest novel by Mrs. Lewes.

The recent reports of the Boston Public Library give evidence of the wonderful influence for good exerted by the annotated catalogue. An increase of 200 per cent in some months, in the reading of the better class of books, was traceable directly to the preparation and printing of such notes. Of it, George B. Emerson said, "I have never seen anything so excellent; and hereafter no large catalogue will be considered complete without something similar appended to it." One of the chief librarians of Great Britain wrote, "I have shown it to some of the profession here, and they are as much astonished at the idea as at the execution of it. I do not think there will be many imitators. The labor of such a work must be enormous, and certainly beyond our resources and methods."

The great need and the difficulty of supplying it are both prominent. The librarians are few, if they exist at all, who are competent in themselves to name the best book for each reader who wishes information. We must have, in convenient form for use, a Manual that will answer these questions. How is it possible to secure it?

Few libraries have the means, as few the men, to do this work as it should be done. At present, by much the wisest course is to "pirate" the best notes from the Boston, Quincy, and similar catalogues; but to secure the best results, this thieving should be reduced to a system. When the best man makes a note on any book, all the libraries should have that note to use, and if the best man don't do it, he or the next best should in some way be induced to do it.

To succeed fully, it is necessary that the work be done by the Association, and not by an individual. First, because an individual could not command the aid of the specialists and experts who would be willing to give their labor to the Association, and thus the preparation would be unsatisfactory; and, secondly, because when done by an individual, even though he had secured in this way much outside aid in making the notes, the work would not be received so heartily and with so much confidence, and, most important of all, it would not be considered the property of each member, who should, on that account, contribute his share towards its perfection. A simple bibliography can be made readily by an individual, for he has only to copy accurately and arrange by some good system the titles of all the books he can find recorded on his subject. The fully annotated Manual, which we esteem bibliography of the highest sort, must be done by the co-operation of a number of those best qualified to make it.

The following plan can be made to work. If it is improved, so much the better.

Let the Association appoint with great care a committee of five to take entire charge of the Manual, a majority vote deciding questions that arise. The committee may then prepare a list of say 10,000 volumes, the best that they are able to select, for a general library in an average community. A Manual of this kind must of necessity disregard local peculiarities, which can be provided for by each library for itself. This work of selection will be freed from much of its drudgery, because there are in print a number of lists representing selections by our most competent experts. These catalogues or lists can be checked by the committee by means of colored pencils, or by conventional signs to indicate the rank each would assign to each book. The lists collated could be consolidated into one alphabet, representing the best judgment of the entire committee. The different members would make notes for many of the books, would select, from notes already in print, such as they approve, and would receive offers of notes from librarians and others interested in the work. As in the selection, most valuable material is ready to the hand of the committee in the work already done in this direction, specially by that library which, through the genius and energy of its superintendent, has become known throughout the world as doing most at once for itself and for others. Though so much has been accomplished, it seems impracticable to ask more of an individual institution than the free use of its material, and the Association must for itself put that material in proper shape for its own use, adding to it what is needed. Much is done already for the committee by individuals, pre-eminently by Mr. Perkins, in his admirable "Best Reading." But probably no man living can, unaided, make such a selection and notes as are wanted, and if he could it is perfectly certain that it would not be so received. The authority of the committee of five experts, representing the entire Library Association, would be great enough to make a place on their list of books something to be aimed at by both authors and publishers, and an incidental advantage of no mean importance would thus be secured.

The first edition of the Manual might be made more rapidly than so important work would seem to demand, because it should be looked upon at first, not as final, but as proof for criticism.

The selection and a part of the notes being ready, and a convenient page, type, etc., chosen, the Manual may be put in type. No plates should be made, but it should be kept standing. Whenever an error is found, or discoveries are made that require any addition, omission, or correction, let it be done in the type. Only small editions being printed, the work is thus kept closely up to date, and embodies the result of the latest researches. As fast as in type, proofs should be submitted to the Association, or to as many of its members as desired, and to such others as might render valuable assistance or advice. The committee should then meet and pass upon the criticisms and suggestions received from these proofs, and the type being corrected in accordance with their decision, a first edition should be printed.

The Manual would then be before the Association as its property, and it would be the duty of every member to report to the committee any correction or suggestion that could possibly be of any service in perfecting the work. As soon as the first edition was exhausted, the committee should again meet and pass upon the criticisms and suggestions sent in. These should be in writing and as briefly worded as is consistent with clearness. One will object to a certain book included among the best, and give reasons which may possibly have escaped the attention of the committee. Another brings forward arguments for adding to the list a work omitted. Another calls attention to an error in fact or in judgment in some of the notes. In short, the brief written suggestions sent in should include everything that may in any way tend to improve the common property of all. These, read before the committee, can be acted upon, and the type, corrected to accord, would be ready for a new edition. Between each edition, some books would be published worthy to take the place of some before put on the list, and so the Manual would be in a constant state of growth, representing as perfectly as possible the combined judgment of the Association upon the best books on the given subjects.

This would require labor and money, but only a small fraction of what would be expended to accomplish the same results in any other manner. Who will pay for doing the work? Who can afford to give the labor required? Well, the work will deserve pay; perhaps it would be well to give the committee taking it in charge a certain copyright, for the Manual would have a very large sale, both as a library catalogue and for individual use. But if the labor were given outright and the entire proceeds put into the treasury of the Association, it would be economy for the libraries whose librarians spent their time upon it. If Mr. Brown does one fifth the committee work on such a Manual, his library gets the benefit of five fifths, and it would be a very short-sighted board of trustees that would not heartily approve of such work in library hours. The large libraries need it quite as much as the smaller ones, for the number of their volumes makes it all the more necessary to choose the best. The small ones want it to guide them in purchasing as well as in reading. Such a Manual would remove at once all necessity for libraries newly starting to pay a bonus of several hundred dollars to some expert who should name a list of books to be purchased. A better list than any individual living could prepare would be ready to their hands.

The preparation of such a Manual would mark an era in library history. The manifold uses to which it would be put must be apparent to every reader,—for individual use as a guide to reading, free from the strong objections urged against all "courses of reading;" as a guide in the purchase of books for either private or public collections; as the main catalogue of many of these libraries. For the latter use, the call numbers of the books in each library could be written in the margin, or if enough copies were wanted for distribution, the call numbers could be easily set in the margin, and a special edition could be printed at small expense. Each library would have then to issue a catalogue only of the books not included in the Manual. The experiment can be tried best with a small selection. Perhaps 5000 volumes would be large enough. Its success established, it would be easy to introduce new titles, with their notes, to any extent desired.

The plan is for ready-made catalogues, and that something of the kind must soon be done is evident from recent discussions. The statistics of the amount of money spent in making catalogues are somewhat alarming, and though the proposed plan aims to relieve only the smaller libraries largely from this burden, when put in operation, it will have prepared the way for our co-operative cataloguing, which *will most effectively reduce the cataloguing expenses of the larger institutions.*

The catalogues are well worth all they cost, even under the present wasteful system of making them. But it requires no little portion of the professional time to make the public and specially financial committees understand this worth. That trained cataloguers at higher salaries must be obtained, and that several thousand dollars must be appropriated by libraries of only a few thousand volumes, requires some reasoning to prove to the average committee-man. But the librarian who understands his work knows that even this pays. Can we not accomplish much better results at a much lower expenditure? The catalogues thus made are only lists of titles. What cataloguer seeking a situation is prepared to make, on all the varying topics, notes such as experience proves to be invaluable?

The gravest difficulties of the multitude of small libraries, already started and springing up almost daily, are found in the selection and cataloguing of their books—most important, most difficult, most botched, of all things connected with these great companions of our schools. The Manual gives the best possible selection to purchase. If so many books cannot be had at first, it is the best possible basis on which to check off those to be purchased. With the notes to assist, and knowing the special wants of the community, the selection of a thousand volumes from the list of five or ten thousand would be trifling compared with the present methods. An expert could go through the catalogue, after having the circumstances explained, and mark in blue those books needed most and in red those needed least, and thus prepare in a single day a better guide for the purchasing committee than can now be made in a month's labor. The librarian has merely to mark the shelf-mark in the margin of the Manual, and the book is catalogued beyond improvement for the public.

The scheme is not a day-dream. Neither is it a "flying machine." It has been under consideration, and to a certain extent discussion, for several years, and there are no obstacles yet brought forward to hinder its speedy and economical execution. There are responsible printers who will undertake the typographical part. There are able librarians, *literati*, and specialists, who will lend their assistance in making the selection and the notes, and in keeping them corrected up to date. The whole question of the usefulness of our libraries is here summed up. "How shall we give the best books to inquirers?" It has been proved that the best means yet known are classed lists with carefully-prepared notes. The libraries want them and must have them, if their highest work is to be done. With hardly an exception, they cannot make them for themselves for lack of men and money. The plan submitted will secure the result, and is entirely practicable. If there be a better way, quicker, cheaper, more satisfactory in any respect, let us have it. If not, let us take the first steps towards carrying out the plan submitted, and put in the hands of our librarians a ready-made *vade mecum* which we feel sure is to be the Coming Catalogue.

25. PRINTED CATALOGUE CARDS FROM A CENTRAL BUREAU

Probably no other question in library administration is more practically important to most libraries and pre-eminently so to a state or other central library having supervision of smaller libraries, than that of reducing cost of cataloguing and increasing utility of catalogues by means of printed cards. The expense item which causes most anxiety to library trustees and most criticism from the uninformed, is almost always the cost of cataloguing. The ablest librarians of the world have been studying for fifty years the problem of securing necessary results at lower cost. There is entire agreement that a library is practically useless without good catalogues, and that whatever the cost it must be faced; so that we hear no discussion by competent judges about getting on without these indispensable keys, but merely of how to reduce their cost by co-operation and better methods. The problem grows yearly more serious with the steadily increasing number of books published, and of readers not satisfied with what they may find in their own library, but insistent on knowing what can be had on the same subject elsewhere. The American Library Association has recognized the gravity of this problem for years, and given it close attention through its strongest committees and its publishing board. A score of libraries have made more or less extended experiments, notably the Boston Public, Harvard College, Columbia University, John Crerar, Princeton University, and the 'Publishers' Weekly' office in New York, where the official bibliographic records of the book trade have centred from their origin. Certain definite results have been attained. Possibly future discoveries may modify some conclusions that now seem clear; but the same possibility hangs over decisions on any subject, so we may safely accept these premises.

1. A card well printed in clear type will be used; not a duplication of manuscript or typewriting, for no duplicating process will give as legible results as good printing. Entries on cards in trays and drawers are more trying to the eyes than in book form, and it is absolutely necessary that the highest practical legibility be secured for the general public. Another reason for printing is the greater economy with which many copies can be made for distribution.

2. These cards must be printed and distributed to subscribing public and private libraries by some central bureau. Cost of type-setting and necessary preliminaries, and, more important, the heavy expense of preparing satisfactory bibliographic titles, necessitate preparing and issuing from one central point, and dividing expense among the libraries benefited. Every year the public and librarians recognize more fully the almost incalculable value of brief notes added to book titles, and epitomizing the most valuable information or suggestion which an expert familiar with the literature of that subject could give to one trying to choose from a great library the book then and there and to him most useful. It would be difficult to over-estimate the practical value of these annotations or 'evaluations,' yet obviously very few libraries could find persons competent to make satisfactory notes on all subjects, or having found them, could afford to prepare and print the notes, except by dividing the cost with other libraries to which they would be exactly as useful.

If the cards must be printed and distributed from a central bureau, the only question left to the New York state library is whether it should do this work in virtue of its relation, as the central library for 7,000,000 people with over 1,000 libraries more or less closely connected with or tributary to it, or whether the central cataloguing bureau can be moved one step farther back, and serve not only for this but for other states. On this account we have postponed for ten years the question of printing our own cards, hoping for a solution that would relieve us of part of the labour and expense. The library committee has always recognized the importance of this question, and had our other work not been so pressing we should doubtless have felt forced before this to begin printing for our own use. But while we have been doing other important co-operative work, the results of which we have given freely to other libraries, they have carried on practical experiments in printing, and

Source: Melvil Dewey, "Printed Catalogue Cards from a Central Bureau," *The Library* 2:2 (1901): 130-34. Permission to reprint obtained from Godfrey Dewey.

we have hopefully watched the results. There are two solutions, either of which would be better than for us to do this work, and one of which is almost sure to be reached within two or three years.

1. Organization of the co-operative cataloguing bureau at some central point, probably in connection with the extensive allied work now carried on by the 'Publishers' Weekly' office in New York. This would be supported by contributions of co-operating libraries which would guarantee its expenses, and by subscriptions from smaller libraries willing to pay for their printed cards, but so situated as to be unable to assume more direct responsibility.

2. Vastly better than this, and the solution to which I have looked for more than twenty years, is that these cards shall be printed by the national library in Washington as part of its proper functions as the library centre for the whole nation. It receives all books copyrighted in this country, besides buying foreign books heavily, and receiving more in exchange than any other American library. It therefore would be the best centre for material to be catalogued. Under its new administration it certainly will soon have unexcelled facilities in its bibliographic apparatus, and in its staff for cataloguing, classifying, and annotating.

The national library would thus, in cataloguing its own books, printing the titles as it would have to do in any case, add the trifling cost of printing extra cards when the type was on the press, and of distributing to libraries according to their needs. No other equal expenditure could possibly accomplish so much as this for American libraries, and it certainly would be a very insignificant minority that would criticise the plan either in theory or practice. Now that the educational world has formally recognized that the public library is as much a part of the educational system as the public school, no one could criticise using the United States' mails for distributing cards to such libraries as maintain standards entitling them to recognition as distinctly educational institutions. Washington is a particularly favourable centre because of the great number of government departments, universities, and other institutions which would be available for assistance, specially in preparing notes on books on a great variety of subjects.

Whether the mechanical process adopted shall prove to be linotype slugs or electro shells, or ordinary stereo plates or papier-maché matrices is merely a question mechanical and financial, to be settled by those in charge. The essential is that cataloguing, annotating, and printing standard cards (7˙5x12˙5cm., now almost universally adopted for bibliographic work) be done for American libraries either at the Library of Congress or at a central bureau, preferably in New York. In my judgment we should devote our own efforts to reaching at as early a day as possible one of these two solutions, of which the national library plan is incomparably the better.

Some will heartily approve utilizing the national library cataloguing and printing, but object to public distribution, and urge that the cards should be bought by some business house or bureau organized for the purpose, and distributed independently of the national library. This means maintaining a double staff, a double stock of cards (for the national library must have its own reserve for it own uses), and in many ways an extra expense, with no gain except gratifying the theory of those who think such distribution not a proper function of the national library. If the narrow view is to prevail that the Library of Congress is not a national library, but merely for the use of senators and representatives in congress, then this argument holds. That idea was, however, repudiated by erecting the finest library building in the world at considerable distance from the capitol, making a great object-lesson to every visitor that it is in fact a library for the nation and not for congress alone. No one will question that this work can be done more conveniently and more cheaply there than by duplicating facilities elsewhere; and I feel sure that in the end this opinion will prevail, even if some other arrangement is forced on us as a makeshift. Use of printed cards for catalogues is just as inevitable as the general use of typewriters and electric light. We certainly should not be discouraged because objections made to other other labour-saving inventions are urged against this greater one, a printed catalogue card for general use. If one in five of the 5,000 public libraries of the country should buy an important new book, it would mean that the heavy expense of cataloguing, and of printing or copying the cards and making notes must be incurred 1,000 times over, or else that some of these libraries should lack this invaluable aid. Hardly anything in modern life will appeal more strongly to a practical business man than the increased economy and efficiency, and therefore, the practical necessity of doing away with the present duplication of labour, and having cataloguing, printing, and annotating done, once for all, in one place, for all libraries for these books, every copy of which is an exact duplicate of every other.

26. [CHANGING CATALOG RULES]

Some librarians seem to feel toward their rules as they do toward their clothes, that they are liable to be commented on unpleasantly unless they have something new each season. Whenever a few come together there is the tendency to propose alterations with the same freedom that they would try experiments in other directions, forgetting that the card catalog is the worst place in the world to make new changes, because new work is inserted at irregular places, destroying consistency and harmony, and reflecting unpleasantly on the ability of those who have done the work. When Panizzi made his rules 50 years ago the field was comparatively new. With a quarter century experience we took up the matter again when the A. L. A. was organized and the ablest librarians and catalogers gave protracted study to agreement on a code. This has been very widely adopted, and we are approximating a general uniform practice. Certain restless spirits will always be clamoring for change, and unless care is exercised will destroy much of the symmetry and consistency of the older work and all hope of uniformity. No librarian with much respect for his catalog will consent to continual changes in his rules, even if he is anxious to keep in harmony with A. L. A. committees, library schools, and the practice of printed cards.

Catalogers now change so often from one piece of work to another that the importance of recognized standard rules for cataloging constantly grows. Our one hope of seeing such rules is to stand firmly by a reasonable ground that no changes are to be made without overwhelming evidence that the change is not only an improvement, but a great enough improvement to justify its cost and the inevitable confusion that must result from it. The best service that those who understand this question can render librarianship is to fight vigorously against the tendency to continual changes and modifications.

I certainly am not by nature over-conservative. I should regret of all things to see the library profession put itself on a plane with some theologians who object to all revision, who refuse to believe that we know more now than we did a generation ago, and who insist that changes must necessarily be harmful. But the American tendency for some new thing, to run after alleged improvements, is peculiarly dangerous in our cataloging work. We may change rules at the loan desk and in the reference department and for almost anything else, but those that affect the card catalog are like changes in the architecture of a great building after it is half done. They may make it more picturesque, but are much more likely to make it ridiculous in the eyes of an expert and are usually very costly. The question whether certain words shall begin with capitals or small letters is but dust in the balance whichever way it is settled, though it is only fair to say that the steady and rapid trend of the English language is to use fewer capitals, that the publishers and printers who have the widest reputation for good taste are leaders in this movement, and that if any change is made it should be to use fewer capitals, or otherwise we are working toward the middle ages instead of looking to the future, and are simply making a change that will inevitably be changed back again a few years later.

Source: Dewey's Remarks in the American Library Association, "Proceedings," *Library Journal* 27 (1902): C196.

27. [UNITY AND COÖPERATION IN LIBRARY WORK]

· · · · · ·

I am going to talk to you about unity and coöperation, I am going to say the same old things. I have been harping on them for thirty years. You know what Holland said, that every bird has to sing his own song, the robin repeats the two double notes, the meadowlark whistles his one refrain, and steadily over and over again the same song swells from a thousand birds. I have always believed and preached coöperation. Perhaps it will be monotonous. You may say I am an idealist, as the lady said about her husband. She said, "My husband is an idealist. He goes around with his head in the clouds all the time, and sometimes I wish he would draw his feet up also." (Laughter) But, coöperation means civilization. Without coöperation there could be no railways, no steamboats, no churches, no schools, no hospitals, no life. Without coöperation a man may live in a cave and dress in the skins of beasts, but there can be nothing more without coöperation, and the man who says he does not believe in coöperation, librarian or whoever he may be, does not believe in civilization and does not believe in life. I take it for granted that we who are here, by our very presence believe heartily in this thing that has been the watchword of the A. L. A. from its beginning thirty years ago.

Now, coöperation means more things than to coöperate in our buildings and our books. The man who does not coöperate would have to write his own books and to print them. It goes further than utilizing each other's experience as to methods, systems, and cataloging. Without touching on those things I am going to speak of two or three little matters in this line and just try to emphasize one general thought. We must have more coöperation in cataloging than in the past. You will understand the importance of printed cards, bibliographies, indexes, and the work of our Publishing Board, and the other things that are connected with the work, but beyond that I think we can realize that we must have more central catalogs. We are starting in my own library what we call a universal catalog. All the printed cards that we can find anywhere in the world we are buying and consolidating into a single great catalog. We are getting all the slips of the British Museum, the cards of our own National Library, and the cards that are printed in various parts of the world, massing them together in a single catalog. It takes a great deal of space and a great deal of time to separate those cards accurately and to guide them. Few libraries can afford to do this and such work must be done from a central library.

There is a certain thing we want to do, we want to bring to all readers the book or pamphlet or magazines or whatever it may be that will be more useful. That is what the cities pay us to do, and we must do it in the best way, the quickest and the cheapest way. This is an age of organization and of system, of concentration. There are centrifugal forces at work. The cities are pouring out through the trolley lines into the country, but at the same time movements are coming to the center. We have learned from the industrial captains that work can be done cheaper and better if it is concentrated; and if we are to take our part in this great world movement we must coöperate, we must work with our associates. Now, the time has come when we need, and the need is growing every year, a national headquarters. There is work of great importance to be done that cannot be done by individual libraries, or by voluntary service. I look with confidence, within five or six years at the longest, to an endowment of not less than a million dollars for our library work, and we can spend the income of it economically. I should like an opportunity to prove to any millionaire that he cannot put a million dollars into any university or hospital that will be so far-reaching in its influence as it would be if given to the A. L. A. or its representatives to organize a permanent headquarters that shall undertake the work that belongs to librarianship. Do not forget what librarianship means—that civilization itself is simply the accumulation of the wisdom and the experience of all the world as preserved in books, that the book is the most wonderful thing that has been evolved in all the history of the race? Wireless telegraphy and telephones and telegraphs are incomparable in effect to this marvelous thing; and the professional custodians of this power are the librarians. How is it in my own state, in Niagara where they have harnessed the falls, that for thousands of years have been carrying that

Source: Melvil Dewey, "[Unity and Coöperation in Library Work]," *Library Journal* 30 (1905): C180-C184.

enormous power, until it has now been made available? Do they content themselves simply with selling that power for electric light? No. It runs trolley lines, furnishes heat, it cooks, it furnishes power for factories, anything that electricity can do better, quicker, cheaper, or easier than other powers that company undertakes to do.

Anything that we can do with books is a part of the work of the library–broadening all the time–and yet you meet men who have to do with books all the while who do not appreciate or understand this. You will meet librarians who have been perhaps a quarter of a century engaged in library work and they will utter commonplaces in regard to it, and have no comprehension of its real meaning, and people will say, "they ought to know; they are librarians, and they do not believe in these things that certain idealists and extremists talk about." Because a man has been dealing with books, it does not give him a right to express an opinion. Mere association with such things is not enough to make him an authority. It occurs to me here in this church, that if there were an insect boring its way through one of these roof timbers you would not take him as a safe guide in an ethical or theological question because he could say, "Why, half my life I have been engaged in work in the church." (*Laughter.*) And in the same way a man who has been in a library or in literary pursuits, if he has never opened his eyes, has no right to pass judgment on these things. Some people, librarians as well as others, are like owls–I say it with all due respect. The owl is a very wise appearing bird and is ornamental in the study. I like him stuffed better than in active service. The bibliographical owl, like his kin, is happiest in the dusk, but in the light he won't always retire to his perch and be as quiet as the real bird.

You know what Walter Savage Landor says, that in the intellectual [sic] as in the physical world men creep close by your side and hold you fast by the hand while you lead them in the darkness, but when you lead them in the light they start and leave you. That is often true and people who dare look forward, who see farther, are often accused of extreme views; they are often called cranks; but it is one of our greatest needs to have more cranks of that kind. My thought goes back to a white-bearded crank whom I knew and loved for years, Henry Barnard, of Hartford, Conn., who, just fifty years before the library school was started, started the first school for training teachers, and in the very year that I was born started the first normal school. In his work in five years, while he was secretary of the board of education in Connecticut he delivered 1300 addresses, preaching the doctrine that the state and the community ought to have an organized public school system. How many of you in this room can comprehend that a man touching our own time so closely, who died only a year or so ago, went to nearly every legislature in the country, was by courtesy accorded the privileges of the floor, and urged the need of public schools, as you and I are urging at the present time the need of library commissions and the recognition of the library as an essential part of a civilized community? The new Secretary of the Navy some years ago presided in Baltimore over a great meeting, I think it was the National Association of Charities and Corrections, and he spoke on the subject of cranks. He introduced the subject by saying that he had noticed when he went into a great machine shop where they were building engines that they took the regular material as it came along and built all the parts of the engine, and then the foreman went around and picked out the very best piece of metal that he could find in the shop and out of that they made the crank. It was the thing that turned the engine, the thing that must not break; it was of the very best material. And I never think of Henry Barnard and the work that he did without hoping that we shall have many men and women who will do similar work in similar ways, perhaps on a smaller scale, but still in the same spirit that Barnard did his work.

Now, we are working with each other and we are taking advice and suggestions from each other. In the wisdom of the East there is a proverb that applies as well to librarians– "All are divided into two classes, two that know and two that know not. If a man knows not and knows not that he knows not, he is foolish; shun him. If he knows not and knows that he knows not, he is ignorant; teach him. If he knows and knows not that he knows, he is asleep; wake him. If he knows and knows that he knows, he is wise; follow him." And so when I come to these conventions and I hear from different people I have a great deal more faith when Miss Stearns or Miss Tyler or some of the people who are working in the same spirit that Henry Barnard worked, in different places, tell me of their actual experience, than I do when somebody who has never tried the experiment says, "it is extreme"; he does not know, he is not entitled to give testimony on that subject.

I take it that the great work that is before us is to sow the seed of this new library movement, to make people understand what it means. Just as the custodians of the great Niagara power have in their hands one of the most marvelous forces that the human mind has had to deal with, we as custodians of books and of libraries have in our custody the greatest power that there is in its effect on civilization and on the world. We ought to use it to the full extent. We have had a marvelous development in these past few years. I am confident that the next ten years holds more in store than all we have done in the past quarter of a century. There is no movement in human history of which I have ever read that has spread so steadily and so rapidly, that has had so little opposition, that has met with so much commendation, that has had as liberal gifts from private sources, that has had as liberal laws. We ought to keep these things steadily in mind. When anyone begins an address on the library and says the library is as important as it is to have good streets, good roads, lights, water supply service, drainage, I respect all that—but it stands on a different plane. You can get on without these things, but you cannot get along without education. It does not pay a community or state to deal in raw material. In Massachusetts, the state that has the most libraries, you find the largest averages in the savings banks. Go to the Patent Office and you will find that in Massachusetts one man in twelve has a patent; in New York, one in 18; in North Carolina, one man in 19,000; in South Carolina, one man in 24,000. Take an example: here was a woman with what the New Englanders call "faculty;" her husband had been saying things unfit for publication because he couldn't get his collar button in. She used her brains on the problem and invented a new kind of collar button, and she has made a million dollars out of it. She could not make that collar button without increasing the wealth of the community and reducing the profanity of all men.

Education pays. Education is in two halves, school education and the education that you get at home, and education centers around the public library and the great school system for which we spend countless millions of dollars. There are no taxes that people are so proud to pay as taxes for schools, there is nothing that they are more proud of than their expenditures either for the state university or for the cross-roads school house, and our petty income for libraries is going to be doubled and trebled and quadrupled, because we are going to learn the lesson the library pays. Do you remember reading Sir Norman Lockyer's address before the war between Japan and Russia opened, to the British Association of Science? He talked plain English to them; he said that England would lose her supremacy unless they spent more money in training and educating citizens. He pointed out that they had lost two hundred and fifty millions of dollars a year to Germany, because Germany had spent money and carried on advances in chemical industries that had given her so much advantage over England. Bismark said that Sedan was won by the schoolmaster. "Why," someone answered, "it was the German needle gun that cost us the victory." He replied, "It was not the German needle gun, but it was the German soldier who held the German needle gun; and it was the German schoolmaster who made the German soldier;" but it was the German university that made the German schoolmaster. Now when we go to our legislatures, it is not a question of books being useful and beautiful. We shall say, here are great things to be done, here is the information— the books that inform and build material prosperity, the books that inspire and build character, the books that count in making the world move on successfully. A nation or community or state that wishes to be great has the problem before it to raise officers instead of privates, to turn out the finished product instead of the raw material, and if we put this question on the lowest plane of mere material prosperity, *it pays* to do the work of general education. This movement is going to grow still more. With a man or a librarian—tree, or man, or movement—when it ceases to grow it begins to rot; it is dead. When a librarian has learned it all and does not grow any more he ought to resign, his usefulness is dead. Every man according to his ability must contribute his part, and every woman. You sow a little bit of seed and it comes back a thousand fold. Perhaps you drop an acorn in the ground. By and by the next century, there is a great oak. You did not create the oak. Back of it all is the God who gives the increase. The message I have to-night for us and our associates of the A. L. A. on coöperation is to sow this seed as we have opportunity, never knowing where it shall bring forth fruit. I would be more glad if I could express more clearly—the question of being out of wind or supper has nothing to do with it—the things of which my heart is full. I have said a good deal; I am ashamed of having said so much, but if you knew how much I wanted to say and had not said, you would think I was temperate.

. . . . . .

We have a long work before us; it will last as long as life; it is a great world movement, wide as the world, resistless as the sunrise, illuminating the whole earth. And the great thing is, it seems to me, that we should be full of hope and confidence. Great things have happened in the past. Let us look forward and not back, up and not down, and lend a hand.

H. CLASSIFICATION

Dewey's ingenious idea of a book-arrangement system based on relative, in contrast to fixed or absolute, location came to him while he was at Amherst. The plan did not spring full-grown from Dewey but was rather the result of a thorough inquiry, search, and experimentation. That his plan resulted in a classification system that has flourished for one hundred years and that was being readied in 1976 for a nineteenth edition attests to its enduring qualities. Since the Decimal Classification is widely known and used and since a careful study of its evolution is available, the selections below pertain to Dewey's ideas rather than to specific modifications or changes in the various editions, or to the specific criticisms of each edition as it was issued.

Though Dewey wrote little in his "Journal" of the challenges he was encountering as he designed and developed his Classification, in a 1920 essay he recalled factors that prompted his action and reflected on the origin of his decimalized notations.

Dewey's dissatisfaction with fixed location as a shelf arrangement for books developed soon after he became an assistant in the Library. On May 8, 1873, he submitted to the Library Committee of Amherst College a proposed *notational* structure based on the decimal principle, for classes and sub-classes which achieved flexibility of location. His formal proposal for a "Library Classification System" describes the merits of the notation.

What was lacking in the proposal, however, was a plan for the order of the classes and for the meaning of the sub-classes. In determining the order and meaning, Dewey sought help from others to whom he acknowledged his indebtedness in 1876; he referred specifically to "specialists in many departments, and nearly every member of the [Amherst] Faculty." In 1882 he again disclaimed responsibility for the content of the classes, stating that

As to the filosophical or rational divisions [of my Classification] my opinion is not valuable, the Amherst faculty being the authors of most of this part of our scheme.

Dewey's own pragmatic views are evident in the "Preface" to the 1876 edition, in which he stated that "philosophical theory and accuracy have been made to yield to practical usefulness." The "Preface" includes information on the order of the classes, mnemonics, book numbers based on order of acquisition and on the "Alphabetical Subject Index," identified in Edition 2 as the "Relativ Index." Dewey's letter seeking copyright, dated April 2, 1876, accompanied by a title page as required, precedes the "Preface." The title page, different from the title page as finally published, indicates that copyright number 4897G was assigned on April 22, 1876.

From the beginning of the use of Dewey's Classification, libraries began to modify it. Dewey expressed his concern over personalized changes within two years after the publication of his scheme, noting that

A scheme can be satisfactory in *use* only to those who realize these inherent difficulties and are satisfied because of their knowledge that a plan free from annoying difficulties is wholly unattainable.

Dewey's plea for uniformity in use appears in the essay entitled "The Amherst Classification," which is selection number 32.

That the classes as originally designed have remained constant is a tribute not only to those who assisted in the analysis of subject relationships but even more to Dewey, who felt compelled to retain their integrity of meaning. The original ten classes, whose headings differ from those in later editions only in terminology, were:

0-90	[Bibliography, Book Rarities, General Cyclopedias, Polygraphy, General Periodicals, General Societies]
100	Philosophy
200	Theology
300	Sociology
400	Philology
500	Natural Science
600	Useful Arts
700	Fine Arts
800	Literature
900	History

Modifications and expansions were made rather extensively in Edition 2 at the divisional and sectional levels but not in the meaning of the classes. Dewey acknowledged in 1893 that he himself had been tempted to make modifications by "transposing classes 4 and 9, so as to bring sociology and history, philology and literature, together." He refrained from making such changes, however, stating that

> We should also make some minor changes if it were possible to start anew; but it is clearly vastly better to use as now than to sacrifice the great gain that comes from using a system in common with several hundred libraries.

The continuing problem with any viable bibliographic classification is inherent within the Decimal Classification as within other classification systems designed for the analysis of content: the conflict between the need to re-evaluate subject relationships and to change or expand and the pressure from users to retain the integrity of notation. Dewey grew increasingly aware of the conflict, concluding that "it is clearly undesirable to make frequent changes or to ignore growth." He added that:

> Apparently a revision about every quarter century would be the golden mean between the costly and impractical changes if an effort were made to keep up to date, and the opposite extreme which would in time make any scheme seem medieval.

In 1931 Dewey offered his final advice on the Classification as a practical and not a philosophic scheme. His statements, written on March 11, 1931, and March 13, 1931, from the Lake Placid Club in Florida, reiterate his conviction that "DC is a praktikal tool, not a filosofik sistem."

While the similarities between the Decimal Classification and the Universal Decimal Classification are evident, the reasons for the similarities are less known. The Otlet/Dewey correspondence, included as entries 35, 36, and 37, indicate that Paul Otlet of the Office International de Bibliographie, Bruxelles, wrote to Dewey on March 24, 1895, inquiring if his Classification could be used as "a basis of the Universal Bibliographic Repertory." Permission was granted generously by Dewey, with the limitations noted in his response of June 29, 1895.

28. DECIMAL CLASSIFICATION BEGINNINGS

My first boyish idea of becoming a college professor and my early college plan of being a missionary to Turkey were abandoned when I determined to make *popular* education my life work. Then I set about studying educational agencies as a whole to learn which most needed development. Statistics showd that 90 per cent of Americans went into bredwinning pursuits directly from elementary schools and that of their few precious school years, 3 wer worse than wasted thru our stupid and antiquated spelling and jumble of weights and measures. To overcome these chief obstacles to elementary school efficiency, Ipland, [sic] and later started in 1876 at the Philadelphia Centennial, 2 national societies, the Spelling Reform Ass'n. and the American Metric Bureau for introducing the international decimal weights and measures.

As secretari of both S R A and Metric Bureau my work and interest hav continued all the 44 years. My faith grows stedily stronger that the chief problem in popular education and Americanization is to save 3 years and make sure that every man, woman and child can easily get the author's meaning from the printed paje of English. Great progress has been made in both reforms. Nearly all the world now uzes the metric system just as they finaly abandoned roman numerals for the simpl decimal arabic, and recently in 4 years activ work of our Simplified Spelling Board, for which Andrew Carnegie gave over $150,000, we secured from 556 periodicals circulating 18,000,000 copies, adoption for regular use of the N E A 12 words: catalog, decalog, demagog, pedagog, prolog, program, tho, altho, thoro, thorofare, thru, thruout, and most of our list of 300 simpler spellings. Similarly, 460 universities, collejes, and normal schools either uze them in official publications or authorize students to uze them, and 173 of them including 19 state universities hav formally adopted more than 200 better spellings, mostly by faculty resolution.

Since the mass of people must gain what real education they had from reading, the free public library stood out clearly in my mind as the true peoples' university. The free public school had won its place as an essential of civilization and progress. My campain was to prove that the library was just as essential and just as much entitled to support by taxation and to take its place as a nesesari complement to the public school: that school taut to read; libraries must furnish and guide that reading.

I became profoundly imprest with the idea that education was in 2 parts of which the public had very little appreciation of the more important. Most people thought of education as a system from kindergarten to university and as completed on final graduation. This was education for a limited period and for those who as a rule gave up their whole time to attending a school. I saw that the other side of education which was not for a few years but for all of life, at home insted of in school, and carried on side by side with the main vocation, was even more important. This home education group is:

1. Libraries or reading including not only books and pamflets but magazines, papers and all reading from conventional symbols.

2. Museums or seeing. The education that comes from reading natural language: scenery, pictures, scientific specimens, and all we lern by studying a thing or a picture insted of printed words about it.

3. Clubs, or education from mutual help of those interested in the same study.

4. Extension teaching, including not only university extension courses, correspondence teaching, lyceum lectures, but all instruction where one more advanst assists the student.

5. Tests and credentials. The intellectual yardstick applied to the work as a stimulus for more ernest and persistent work than is possible to most people without some definit goal.

Of these 5 elements, the library is so vastly the most important and the natural center round which the rest clusterd, that we often speak of libraries as including this whole field of home education as in speaking of 'schools' and we include elementary, secondary, colleges, professional and technical schools, and universities.

Source: Melvil Dewey, "Decimal Classification Beginnings," *Library Journal* 45 (1920): 151-54.

In visiting over 50 libraries, I was astounded to find the lack of efficiency, and waste of time and money in constant recataloging and reclassifying made necessary by the almost universally used fixt system where a book was numberd according to the particular room, tier and shelf where it chanced to stand on that day, instead of by class, division and section to which it belongd yesterday, today and forever. Then there was the extravagant duplication of work in examining a new book for classification and cataloging by each of 1000 libraries insted of doing this once for all at some central point.

The vision of wonderful possibilities before libraries was inspiring, but money available for the work was not 1 per cent of what was needed even with greatest economy, and even this little money seemd hardly 50 per cent efficient becauz of wasteful duplication and crude methods. For months I dreamd night and day that there must be somewhere a satisfactory solution. In the future wer thousands of libraries, most of them in charje of those with little skil or training. The first essential of the solution must be the greatest possible simplicity. The proverb said "simple as a, b, c," but stil simpler than that was 1, 2, 3. After months of study, one Sunday during a long sermon by Pres. Stearns, while I lookt stedfastly at him without hearing a word, my mind absorbd in the vital problem, the solution flasht over me so that I jumpt in my seat and came very near shouting 'Eureka!' It was to get absolute simplicity by using the simplest known symbols, the arabic numerals as decimals, with the ordinary significance of nought, to number a classification of all human knowledge in print; this supplemented by the next simplest known symbols, a, b, c, indexing all heds of the tables, so that it would be easier to use a classification with 1000 heds to keyd than to use the ordinary 30 or 40 heds which one had to study carefully before using. This was 47 years ago and no one in any country has yet found any other plan so simple, so efficient and so easily understood.

With aid of professors in each department and cooperation of librarians interested, in 1872-76 I workt out the 10 classes and their 100 divisions and 1000 sections, following the inverted Baconian order, but they were not publisht til 1876. Many promptly ridiculed the idea of 1000 divisions in a library as wholly impracticable in use, but when they found with delight that the relativ index, referring not to accidental paje number of a catalog or to a certain inch or more on some wooden shelf, but to permanent class, division, and section to which a book belonged, made closer classification easier than the old way, they began asking for more minute divisions.

So step by step 10 editions printed in 43 years hav grown from 1000 hedings to over 30,000, and not a week passes that some one, in some country, does not request closer division of the subject of his special interest. From cooperation of the Amherst college faculty the work spred til many hundreds hav shared in stedy enlarjment and improvement. Correspondents in all parts of the world send to us at Lake Placid Club new heds for tables, new words for index, and other suggestions. The great inconvenience to all users of having supplement after supplement, led us to incur the cost of keeping the whole work in type so as to insert at its proper place any new material.

Each year someone is troubld becauz we fail to make what he calls 'improvements,' but we chek up with great care all these sugjestions and if a large majority of those whose criticism we hav found reliable, agree that the proposed chanje would do more harm than good, we hav politely to lay it on the table, often to the proposer's annoyance. Some sugjestions would clearly hav been better had they been thought of erlier, but when many thousand libraries ar numberd on a uniform system, only gravest reasons justify chanjing numbers and introducing confusion that destroys the very great advantaj of numbers having the same meanings in every civilized country. In fact, at a World Conference in London, discussing an international languaj, an expert declared that D C numbers wer the only languaj known among all civilized people with a perfectly definit meaning. The advantaj of this harmony, in addition to other D C merits, led in scores of cases to entire reclassification of libraries that had adopted schemes of their own. Here and there some D C user is sure he could make a better scheme than had resulted from cooperativ work of hundreds of people in various countries for 40 years. After a few years' trial, many hav thrown away their 'improved' systems, which they found after trial to be inferior to standard D C. The main consideration is however no longer whether D C is the best system devisable. One could surely today make a better classification than yesterday. No classification can be perfect and much valuable cooperativ work is based on D C, so the paramount question now is between:

Great delay (to make a good classification takes many years) for the sake of possible betterment;

Acceptance of a tried and practical system (necessarily with some imperfections) but carrying immense advantages of uniformity with thousands of libraries and individual users and of worldwide and growing cooperation.

Chanjes clearly worth their cost ar incorporated in tables and index, and recorded owners of erlier editions ar notified so as to keep uniformity of usage. But no number is altered merely to fit a new theory, for theories ar constantly chanjing and a shifting classification is impracticable for libraries. If a scheme brings related subjects together, provides for adding new topics, and enables books on the same faze of the same subject always to be clast together and found quickly when wanted, it is of comparativly little moment whether exact sequence on shelvs accords with the latest theory.

Miss May Seymour became my assistant at Columbia university 33 years ago. From the first she specialized on D C. 13 years ago she moved to Lake Placid Club to devote herself to growing D C demands. She has here 2 rooms with needed assistants and equipment, and has acumulated a mass of sujjestions and reports of experiments and experiens astonishing to one who never attempted the serious work of tabulating all printed nolej.

For 25 years the International Institute of Bibliografy with central offis in Brussels has done a vast work in focalizing D C experience of a score of countries, and with rare unselfishness making all their results availabl to all the world. 2 years ago the A L A establisht a committee of classification experts to cooperate with each D C revision so that we hav their invaluable advice on all mooted questions.

For 43 years we hav carefully protected each revision by Copyryt not as a source of income but simply to protect against garbled reprints that wud destroy much of their usefulness by introducing confusion in meanings of numbers that ar now definitly intellijible thruout the world. In these 43 years we hav never accepted a dollar for any reprint in any languaj, and our wils wil insure that the copyryts pass under control of the A L A, I I B or some similar noncommercial body, so that they shal be used forever, solely for the public good. If, as we hope, someone appreciating its usefulness, endows or subsidizes our work so the enormus expense of constant revision can be met, we plan to hav the book available to all in varius languajes at the mere cost of manufacture.

So many thousand libraries in a score of cuntries now use it and D C numbers hav been printed in so many million pajes of catalogs, indexes and other works, that it seems impossible that it shud not go on permanently in spite of the fact that if we cud start anew today we shud mak varius changes, e.g., abandon the Baconian order theory and transpose classes 4 and 9 so that history wud follow sociology and philology wud stand next literature. But in fact it is simple to transpose these great classes bodily in a library, without change of numbers, while it wud be quite impossible to alter millions of entries where history is always 9 and language 4, not only in main classes but in hundreds of derivativs. Every expert knows that our boasted decimal system wud be improved wer it duodecimal and so divisible by 2, 3 4 and 6, insted of by 2 and 5 only, but no one thinks such change now possible. So we content ourselvs with the thot that the D C, like its foundation the Arabic decimals, while not perfect, has yet renderd and seems destind permanently to render, invaluable servis.

29. PROPOSAL FOR A LIBRARY CLASSIFICATION SYSTEM

Select the main classes, not to exceed nine and represent each class by one of the nine significant figures (ten digits). Subdivide each of these main heads into not more than nine subordinate classes, and represent each sub class by a digit in the first, or ten's, decimal place. Sub-classify each, or any, of these eighty one (hundred) classes, into not more than nine subclasses; and assign to each, one of the digits in the second decimal place. Thus the subclasses may be increased in any part of the library without limit; each additional decimal place increasing the minuteness of classification ten-fold. Arrange the classes numerically; (omitting the decimal point but arranging as if it were written after the first figure) and the books of each class alphabetically by authors under that class—the books standing in the same order on the shelves as the titles of the same in the catalogue. Enter in each volume in place of the number of the shelf as usually entered, its class number as far as assigned. For convenience of runners, enter, in the usual place of 'number on shelf', the authors name (if anonymous the letters or words as in the catalogue) spelled as it should be in the catalogue. Readers will call for books thus located by their 'class number' (instead of 'shelf') and author's name as printed in the catalogue (instead of 'number on shelf').

When the number of volumes in any alphabet increase enough to warrant, select from it all of a like character and give them a place together (alphabetically of course) e. g., If the class were 47 (see top page) add to each volume selected for the new subclass a digit making the class number 4.71. The next subclass picked out would be 4.72 thus allowing ten new subclasses instead of the original class 4.7. Books of a general character, embracing more than one topic or subject would remain in the general class e.g., A Dictionary of Science would receive no subclassification but remain simply 4 with main class number. If it were a work treating of the subject 4.7 generally; not limited to any of its subclasses it would take 4.7 only as its alphabet number. Large sets, pub doc serials, periodicals etc should be given a distinct no for each set, then the alphabet word may be omitted & simply the class no & vol. attached to each book. Of course the subdivision of the class should be carried far enough to entitle the set to a distinct number. The cipher has its regular zero power i. e, indicates no classification e. g., 0 would be the class no of a general cyclopedia which covers all the nine classes. 470 would indicate that the work embraced several or all of the subheads 471.2 & hence 0 indicates no further classification.

It is desirable to fill out the scheme fully when an additional class is made since there would be danger of confusion if only 471 (e.g.) were chosen without knowing what 472.3 etc were to be. If convenient *nine* subheads will be desirable because of symmetry—but the system is not at all affected if only a part of the nine figures are employed, e.g. if seven classes were made, 478 & 479 would not appear in the scheme.

Note: Dawe includes two additional papers, "The Merits of the System" and "Its Special Adaptation our Library" which were also part of the original proposal. Dawe, *Melvil Dewey*, pp. 321-24.

Source: Copy in files of Dr. Godfrey Dewey and Deo B. Colburn, Lake Placid Club, New York.

30. [DEWEY'S LETTERS SEEKING COPYRIGHT . . . 1876]

Amherst, Mass. Mar. 22, 1876

Sir, I wish to enter for copyright a little work just passing thro' the press with the title

"A classification & Subject index with directions for their use" Amherst College Library Amherst, Mass. 1876

I enclose 1.00 for copyright which I beleev costs that amount. Having had no experience in these matters I am not at all sure that I hav made applicasn in proper form. If not please advise me.

Very truly
    Melvil Dewey

Source: Copy in files of Dr. Godfrey Dewey and of Deo B. Colburn, Lake Placid Club, New York.

Amherst, Mass. Apr. 2, 1876

I enclose title page of a little book for copyright—also the 1.00. Please advise me if this authorizes me to print "Copyright &c."

Very truly
    Melvil Dewey

Source: Original in Copyright Office, Library of Congress, Washington, D.C.

31. PREFACE TO *A CLASSIFICATION AND SUBJECT INDEX*

The plan of the following Classification and Index was developed early in 1873. It was the result of several months study of library economy as found in some hundreds of books and pamphlets, and in over fifty personal visits to various American libraries. In this study, the author became convinced that the usefulness of these libraries might be greatly increased without additional expenditure. Three years practical use of the system here explained, leads him to believe that it will accomplish this result; for with its aid, the catalogues, shelf lists, indexes, and cross-references essential to this increased usefulness, can be made more economically than by any other method which he has been able to find. The system was devised for cataloguing and indexing purposes, but it was found on trial to be equally valuable for numbering and arranging books and pamphlets on the shelves.

The library is first divided into nine special libraries which are called Classes. These Classes are Philosophy, Theology, &c., and are numbered with the nine digits. Thus Class 9 is the Library of History; Class 7, the Library of Fine Art; Class 2, the Library of Theology. These special libraries or Classes are then considered independently, and each one is separated again into nine special Divisions of the main subject. These Divisions are numbered from 1 to 9 as were the Classes. Thus 59 is the 9th Division (Zoology) of the 5th Class (Natural Science). A final division is then made by separating each of these Divisions into nine Sections which are numbered in the same way, with the nine digits. Thus 513 is the 3d Section (Geometry) of the 1st Division (Mathematics) of the 5th Class (Natural Science). This number, giving Class, Division, and Section, is called the Classification or Class Number, and is applied to every book or pamphlet belonging to the library. All the Geometries are thus numbered 513, all the Mineralogies 549, and so throughout the library, all the books on any given subject bear the number of that subject in the scheme. Where a 0 occurs in a class number, it has its normal zero power. Thus, a book numbered 510, is Class 5, Division 1, but *no* Section. This signifies that the book treats of the Division 51 (Mathematics) in general, and is not limited to any one Section, as is the Geometry, marked 513. If marked 500, it would indicate a treatise on Science in general, limited to *no* Division. A zero occurring in the first place would in the same way show that the book is limited to *no* Class. The classification is mainly made by subjects or content regardless of *form*; but it is found practically useful to make an additional distinction in these general treatises, according to the form of treatment adopted. Thus, in Science we have a large number of books treating of Science in general, and so having a 0 for the Division number. These books are then divided into Sections, as are those of the other Classes according to the form they have taken on. We have the Philosophy and History of Science, Scientific Compends, Dictionaries Essays, Periodicals, Societies, Education, and Travels,—all having the common subject, NATURAL SCIENCE, but treating it in these varied forms. These form distinctions are introduced here because the number of general works is large, and the numerals allow of this division, without extra labor for the numbers from 501 to 509 would otherwise be unused. They apply *only* to the general treatises, which, without them, would have a class number ending with two zeros. A Dictionary of Mathematics is 510, not 503, for every book is assigned to the *most specific head that will contain it*, so that 503 is limited to Dicionaries or Cyclopedias of Science *in general*. In the same way a General Cyclopedia or Periodical treats of no one class, and so is assigned to the Class 0. These books treating of no special class, but general in their character, are divided into Cyclopedias, Periodicals, etc. No difficulty is found in following the arithmetical law and omitting the initial zero, so these numbers are printed 31, 32, etc., instead of 031, 032, etc.

The selection and arrangement of the thousand headings of the classification cannot be explained in detail for want of space. In all the work, philosophical theory and accuracy have been made to yield to practical usefulness. The impossibility of making a satisfactory

Source: Melvil Dewey, *A Classification and Subject Index for Cataloguing and Arranging the Books and Pamphlets of a Library* (Amherst, Mass., 1876). pp. 3-10. Permission to reprint "Preface" granted by Forest Press, Inc.

classification of all knowledge as preserved in books, has been appreciated from the first, and nothing of the kind attempted. Theoretical harmony and exactness has been repeatedly sacrificed to the practical requirements of the library or to the convenience of the department in the college. As in every scheme, many minor subjects have been put under general heads to which they do not strictly belong. In some cases these headings have been printed in a distinctive type, e. g., 429 SAXON, under ENGLISH PHILOLOGY. The rule has been to assign these subjects to the most nearly allied heads, or where it was thought they would be most useful. The only alternative was to omit them altogether. If any such omission occurs, it is unintentional and will be supplied as soon as discovered. Wherever practicable the heads have been so arranged that each subject is preceded and followed by the most nearly allied subjects and thus the greatest convenience is secured both in the catalogues and on the shelves. Theoretically, the division of every subject into just nine heads is absurd. Practically, it is desirable that the classification be as minute as possible without the use of additional figures, and the decimal principle on which our scheme hinges allows nine divisions as readily as a less number. This principle has proved wholly satisfactory in practice though it appears to destroy proper co-ordination in some places. It has seemed best in our library to use uniformly three figures in the class number. This enables us to classify certain subjects very minutely, giving, for example, an entire section to Chess. But the History of England has only one section, as our scheme is developed, and thus the two might be said to be co-ordinated. The apparent difficulty in such cases is entirely obviated by the use of a fourth figure, giving nine sub-sections to any subject of sufficient importance to warrant closer classification. In history where the classification is made wholly by countries, a fourth figure is added to give a division into *periods*. As the addition of each figure gives a ten fold division, any desired degree of minuteness may be secured in the classing of special subjects. The apparent lack of co-ordination arises from the fact that only the first three figures of these more important heads are as yet printed, the fourth figure and the sub-sections being supplied on the catalogues in manuscript. Should the growth of any of these sub-sections warrant it, a fifth figure will be added, for the scheme admits of expansion without limit.

The arrangement of headings has been sometimes modified to secure a mnemonic aid in numbering and finding books without the Index. For instance, the scheme is so arranged that China has always the number 1. In Ancient History, it has the first section, 931: in Modern History, under Asia, it has 951: in Philology, the Chinese language appears as 491. After the same manner the Indian number is 2; Egyptian, 4; English, 2; German 3; French, 4; Italian, 5; Spanish, 6; European, 4; Asian, 5; African, 6; North American, 7; South American, 8; and so for all the divisions by languages or countries. The Italian 5, for instance, will be noticed in 35, 55, 450, 755, 850, and 945. This mnemonic principle is specially prominent in Philology and Literature and their divisions, and in the *form* distinctions used in the first 9 sections of each class. Materials, Methods, or Theory occurring anywhere as a head, bears always the number 1. Dictionaries and Cyclopedias, 3; Essays, 4; Periodicals, 5; Associations, Institutions, and Societies, 6; Education, 7; Collections, 9. In the numerous cases where several minor heads have been grouped together under the head Other, it always bears the number 9. Wherever practicable, this principle is carried out in sub-dividing the sections. For instance, the Geology of North America, which bears the number 557 is sub-divided by adding the *sections* of 970 (History of North America). The Geology of Mexico then bears the number 5578; mnemonically, the first 5 is the Science number; the second 5, Geology; the 7, North America; and the 8, Mexico. Any library attendant or reader after using the scheme a short time will recognize at a glance, any catalogue or ledger entry, book or pamphlet, marked 5578 as something on the Geology of Mexico. Users of the scheme will notice this mnemonic principle in several hundred places in the classification, and will find it of great practical utility in numbering and finding books without the aid of Catalogue or Index, and in determining the character of any book simply from its call number as recorded on the book, on all its catalogue and cross reference cards, on the ledger, and in the check box.

In naming the headings, brevity has been secured in many cases at the sacrifice of exactness. It was thought more important to have short, familiar titles for the headings than that the names given should express with fullness and exactness the character of all books catalogued under them. Many subjects, apparently omitted, will be found in the Index, assigned, with allied subjects, to a heading which bears the name of the most important only. Reference to this Subject Index will decide at once any doubtful points.

In arranging books in the classification, as in filling out the scheme, practical usefulness has been esteemed the most important thing. The effort has been to put each book under the subject to the student of which it would be most useful. The content or the real subject of which a book treats, and not the form or the accidental wording of the title, determines its place. Following this rule, a Philosophy of Art is put with Art, not with Philosophy; a History of Mathematics, with Mathematics, not with History; for the philosophy and history are simply the *form* which these books have taken. The true content or subject is Art, and Mathematics, and to the student of these subjects they are most useful. The predominant tendency or obvious purpose of the book, usually decides its class number at once; still many books treat of two or more different subjects, and in such cases it is assigned to the place where it will be most useful, and underneath the class number are written the numbers of any other subjects on which it also treats. These *Cross References* are given both on the plate and the subject card as well as on the cross reference card. If a book treats of a majority of the sections of any division, it is given the Division number instead of the most important Section number with cross references.

Collected works, libraries, etc., are either kept together and assigned like individual books to the most specific head that will contain them; or assigned to the most prominent of the various subjects on which they treat with cross references from the others; or are separated and the parts classes as independent works. Translations are classed with their originals.

The Alphabetical Subject Index is designed to guide, both in numbering and in finding the books. In numbering, the most specific head that will contain the book having been determined, reference to that head in the Index will give the class number to which it should be assigned. In finding books on any given subject, reference to the Index will give the number under which they are to be sought on the shelves, in the Shelf Catalogue, or in the Subject Catalogue. The Index gives after each subject the number of the class to which it is assigned. Most names of countries, towns, animals, plants, minerals, diseases, &c., have been omitted, the aim being to furnish an Index of Subjects on which books are written, and not a Gazetteer or a Dictionary of all the nouns in the language. Such subjects will be found as special chapters or sections of books on the subjects given in the Index. The names of individual subjects of biographies will be found in the Class List of Biography. Omissions of any of the more general subjects will be supplied when brought to notice.

In arranging the books on the shelves, the absolute location by shelf and book number is wholly abandoned, the relative location by class and book number being one of the most valuable features of the plan. The class number serves also as the location number and the shelf number in common use is entirely dispensed with. Accompanying the class number is the *book* number, which prevents confusion of different books on the same subject. Thus the first Geometry catalogued is marked 513.1; the second 513.2, and so on to any extent, the last number showing how many books the library has on that subject. The books of each section are all together, and arranged by book numbers, and these sections are also arranged in simple numerical order throughout the library. The call number 513.11 signifies not the 11th book on shelf 513; or alcove 5, range 1, shelf 3, as in most libraries, but signifies the 11th book in subject 513 or the 11th Geometry belonging to the library. In finding the book, the printed numbers on the backs are followed, the upper being the class and the lower the book number. The class is found in its numerical order among the classes as the shelf is found in the ordinary system: the book in its numerical order in the class. The shelves are not numbered, as the increase of different departments, the opening of new rooms, and any arrangement of classes to bring the books most circulated nearest to the delivery desk, will bring different class numbers on a given shelf. New books as received are numbered and put into place, in the same way that new titles are added to the card catalogue.

The single digit occasionally prefixed to the book number, e. g. the 3 in 421.3.7 is the nearest height in decimeters of books too large to be put on the regular library shelves, which are only 2½ decimeters apart. The great mass of the library consists of 2-decimeter books, the size numbers of which are omitted. Books from 2½ to 3½ decimeters in height have 3 prefixed to the book number, and are found on the bottom shelf of each range. The larger sizes are prefixed with 4, 5, &c., and are found on the special shelves provided, in order to avoid the great waste of space otherwise occasioned by the relative location. By this use of the size numbers a close economy of space is secured.

Thus all the books on any given subject are found standing together, and no additions or changes ever separate them. Not only are all the books on the subject sought, found together, but the most nearly allied subjects precede and follow, they in turn being preceded and followed by other allied subjects as far as practicable. Readers not having access to the shelves find the short titles arranged in the same order on the Shelf Catalogue, and the full titles, imprints, cross references, notes, &c., on the Subject Catalogue. The uncatalogued pamphlets treating of any subject bear the same class number and are arranged on the shelves immediately after the books of each section.

In both the Author's Catalogue and the Subject Index, brevity has been studied because of the economy, but more because of the much greater ease of reference to a short title catalogue. The custom of giving full titles, etc., under authors, and only references or very brief titles under subjects, has been reversed. A reader seeking a book of a *known author*, in the vast majority of cases, wants simply the number by which to call for it, and can find it much quicker in a brief title catalogue. In the rare cases where more is needed the class number refers instantly to all these facts on the cards. On the other hand, a reader seeking books on a *known subject*, needs the full title, imprint, cross-references, and notes, to enable him to choose the book best suited to his wants.

The Subject Catalogue is a full title Shelf List on cards and is for the use of the public. The Shelf List is a short title Subject Catalogue in book form, made of separate sheets laced into an Emerson binder, and is for official use. We thus have without extra labor, both full and short title Subject Catalogues and Shelf Lists. The public Authors' Catalogue is a printed volume; the official Authors' Catalogue or Index is on cards. As a result each of the public Catalogues is checked by an official Catalogue; each of the card Catalogues by a book Catalogue; each of the brief title catalogues by a full title catalogue—an advantage that will be appreciated by all librarians desiring accuracy of administration and catalogues.

The arabic numerals can be written and found quicker, and with less danger of confusion or mistake, than any other symbols whatever. Therefore the Roman numerals, capitals and small letters, and similar symbols usually found in systems of classification are entirely discarded and by the exclusive use of Arabic numerals in their regular order throughout the shelves, classifications, indexes, catalogues and records, there is secured the greatest accuracy, economy, and convenience. This advantage is specially prominent in comparison with systems where the name of the author or the title must be written in calling for or charging books and in making references.

Throughout the catalogues the number of a book shows not only *where* it is but *what* it is. On the library accounts the character of each person's reading is clearly indicated by the numbers charged, and the minutest statistics of circulation in any subject are made by simply counting the call slips in the check box, and recording the number against the class number in the record.

By the use of size numbers the greatest possible economy of space may be secured for the size distinction may be made for every inch or even less if desired, and this without additional labor, as it will be seen that the size figure, when introduced, requires one less figure in the book number, and so does not increase the number of digits as would at first appear.

Parts of sets, and books on the same or allied subjects, are never separated as they are sure to be, sooner or later, in every library arranged on the common plan, unless it be frequently re-arranged and re-catalogued. The great expense of this re-cataloguing makes it impracticable except for a few very wealthy libraries. In this system the catalogue and book numbers remain unchanged through all changes of shelving, buildings, or arrangement.

In addition to its own peculiar merits, this plan has all the advantages of the card catalogue principle and of the relative location, which have been used and very strongly approved by prominent libraries.

As in the card catalogue system there is room for indefinite expansion without devices or provisions. Space is the only requisite and if the shelf room is exhausted, the floor space is equally good, except for the inconvenience of stooping.

Some prominent opponents of classed catalogues have admitted that the Subject Index, in deciding where to class a book at first, and where to look for it ever afterwards, has removed their strongest objections. Certainly it would be impossible to make an Index more cheaply or more easy of reference, it being a single alphabet, of single words, followed by single numbers.

These class numbers applied to pamphlets have proved specially satisfactory. The number is written on the upper left corner and the pamphlets are arranged either in pamphlet cases with the books on the same subject or on special shelves divided every decimeter by perpendicular sections. As each pamphlet is examined when received into the library, it is the work of a single moment to pencil on it its class number. There is no expense whatever incurred, and yet the entire pamphlet resources of the library on any subject can be produced almost instantly. The immense advantages of this plan over those in common use, both in economy and usefulness, will be appreciated by every librarian caring for a pamphlet collection. A catalogue of authors may be made on slips if desired. The pamphlets themselves are the best Subject Catalogue.

Though designed wholly for library use, the plan has proved of great service in preserving newspaper clippings in large envelopes arranged by class numbers; and more especially in taking the place of the common note-book and Index-Rerum. Slips of uniform size are used with the class number of the subject written on the corner. Minute alphabetical headings are used under each class number, the slips being arranged in numerical order like the Subject Card Catalogue. Clippings and notes arranged in this way are at all times their own complete index, and have the same advantages over the common scrap and note-books that the Subject Catalogue has over the Accessions Book, in looking up the resources of the library on any given subject. Those who have tried this method are so enthusiastic in its praise that it seemed worthy of mention in this place.

The plan was adopted in the Amherst College Library in 1873, and the work of transferring the entire library to the new catalogue at once commenced. It was found entirely practicable to make the change gradually, as means allowed, without interfering in any appreciable degree with the circulation of the books. The three years trial to which it has been there subjected has more than justified the claims of its friends, and it is now printed with the more confidence on this account. It has been kept in manuscript up to this time, in order that the many minor details might be subjected to actual trial and modified where improvement was possible. The labor involved in preparing the Classification and Index has been wholly beyond the appreciation of any who have never attempted a similar task. Much valuable aid has been rendered by specialists in many departments, and nearly every member of the Faculty has given advice from time to time. Among the many to whom thanks are due, special mention should be made of Mr. C. A. Cutter, the librarian of the Boston Athenaeum, and Prof. John Fiske, of the Harvard University library for valuable suggestions and appreciative criticism. While these friends are in no way responsible for any remaining imperfections in the scheme, they should have credit for many improvements which have been made during these three years of revision. The essential character of the plan has remained unchanged from the first. Doubtless other improvements are still possible, and it is hoped that users of the scheme will call attention to any proposed change in the naming or arrangement of the headings, or to any omission which should be supplied in the Subject Index.

Before printing, the plan was submitted to quite a number of librarians for criticism. Among the hundreds of points raised as to its practical workings and usefulness there was only one in which it was not shown to be equal or superior to any other system known. This objection applied only to the arrangement on the shelves; not at all to the catalogues or indexes. It was, that in this relative location, a book which this year stands, e. g., at the end of a certain shelf, may not be on that shelf at all another year, because of the uneven growth of the parts of the library. This slight objection inheres in any system where the books are arranged by *subjects* rather than by windows, doors, shelves, and similar non-intellectual distinctions.

In this hurriedly prepared account of his plan, the author has doubtless failed to meet many objections which may be raised and which he could easily answer. He would therefore ask the privilege of replying personally to any such objections, where they arise, believing that it will be possible to answer, if not all, at least a very large proportion.

In his varied reading, correspondence, and conversation on the subject, the author doubtless received suggestions and gained ideas which it is now impossible for him to acknowledge. Perhaps the most fruitful source of ideas was the *Nuovo Sistema di Catalogo Bibliografico Generale* of Natale Battezzati, of Milan. Certainly he is indebted to this system adopted by the Italian publishers in 1871, though he has copied nothing from it. The plan of the St. Louis Public School Library, and that of the Apprentices' Library of New York, which in some respects resemble his own, were not seen till all the essential features were decided upon, though not given to the public. In filling the nine classes of the scheme the inverted Baconian arrangement of the St. Louis Library has been followed. The author has no desire to claim original invention for any part of his system where another has been before him, and would most gladly make specific acknowledgment of every aid and suggestion were it in his power to do so. With these general explanations and acknowledgments he submits the scheme, hoping it may prove as useful to others as it has to himself.

Amherst College Library,
June 10, 1876

Those interested will find fuller explanations and remarks in the Library volume now being printed by the Bureau of Education at Washington.*

---

*Melvil Dewey, "A Decimal Classification and Subject Index." In U.S. Bureau of Education, *Public Libraries in the United States of America: Their History, Condition, and Management,* Special Report, Part 1 (Washington: Government Printing Office, 1876), pp. 623-48.

32. THE AMHERST CLASSIFICATION

The number of libraries, public and private, that have adopted this scheme, and the very large number of inquiries and suggestions constantly coming to the author, have made it necessary to break the intentional silence of the *Journal* on this subject. It is no longer possible to attend to these many demands by correspondence, and it often happens that much labor and ingenuity are wasted through lack of a few words of caution or explanation. The part of the author in organizing the first conference and establishing the *Journal*, made him specially sensitive to any thing that could be construed into a personal motive for the work done, and he therefore carefully kept in the background every thing pertaining to his system. Its growth in popular favor has been entirely without his effort or attention; and in some suggestions and results of experience in making and using the classification and subject index, in preparation by him for succeeding *Journals*, the entire subject will be treated as if it were the work of another. The article or articles will be written simply because there is a demand for them from a considerable number of readers and supporters, and because it is thought that no little labor will be saved to other librarians by giving them the results of three years' constant experiment in one of the most important branches of library economy. In fact, there are several articles and communications now pigeon-holed in the *Journal* office, which are nothing more than partial repetitions of these experiments, in which the same ground has been traversed by others who have reached the same results as far as they have gone. Limited space will make it necessary to supplement rather than duplicate the matter on the same subject published in Chap. 28 of the Government Report.

The author desires with this announcement to distinctly express his conviction that any efforts towards improvement in this important particular of classification will be infinitely more fruitful if directed towards greater uniformity in the use of the different libraries and catalogues rather than towards an impossible ideal set up by one person, accepted by no other, and never realized by the author. Long study of the subject makes it clear that a classification satisfactory in *theory* is, in the nature of things, an impossibility, and that a scheme can be satisfactory in *use* only to those who realize these inherent difficulties and are satisfied because of their knowledge that a plan free from annoying difficulties is wholly unattainable. Until the mind of every author runs in the same grooves, and these the ones laid down by the classifier, the books will in their nature present a certain number of unsolvable problems in classification. Combine in one the philosophic merits and logical consistencies of all the hundreds of schemes that have thus far been proposed, and there will still be found books that must be taken entirely to pieces if they are satisfactorily assigned to proper categories. A very little study of the subject will convince any doubter of the impossiblity of making a scheme free from defects. It therefore seems wiser to attempt something possible and practical, like greater uniformity in shelves and in catalogs, and the author of the Amherst system begs leave to say to all interested that his desire for such practical results is much greater than his gratification at any merits found in his own plan, and that therefore he would gladly forget his own and unite on any other system that should win general approval as the best. The "Suggestions" will, therefore, be offered as a contribution to the solution of this practical question rather than as directions to the users of the Amherst scheme, though for convenience they will be based on that as a text, and will be most applicable and interesting to those employing that plan in any of its various applications.

. . . . . .

Source: Melvil Dewey, "The Amherst Classification," *Library Journal* 3 (1878): 231-32.

33. FUTURE OF DC

Sum day befor long Biscoe & I & DF will go west & we ar stil gesing who wil take our places. . . . After 50 years I naturali feel keenli the dilema we ar in & hav had a growing conviktion that we wer in danjer of a grave mistake. Isaac Pitman almost ruined his short-hand by his frequent chanjes & Ben Pitman, Howard & a skor of others broke away from him & started a lot of sistems as bad as our litl church denominations. . .

It's a big lyf work for an abl man with a good deal of muni & with a good staf to undertake a nu DC. My 58 years on it convinces me that the onli safe & sensibl plan is for us to concentrate on the DC used in 20 cuntries by 14,000 peopl as much the simplest & most praktikabl sistem. Ad to it nu subjekts that ar wanted lyk aviation, radio, motors etc so that peopl wil hav a place to put the nu books. But at the 1st, my conception & my experience proves I was absolutli ryt, was that we made no pretension to filosophik akuⱥasi or completenes & that we had 2 things to do; to no wher to put a book when it came up & then to no wher to fynd it agen whether next day or a centuri later; that the endles diskusions & theories wer of no praktikal valu whatever to us. I dout if 10% of our users wd undertake the frytful cost of chanjing numbers. It sureli wd be mor lojikal if we chanjd places with 400 & 900. But it wd be stupid to try such an overturn.

DF's* propozal to chanj places with 130 & 160 is much the same thing. As to which place lojik is is a mere whim & when yu start to do that for lojik yu open the way to 100s of others & the great merit of DC is destroyd. My jujment is clear that whyl we may make aditions that our principl is ryt that we won't tear to pieces to gratify specialists. It is uterli imposibl to get them to agree among themselvs & DC is not a filosofik skeme but mereli a praktikal working method to no wher to put things & then to fynd them agen. & I believ its valu will be larjli rekt unles the Foundation stiks by the onli praktikal method, spending tym & muni on the old DC, frankli rekognyzing its faults & that it gets out of date.

Its existence depends on constant sales of nu editions & we wil ruin this incum when we ignore the praktikal needs of the great bodi of users & try too to gratify the critiks of which a nu crop springs up at least anuali. I strongli urj that we abandon eni such eforts, that we provyd for nu subjekts cuming up by ataching them to the most clearli alyd & say frankli as we hav for over 50 years that DC is a praktikal tool, not a filosofik sistem, & that our duti to the publik compels us to make each nu edition mor fuli meeting this praktikal want & refusing to gratify an occasional critik by making obvius improvements in his subjekt at the cost of anoying & confusing the great bodi of users.

I am surpryzd that DF sujjests leaving the other divisions & chanjing places with 130 & 160. If it wer a complete explosion of 100 throwing away all that is dun it wd pleaz sum peopl but to mereli shift 130 & 160 wil pleaz a fu, anoy & disgust & cripl thousands. Richardson's proposal to decimalyz LC skeme is lyk other crazi propositions, amusing for skolars to think over & work over but entyrli impraktikabl. DC has no endowment, can liv onli by provyding what its users want & seling edition after edition. I urj therfor that we plant our feet solidli on the old ground & waste no tym & muni over eni fyn spun theories.

Melvil Dewey

7 11Mr31

---

*Dorkas Fellows, then editor of the Decimal Classification and Relativ Index.

Source: Copy in files of Dr. Godfrey Dewey and of Deo B. Colburn, Lake Placid Club, New York.

Don't misunderstand my yesterday's note on this. I firmli believ it unwys to tinker with DC in an efort to pleaz specialists who never agree among themselvs & never wil. But I realyz that ther has been much dissatisfaction with 100, & it may be wys to recast it. Lukili meni libraries hav fu 100 books. But it seems to me much wyzer if it must be remade, not to knock our old numbers to pieces for so slyt a chanj as transposing 130 & 160. Most of the old criticism wd stil remain. I am too much away from aktiv contak to stres my own feeling & am qyt content to be satisfyd with what DC ofis & its wyzest advyzers desyd. But all my experience confirms the belief that we ar lost if we try to meet all plauzibl criticisms. The chief valu is in its great simplisiti, economi & wyd use. Nearli everi specialist wd lyk to rewrite his subjekt & can point out difikulties in existing numbers; but our rule for 50 years is best, 'stik by old numbers & provyd for nu subjekts by ataching them to the most nearli alyd' & answer critiks by saying 'our rule always has been praktikal usefulnes, larjli dependent on veri wyd use of numbers with the same values.' It is absolutli imposibl to make eni skeme that a lot of prominent people won't sharpli criticyz in their special field. Don't try to satisfy them & don't cripl the proved wyd-spred usefulnes by tinkering in an efort to be mor lojikal. So my experience of 50 years leads me to urj Foundation trustees strongli to say 'no' to these propozals for chanj & improvement except as a place must be found for nu subjeckts that cum up. If libraries can hav a number to asyn wher they can fynd the book quikli when wanted 99% of usefulnes is secured.

Cordiali
Melvil Dewey

7 13Mr31

Source: Copy in files of Dr. Godfrey Dewey and of Deo B. Colburn, Lake Placid Club, New York.

35. LETTER FROM PAUL OTLET, 24 MARCH 1895*

Mr Melvil Dewey:

Being very much occupied with all that can contribute to the progress of bibliography and classification of books, I have made the acquaintance of your work with the keenest interest. Your Decimal classification is truly a masterpiece of ingenuity. I have studied it for several weeks with the intention of making it the basis for our bibliographic office, and on this occasion I take the liberty of addressing to you the following questions:

1 In your opinion would the Decimal classification be applicable to a bibliographic arrangement, and what modifications should it undergo for this application?

2 I send you with this letter a notice on the office of sociologic bibliography which we have founded at Brussels, and specimens of two bibliographic reviews that are published regularly. These reviews have adopted a classification entirely conformable to European ideas for law and sociology. According to your idea how would it be possible to apply your system to these subjects? Your work scarcely furnishes enough subdivisions in law and sociology. If our office adopted your system for the publication and which would result in acquainting Europe with your idea—could you put yourself to the task of introducing into your Classification, with our collaboration, all the divisions and subdivisions for law and sociology which are now lacking?

3 Could we proceed to a French translation of your Decimal classification, and on what terms?

4 We should like to know by how many libraries your system has already been adopted, and if it finds a serious rival or an auxiliary in Mr. Cutter's system.

5 We should also like to know if there is not in the United States a question of applying your system to the classification of some published bibliography; for example, to the new editions of Poole & Fletcher's index.

6 Could we not receive the reports of the American Library association on classification? It is impossible for us to procure these works in Belgium.

I thank you sir for the reply which you will kindly make to these questions, and I again ask pardon for the liberty I have taken in asking them of you.

Paul Otlet

---

*Translated from the French.

Source: Copy in file of Dr. Godfrey Dewey and of Deo B. Colburn, Lake Placid Club, New York.

36. LETTER FROM PAUL OTLET, 8 JUNE 1895*

Monsieur Melvil Dewey
President of the American Librarian
      Association
New York state library.

Sir.

Our International Office of Bibliography, under the high patronage of the Belgian Government, has been for several months past studying an extensive scheme of universal bibliography and is at present nearly arrived to the accomplishment of its work.

Amongst the numerous systems of classification which attracted our attention, your valuable work upon "Decimal Classification" has been found the most practical as well as the most universal, and our purpose would be to make use of it as a basis of the Universal Bibliographic Repertory. We shall have, in a few days, the honour of forwarding you a complete exposition of our organisation which comprises:

1rst. an international agreement between all Governments towards affording patronage and eventually subsidies to the new scientific institution.

2o Creation of a central bibliographic institute, being a kind of international confederacy of all associations interested in bibliography such as universities, public offices, learned associations, librarian associations, printers and Editors associations.

This institute is intended to take charge of the foundation of international bibliographic unities and of the decisions to be taken on all questions concerning the scientific organisation of the repertory.

3o An international office of bibliography being the administrative and executive organ of Governments and of the institute of bibliography, entrusted with all that concerns the realization and publishing of the repertory.

We take the liberty of soliciting your kind support for our undertaking and also leave from you to translate in french, german [sic] and Italian your work on "Decimal Classification."

Being desirous of creating in each Country a provisional committee with which to enter in direct correspondence, we should be very happy if you would accept the presidence [sic] of the Committee for the United States and shall gladly receive your affirmative answer.

We have caused a comprehensive and careful study of your classification to be made by several competent persons who gave us every assurance of its undoubted merits and usefulness, but at the same time suggested a certain amount of possible improvements in details, bearing principally on additions to be made to the work. As soon as we shall be favoured with your answer, we shall have the pleasure of forwarding these notes and reports, begging that you will peruse them and tell us wether they meet your views.

We remain meanwhile, Sir,

      most sincerely yours,

      Paul Otlet

P.S. It is in connexion with the *Union litteraire internationale* of Bern that we are carrying out our scheme, as described above.

---

*Translated from the French.

Source: Copy in files of Dr. Godfrey Dewey and of Deo B. Colburn, Lake Placid Club, New York.

37. LETTER FROM DEWEY TO OTLET, 29 JUNE 1895

Paul Otlet
Brussels, Belgium

Dear Sir,

Your letter of June 8 announcing that you had found our Decimal Classification the most practical as well as the most universal in use, and that you wished to make it the basis of the International Bibliographic work, gives me great pleasure.

You will see in the enclosed handbook of the American Library Association that at the time of our world's fair meeting, the last year of my presidency, I emphasized the fact that the most important work before us now was bibliography. We have given our time largely to administration and have cleared the way for bibliography. I esteem it of the first importance that we should have not only cooperation throughout our own state which we are rapidly effecting, and through our country, but also internationally. I am at present chairman of the cooperation committee of the American Library Association and shall make this an important feature in my report and recommendations. I am also president of the publishing section of our association where we are engaged in bringing out bibliographic publications through cooperation. You will find us ready on all sides to join in any practical and practicable work.

I shall gladly give to the association permission to translate the classification as you request into German, French, Italian and any other of the languages where it may seem desirable, leaving the terms entirely to the officers of the association. I should be very glad if the sales of the book should result in a profit that could be used for advancing bibliographic work. My interest in classification you know, of course without assurance, is not commercial, but that it may do the largest possible good. I found however that it was absolutely necessary to retain the control and ownership of the copyright to prevent garbled editions which would be very mischievous.

I shall accept with pleasure the proffered presidency of the committee for the United States and be glad to receive promptly everything that you may publish bearing on this work. Answering more definitely some of your questions. I should say that the D. C. (the universal catch name for the decimal classification used among our library people) has been found specially applicable to bibliographic arrangement and reference. We have felt the need of very great enlargement in law and sociology, and not a little work has already been done. We shall be very glad to have the suggestions from you as to what would best meet European needs, and we shall willingly undertake the task of enlarging these departments to any desired extent. You will know that the classification has grown very irregularly, being enlarged not symmetrically but here and there as demand arose, each edition including some enlargements not in the preceding.

Judging from our list of libraries that we know to be using the classification and the number that we find from time to time not included in that list, I presume that, large and small, there must be 1000 libraries at least now using it.

Your question as to whether it finds a serious rival in Mr. Cutter's system I can answer freely, as Mr. Cutter is one of my most intimate friends. In fact, his system was announced first in 1877 in the Publishers Weekly as Dewey & Cutter's, he undertaking the work of filling out the heads while I furnished the general plan. That work proved much longer than we anticipated and my name was by mutual consent dropped, but we have kept up the most intimate relations. He says, laughingly, that his system is a great deal better than the D.C., but that people can not be made to believe it and keep on using mine. We have had scores of cases where committees have taken up elaborate comparisons, and the report is uniformly in favor of the Decimal, because of its greater simplicity, and chiefly it is the easiest to administer of any Classification now extant. In practical experience it has been found of the greatest value. Of course, as I say in my preface, I appreciate probably more keenly than any one else many of the shortcomings, but it would be impossible to make

Source: Copy in files of Dr. Godfrey Dewey and of Deo B. Colburn, Lake Placid Club, New York.

any classification that would suit any large number of people in all respects. This has been found of the greatest practical value in 20 years trial. It is constantly being applied in this country to various uses, to indexes, bibliographies, catalogs, newspaper clippings, manuscript notes, etc.

I hope that the effort to secure international cooperation in bibliographic work will prove a complete success.

Yours very truly
Melvil Dewey

I. GOVERNMENT DOCUMENTS

Even though librarians of today have access to indexes to documents and a distribution pattern undreamed of when Dewey first wrote of problems associated with public documents, they may endorse the intent of his 1876 criticism (here reprinted) of the state-of-the-art and his recommendations.

Dewey was not alone in his concern. The editors of *Public Libraries in the United States of America* reviewed the problems of "Copyright, Distribution, Exchanges, and Duties," and they included a brief chronology of congressional activities relating to the distribution of documents. The editors frankly stated that though Congress had "ordered that a copy of the public journals and documents of that and every succeeding Congress should be sent to each college, university, and historical society" as early as 1813, the law had not been implemented fully. Thus, Dewey's concern with documents reflected a commonly held view among those informed. His essay, however, alerted librarians who had not been able to read the *1876 Report* that the distribution program of national, state, and foreign documents needed vast improvement. He identified two great needs of librarians—needs that have not yet been completely filled—as being "larger, fuller, and better indices and an improved system of exchange."

In 1896, twenty years later, during the hearings on the "Condition of the Library of Congress," Dewey criticized the distribution program whereby libraries were receiving duplicate copies of documents, especially of duplicates "bound in full sheep" bearing "a little different title page or label on the back." He also urged that a documents department be placed in the Library of Congress and that it

> include not alone the distribution of duplicates . . . but the great work of having in one place in the hands of experts a complete collection of everything published by the National, State, and local governments of this entire country.

38. PUBLIC DOCUMENTS

As a general rule, the public documents have been a despised class of books. Especially has this been true in our smaller libraries, which have hardly yet learned to appreciate them. Till within a comparatively few years they were hardly preserved at all. In 1848 it was said of the Vermont State publications, "So little regard has been had to the preservation of our most important documents that no one of the public libraries of this State (not even our State library) contains a complete set of the published laws and journals of our legislature." At the present time the case is much improved, but yet there is a chance for still greater advances. A few United States documents are regarded as valuable. Specialists have learned that they contain much which is of the utmost importance to them, and which they can obtain nowhere else. The reports of the Patent Office and of scientific men attached to the various exploring expeditions are perhaps the most prominent illustrations. Yet so many of these latter are hidden away in entirely unexpected places, sometimes in the report of one government officer and again in that of another, that without some clue to guide us through this labyrinth we are entirely lost.

The first great need, then, is some full index, brought up and kept up to date—an index of reports and also one of subjects treated of in the reports, the fuller the better. At present there is no such thing. We would not ignore the work which the Boston Public Library has done and given to the public. But its printed index is now a dozen years old, and though its written catalogue may be kept up, that is small consolation to others who have no access to it. There are also indices published by government of some portions of the United States documents—e. g., the executive documents of the House of Representatives—but they are poorly compiled and of very little value. Of the Massachusetts documents there is no general index, and I presume none for those of the other States. Thus it is still true that we have no such catalogue as we need.

A further cause of the contempt with which public documents are regarded is the careless lavishness which they are scattered about the country. There seems to be no desire to send them to those who are interested in them and will use them, but they are cast indiscriminately abroad. As a result they are thrown into the paper-basket, or used for scrap-books, or something else equally important. This waste is perhaps not so common now as in former years, but still it is sufficient to urge upon us some better disposal of them. The report of the Commissioner of Education for 1872 mentions about forty libraries having over 25,000 volumes apiece. This number must be quite largely increased now; perhaps, for lack of more definite information, we may call it one hundred. If, now, all the States of the Union would supply each of these hundred libraries with copies of their State publications, it might be of as great service in spreading information in regard to the States as the elaborate preparations of some of them at the Centennial Exhibition. It certainly would not be very expensive—the mere cost of paper, press-work, and binding. If, in addition, the United States Government would institute, or rather *extend*, its system of exchanges with foreign countries so as to supply these one hundred libraries in all parts of the land with a copy of the government publications of the principal nations of Europe, we would gain valuable books and make them reasonably accessible to large numbers of people. There must be many libraries abroad which would desire our publications in return, and this would give to those countries better and more reliable information concerning our own land, which they so often fail to appreciate.

This system of exchanges is, of course, nothing new. Its many advantages and great simplicity have been urged long since by M. Alexandre Vattemare, and it was, at least partially, carried into effect. I urge it here, at the beginning of our new enterprise, as something in which all librarians should be interested, hoping to stir up renewed discussion and *action* upon the subject. The two great needs of our libraries in regard to public documents are larger, fuller, and better indices and an improved system of exchange.

Source: Melvil Dewey, "Public Documents," *American Library Journal* 1 (1876): 10-11.

J. COLLEGE LIBRARIES

Though Dewey's initial library experiences were at Amherst College and later at Columbia College, he wrote surprisingly little about the academic milieu. While the work for which he is universally known—his Decimal Classification—was designed during his Amherst years, the Classification was not limited in application to a college library collection. Because of the Classification, however, he was involved primarily with developing, testing, and readying it for publication during the years 1873 to 1876.

While serving as Managing Editor of the *Library Journal*, after leaving Amherst, Dewey designated one issue (volume 2, no. 2, October 1877) as a "College Number." Though he could have taken the opportunity to write about Amherst or to anticipate developments in college libraries, Dewey chose not to do so. Among the essays included, however, was "Hints for Improved Library Economy, Drawn from Usages at Princeton," by Frederic Vinton; this was an area in which Dewey was to seek improvement during his years at Columbia College (1883-1889).

The years as Professor of Library Economy at Columbia College were active and turbulent for Dewey, and his impact is evident in the "Librarian's Reports," circulars, letters, and other writings primarily for internal use. Among his accomplishments were the reorganization of the entire library following the move into the new building, the merging of six libraries into one making it possible to unify management of the library collection, the design of a "Code of Standing Rules," endorsed soon after his appointment, the preparation of a subject catalog, and the implementation of his plan for his School of Library Economy.

While at Columbia College Dewey delivered an address in 1886 before the Association of Collegiate Alumnae on "Librarianship as a Profession for College-Bred Women"; its content, however, did not relate specifically to the college library. In 1886 he began to edit a periodical, *Library Notes: Improved Methods and Labor-Savers for Librarians, Readers and Writers*, but its advice and guidelines were applicable to all types of libraries, not to the college library alone.

The second edition of his Classification, with its recognizably decimal structure, was published in 1885 as the *Decimal Classification and Relativ Index*. The Columbia College Library was the laboratory in which the Classification was applied and expanded—largely by Walter S. Biscoe, who was Librarian in charge of Classification and Catalogs. As with *Library Notes*, however, there was no intention that the Decimal Classification be limited to the college library.

Thus, it can be seen that Dewey always considered himself interested in "libraries," despite his specific role at any given time. The two essays below do relate to the college library. The first reflects Dewey's view of the internal expansion of reference services through the creation of a "faculty library"; the second, his conviction that the college library could contribute to his concept of the library as an instrument of education for the masses.

39. THE FACULTY LIBRARY

There has been marked increase in the last ten years in the number of reference librarians appointed; for we have learned that no system of catalogues, indexes, and bibliographies can possibly take the place of personal help. The rapid growth of universities has accustomed the public mind to great expenditures for educational purposes. When Columbia University requires over $1,000,000 for its annual expenses, New York State will be less alarmed at a reasonable appropriation for its great library than in the time when a million dollars would have been considered a princely permanent endowment. All thoughtful students have noted the remarkable similarity in development of the school and library movements, the library naturally following a generation or so behind the earlier school. In the United States the tax-supported high-school has almost entirely replaced the former prosperous academies, just as the tax-supported public library is replacing most of the subscription libraries. In each case a few of the strongest institutions under favourable circumstances will be maintained, but hardly more than enough to prove the rule. Modern demands for great equipment and large faculties of necessity have brought about the development of the few real universities, Columbia, Harvard, and Yale, having all recently taken that name. On the other hand, many so-called universities and colleges have been compelled to close their doors. Others have taken a simpler and more truthful name, and adjusted their work to new conditions and to their more limited income, while each year the great universities grow larger and demand more and more for their support. I recall being laughed at as an enthusiast or dreamer because, not many years ago, while at Columbia, I prophesied that there would be within my lifetime four thousand or five thousand students, and yet to-day it is safer to prophesy that the number will be more than double this, for already a half-dozen institutions are nearing the five thousand mark.

Evidently circumstances will force a similar development in libraries. The rapid increase in annual publication is making it beyond the capacity of poor libraries to care for a large proportion of these books even if they were given to them. Even a poor man can buy a horse. The financial problem is 'his keep.' Every book must be lodged. It must be shelved, catalogued, inventoried, and cleaned. For books wanted only at long intervals it is cheaper to supply the demand from a central library by utilizing mail, telephone, and express, than to undertake to keep the books at hand, just as it is folly for the ordinary high-school or country college to offer instruction in Russian, Chinese, and various other subjects of human learning, for which the students are very few. Even the most economical will not question that somewhere, available in case of need, a copy of everything published ought to be preserved. This function will more and more go to the state and national libraries, and to the great universities and the few public libraries at central points, where there is sufficient income for this costly work.

In this limited number of great libraries the comparatively modern notion of the reference librarian is bound to develop into what I think we may wisely call the 'library faculty.' One man cannot possibly do the reference work for a large library from lack of time, and no man since Humboldt presumes to be a specialist on all subjects. A process of evolution is inevitable. As demand and income warrant we shall have reference librarians each limited to history, science, art, sociology, law, medicine, education, or some other topic, till we shall have in the library, as in the university, a company of men each an authority in his own field. Such a corps is obviously best named a Faculty, and for a library equipped with such a staff of specialists I propose the name of 'faculty library.' This is another step toward making the library the real People's University. Though these reference librarians will as a rule hold no classes, they will be available not only personally but through correspondence, and with the telephone which is so rapidly becoming universal, the smaller libraries depending on the faculty library, and individual students, as well as schools and teachers, can all readily

Source: Melvil Dewey, "The Faculty Library," *The Library* 2:2 (1901): 238-41. Permission to reprint obtained from Dr. Godfrey Dewey.

inquire of the library specialist as to the best books to buy, read, or consult for any purpose on any topic. This Library Faculty will be the source of our best bibliographies, and, most important, of the annotations destined to make bibliographic work of the future infinitely more valuable than the mere collection of titles without evaluation. Perhaps some man who recognizes the present trend and magnificent possibilities will endow such a library and give an object lesson of what it may do a generation earlier than would be possible through slow natural evolution, retarded by lack of means, instead of stimulated by removal of all obstacles. It is certain that reference work must be closely divided if it is to be of high value. It is also certain that a library faculty can do the work much better than the professors in the same subjects in the university, because library questions refer to the literature of the subject, while the professor deals with the subject itself. The work of the university professor is to extend the field of knowledge in his subject, to lecture to his classes, and to publish results. The work of the library specialist is to know of everything available in print in all languages on his subject, and its value for different readers and students, so that he shall be the best possible adviser as to what to read, whether for one seeking a single fact or a student carrying on the most exhaustive studies. He must be a bibliographer in the broadest sense. The college professor will naturally know much bibliography, and the library specialist cannot be a competent adviser without a very good knowledge of the subject, but the kinds of work are essentially different; and just as we need both schools and libraries to cover the educational field, we need on special subjects college professors and library specialists. Probably the latter will combine authorship with their official duties more largely than the former, specially compilation, condensation, and other literary work most closely allied with bibliography. To be sure in both subjects the library is the laboratory of the professor; but the chemist, whose heart is wrapped up in research, or whose chief interest is in lecturing, is less likely to be the best guide in a library for all possible questions in that subject than a man whose whole life is devoted to knowing the literature of his subjects in all its bearings. Trial and experience may modify more or less this general plan; but one of the great educational institutions to be developed in this new century is the 'faculty library.'

40. THE RELATION OF THE COLLEGES TO THE MODERN LIBRARY MOVEMENT

First, what is the modern library movement? Libraries are of three kinds–storage, recreation and laboratory libraries. Of course, every library must have its function as a reservoir for storing literature. Certainly it is a proper function for public and many other libraries to furnish the highest kind of recreation. The conception of the library as a laboratory is comparatively new, and is an essential part of the modern library idea. There was a time when only chemists considered a laboratory as essential to their college work. Then we found the necessity of laboratories for physics, mineralogy, geology, biology, botany, zoology, etc., and Professor Stoddard just now voiced the feeling of every first-class instructor with the modern spirit when he demanded for his department an English literature laboratory.

As we glance over the field of philosophy, theology, political and social sciences, philology, art, literature and history, we find that for everyone the library is the laboratory, and that even in science where certain apparatus is necessary the library is also the laboratory in supplying in books and serials the result of the world's experiments.

The functions of all libraries are threefold–to get, to keep, and to use. The old librarian had the miserly instinct of *getting* as many books and pamphlets as possible, usually also of *keeping* them safely; but it is a large item in the modern library idea to *use* this material to the fullest extent. To get, to keep and to use, but the greatest of these is to use.

The modern librarian is proud to show how much his books have been worn by legitimate use. The old librarian was distressed to see his books show signs of wear. Indeed I knew of one case in which a college librarian sent a request for the president to read in chapel, that the students should abstain from reading a certain article in the Encyclopaedia Britannica which a professor had commended, because those leaves showed signs of special wear and detracted from the beauty of the volume.

Most libraries have also the threefold departments for reference, the news-room for serials, and the circulating department for home use.

As the next text, note–without exact chronological order or anything more than suggestion–how marked and universal has been the movement in developing the scope of education. It was once for the rich alone; now for the poor as well. It was for the nobility; now for the common people, so that often the education of a modern bootblack would put to shame that of a mediaeval knight. The old education was for males only; to-day some of the best higher work at home and abroad is being done by women and women's colleges. The old was for the bright; the new also builds schools specially for the feeble-minded. The old was for those with all their faculties and senses; the new includes the blind and the deaf, and astonishes the world with the results attained in spite of what once seemed insuperable obstacles. The old was for natives only; the new concerns itself with immigrants, the Chinese, etc. The old was for the white; the new is doing famous work for blacks and Indians. The old conceived of only elementary education for the masses; the notion is now abroad that something higher belongs to every citizen, regardless of nativity, color or sex.

Now mark the two distinctions that are most modern, for all these that I have named have been already generally received. The old education was for the young; the new will provide for education all through life. Last, the old education was thought of as confined to schools and colleges, and when students left them the idiom of the language had it that their education was "completed." The modern library idea assumes that education is not for the young only, but is to last all through life, and that it is to be given not alone in the schools, which furnish the best tools for carrying on an education, but that it is to be given at the home and in connection with the regular work of life.

We find circumstances exactly adapted to these new ideas, for there is a growing difficulty in keeping students in schools and colleges long enough to complete satisfactory courses; but at the same time there is growing opportunity for out-of-school education because of shortened hours of labor.

Source: College Association of the Middle States and Maryland. *Proceedings of the Second Annual Convention. . . . Held at Princeton College, N.J., Nov. 28th and 29th, 1890.* (n.p.: Globe Printing House, 1891), pp. 78-83.

The modern library idea recognizing all these conditions would provide, with the library as the central and most important part of the institution, what we call the people's college in every community of any size. If this idea were housed in a building in the form of a Greek cross, one wing should be devoted to the library, another to the reading-room, a third to the museum of science, and the fourth to the museum of fine art; for our conception is clear that with the library in the people's college should go the museum, including not only science and art, but historical and other museum collections which help to educate by exhibition. When we take a book from the library we learn by holding the printed page before the eye and taking in new ideas; when we stand before the picture or marble, or case of scientific specimens, we are simply taking in ideas through the eye by reading not from the printer's book, but from the book of nature or art. The second story of our building would provide lecture and seminar rooms for university extension courses, classes and other agencies essential in completing the work of the people's college. To illustrate the growth of this idea, I mention that Milwaukee hopes in its new library, for which plans are now being drawn, to include in its upper rooms a feature, as yet untried, as a part of their musical library in which texts of the best music will be provided. Remote from the reading-room they hope to have a piano, violin, guitar, flute and other instruments so that musicians consulting the musical library may have an opportunity to read the music they are consulting, each by aid of the instrument which he plays.

The work to be done by an ideal library is threefold. First, it should make more readers than ever before, inducing those to read who have not acquired that priceless habit. Second, it should teach its readers better methods, in order that they may obtain more from their reading, learning how to get the most out of a book in the shortest time. Third, it should teach them to read better books. The ideal will only be attained when a librarian may closely approximate to giving to each reader at each visit to the library the book that then and there, and to him, will be most useful.

The duty of the college. You should first make your own library include the modern and most important functions—to be in the best sense a laboratory. The college as well as the university is responsible for this work which some at first thought consider as belonging wholly to the university. But college training is to give tools for getting further education, the most essential of all being the ability to use libraries effectively. Every reputable college owes it to its students to give them not only experience in a laboratory library, but also instruction in the use of bibliographical apparatus. To make your libraries what they ought to be, you must, of course, provide the best books and serials. Will each of you think for a moment of your own library, and estimate what per cent of the books now in it you would buy as the best, if beginning anew to-day? You will be astonished to see how small a percentage of the volumes which you report you would dare call the best existing for your purpose.

The college library should be like the college well, open to the students whenever they are in the mood to use it, and not at fixed and limited hours. From eight in the morning until ten at night, including holidays, the doors should be open for all who wish to come. Too many are as I found the New York State Library two years ago—it was carefully locked till the hour when every officer and clerk in the capitol must be at his desk, and was as promptly locked again when they were released, so that throughout the year it was ingeniously arranged that they never had access to the books. It is now open for twice as many hours, including all holidays and vacations.

Another important feature for which the scholarly mind is in danger of feeling too little respect is the provision of physical facilities. Library rooms in light, heat and ventilation, in tables, chairs and all conveniences for work, should be carefully arranged to avoid distracting the attention of the busy worker. A man cannot do his best work in an uncomfortable chair or in a bad light or in an unventilated room.

Your students should have more liberal access to the shelves. It will cause some confusion and make extra labor for your librarian. You may even sometimes lose a book, but suppose you lose twenty or fifty or one hundred dollars' worth (which experience proves you will not), the privilege is worth tenfold that cost to the body of students in whose general education it will play so large a part to be able to handle the books for themselves whenever they can command a leisure hour.

The books and physical facilities must be supplemented by bibliographical aids, by the best catalogues, classifications and indexes, by shelf-labels, guides and by notes and ample cross-references. Stop and think what this means, and you may avoid a common and grave mistake of expecting too much in too short a time. It takes time, money and sympathy with this great work for even the best librarian to get his collection in complete working order. We have seen repeatedly, when some college or board of trustees were a little stirred on this question and determined to do something to improve the library, the most ridiculous expectations as to early results. It is a great undertaking to so arrange and administer a collection of 100,000 volumes that to any man it will be possible, within a few moments, to give from that collection not only the book or pamphlet, but the article hidden away in some volume of transactions, or in some periodical, which to him, then and there, is the thing he most needs. It requires almost infinite labor, but it is well worth the cost. Think of this, and do not, after a new librarian with the modern spirit has undertaken this herculean work, expect in a few months or even years that he can transform a great collection, as if by magic, properly catalogue and prepare all the new material received, and also go back and do the work that has been left undone perhaps for fifty years. It is as foolish as if a family living in tents should begin to build a splendid hall of stone, and before the foundations had fairly risen above the surface of the ground should pass judgment, saying this new plan that promised such extravagant things is a failure, for it is no warmer or more comfortable than in the old tents.

That the colleges are turning their attention in this direction is evident when we look about and see that nearly all the leading institutions have, within the last few years, built new and greatly improved library buildings, and yet hardly one of them has by any means realized the ideal. Harvard, Yale, Columbia, Cornell, Amherst, Dartmouth, Williams, the Universities of Michigan, Vermont and Pennsylvania, Syracuse and Colgate are among those that occur to me on the spur of the moment.

But the colleges have a responsibility beyond making their own libraries what they should be and showing their students how much can be accomplished in liberal education in a well-administered library without other aids. You ought to send your graduates out with such an appreciation of what it is possible for a library to do as will make each a missionary in the town where he may live, earnest and active in seeing that it is provided with what the modern librarian calls the people's college. I see here a graduate of Amherst, whom I have not seen for fifteen years, who recalls a classmate who wrote me this week that he had remembered the seed sown in one of my lectures before his class in 1875; that he was now a lawyer in an inland town and trustee of its academy; that he had contributed largely himself and succeeded in raising from others sufficient money to make a creditable beginning on a library which they meant to make something near the ideal which I had set before him so many years ago. This illustrates my point, that if the subject is properly presented, sooner or later the seed sown will bear fruit. The colleges owe it to the public in every way to aid this great educational movement.

As pointed out yesterday, university extension work, which is an essential part of the modern library movement, is revolutionizing the face of England, bringing old Oxford and Cambridge into relations with the general public such as have never existed before. With us, we are giving great privileges to our colleges. In New York we have repealed the old laws limiting the power of holding property to $4,000 for academies, and to 40,000 bushels of wheat for colleges, and raised the limit to $250,000 of annual income. We have freed them from taxation. We last year freed them from the five per cent collateral inheritance tax, and are constantly, by law, giving them great powers and privileges. To them much has been given, and of them much will be required. The colleges cannot, in justice or with safety, much longer neglect the higher education of all the citizens, and confine their efforts to the favored few able to bear the cost of four years' residence.

To accomplish these results two things are needed. First, money for buildings, books and equipment. If the right brain guides its expenditure this will accomplish much, but it is not the most important factor or the one most difficult to-day to secure. However fine your library and its equipment, it will never be more than a half success unless there is behind it a large, strong, earnest human soul which will supply the vital force that makes all the plant efficient. It is as if every building on this campus was equipped most splendidly with chandeliers and electric lamps, beautiful in form, perfect in model, and lacking nothing but the dynamo. Without that connection they are cold, dark and useless, in fact as well as technically "dead." The librarian holds a similar relation to even the best equipment. To spend money on the plant without securing the man is as unwise as to build the finest and largest cathedral organ and then put on the bench a young girl who can only pump out Moody and Sankey hymns. You will never know the almost divine possibilities of the instrument until there sits down to it a master of every stop and pedal.

Realizing all this for many years, we who had most at heart this modern library idea four years ago established a school for training librarians* for their peculiar work. It started with a twelve weeks' course which rapidly developed, as it only partially met the demand, to six months, a year, and after one season to two years.

It has drawn candidates from Maine to California. Its standard has been raised each year. We have to-day thirty pupils at Albany, coming from some fifteen different States and representing many of our best colleges, but yet we have not enough of the best material to meet the demand which is increasing all over our land. The duty that I wish most strongly to urge upon the colleges to-day is that you should present or allow some of us who are interested to present to every class the unequalled opportunities of usefulness offered by the librarian's profession at just this critical time when it is developing so rapidly. We probably do not want one out of a hundred of your graduates. We reject each year scores of candidates. We have no place for the men that will probably not succeed in law, or medicine, or in the pulpit, but we do wish above all things to secure the occasional man whom nature has fitted for the highest success in this peculiar and inspiring work; a man with capacity that would command success in business or in the learned professions and who will welcome this great opportunity. If you can send us such men you will not only do them the greatest service in finding for them an ideal life-work, but in the end, in the far-reaching influences, in the work accomplished for higher education by their agency, all that it has cost you will come back ten, or twenty or a hundredfold.

* A reference to the Columbia College School of Library Economy (1887-1889) which, when Dewey made this speech, had been transferred to Albany where it became known as the New York State Library School.

K. A GREAT NATIONAL LIBRARY

In 1896 as the imposing Italian Renaissance building designed for the Library of Congress was nearing completion, the Joint Committee on the Library (54th Congress, 2d Session) convened, from November 16 to December 7, to inquire "into the condition of the Library of Congress."

The member of the Joint Committee who led the questioning was the Hon. Lemuel Ely Quigg, Representative from the State of New York, who had served in Congress since January 30, 1894. His political qualifications were impressive in 1896, since he had been serving as chairman of the Republican State Convention and was a delegate to the Republican National Convention. His knowledge of libraries, however, appeared limited. While he did not identify it as his personal appraisal of libraries, his inquiry as to what libraries could do, if properly equipped, "other than haul books down off the shelves for the benefit of readers" may well have reflected his or a commonly held view.

Among those invited to appear before the Committee were Herbert Putnam, then Librarian of the Boston Public Library and later Librarian of Congress (1899-1939), Dr. William T. Harris, Commissioner of Education, and Melvil Dewey. While Dewey spoke in a "slightly rapid gait" as was his custom, he responded to the questions of Representative Quigg with remarkable clarity, continuity of thought, frankness, and imagination, envisioning new dimensions of service for the "National Library." The concept of a national library was not original with Dewey; others had projected it earlier, notably Charles Coffin Jewett in 1848 and Ainsworth Rand Spofford, Librarian of Congress (1864-1897). Not only had Spofford viewed the Library as a national library requiring a collection "universal in its range" which reflected an acquisition policy of inclusiveness, but he had guided the Library toward achieving that goal during his many years as Librarian. It was Dewey, however, who characterized the national library as "a center to which the libraries of the whole country can turn for inspiration, guidance, and practical help."

The scope of the questions addressed to Dewey was comprehensive, covering such matters as cataloging, classification, management, staffing needs of the Library, education for librarians, women as librarians, competitive examinations, and library activities in New York State. His answers reflected not only his experience but also his pride in the University of the State of New York, its Board of Regents, and the achievements of the New York State Library, particularly its program of traveling libraries, a service he had devised and implemented.

The full report is a major contribution, long neglected, to the literature of the profession. It offers a rare insight into nineteenth century librarianship and into Dewey's blending of practicality and vision. Extracts from Representative Quigg's questions, which elicited from Dewey his views on what today would be called a national network of library services with the Library of Congress as the centrifugal force, follow.

41. [DEWEY'S TESTIMONY ON THE CONDITION OF THE LIBRARY OF CONGRESS]

Rep. Quigg: . . . Tell the committee, if you please, why the functions of the Librarian require such training and such education, and what can be accomplished as the result thereof. . . . Supposing we have got all the books and everything that your brain can devise for us, and the question is, What good is it going to do the people?

Mr. Dewey. The modern library is a totally different institution, or should be, from that of the past. It is only a fraction of its work to acquire with skill from all sources every book, pamphlet, serial, or other article pertaining to its collections and to keep them safely housed in your new building. The old idea was that the librarian had to get all he could and keep what he got, but that is only a small part of the duty of the modern librarian, as it is conceived by the best thinkers, not simply among librarians, but among educators and all who have studied the problem. I can only answer your question by going back to some fundamental principles. I will be very brief and say in minutes what could be fully explained only in hours. These last years of the nineteenth century are surely to be known in history as distinctively the library age. A generation and more ago the schools were passing through just such an experience as the libraries are going through to-day. I have a venerable old friend still living in Hartford, Henry Barnard, who nearly a half century ago went to about twenty-seven different States and by courtesy of their legislatures urged upon them the importance of maintaining a distinct department of public schools. We in this generation find it difficult to understand how any State or city or village can think of a government which does not consider liberal provision for public education one of the most important of its functions, and yet there are men living who remember the public school societies which were organized to urge upon the public the recognition of the function of the public school in our American civilization. We are now repeating exactly that experience with the public libraries.

The American Library Association was founded twenty years ago, at the time of the Centennial, and we have now a score of auxiliary societies in leading States and cities of the country all trying to bring about that era when the library shall have the same recognition now accorded to the other part of education as represented by the schools; for schoolmen as well as librarians all agree—I believe no student of the subject pretends to hold a contrary opinion—that the most the schools can do is to give the tools with which to acquire an education and teach the masses to read intelligently, to take the author's meaning from the printed page, so that by holding before the eyes the sheet of paper with the conventional marks in ink upon it the author's thoughts and emotions may be repeated in the reader. As a matter of fact, in our States which are proudest of their educational facilities we are hardly holding our own; in fact, in some cases losing on illiteracy. For the great mass of the people the elementary education is all that we can hope to give for many years at least. They must go out as breadwinners.

We all know that the ideas and ideals of most people are shaped not so much by what they were taught in school, nor by what they have heard from the rostrum or the pulpit, as by what they have read. It is clear, therefore, that if we are to educate most of our people, it must be done by guiding the reading after the school age. There is no practical way of doing this except by the free public library, and so libraries are springing up in every community throughout the country, and the time is coming when it will be taken as an insult for a man to ask, as he does now in a village, Have you a public library? as much as it would if he asked, Have you a post-office, or, Have you a school? This is the education that can reach all the people while the schools can reach only a part, and that lasts all through life, while the schools are only for a limited period of youth.

. . . . . .

Source: U.S. Congress. Joint Committee on the Library. *Condition of the Library of Congress.* [Washington: Government Printing Office, 1897]. 54th Congress, 2nd Session, Senate Report no. 1573, pp. 141-43; 145-46; 146-49; 160-61; 166; 168; 268; 269; 270.

We all know that a great work can only be accomplished by competent organization. A successful army must have not only individual soldiers, but companies and regiments and divisions, and, shaping all, a department of war. It is equally true that we shall never accomplish our best results in librarianship till we can have at the National Library in Washington a center to which the libraries of the whole country can turn for inspiration, guidance, and practical help, which can be rendered so economically and efficiently in no other possible way. You have just completed the most magnificent library structure in the world, and we are all proud of it. We have a great collection of books largely inaccessible for want of space, and there is no question that Congress will make appropriations to enlarge it, so that we shall be proud of the extent of our literary resources; but the building and the books are less important than the other work which should properly be done by our new National Library, and it will be a great disappointment to those who know this subject best if in the administration of the new National Library it does not do a work for the people of this country as much superior to that done by any other national library as this wonderful building excels other homes for books.

You ask what ought to be done. You already have the building, which, by careful study, affords opportunity for introducing many features of administration for which no provision has yet been made. You have the books, which, when arranged in their new quarters, will betray sad gaps, and liberal appropriations will be necessary to fill them and to provide for the work which the public will reasonably demand.

I hope that with the new order will come a new name, for the Library of Congress conveys a false impression as much as it would to call the British Museum the parliamentary library. When Congress appropriated $3,000 with which to buy books for the use of the two Houses, it was clearly a library of Congress, and people will always understand by that title the collection of books which, of course, you will keep in this building for the convenient use of the legislative body. Even an act of Congress or the failure of Congress to enact a change of name will never prevent the public from continuing the name by which already the building is so widely known—the National Library.

. . . . . .

Rep. Quigg: . . . If Congress would supply appropriations sufficient to do this work [the making of a satisfactory catalogue], and have that work done—that is work that is very valuable to all libraries throughout the country—would it not be valuable for the students that might care to attend the library?

Mr. Dewey. The first thought is for the readers who come to the Library. It was because it was so unusual a function that I emphasize the importance to other libraries throughout the country of having this catalogue work properly done here. We have perhaps 4,000 public libraries in the country of 1,000 volumes or more. If a book is published that 500 of these libraries will buy, where can you think of a greater waste than that every one of the 500 should have to undertake, each for itself, with, in most cases, limited bibliographic machinery and insufficient force, to catalogue that book when it has been already catalogued in the National Library by the most expert staff in the country, having at their disposal every known resource? Printing is very cheap. Any library willing to pay the cost of paper and postage could have a copy of these cards furnished without extra expense to the Government, which has already paid for making its own cards. This distribution of printed catalogue cards has long been the dream of librarians. By cooperation among ourselves we are now carrying it on to a limited extent under great disadvantages. It would mark an era when the National Library was ready to do this incalculable service to the libraries and students of the country.

Rep. Quigg: Tell us what else could be done in a national library; to what work the Congressional Library could best devote its time and money.

Mr. Dewey. There are scores of important things that might be done. On the spur of the moment I will suggest some that occur to me as specially important.

You ought to have here for the nation what we maintain in New York, a paid-help department, or a correspondence library. Any person in the United States should be at liberty to send to this Library, provided he is willing to pay the actual extra labor thrown upon the assistant, for extracts from any book carefully typewritten and verified before a notary; for translations; for any bit of literary work which a skillful assistant could do in the Library. Often a scholar must have access, for an hour or two before he can go on with his work, to something to be found only here. If he has to ride 1,000 or 2,000 miles away, the time and cost of the journey may be prohibitive, but at an extra expense to your Library of a single hour of an assistant's time, costing perhaps a single dollar, the whole purposes of the journey could be served.

It is little less than a crime against scholarship not to provide such facilities. It would be absolutely no burden to the taxpayer, and if skillfully organized, thousands of such applications would come in every month. There is not only the great saving in the time and expense of a journey to the Library, but a staff here properly trained would have among its members some person who could often do in an hour more than the reader in person could do in a day or a week. I do not advocate making such services free, because the privilege would be sadly abused; but if the full time given by any member of the staff is paid for at the rate of his annual salary, so that only the facilities of the Library are free to all readers, this collection of books is not a library for Washington and the Government officials residing here, but becomes in fact a national library directly available to every inhabitant of every State. In many cases this service can be rendered by telephone or telegraph without even the short delay of the mails. Here is one magnificent opportunity for usefulness that would be appreciated and commended even though it should involve a large expense, and properly organized it need not cost a dollar. I would venture to defend the thesis that such a department could be made more useful than any single university in America.

As we study this question it will be more and more apparent that the great national university which we need is really an ideal library administered not on the old lines of getting and keeping and serving a constituency at the door, but with the conception that the true university of these times is a great collection of books and that its students may be scattered all over a great nation. The difference between this library and the old is the difference between the manuscript volumes carefully chained in the monastery, to read which one might have to travel hundreds of miles, and the modern book which may be multiplied indefinitely and had in any part of the world for the price of a single meal.

Rep. Quigg: Do you think they should have more money to spend for books?

Mr. Dewey. Unquestionably. I see in your appropriation bill the beggarly item of $4,000 for books, or, including allied expenses, a total of $11,000. This is a great, rich nation, of which we are very proud, and yet in its snug little island England feels that she is not doing enough when she gives ten times this amount for books to the British Museum, some $45,000 if you limit it strictly to the book account, or over $100,000 if you count in the allied expenses as in making up the meager $11,000 at present granted to our National Library.

· · · · · ·

Rep. Quigg: What do you mean by the distribution of duplicates?

Mr. Dewey. You have on a rented floor over the post-office in your city a public-document division which is doing admirable work in distributing to the libraries of the country Government publications. It has on hand some 300,000 volumes, I think. It is collecting from libraries and other owners United States publications which they no longer require, classifying and shelving them so as to supply to other libraries books greatly needed to complete sets and meet real wants. This work is naturally a part of the National Library. You have empty shelves that will hold all the books, and rooms for the small staff employed, and you would bring together the work that belongs together. Besides the Government publications, there will be received great quantities of books as gifts, many of which will duplicate those already in your collection.

The National Library should have full power to place these extra volumes where they will do most good to the country, exchanging some, giving others to small libraries, and when they get books so much worn or so commonly duplicated as not to be worth further preservation, sending them to the paper mill. This is a function which it is very dangerous to trust to any but the most skillful, for they will send to the mill to-day, under the guise of trash, books that next year or in the next generation will be eagerly sought and highly valued. It ought to be known to every library and to every private book owner that he may send by cheap freight to the National Library any literary material with the assurance that under its skillful management it will be sure to accomplish the maximum amount of good, and that nothing of value will be wasted. Much of this work could be done, as we are doing it in New York, by the State library, but there is a very large field that is national rather than local in its scope, and there are many who will give their books to the finest library in the world as a matter of sentiment or national pride when they would not give to their small and modest local library.

Rep. Quigg: . . . Will you show me what we can do in transferring to libraries throughout the country—what we have to accomplish in the way of cataloguing books, so that readers everywhere throughout the United States can have the benefit of our complete system? What else can you say?

Mr. Dewey: One of your largest fields which I have not yet mentioned is bibliography.

Mr. Cummings: What do you mean by bibliography?

Mr. Dewey. A bibliography differs from a catalogue in that it gives, not the list of the books in a given collection, but a list of all the books that have been written, or of a selection of the best books regardless of whether they are in the library. Bibliography is coming to be one of the most important of the sciences. The field of human learning has become so vast, the product of the press so overwhelming in numbers, that without the aid of bibliography a large portion of scholarly endeavor would be lost. A man to be safe in pursuing any new investigation must know what has already been done in that field, or perhaps after ten years of the most earnest effort he produces something which has been already equally well done and his life has been wasted.

Even more important is the service bibliography renders to the inquirer who with the time at his disposal wishes to find the best publication. You recall that during the present summer there has been held in London an international congress to which you sent delegates in recognition of the duty of civilized nations to promote bibliography, or the preparation of trustworthy lists of the publications available on all subjects. This work should properly center in the National Library. It can be done only with great resources of men and books, like many other proper functions of this Library which are impracticable in municipal collections, for the taxpayers would justly resent the expenditure of their money for the benefit of people in distant communities. We are doing at Albany much work of this kind, because we are maintaining a library for the benefit of a great State, having nearly 1,000 other libraries in its borders which may profit by our work, but it would save much time and labor that we could use directly for New York interests if the National Library were so situated as to perform its proper functions.

In saying this it implies no shade of criticism on the Librarian of Congress who has, in thirty-five years of service, won the admiration of all who know how helpful he has been to Congress and how much he has done in the most discouraging surroundings. He has had neither men, money, nor room adequate to the functions. He may justly be proud that he has done so much, and I am sure he will feel it no criticism when I insist that the National Library hereafter ought to do one-hundred-fold more. Every library in the United States— yes, every student, should feel free to write or telephone or telegraph to the National Library and have a prompt response as to any book on any subject, if here; and if not, information in what library it could be found. It involves great labor and great expense, but so does the Patent Office and the Pension Office and many other Departments of the Government, for which the people are willing to pay when they consider the aggregate benefit to the whole country.

Rep. Quigg: . . . You say that there may be books somewhere that we can not get; that our libraries should contain not only a complete catalogue, but a complete enumeration of the books we have and of books that other libraries have, and that we have not, all over the world; that the enumeration should be supplemental to the catalogue of each book, so to speak, and that the libraries all over the United States should have the benefit of that enumeration of books and of that complete cataloguing of their contents, showing that they are available here, or if not here, then in London, or Paris, or Boston, or New York, or somewhere else. . . . You must have found out what it is that libraries can do if properly equipped with books and men other than haul books down off the shelves for the benefit of readers that come in and ask for books, to tell us what more to do . . .

Mr. Dewey. I have not mentioned the exceedingly important element of annotation of catalogues and bibliographies. This is another ideal to which we have not attained for lack of what we now expect to have in the National Library. You can understand the value to a young reader if when he took the book from the shelf a wise man who had specially studied that subject should touch his shoulder and say the few words that would be most helpful to him in using the volume, and without which he might get a wrong impression which would go with him through life. Suppose it is a history that was written from the standpoint of some particular party or some religious sect. How infinitely important that the young man should know that before he studies the work as an impartial statement. Suppose it is a book valuable for its style but untrustworthy in its facts, or vice versa; suppose it has been superseded by something in every way more reliable; you can think of hundreds of circumstances where a few words of expert advice would be invaluable. Now what we wish is to have that advice condensed into a note appended to the title in the catalogue or bibliography so that not only the reader who is happy enough to have a wise friend at hand, but every reader who has access to the printed catalogue may have the benefit of this expert advice. Such notes to be valuable must be prepared by those with leisure to become thoroughly familiar with the literature of their chosen field. This means a staff of specialists so large that no local library has dared to attempt it. They have only two, in some libraries a half dozen, who do this kind of work, but only in the National Library can we hope for the organization of an adequate staff of specialists.

Rep. Quigg: Are you suggesting a line of original inquiry—of original investigation—[assuming that the Library has a staff of specialists which Dewey had proposed] about these libraries?

Mr. Dewey. Oh, no indeed. I would not confuse the function of the university with that of the library. The library expert would make his investigation not about the facts or the things, but about the books concerning them. He would, for instance, know all about the literature of chemistry, but he would not have a laboratory and be himself an investigator. We should raise these things to the second power and have on the library staff the men who can tell the investigators what has been written in the various languages up to date on the subject which they are studying.

. . . . . .

Rep. Quigg: Have you anything else to suggest?

Mr. Dewey. The National Library ought, under certain circumstances, to lend books all over the country. I do not mean that it should take the place of local or State libraries, but there are certain books obtainable only here which must in some cases be used for several days or weeks by scholars at a distance who can not get what they need through the paid help department or by employing library assistants in the building. Under proper restrictions there should be a system of lending to libraries and students throughout the country. For the cost of mail or express a student may often save an expensive journey, and we have now perfected means of packing and sending books with little danger of injury, and the risk of a fire in a mail or express car is really very small. Of course, many things are so valuable that they could never leave the fireproof building, but there are many others that might be used in this beneficent work.

. . . . . .

Rep. Quigg: ... This Library is the property of Congress. ... I would like to know from you what suggestions you would make to this committee as to the present legislation looking to the supervision of the Library.

Mr. Dewey. I see only one course; that is, to express frankly my present opinion in regard to it, though there may be circumstances not now known to me which would influence it, the public feels that this really ought to be the great national library, not simply the Library of Congress, which it understands to be for the direct daily use of the Senate and House.

......

It seems a misnomer for the great national library to bear the limited legislative name. It is not a serious matter, but the people are getting to think of this entirely as a national library. You will see it called so in papers. It seems to me that the spirit of the law creating this vast building with all its possibilities and responsibilities did not intend that the entire administrative and executive detail should continue under one man, as was proper with the original $3,000 library. The Library has now few statutes, no particular rules, and the Librarian is appointed and goes on with his work really independently of any trustees.

......

It seems to me a mistake where it really is a national library that it should be considered as only a library for or of Congress. It should not be shut out from the application of the civil-service law on the ground that it is not in the executive department, when its chief functions are really no longer legislative but administrative and executive.

Rep. Cummings: It was originally the Library of Congress?

Mr. Dewey. Yes; the first appropriation was $3,000 to buy books for the two Houses to use. I think it has changed from that to the great National Library. But Congress still needs in the Capitol a library of all the books in daily use. This can best be treated as a branch of the National Library. You have a tunnel across to the building, and with telephones and pneumatic tubes can get any book required in a minute or two longer than it would take if the Library were in this building. The national Library I am sure will take on many new and important functions which are in no way connected with Congress. We had the most similar problem in the country in New York, of course on a smaller scale. Our State library till 1844 had no trustees, as now. From the year it was put in charge of the regents there was marked improvement, and it now stands far in advance of any other State library in the country. Adjoining it we had the senate and assembly libraries carried on by legislative committees. Some years ago an inventory showed a loss of over 50 per cent of all the books that had been bought for them while our library had lost almost none. With constantly changing committees and librarians, a suitable and safe administration is hardly practicable.

......

Rep. Quigg: ... Has anyone devoted any attention to the collection of a fine art exhibition or exhibit? Do you think that any effort in that direction ought to be made in connection with the new Library?

Mr. Dewey. I do, very decidedly. The feeling is general among the best educational thinkers of the country that we have got to educate the people through the eye, not only by reading the conventional language as printed in books, but also the natural language as shown in works of art and objects of scientific or historical interest. We are outgrowing the curious notion so ingrained in many people that education is something to be had only from the printed page. To be sure that is the principal agency, but this nation ought to recognize the immense part to be played by art, and it is far enough along in its second century to feel ashamed that it has not more to show when compared with the European countries to which we boast our superiority.

......

Rep. Quigg: . . . Is there anything else that you would like to say . . . that you have not said, Professor?

Mr. Dewey. Yes, I should like to talk to you two weeks about these matters. You ought to have a music room adjoining and in connection with the musical library, with a piano, violin, and other instruments so that people could come in and try the scores. I think that would be an inexpensive and practical thing. Many expert musicians can read a score and get all they wish from it by eye without the ear. Others whose wants should also be met must play it on some instrument or it does not serve their purpose. Of course the instrument room should be shut away from the other to prevent annoyance. You will have an immense collection of musical scores here, and it would give it a practical character as a national musical library.

I think there will be great disappointment when your library gets into the new building, for it will be found very poor in many directions. I do not see how it can be otherwise, since the amount of your appropriations has been so small and so much has been necessary to keep up the work of binding periodicals, etc. When you say 740,000 volumes you have to bear in mind the large number of copyright duplicates.

One other thing of many and then I will stop—that is, the deposit by the other Departments of the Government in the Congressional Library of books, pamphlets, maps, prints, manuscripts, or anything else that properly belongs there, which the head of the Department no longer needs in the administration of his office. We found in our State that an immense amount of valuable material went to the paper mill—material which the present administrative officers no longer used. One office sent 40,000 volumes in one year to the paper mill, at $5 per ton. There is only one safe place for preserving such works—a fireproof library in charge of officials who realize the danger of destroying any literary work, because what to-day is voted rubbish by one official may in future years prove to be a treasure to another. Care of such property is a science by itself, and it is unsafe to trust it to library novices.

[Following Dewey's statements Rep. Quigg sought the views of other witnesses on many of the ideas earlier stated. The responses of Putnam, for example, were more restrained and occasionally in conflict with those of Dewey. With the other witnesses, too, Rep. Quigg was somewhat more aggressive than he had been with Dewey. Toward the end of the hearings Dewey spoke briefly again; excerpts from his comments follow:]

. . . I come into librarianship not from the side of books, but of education. For twenty years I have been studying certain phases of librarianship on general lines, and for the past eight years have had an experience in New York which gives me confidence in the suggestions made. They are not mere matters of theory given on the impulse of the moment, but the result of years of study and experiment in very similar lines.

. . . . . .

But the function of art as an educating force ought to be recognized in this country, and it is a broader and better view to treat it as an ally of the library.

. . . . . .

There should be collected here the finest bibliothecal museum, illustrating everything pertaining to libraries, and so displayed and annotated that students could readily get from it the practical lessons which such a compendium of experiment and experience could teach.

Attention has been called to the tremendous expense involved in printing catalogues. The more one emphasizes the difficulties the more important seems the function of the National Library in meeting them, for the local libraries have not the means to pay for this important work and it must be done here or not at all. The tremendous growth of literature staggers those who study the statistics, and the new shelving required in the larger libraries seems beyond belief. No one who is not prepared to begin lapsing into barbarism would deny that at least in one place in the country there should be an all-inclusive library that would preserve at least one copy of every obtainable book and pamphlet printed, so that students in the future could get access to it if needed. This problem is growing so costly and difficult that it can hardly be attempted except by the National Library.

Judging from the experience of other great libraries which have moved from cramped into ample quarters, you are sure to have an immense increase in the number of readers who frequent the library daily and consequently a corresponding increase in the duties of the reference librarian. You will find as you move into the new building thousands of ugly gaps to be filled in making a well-balanced library, and an immense additional burden will be thrown, specially in the next few years, on the Librarian in making his selection of books to be bought. With this increase will come, under proper management, thousands of gifts, large and small, that will swell the work of cataloguing current accessions beyond any proportions yet suggested.

L. TRIBUTES TO COLLEAGUES

Dewey's tributes to his peers were somewhat rare despite his wide acquaintance in the profession. His memorial statements made for those who had differed with him have a refreshing frankness and honesty. He could, in contrast, be effusive and flattering to those with whom he had close personal relationships. The following tributes represent Dewey's varying attitudes toward Mary Eileen Ahern, Frederick Morgan Crunden, Frederick Jackson, William Frederick Poole, and May Seymour.

42. A NOTABLE RECORD
[MARY EILEEN AHERN, 1865?-1938]

Miss Ahern in the past 36 years has completed 36 volumes of which eni leader myt justli be veri proud. In all thez years she has been 'featured' in the stedi succesion of librari 'movies.' Her interests wer nation-wyd. She was a frequent visitor to skors of librari centers & knew personali perhaps mor librari leaders & workers than eni other ALA member. Her keen Irish wit & sense of humor made her always interesting. Her outspoken franknes ofen got on the toes of the supersentitiv [sic]. Her lance was bryt & keen & was always in poise when needed. Her keen mind & fasil pen wer enlisted promptli in everi good librari cauz. If we had to elekt a 'librarian militant' she wd be sure of the votes.

It seems onli yesterday that I diskust with her ernestli the policies & form of the nu periodical which was to ask & receiv the suport of the profesion. Her mind was a hy speed enjin that never stalld. She was usuali a warm suporter of enithing that gave promis of helping the librari profesion to a hyer plane, & it was never dificult to find out why she withheld her suport from mezures which her keen mind cd not aprove.

She has always abyded by the program I urjd when as founder of Library Bureau I was consulted as to the nu journal. Its syz & larj, clear typ in dubl columns have made it always a fizikal delyt to read.

Libraries under another editor cd never be just the same. From the 1st number her personaliti has been stampt on her magazine & ther is a fitting digniti in marking her retirement by clozing her 36 volumes as a stori completed.

The editor has laid down her fasil, efisient & sumtyms militant pen but we all hope that her voice for meni mor years wil be herd in librari counsel in which she has so long playd so prominent a part.

Source: Melvil Dewey, "A Notable Record," *Libraries* 36 (1931): 438.

43. TRIBUTE TO MR CRUNDEN
[FREDERICK MORGAN CRUNDEN, 1847-1911]

A little after we founded the A. L. A. in 1876, there came to us from St Louis the brain and big hart that won instant recognition and enduring leadership. For years he has been our senior living ex-president. For a third of a century I have workt intimately with the rare man who has just left us. We have discust a thousand matters but never once have I heard from his lips an argument or suggestion based on selfishness. His thought was ever the greatest good of the greatest number and for that he was always redy to sacrifice his own interests in a way sadly rare in these days of self-seeking. Those who shared his friend-ship are better men and women; the A. L. A. is stronger and has higher ideals; and a good bit of the Master's vineyard is a better world to live in because of the influence of his earnest life.

After the awful blow fell and he went out of our lives without a moment's warning, we who loved and admired him, and that ment all that had the rare privilege of his friendship, hoped against hope that he might come back to us. After five weary hartbreaking years there was a rift in the black clouds as if he had been permitted to return to earth long enough to see with mortal eyes some of the wonderful fruitage from the seed his hand had planted.

He saw the beautiful F. M. Crunden branch library, a conspicuous leader among similar institutions because of services to all the people, unusual even for the best of these People's Colleges. He saw the great central bilding, the crowning monument of his long lifework, the special pride of the St Louis for which he did so much.

He saw carvd in granit above the main entrance of this temple a motto chosen by a wise committee from the whole field of literature, a telling extract from one of his own many addresses.

He saw a whole great city loyal still to the memory of the man whose life had made that city a better home.

It was not for him to remain thru the harvest that came from his planting, but like Moses, he had his brief space on the mountaintop and at last his eyes swept over the promist land to which he had so strenuously led his people. Then after this brief inspiring vision his great hart sweld out in a prayer that was quickly answerd, "Now, Lord, lettest thou thy servant depart in peace, for mine eyes have seen the growing fruit of all my labors."

Source: Melvil Dewey, "Tribute to Mr Crunden," *Public Libraries* 16 (1911): 437-38.

44. IN MEMORIAM: FREDERICK JACKSON [1841-1886]

Members of the A. L. A. and readers of the *Journal* will feel the loss of Frederick Jackson, who died at his home in St. Paul, Minn., Monday evening, 11th October, after six weeks' illness from typhoid fever, with an attack of erysipelas. Mr. Jackson left his pressing business in St. Paul to come down to Milwaukee and welcome the A. L. A., and it was he who organized the cordial welcome which we received at St. Paul on our western trip,—three of the party being entertained at his home. About the 20th of August he accepted my earnest invitation to come to Green Lake, Wis., for a quiet post-conference rest. He was indisposed on his arrival and during his entire stay, and after ten days started for home, going by way of the Dells, to enjoy the trip which he missed when the A. L. A. party were there. He seems to have taken to his bed almost at once on reaching home. Only a day or two before his death I received a playful note, announcing the long confinement, in a tone that implied that he was over the worst. The funeral was at St. Paul, where he was buried. He leaves a wife, three daughters, and one son, the eldest being but 14.

Mr. Jackson was 45 years of age, and was born in Newton, Mass., where he was for several years Superintendent of its famous Free Library, much of the success of which was due to his earnest efforts in its earlier years. He studied at the Lawrence Scientific School of Harvard College, but did not graduate; he always retained a strong interest in literature and science. He served one term of the war in the 44th Mass. Regiment, and was wounded in a skirmish in North Carolina. After the war he bought a plantation, and spent some time in South Carolina.

Mr. Jackson was at the first conference in Philadelphia, and was a regular attendant on all meetings of the A. L. A. or the Executive Board, of which he was, till he removed to St. Paul in 1881, a member. He was chosen treasurer when the office was separated from that of secretary, and was an active member of the Coöperation Committee. He made his headquarters in Boston, at the A. L. A. offices, 32 Hawley street, and shared with me the development of the Supply Department into the large business done in 1879-80.

In 1881 large investments in St. Paul led him to accept the financial department in the wholesale hardware house of Farwell, Ozmun, & Jackson, which in the past five years has built up one of the largest hardware businesses of the country, as was testified to those of us who visited the immense store filled on all its five floors.

At Green Lake he told me that he had decided to withdraw from active business with the new year, in order that he might gratify his taste for reading and study, and have more time for congenial pursuits. It was a pleasure to find a man that, after an unusually successful business career, was satisfied with his earnings, and prepared to give himself to culture rather than money-getting. It makes his early death doubly sad, that he who had decided in the hight of prosperity to leave active business,in order to give his time and strength to a life of higher enjoyment and usefulness, should not have been permitted even to enter that promised land.

There was no more loyal friend than Frederick Jackson. I have known him intimately during these ten years, and only to find his friendship to wear like pure gold. And my experience was not peculiar. I remember, in 1877, when our party spent two months abroad at the time of the Library Conference in London, that I amused myself towards the end of the trip by asking the individual members of the party, which had grown most in the estimate of the rest, on that closer acquaintance which our constant travel together insured. And all answered Frederick Jackson. Of that delightful party Mrs. Cornelia B. Olmsted, of the Wadsworth Library, Geneseo, N.Y.; Charles Bradbury, of Boston (Mr. Cutter's brother-in-law); Lloyd P. Smith, of the Philadelphia Library, and now Frederick Jackson, have gone over to the majority. Had we selected the four most genial, whole-souled, lovable members from the twenty-two, I think we should have chosen just these four.

The last I knew best, and I wish to lay on his grave the tribute due from one who as he knew him better could not but love him more and more.

Source: Melvil Dewey, "In Memoriam: Frederick Jackson," *Library Journal* 11 (1886): 478.

45. WILLIAM FREDERICK POOLE [1821-1894]

MELVIL DEWEY.—Mr. President, I want to say what I so often have said to the students in the Library School about Dr. Poole, and what you have already said here to-day, that this later generation did not realize how much Dr. William F. Poole had been and done in the American library movement a quarter of a century ago. He was the man that stood most for the stimulating element in organizing new libraries and giving them some tangible method, and a great many who knew him in these last years after he had worked for so many years as the leader and recognized expert (he said sometimes in our meetings with more frankness than modesty, that he thought he knew all that was worth knowing about librarianship), forgot that for many years he stood for as much as almost all the rest of the librarians together.

Another thing is to me a very delightful memory; his best friends were those who knew him best. His associates were his most loyal and enthusiastic friends. He was a born fighter. Nothing would bring him to his feet so quickly as a chance to attack something. When we were in England seventeen years ago, we were all proud when Dr. Poole took the floor to make an address. With his fine presence, his strong voice and earnest manner, there was no man in either Association that made so splendid an impression as he. Those of us who used to have frequent tussles with him have always retained our affection for the man, though we may have differed on some question of policy.

I remember well my first meeting with Dr. Poole. He brought out his index the year that I was born, and I had from boyhood known his name as the great librarian. When coming out of college in 1876 the notion took possession of me that we should have a library association, but I was very shy about the first approaches for calling a meeting. The same was true of Mr. Winsor. The one man who from the first, through the whole history of the Association, has always had faith, not only said, "I think it can be done," but also "I will help," and did help, was Charles A. Cutter of the Boston Athenaeum. The other older librarians were often in doubt, but Mr. Cutter never failed to join heartily in every advance movement. In the early years, especially, as some of you know, there was a great deal of distrust as to what we should accomplish, and Dr. Poole was very shy indeed. At first he withheld his name entirely, but, at the last, consented to have it appear on the organizing committee with that of Mr. Winsor, Mr. Lloyd P. Smith of Philadelphia, and myself.

We met first in Mr. Smith's house, and it was the first time I ever saw Dr. Poole's face. As I came into the parlor late in the evening, he came across the room and drawing himself to his full height burst out laughing. "Well," he said, "Dewey, you are a better looking man than I thought you were. I had a clear picture in mind of you as about 70 years old, with white hair and glasses and round shoulders." In fact I was then the youngest man in the association. My picture of our Nestor was equally wide of the mark. Dr. Poole's soldierly bearing gave me the impression of a generation younger than I had been prepared to meet. The surprise was a most delightful one to me, and from that time till he died I always enjoyed very much my relations with Dr. Poole. When an issue came up you did not lose your affection for him if you voted on the other side or differed from him. If the people who work with a man and know him intimately like him best, it is a very good sign. I am afraid of the man who is liked best by those who know him least.

William F. Poole, far above all others, was the apostle of the modern library movement for many years. Nearly a quarter of a century ago he stood almost alone in his active and earnest efforts for the library advancement. As I have dipped here and there into the history of American libraries this fact has continually come back to me, as I have found traces of his work in stimulating and shaping their growth. No other man deserves so much credit for those early years as our dear friend, Dr. William F. Poole.

Source: American Library Association, "Proceedings, 1894," *Library Journal* 19 (1894): C169-C170. Referred to as the "Lake Placid Conference."

46. MAY SEYMOUR [1857-1921]

Only those in the inner circle will realize how great a loss the profession has met in the death of May Seymour. She was so insistent on keeping herself in the background that few realized the extent or value of the admirable work she has been doing for 34 years.

She was a prominent graduate of Smith College in the 2d class, 1880, and was perhaps the first to matriculate in the first library school at Columbia. She took in this school the same foremost place that she has held in every position.

Except for a few months spent in helping to organize the Osterhout Library in Wilkes Barre, she has workt constantly as my personal assistant for 34 years. She went to Albany April 1, 1889, in charj of classification. During her 17 years in the State Library no member of the Library School faculty was more interested or efficient in developing the new school. Her unusual ability very soon won her appointment as secretary's assistant in the Regents' office which placed her next to me as the executive officer of the University of the State of New York. Beside her work in the library and school, her marvelus mind very quikly graspt the broader problems of the University, and no person, of several hundred on my staf during those 17 years of re-organization, helpt me more, not alone by loyal co-operation and servis, but in practical suggestions based on thoro study and most unusual bredth of comprehension of the great educational problems of the Empire State. She workt with me constantly as State director of education for the Chicago World's Fair. She was the editor and executiv for the A L A catalog which is a monument to her ability and industry. She soon relievd me of most of the work of the successiv editions of the Decimal Classification, and for the last 17 years has been the responsibl editor, doing all the work, coming to me only for occasional consultation. She had recently completed the 10th edition. This spring the long talkt of Abrijd D C was publisht and she had sent the last ms with instructions to print only a few days befor her deth.

She shared fully my enthusiasm for simplifying English spelling, and for the introduction of decimal weits and measures. She shared with Mrs. Dewey and me, mor than anyone else, in formulating the ideals and working plans for the Lake Placid Club. 15 years ago, soon after I left Albany, she came to Placid, and has from that time livd with us like an own sister, and yet more efficient than any salaried officer.

In my 70 years experience I can recall no woman with a finer intellect, or with a loftier caracter. By birth and training pre-eminently a scholar, she had an impatience of inaccuracy, or mental sloppiness or indolence that made her a terror to the incompetent. Many very able peopl never knew her wel enuf to realize her unusual qualities, but those who did, found bak of that somewhat prim exterior and the critical mind, a welth of qualities of which they had litl dreamd.

Source: Melvil Dewey, "May Seymour, August 31, 1857-June 14, 1921," *Library Journal* 46 (1921): 606-607. Reprinted from *Library Journal* 1921. Published by R. R. Bowker Co., a Xerox company. Copyright © 1921 by Xerox Corporation.

M. THE FUTURE . . .

Dewey can be identified readily as a futurist among his peers, for he was surveying constantly the horizon for new trends and further extensions of services. Even in adversity, he anticipated things yet to come with an optimism not always shared by others in the profession.

As the twentieth century dawned, Dewey, like others, found it inviting to survey the past and meditate on the future. In 1901 he participated in a symposium on "Libraries in the Twentieth Century," making predictions on "libraries as bookstores," "libraries as publishers," "pictures," and "home education." Having thrust his audience into the future, he made the following comparison:

> When we look back a quarter century and realize that we have been living in what is distinctivly the library age of the world, we are amazed at the growth. To him whose vision is as keen looking forward as looking backward the magnificent results already accomplisht are exceeded by the almost sure promise of the still better things which are soon to be.

Such comparisons were typical of his enthusiasm and faith; once again in 1904, reporting on "Library Conditions in America," he concluded with the following vision of the future:

> We look back with pride and amazement on the progress of the last quarter century, but he is but a superficial observer of things bibliothecal who does not see that great as has been the accomplishment of the past there are in the quarter century just before us still greater things in store, plausible, practicable, more than probable.

When invited in 1903 to address the meeting of the Massachusetts and Western Massachusetts Library clubs, Dewey chose as his topic, "The Future of the Public Librarian." Through his imagery a new librarian emerged, an information expert, providing also inspirational and recreational materials, multi-media oriented, one who would "do his work, not by hand, but by machinery." Though he was not technologically skilled enough to predict the computer age, there is little doubt but that he would have welcomed it as readily as he had telephones and typewriters, the time-savers of his day.

Though long withdrawn from active involvement in the library profession, in 1926 he was invited to attend the Fiftieth Anniversary of the American Library Association and was among those "Five Men of '76" honored. Dewey was then seventy-five years old but remained young in spirit for, according to his birthday letter, he was "attacking . . . new and constantly broadening problems with the zeal and faith of twenty-five years ago."

With that zeal and faith Dewey delivered at the anniversary meeting what became his farewell address to the library world, "Our Next Half-Century." It was a symbolic and glorious finale for Dewey, reflecting the "clear, far-seeing vision of the dreamer" and the doer. His final question in his address continues to compel response from the generations that have succeeded him:

> Men and women of the American Library Association, what will you do with this stupendous fifty years ahead?

47. THE FUTURE OF THE PUBLIC LIBRARIAN

The future of the public librarian is largely dependent on the future of the book, the library, the reader, and the trustees—the factors with which he has largely to deal. Recent investigations on large numbers of children have shown that the chief influence on the life of the child, and through him on the citizen of the future came not from father, mother, teacher, or school, but from the reading of childhood. The librarian of the future, who guides more than any other force the reading of the community, therefore, holds in his hands the longest lever with which man has ever pried.

The old librarian stayed at home, usually both from preference and necessity. Now, and still more in the future, he travels, broadens his horizon, utilizes the experiments of others, and accomplishes more for his constituency with the time and money at his disposal by keeping in touch with what others are doing.

The librarian of the future in all the larger institutions will become a faculty just as the single teacher has developed into the college faculty, and he will use labor-saving devices and appliances wherever they are found practicable in saving time or money, so that we may fairly say that he will do his work, not by hand, but by machinery. Telephones, typewriters, card systems, fountain pens, and every practical aid will be brought into play as freely as they would in a manufactory or commercial office, for the librarian of the future will break loose entirely from the mediaeval traditions that seem to make it unprofessional for him to study minute economies. In the library, the reference librarian, himself a very recent and very valuable invention for helping the public, must be differentiated by subjects, for the demands of the public are so exacting that no human being could even pretend to be thoroughly familiar with the whole range of literature on a great variety of topics. The great libraries are assigning specialists to one department after another, as public demands warrant and we are developing in the national and in the leading states, and great central libraries, a system of library faculties destined to revolutionize some of our professional work.

Librarians are rapidly taking on their proper functions as book experts for their various constituencies. But the librarian is rapidly outgrowing the idea that he is concerned with books alone. The public pays its money, not to dignify books as such, but because it wishes information, or, still better, inspiration or innocent recreation, afforded in the best and cheapest way. This is oftenest through books, but pictures, specimens, classes, and lectures, and other means are found sometimes to be more effective or desirable. The library of the future is the recognized head of all these agencies, designed for old and young alike, to be had at home while engaged in other duties, as contrasted with the school education, designed only for the young for a limited course, and for those whose main business is to go to school.

Source: Melvil Dewey, "The Future of the Public Librarian," *Public Libraries* 8 (1903): 327-28.

48. OUR NEXT HALF-CENTURY

I am not sure in which capacity I am here. Forty-nine years ago in England, at every place we stopped, I was asked if I was the son of Melvil Dewey who had been so persistent in library work and now I meet people who ask if I am the father of the hard-working Melvil Dewey who is still under the harrow.

I have a little box in which I have been putting for some time notes of things I would like to say to the American Library Association and when Dr. Belden asked me to speak for thirty minutes at this meeting on Our Next Fifty Years, I said nothing would please me more. I took those notes out as I was leaving home, condensed them into five large pages of shorthand notes, and found if I were to tell you even briefly all the things I had saved up to tell you, my speech would not end till after the Sesquicentennial was closed for the season. So I am going to cut it down to one-tenth the amount (the decimal system, you know) because I found that even condensed, it would last till the Sesqui closed for the day. Therefore, I have put on a post card only a few of the topics that I wanted to mention briefly.

But first I can't resist telling you two stories of this famous city. Fifty years ago I came here to see the magnificent Ridgeway Branch Library just completed. I had urged that it be put in a more central location where readers could drop in most conveniently. But they built it off center. When I went in there with Lloyd P. Smith, the librarian, and looked over the great reading room expecting to see two or three hundred people busily at work I saw only three or four and said, "Is this the average attendance?"

He answered, "Dewey, there is scarcely a day that *somebody* doesn't come into this library."

Dr. Talcott Williams, long editor of the Philadelphia *Press*, was my assistant fifty-two years ago in Amherst College Library. He told me that one day a noted criminal for whom the police of the entire country were searching was in Philadelphia. This man alone had information which Dr. Williams knew would give him a great "scoop" over all the other papers of the country and a contract was made that that information should be given if Dr. Williams would securely hide the criminal from the police where he could not be found for 24 hours. Dr. Williams gave him a novel and sat him in the center of the big reading room and no one detected him.

Mr. Bowker's comments on Mr. Poole lead me to say that we ought today to pay our tribute to that Nestor of the library profession. We were often in antagonism, but he was a broad-shouldered, hard-hitting man who started many libraries and encouraged many librarians and in his day was easily the leader, and yet, Dr. Poole looked on this iridescent dream about the American Library Association and the things it might do with a feeling that the movement had one foot in the grave and the other foot on a banana peel. He declared that while our 1876 conference had been a great success we could not hope for another before 1900. I, the youngest of the delegates, insisted that our great possible future needed at least an annual meeting and that if five others would come we would hold it. And we did though once there were only thirty of us. You can imagine my joy in looking over this greatest audience in library history and seeing what the little movement has grown to. Fifty years of the past have put down the roots and brought bud and blossom and the fifty years to come will bear the fruit, if you who carry on the torch do your part. An Association like this is like a tree; when it ceases to grow it begins to rot. The tree may live on for a year or two, but the vital force is gone. It is dead. So we may not grow in numbers but unless we grow in strength and usefulness, A. L. A. is dead like the trees we sometimes see that are really dead though they may still put forth their leaves.

As I look forward to the next fifty years (I had a couple of hours of prophecies I wanted to make in my thirty minutes and I must get them into five minutes for my predecessors on this program have already used all my time), I think the first important step is to win complete public acceptance of the theory we have been preaching for fifty years, that this world will never be made better by mere police and soldiers and legislation. It can be done only by making people wish the better things, and that process *is* education.

Source: Melvil Dewey, "Our Next Half-Century," *ALA Bulletin* 20 (1926): 309-12. Permission to reprint obtained from the American Library Association.

We must make the public understand that the things that center round the library are just as much a part of complete education as are the schools. Many people think of schools as being the only source of education. But they are not. On the other side are the libraries, the museums, study clubs for mutual help and extension teaching. When the public realizes this broader conception of real education and gives it proper support, we shall see repeated the process which has been going on during all the growth of the public school system.

Long ago we had private schools, church schools, public school societies, and endowed academies. Even in my own time, I remember when public education was finally recognized as the most important thing that could be done for the Empire State and so should be paid for by the state. "The public schools are free" was sung in every town when Victor M. Rice won his fight to abolish tuition. And libraries are going through just the same evolution.

We had various libraries, club, society, church, college, proprietary, circulating, and subscription as we had had all kinds of schools. But the library free to all was a great new idea that is spreading all over the world.

We had public library societies and associations just as we had had similar public school societies to convert the tax payers to the free school idea. Thus in the fifty years we celebrate today, the public has, and chiefly through A. L. A. influences, largely come to recognize the free public library just as important as the school.

From the infancy of the race there are certain things every child surely calls for. "Give me a ride." His mother carries him in her arms or rocks him in the cradle. This instinct to ride has evolved into canoes, sail and motor boats, submarines and steamships; into baby carriages, coaches, motor cars, railways and pullmans; into airplanes and dirigibles.

"Tell me a story!" Mother's simple narration has evolved into the entrancing tales of biography, travel, and history and supremely into the short story and novel and the modern magazine and weekly circulating millions of each issue.

"Sing me a song!" That is the part of library work that now most needs rapid development. From it have grown all musical instruments from the Pipe of Pan to reproducing pianos, victrolas, and radios and supreme in this kingdom of harmony pipe organs and symphony orchestras.

Then as the child grows older, "Tell me the news!" From that has evolved the miracle of the newspaper giving for a cent or two news from the entire world at each breakfast table.

Next came the questions "What?" ' How?" and from them have come the information desk, the cyclopedia, and reference books that give information and build power and efficiency.

Then seventh, that greatest question to which human souls demand an answer. "Why?" And the reply must be sought in philosophy, religion, and their handmaids.

Satisfactory answers to these seven fundamental needs must be sought for all (except the riding) in the library of the future. The name library will stand although the thing may change very much.

This library of the future has as its chief function to find and train leaders. The world has learned that government by inexperienced councils or committees whose chief ability is to get elected is inefficient and wasteful. City managers, club managers, who are real leaders and are allowed to lead are giving the best results. Many a librarian is crippled by "too much trustees." Nathan Hale of the Boston Public Library used to say, when the board was about to pass some unwise vote: "Boards are long and narrow; they are made of wood." But I must add my tribute to the many trustees who serve the public best by loyal support of the executive wisely chosen to guide the work.

Our greatest need in librarianship is real leaders and to such should be given the power to lead.

Look at Italy, Spain, Turkey, and Belgium and the spreading movement that in all large affairs is calling for men big enough to hold the helm with a strong hand. When I say "men" I think of the majority of them as women for they have learned and are doing more and more executive work. In my own experience for sixty years, I have found woman most unselfish, most willing to give her life work for the highest public good. In the future great library concert, above the notes of bass and baritone the soaring dominant note will be a clear soprano.

For our jubilee librarianship has this year received great gifts of four millions that our work and chiefly our library schools may go on with new strength and efficiency. Their chief work now is to train leaders, captains, colonels, and now and then a great general. Experts say the world's destiny is shaped by not over one in a million. If this startles you, write down for our one hundred and twenty million Americans the one hundred and twenty names of men and women whom you consider our greatest leaders. Then think how if you blot out their whole influence you would change the history of this great nation and of the world. It was not till they made Foch the leader that we won the Great War. The thing librarianship needs more than anything else is great leaders who are inspiring. Had it not been for the Civil War, Ulysses S. Grant would be unknown. Yet when another great strife came, we cried, "God grant us another Grant." We must hunt for undeveloped genius for often it has no self-starter.

Fifty years ago when it was suggested that we throw away books no longer in use, we laughed at it as ridiculous for a normal librarian's instinct is to keep every book and pamphlet. He knows that possibly some day, somebody may want it. But in many places we are facing physical limitations. At the recent meeting of the British Association, it was said "the greatest concern of scientists is about cemeteries and libraries." Cremation solved the problem of growing cemeteries, but the mind is appalled to see what will be later when there are now 23,000 scientific periodicals published every year.

President Eliot expressed the fear based on the rapid growth of the card catalogs of Harvard and the Boston Public Library that they would some day meet about the middle of the Charles River bridge.

Most librarians are inclined to make a book something sacred. But we ought to recognize and employ it as a tool to be used not a fetish to be worshipped. The public wants certain things done the way they can be done best, cheapest, and quickest, and if libraries can do this, then that is the proper function. At least a small library should be in easy reach of every citizen. A storehouse library to preserve books very seldom needed should be in every state or great university. But if a competent jury sat on all that is printed in books, magazines, and newspapers, more than ninety per cent of it would go back to the paper mill.

Perhaps the library of fifty years from now will have outgrown the present book and relegated it to the museum with the older inscriptions on clay. The enemies of the book and of reading grow apace. Radio, movies, and various devices are making short cuts to what books have been doing. Our great function is to inform or to inspire, or to please; to give to the public in the quickest and cheapest way information, inspiration, and recreation on the highest plane. If a better way than the books is found we should use it.

In his report on the movie theater, published recently, Will Hays said that there are 23,000 of them with ninety million people attending them every week, with an income of a thousand million dollars each year and growing rapidly. I have this week heard the Vitaphone, where the moving picture speaks in natural tones, synchronizing perfectly with the action. If we can carry information or inspiration or recreation to human beings better or quicker or cheaper, we are bound to adopt that means.

I am a thorough optimist. They say that the optimist makes stepping-stones of obstacles to find his way to the other side of the stream that bars his way. The optimist finds the wolf at the door and comes out next day with a new fur coat.

If the movies are teaching so many millions a week *not* to read, let us utilize this great method, for the motion picture, decried and abused by many is one of the greatest agencies for education man has yet devised. A bad book is as efficient for evil, as a good book is for good, but no iconoclast preaches against books as books. It is only against their misuse.

If I were to say one-tenth of the things that are crowding into my mind on this subject, you would lose your lunch and your patience. But I must add that the American Library Association has made a wonderful record in the fifty years past. Its future is still larger and better. When we think of what has been done in the past and what is being done in our own time, we should not be staggered at anything that is good however fanciful it may seem at first.

Harvard recently announced a new measurement on the far confines of the universe beyond all our dreams. If you put on this new chart the distance from the earth to the sun, what our minds would grasp as one inch in distance would be twelve million miles.

Everywhere we turn, science is making these astounding strides that seem like Munchausen tales. Harvard has succeeded in measuring the heat of a candle fifty miles distant, and our U. S. Bureau of Standards easily measures the added weight of a dot on i. When proven science shows us these startling things we ought not to fear to look at fifty library years ahead, which will be vastly more fruitful than the fifty that are behind in which we justly take so much pride. We should adopt the motto of the Fabian Society of London. "For the right moment you must wait most patiently as Fabius did when warring against Hannibal though many censured his delays. But when the right moment comes, you must *strike hard*, else your waiting will have been in vain and fruitless."

There is a tremendous work in this broader education to be done. To do it is the birthright of the American Library Association, and unless we do it, the other agencies—voluntary societies, churches, and others—may attempt it. It is a great work and it will require persistent patience and steady application for many years after we veterans of the old guard have gone into the silence.

"Heaven is not reached by a single bound;
But we *build* the ladder by which we rise
From the lowly earth to the vaulted skies,
And we *climb* to its summit round by round."

The A. L. A. has this wonderful opportunity. If you look at the library problem of the next fifty years, serene, clear-eyed, and unafraid, you will see it.

Men and women of the American Library Association, what will you do with this stupendous fifty years ahead?

N. THE REMEMBERED PAST

With the commencement of his sixteenth year (1866) Dewey began to keep a journal of his activities and his thoughts. While the entries became less frequent between then and 1877, for a few years he wrote a summary statement on each birthday—an inventory of his possessions, of his financial status, and of his height and weight.

His thoughts written on the eve of his eighteenth birthday indicate that the young Dewey had decided definitely not to enter the ministry, and he repeated his wish made earlier to devote his life to "a higher education for the masses." Thus his pattern of recording something very personal on or near his birthday was established before he went to Amherst.

In his seventy-fifth birthday letter, dated New Years 1927, he mused:

> The secret of my perennial youth is becauz I hav from child hood always workt fast and long hours, but hav never worried. I hav always been a total abstainer from liquor, tobacco, tea, coffee and condiments, and hav been a small eater and larj sleeper. I used [to] tel my college classes that the old rule was 6 hours for a man, 7 for a woman, 8 for a child, 9 for a fool. I like 10. Perhaps becauz I believ so firmly in decimals, of which I hav been a life-long advocate and activ missionary. I was born Dec. 10, 1851, the anniversary of the deposit of the prototyp meter in the Palace of the Archives in Paris. In 1872 I devised my decimal classification and publisht it 1st in 1876. It is now used by 14,000 public and private libraries, studies and offices in a score of cuntries. I am so loyal to decimals as our great labor saver that I even like to sleep decimally.

He concluded the letter with the observation that:

> You naturally myt expect a swan song, but here I hav written not an obituary but a prospectus.

In reality it was the eightieth birthday letter that was his "swan song." In it he summarized, in his very special hyperbolic style, his achievements of the preceding decades. Perhaps the things he identified were the things for which he wanted to be remembered. Curiously he omitted references to his founding of the Columbia College School of Library Economy or its transfer to Albany as the New York State Library School, except in the postscript to his letter; instead he made a passing reference only to "my old librari skool graduates." Omitted also are references to his contributions to the educational reforms and library developments in New York State, his years as Secretary to the Board of Regents of the University of the State of New York, or to the New York State Library. Despite these curious omissions, the letter remains a striking example of Dewey's vitality and indestructible optimism.

The final selection in this book is Godfrey Dewey's remembrance of his father, a short essay prepared for the 75th Anniversary celebration of the American Library Association and the centennial year of Melvil Dewey's birth.

49. [MELVIL DEWEY'S EIGHTIETH BIRTHDAY LETTER]

80th birthday letr 10 Dec 31, to a fu personal frends
from our Florida branch,
7 Lakes, Lake Placid, Hylands Co, Fla

Today starts my 9th decade. When my Albany staf celebrated my 5th decade I felt fairli mature.

At 80 owing to the 5 winters I hav spent in this best clymat on erth I don't feel as old. My jeneral helth (& Emily's) is betr than for years. I can't (& don't) run as fast or as far, don't work 3 ½-days a m, p m & eve, can't stand as long hours, take a nap except when I forget it, having lernd that mor can be dun by not crowding the 80 year old machine too fast. My purpose all thru thez 80 years has been to shape my personal habits so to get qualiti & quantiti results. 2 shorter ½ days at my big desk made for me 40 years ago ar reducing arears of mani things I thot important to clean up whyl I stil hav my apetyt for work. So whyl the world has mor to wori about than ever befor in human histori I am bizi & hapi, not becauz I am indiferent to thez present problems but becauz my mind is skoold not to wori. I profit by De Stael's dictum:

'The sumit of human hapines is to feel each nyt yu hav made sum progres toward a worthi ideal.'

A glance today over mor than 60 years shows nyt & day, erli & late givn entyrli to what it seemd wd best serv the future. 40 years ago we counted 15 local, state or national organizations or movements of which the chief load was on me & my wyf had ½ as mani mor. Our wyz fizician fearing overstrain or posibl break made us both turn over most of thez jobs to associates.

In all thez most of the real work has been dun by unusuali loyal co-workers. My share has been lyk a gadfly, to prod others into aktion. So the world has always givn me mor than my share of credit. Mani of thez loyal associates hav been jenerus in saying that they wer inspyrd rather than stung into their activ cooperation. Among skors of movements started or led by me 5 ar prominent.

In 1876 youthful zeal led me to start 3 national education societies, American Library Asn, American Metric Bureau, Speling Reform Asn, 3 periodicals, & also Library Bureau. Most of the worthi co-workers who helpt cari on the torch during thez 55 years hav gone into the silence; but a fu with me ar stil holding our forts or trenches.

Librari Critisyzd for trying the imposibl in starting American Library Asn, for 15 years maid of all work & without salari, my burning faith & optimism kept the tredmil turning. Our monthli Librari Journal to which was givn 5 strenuus years, twys in anser to its SOS when the publisher anounst its suspension, was kept alive by great personal sacrifys, til it has gone on to 56 stout volumes that hav playd a great part in the modern librari movement which from our beginnings has spred over much of the world.

Our ambition in 1876 was to get 100 members to an anual meeting. This year ther wer over 3000.

We felt rich with our first $100 gift. Now we count milions in our own direkt work besides hundreds of milions spent on nu libraries.

Since rezyning as NY state direktor of libraries 25 years ago my interest keeps up, but after 30 years on the firing lyn it has been a joy to see from the syd lyns the marvelus progres of this great modern librari movement & the larj fraktion of leadership by my old librari skool graduates & by my former activ co-worker associates.

Decimal Classification This was my chief work in Amherst from 1873 to '76. It was a radical departure from establisht methods but without advertyzing or ajents its great efisiensi has carid it to 14,000 users in 20 nations. The Librari Survey of 1926 found that this great laborsaver was used in 96% of public libraries & 89% of colej libraries; Cutter sistem in 20 public & 4 colej; Librari of Congres sistem in 3 public & 14 colej.

Source: Melvil Dewey, "80th Birthday letr 10 Dec 31, to a fu personal frends from our Florida Branch, 7 Lakes, Lake Placid, Hylands Co, Fla." Copy in files of Dr. Godfrey Dewey and of Deo B. Colburn, Lake Placid Club, New York.

Metric Since we started Metric Bureau in '76 international decimal measures gaind stedili til Japan & Russia recentli completed the list of 55 nations, the whol civilyzd world except Britain & America that shd hav been at hed insted of tail of this reform. But we gain each year & our absurd weits & measures wil soon be replaced by metric. Stedi work from our central ofis, 156 5th av, NY, promises erli succes.

Speling Skolars agree that we hav the most unsyentifik, unskolarli, illojikal & wasteful speling ani languaj ever ataind. But everi year shows progres & old workers of '76 rejoice that all competent educators now admit this to be the most vital problem in universal education & in making simplifyd English the universal world languaj. LP Club has long been headquarters for all 3 national societies for ridding English of its worst obstakls in overcuming illiterasi & becuming the world languaj.

Literari labor savers In '76 my plan was sneerd at as 'Dewey's jimcraks.' Its first year sold a total of $300. This grew to $15,000,000 a year & then merjd with Remington typwriter & other similar concerns. Its growing beneficent servis has spred to most other nations. As founder of Librari Bureau in '76 my presidensi continued 25 years. Since then I hav not ownd a share of its stok. It has been parent of mani imitators but the world stil knows it as first to 'sel methods rather than merchandise.' My experience in Librari Bureau led to my elektion during war tym as president of both national efisiensi societies & also to making our Foundation's chief work Seedsowing including laborsavers.

Lake Placid Club 53 years ago we began planning an ideal vacation home for thoz doing sum worthi work but needing nu helth & strength to cari on efisientli. After 16 years serch for the veri best location we found Lake Placid 40 years ago. There in 1895 we started with onli $500 cash & for peopl who believd in our unusual standards & ideals, what is now known as the leading famili cooperativ club of the world.

From 30 peopl in a rented house on 5 akers it grew to 412 bildings on 10,600 akers & from $4800 total biznes the first year to over 3 milions anuali. Most peopl think of it as simpli a fyn summer & winter resort but in fakt that was my smallest interest. But it has grown so prominent that most peopl forget its real object & carakter. Insted of sending its big Handbook enclozd 8 pajes giv my real object. Remember it has grown rapidli for 7 years since this was printed in 1924.

In 1922 my entyr voting stok was givn to found our LPC Education Foundation. Later everithing els I ownd made up an initial endowment of a milion. My lyf work is thus just geting fairli started. Each year our members giv mor & mor to this Foundation which now owns the entyr group of corporations known as Lake Placid Club.

Northwood, our Club boys skool, is alredi among the veri best.

7 Lakes, our Florida branch Club Frends who had watcht our fenomenal Adirondak growth gave our Foundation 3000 akers on 7 Lakes which we had chosen after long studi & motoring 20,000 myls in the south, as best subtropic location in America for a famili club with our unusual ideals & methods. With other gifts this Florida branch endowment was estimated worth ultimateli a milion. The lejislature chanjd the name of the best location on the famus Florida Rij to Lake Placid & gave with remarkabl powers of control a town charter for 50,000 akers on its 30 lakes.

Here we ar hapili bizi duplicating the parent Adirondak Club. Our counsel who helps us greatli with wyz advys, with mor truth than polytnes sed to our direktors: 'That youth is 80 & just wel started on a nu 50 year job.'

But I tel them *my* job is *Seedsowing*, to plant & start helthi growth but not to wait to see mature trees.

My wyf, Annie Godfrey, was always an equal partner. We began this Club vision at our mariaj in '78. Our beautiful granit chapel bilt as her memorial, resyts she was co-founder of the Club, 'serene, clear-eyed & unafraid.' For 44 years she left on the Club the impres of her practical wisdom, taste & unfaltering faith. We had always agreed that whichever went first the other shd cari on our plans. Her chief associate & closest frend, Emily Beal of Boston, came to us 15 years ago as vicepresident & jeneral manajer. 7 years ago we marid & she also has stampt her personaliti on both parent Club & Florida branch of which she, 25 years yunger than I, is real hed as vicepresident & trezurer.

I hav never graspt the thot that sum day I shd 'retyr.' I am neither just waiting for nor dreding the sumons. I tel my staf that perhaps I wil retyr at 100 thus giving me 20 mor years of activ work. Each day starts exaktli as if ther wer 20 mor years. My vigorus wyf is at the helm & is a skilful enjineer as wel as steersman. We get daili reports from the parent Club wher we hav turnd over activ manajment to the veri efisient gydans of the 3 best vicepresidents that hav grown up with us. Tho in constant tuch with all main Club problems we ar unworid even in thez trublus tyms of world-wyd depresion.

Godfrey, my onli child, now 44, has becum US leader in simpler speling. For 2 years he has givn praktikali all his tym as prime mover in getting the World Olympics at Lake Placid next Feb 4-13 & is president of the Olympic committee. He is deepli interested in most of the work to which I hav givn my lyf. I believ he wil render valiant servis toward making this a betr world.

All thez 'cauzes' for which I hav workt for a lyftym stil ar 'my children' & I am justli proud of what they hav alredi dun & even mor am inspired by the clear vision vouchsafed me of their future.

Each year starting, Oct 15, we motor from Placid north to 7 Lakes, our Florida branch, wher we liv from Nov 1 to May 1. My fizicians tel me (& we ar also certain from 5 years experience) that this best clymat on erth wil ad a dozen years to my lyf.

I just brekfasted in our patio surrounded with brilliant flowers; gorjus flame vine covers the pergola & bronz bouganvillea (rose catalina) drapes the sun porch wher we spend most of our waking hours when not at our desks. 4000 akers of Peerles Placid declared by experts the best of Florida's 30,000 lakes is 800 ft east & 50 lower at the foot of our broad lawns & golf cours. Our grounds border for 1½ myls Lake June-in-winter. We liv ideali in real June days.

Enclozd notes wil giv an idea of wher we liv. We hope to see yu here & also at our big Adirondak Club.

My pet aunt used to tel me 60 years ago that her great ambition was to gro old beautifuli & she did. But mine is not to gro old at all in spirit & faith in the ultimat triumf of the best things. Melvil Dewey is not a watch that wears out to be discarded but lyk a sun dial wher no wheels get rusti or slip a cog or get tired & long for rest. I'l send another 5 years letr on my 85th.

With all compliments of this Xmas season.

Cordiali
Melvil Dewey

PS to my 80th birthday letr.

My mother taut me 'praiz to the face is an open disgrace' & it has been a lyf-long fad to avoid personal compliments. When Grosvenor Dawe, ex-editor of Nation's Business of the US Chamber of Commerce, sugjested that the Quest Society of Fla, (whose objekt is to call atention to thoz who hav renderd unusual public servis) wd lyk to make a pilgrimaj to 7 Lakes on my 80th birthday I begd him as a personal frend not to do it & supozd it was dropt. I mimeod an 8 p letr that I thot sum frends wd read & pland my usual ful day's work.

My usual erli strol to the beach showd a beautiful 30 or 40 year old palm not ther the day befor. My Adirondak staf had wired the state expert on moving trees, he knew of this rare specimen, bo't it, bro't it 60 myls with his big transplanting machine & got it set without my discoveri.

Then came a volume of letrs from my staf that tucht me deepli.

Then the ex-president of the alumni of my Librari Skool came in person to deliver from leading alumni & former associates over 100 letrs magnificentli bound in ful toold turki. Then Quest Society ofisers & leaders apeard with their warm personal greetings & left another volume of letrs from librarians.

On my 75th Fla State Librari Asn gave me a wonderful day at their Orlando meeting. Their ex-president bro't another group over 100 myls for my 80th.

Then came a shower of letrs sent too late for the volumes & a long fusilade of telegrams. Over 300 letrs & 100 wires wer from 40 states besyds the forin cuntries.

What pleazd me most was an undertone runing thru them that they wer not looking bak on a job completed, but had confidence that I wd never drop my harnes & 'retyr' but was starting my 9th decade with my lyf-long spirit of looking out not in, forward not bak, up not down.

Columbia Univ anounst for the 1st Librari Skool in the world which I started ther in 1887, that a founder's day meeting wd be held each Dec 10 hereafter. When I go thru NY each May they hav held a moveabl founder's day & brot together the combynd classes for a full hour's talk folowd by a reception. The skool, now 20 tyms larjer than our 1st year, lyks to meet the old 'pyoneer' & it inspires me to grasp their hands & bid them 'cari on the torch.'

Then came report of anual founder's day at our Northwood skool with its series of adreses by faculti & students renewing their plejes to maintain our unusual standards. Fynali a nu founder's day was started. My 70th was celebrated ther by a jeneral meeting of the parent Club with speeches & gift of a great silver luving cup. They naturali supozd that having past 70 it was my valedictori but evidentli hav desyded that I am an almost permanent fixtur. Besyd other features our direktor of music gave a resytal of my favorit numbers on the memorial organ & also on the Forest Towers chimes.

For 60 years known as leading apostl of decimals, 10 seems to pursue me for even my 8 paje letr has grown to the mistik 10. With television yu myt see me blush with this deluje of items so veri personal.

Thez meni things reali seem to me not my own work, for 60 years ago I anounst dreams of doing varius important things for which my 1 lyf was not enuf. Insted of doing them myself my job was to inspyr others to do the real work so I cd thus raiz myself to the 2d power. If we cd develop 1 nu efisient worker yearli, in 50 years 50 jobs cd be done. So I hav always been indiferent as to *who* did the work or receivd the credit. From the 1st my whol concern was that *sumone* shd do it. I cared mereli for results.

50. GODFREY DEWEY'S TRIBUTE TO HIS FATHER

To sketch in a few words a recognizable picture of as many-sided a genius as my father, Melvil Dewey, is no easy task. Merely to list the major interests with which he was actively concerned, giving a single sentence to each, would take too much space, yet their very number and importance and diversity is a significant measure of the man.

Before he was 25 years old, he had developed and published the first edition of the Decimal Classification, had established the *Library Journal*, and had been the most dynamic factor in the founding of 3 national organizations—the American Library Association, the Spelling Reform Association, and the Metric Bureau (Lj, March 15, 1951, p. 457). Before he was 40, the mid point of his life span, he had established the Library Bureau, which in addition to its primary function, brought into general use for the first time such today universal labor savers as the card index, vertical file, and loose-leaf binder; had created at Columbia University the first Library School and transferred it to Albany as the New York State Library School; had become Secretary of the Regents of the University of the State of New York, in charge of all higher education in the State, and had put thru the Legislature a revision and consolidation of the education laws of the State which affected the Regents; and was at the same time Director of the State Library, the State Library School, and the new Home Education (today we would say Adult Education) Department which he had created. Within 10 years more he had received from the 1900 Paris Exposition, three of the very few Grands Prix awarded to this country—one for his Library Exhibit, one for his Home Education Exhibit, and one to himself personally; and had created and guided thru its early years the institution which for the last 25 years of his life was to become the focus of his immense energies—the world-famous Lake Placid Club.

To summarize briefly the outstanding personal characteristics of an individual as original and forceful as Melvil Dewey, is hardly less difficult, and brief statements must often read like a series of contradictions, for the contradictions were there.

My father had a rare gift of inspiring intense and lasting loyalties on the part of his associates and co-workers and even among more casual contacts. Yet, thruout most of his life, he was rarely witout a harassing number of enemies. Some few of these represented hostility to the scrupulous integrity which he maintained in his official positions. More, probably, resulted from occasional failures in tact or patience. Still more, however, undoubtedly derived from the driving energy which was his most distinctive characteristic and which was constantly insisting on putting thru desirable or desired measures forthwith, regardless of the resistance which might be engendered, rather than to await some vague and indefinitely remote more favorable opportunity. One trait which mitigated somewhat the consequences of these adverse reactions was his longstanding preference for working in the background as secretary of a movement or committee, or in no official position, rather than as president or chairman. Always he was glad to have the credit for any achievement go to anyone who might thereby be motivated to work more effectively for it; for his own motivation, it was sufficient to see that the desired result was achieved.

Determination and persistence in achieving a desired end, coupled with an unshakable confidence in his own judgment, both as to end and means, plus an almost incredible skill in rationalizing his purposes (interestingly described in chapter 13 of Fremont Rider's ALA biography, *Melvil Dewey*) was perhaps the keynote of his personality and achievements. Fortunate it was that his judgment was so often right, for he nearly always, sooner or later, achieved his goal. One did not say "no" to father, unless one was prepared to make a life work of it, and I have often heard him ascribe his success with the unique Lake Placid Club, to having listened patiently to much conventional good advice and then done exactly the opposite.

If space permitted, much could be said of his lifelong passion for efficiency and economy—he called it his "Scotch"—which ranged all the way from Library Bureau and what he called "literary labor-savers" to simpler spelling of English, the metric system, and the world calendar.

Source: Godfrey Dewey, "Dewey, 1851-1951," *Library Journal* 76 (1951): 1964-65. Reprinted from *Library Journal* 1951. Published by R. R. Bowker Co., a Xerox company. Copyright © 1951 by Xerox Corporation.

Finally, among the outstanding personal characteristics summarized in these few brief words it should be noted as helping to explain the extraordinary range of Melvil Dewey's interests and achievements, that creation was always the breath of life to him, his chief reward and satisfaction in life. Once an idea or an organization was established and functioning smoothly, its possibilities measurably realized, let somebody else run it. No more than Tennyson's "Ulysses" could he rest idly on his laurels. Always it was for him, until the end—

> Tis not too late to seek a newer world.
> Push off . . . my purpose holds
> To sail beyond the sunset, and the paths
> Of all the Western stars, until I die.

PART III

BIBLIOGRAPHY

Most of Dewey's manuscripts, including drafts of many of his writings, his correspondence, his business transactions, records of his Columbia College days, his Albany years, and his Lake Placid Club activities, are in the Rare Book and Manuscript Library, Division of Special Collections, Columbia University Libraries, Columbia University, New York. "The Melvil Dewey Papers Calendar" lists 110 boxes (numbers 1-104 plus 6 inserts) and 73 pamphlet boxes (P-1–P-73).

Letters from Dewey will be found also in the archives of the University of Illinois among the papers of Andrew S. Draper and of Katharine Lucinda Sharp; and among the papers of William Dawson Johnston (62-4538) and others at the Library of Congress. Other sources include the archives of the American Library Association, now located at the University of Illinois; the Lake Placid Club; Forest Press, Inc.; and the personal files of Godfrey Dewey and of Deo B. Colburn.

Dewey's enduring contribution to librarianship continues to be his *Decimal Classification*, the first edition of which (1876) has become a classic. Despite this, he wrote little on classification and entrusted much of the continuing revision to his associates, Walter S. Biscoe, May Seymour, and later, Dorkas Fellows. Somewhat ironically, however, Dewey's other writings, ranging from notes of utmost practicality to vast insight into the future, have been overshadowed by the *Classification* and the criticisms which each revision has engendered.

Though remembered as a man of action, Dewey found time to be both an author and an editor, and, in his editorial capacity, Dewey found another outlet for expressing his own ideas or for melding the diversified views of others. Throughout his professional career, he was involved in one editorial responsibility or another, with a brief interlude between the years 1881 and 1886, as 1) editor of periodicals, 2) editor of columns within periodicals, 3) as editor of two books.

EDITOR OF PERIODICALS

Dewey's editorial career extended from 1876, when he became associated with the *American Library Journal* (later *Library Journal*) through 1909, after which time his name disappeared from the title page of *The Library*, a journal with which he had been involved since 1900. The following chart identifies the dates of his association with periodicals and editorial positions held:

Periodical and Editorial Positions Held

1876-1880	*The Library Journal.* v. 1-5. Sept. 1876-December 1880. New York: F. Leypoldt, 1876-1880. Managing Editor: vols. 1-4, nos. 1-6, 1876-1879. General Editor:
	With R. R. Bowker v.4, nos. 7-8–v.5, nos. 1-6, 1879-1880.
	With F. Leypoldt v.5, nos. 6-7 [i.e., 7-8] – nos. 11-12, 1880.
1879-1880	*Readers and Writers Economy Notes.* v. 1-2, no. 4. March 1879-April 1880. Boston: 1879-1880.

Dewey incorporated the Readers and Writers Economy Company in 1879 and served briefly as president, treasurer, and sole manager. In October 1880 he withdrew from the Company, but during his short association he edited the *Readers and Writers Economy Notes*, the first issue of which

Periodical and Editorial Positions Held (cont'd)

was entitled *Economy Club Notes*. Later, one of his editorial columns in *Library Notes* reflected his association with the Company, "Literary Methods and Labor-Savers for Readers and Writers."

1886-1898   *Library Notes: Improved Methods and Labor-Savers for Librarians, Readers and Writers.* Edited by Melvil Dewey. v. 1-4, June 1886-Sept. 1898. Boston: Library Bureau, 1887-1898.

Dewey edited 16 numbers of *Library Notes*, beginning while he was at Columbia College and later after he had assumed his extensive responsibilities in Albany. Not only did he fulfill his chief editorial duties, he was "responsible for all unsigned matter except in the advertising pages."

[1896-1931   *Libraries: A Monthly Review of Library Matters and Methods.* v. 1-36, May 1896-1931. Chicago: Library Bureau [1896-1931]. v. 1-25: *Public Libraries.*

Dewey's unacclaimed sponsorship of the new journal, *Public Libraries* (later *Libraries*), beginning two years before the demise of his *Library Notes*, both published by Library Bureau, suggests that he offered editorial advice and guidance to the editor, Mary Eileen Ahern. Dewey wrote in 1931 that he had "diskust with her ernestli the policies & form of the nu periodical" and that "she has always abyded by the program I urjd when as founder of Library Bureau I was consulted as to the nu journal."]

1900-1909   *The Library: A Quarterly Review of Bibliography and Library Lore.* New series, v.1-10, 1900-1909. London: Alexander Moring, 1900-09. (Reprinted in 1966 by Krauss Reprint, Ltd., Nedeln, Liechtenstein).

Dewey considered himself the American editor of *The Library*, although his name appears on the title page of the issues of the "new series" as "in collaboration with . . . Melvil Dewey." While the extent of his collaboration has not been verified fully, it is evident that he added international prestige, as did the other collaborators. He also contributed essays, one being his "Printed Catalogue Cards from a Central Bureau." In the third series, v. 1-10, 1910-1919, Dewey is listed as a member of the Advisory Committee.

EDITOR OF COLUMNS WITHIN PERIODICALS

The columns he edited reveal Dewey's awareness of the need for pragmatic and current information. However far-ranging his vision, he was able to report

on timely and routine matters, to share his views and experiences, and to welcome
response from readers. The major columns (some of which appeared irregularly),
the dates of his editorship, and the periodicals in which they appeared are listed
below:

Column Title	Dates	Periodical
"Notes and Queries"	1876-1880	*American Library Journal* 1 (1876/1877)
		Library Journal 2-5 (1877/ 1878-1880)
"Editor's Notes"	1886-1898	*Library Notes* 1-4 (1886-1898)
"Library Economy"		
"Literary Methods and Labor-Savers for Readers and Writers"		
"Progress"		
"Library Notes"	1898-1909	*Public Libraries* 3-14 (1898-1909)

EDITOR OF BOOKS

Dewey's name appears as editor of two significant titles: *Papers Prepared
for the World's Library Congress* (1896) and *A.L.A. Catalog: 8,000 Volumes
for a Popular Library, with Notes* (1904).

American Library Association. "Papers Prepared for the World's Library Congress
[held at the Columbian Exposition, Chicago, 1893. Edited by Melvil Dewey],"
In U.S. Bureau of Education. *Report of the Commissioner of Education for the
Year, 1892-93*. Washington: Government Printing Office, 1895. v. 1, parts I
and II, Chapter ix, pp. 691-1014. (U.S. Bureau of Education. Whole Number 217).
(Reprinted as a separate, with Dewey's name as editor on the title page, in 1896).
 The project, initiated by Dewey while he was serving as President of the
 American Library Association (1892/93), was designed as a handbook
 of library economy. William T. Harris, Commissioner of Education, praised
 the "Papers" as "a unique and valuable treatise on the general subject
 of the management of libraries." In addition, the "Papers" furnish a select
 "who's who" of the times and provide valuable information on late
 nineteenth century librarianship. Dewey meticulously exercised his
 editorial privilege throughout the "Papers," not by supplementing or
 modifying the text of each paper, but by adding his observations in
 footnotes.

American Library Association. *A.L.A. Catalog: 8,000 Volumes for a Popular
Library, with Notes*. 1904. Prepared by the New York State Library and the
Library of Congress under the Auspices of the American Library Association

Publishing Board. Editor: Melvil Dewey . . . Part 1: Classed. Part 2: Dictionary. Washington: Government Printing Office, 1904. 2 v. in 1.

> The publication of the 1904 *A.L.A. Catalog* brought to an end Dewey's commitment to make available to libraries a list of the "best books with compact notes indicating scope, character, and value." The genesis of his commitment is found in his 1877 essay on "The Coming Catalogue."* The publication was made possible when the New York State Library assumed responsibility for the editorial work under the direction of May Seymour and the Library of Congress agreed to share in its printing and distribution.

DEWEY AS AUTHOR

It was through his personal writings that Dewey expressed himself freely. Dorothy Parker at one time characterized Dewey as among the few with an originating brain; it was a characteristic confirmed by the vision and scope of his writings in their goal if not always in the realization of their ideas. His writings reflect his skill in detailing routines when necessary, in distilling his own ideas and those of others, in compelling action and reaction, and in foreseeing trends of the future. Though many of his writings are little read and infrequently cited, they contain the origin of, or the stimulation for, many current views and movements—significantly, his commitment to the view that the public library is an integral part of the state educational system.

The accompanying citations are a contribution to a definitive bibliography of Dewey's writings on librarianship. Omitted are references to annual reports which he prepared as Secretary of the American Library Association, his committee reports, his annual reports prepared while at Columbia College and later in Albany as Secretary of the Regents of the University of the State of New York, as Director of the New York State Library and of the Library School. Also omitted are numerous publications bearing the imprint of the New York State Library issued during his incumbency as State Librarian. References to some of Dewey's remarks or comments made during meetings of the American Library Association are included, though a thorough analysis has not yet been attempted.

In 1884 Dewey observed that many of his writings had been unsigned and also that "several little books, published under other names, are also to quite an extent my work." Many years later, in 1931, he informed Margaret Zenk and Roby Blair, who had compiled a bibliography of his writings, that:

> Your list is long but ther ar 100s of anonimus things that hav been printed & which no one has ani record of or ani means of making 1.

---

*Dewey referred to the *Catalog of the "A.L.A." Library: 5,000 Volumes for a Popular Library*. Selected by the American Library Association and Shown at the World's Columbian Exposition (Washington: Government Printing Office, 1896) as an "imperfect first edition without notes" of the 1904 *A.L.A. Catalog*. Though Dewey was supportive of the *Catalog*, his name appears neither in the "Letter of Transmittal," signed by W. T. Harris, nor in the "Introduction."

Their bibliography, dated Pittsburgh, Pa., 1932, is included in G. G. Dawe, *Melvil Dewey: Seer; Inspirer; Doer, 1851-1931.* Biografic Compilation. Club Edition (Lake Placid Club, N.Y.: Melvil Dewey Biografy, 1932. pp. 367-84). Though the bibliography contains some errors and has numerous duplicate entries, it provides a basic alphabetic listing of Dewey's writings.

The bibliography below is arranged chronologically. Within each year the following divisions are used, where appropriate:

> *Books, Chapters in Books*
> *Library Journal*
> *Library Notes*
> *Public Libraries (later: Libraries)*
> *Other Periodical Sources*

Within each division entries are arranged alphabetically. References to reprints of Dewey's essays follow the chronological arrangement. The bibliography is, as Dewey might have noted, a "typwritn movie" of the progression of his ideas during his years in the library world. Omitted, therefore, are references to Dewey's involvement in activities not related to the library world—for example, his association with the American Metric Bureau and the Spelling Reform Association; his editorship of *Metric Bulletin* and *Metric Advocate* (1876-1883) and associate editorship of *Spelling* (1887-1895); his contributions to the total educational program of New York State while serving as secretary to the Regents of the University of the State of New York; and the intricacies of the Lake Placid complex.

1876

Books, Chapters in Books:

A Classification and Subject Index for Cataloguing and Arranging the Books and Pamphlets of a Library. Amherst, Mass.: 1876.

"A Decimal Classification and Subject Index." *In* U.S. Bureau of Education. *Public Libraries in the United States of America: Their History, Condition, and Management.* Special Report. Part 1. Washington: Government Printing Office, 1876. pp. 623-48. (Referred to as the *1876 Report.*)

American Library Journal:

"Notes and Queries." 1:23-24; 194; 232-33; 266-67; 300-01; 377-78; 410; 447.

"The Profession." 1:5-6

"Public Documents." 1:10-11.

1877

American Library Journal:

"The American Library Association.' 1:245-47.

"Book Selections." 1:391-93.

"The Coming Catalogue." 1:423-27.

"Co-operative Cataloguing." 1:170-75.

"Defacing Books." 1:326-28.

"The English Conference." 1:433-34.

"A Model Accession-Catalogue." 1:315-20.

"Notes and Queries." 2:81-82; 308-09.

"Sizes, Committee on: Report of the." [Dewey member of the Committee]
1:171-81.

1878

Library Journal:

"The Accession Catalogue Again." 3:336-38.

"The Amherst Classification." 3:231-32.

"Book Supports." 3:192.

"Charging Systems: A New Combined Plan and Various Details." 3:359-65.

"Charging Systems Based on Accounts with Borrowers." 3:252-55; 285-88.

"Colored Guide-Blocks." 3:192.

"Delinquent Notices and Check-Boxes." 3:370-71.

"Experiment and Experience." 3:301-02.

"Injuries to Books." 3:259-60.

"Manila Paper in Libraries." 3:159.

"Mr. Cutter's Bulletins and the Coming Catalog." 3:269-70.

"Notes and Queries." 3:31-32; 77-79; 126-27; 164-65; 200-01; 271; 310-11;
349-50; 380-81.

"Numbering: Rejoinders to Mr. Schwartz." 3:339.

"Principles Underlying Charging Systems." 3:217-20.

"Size of Books Without Marks." 3:372.

"The Use of Colors in Libraries." 3:65.

"Young Men's Lib. Assoc., Ware, Mass. Catalogue of the Library." [Review]
3:264-65.

1879

Library Journal:

"Apprenticeship of Librarians." 4:[147]-48.

"Arrangement on the Shelves—First Paper." 4:117-20.

"Arrangement on the Shelves—Second Paper." 4:191-94.

"Book and Reader Accounts." 4:131.

"Duplicating Processes." 4:165.

"Library Hours." 4:449.

"The Mass. [Massachusetts] State Library Bill." 4:130.

"Months in Brief Entries." 4:93.

"Notes and Queries." 4:24-25; 61-62; 100; 137-38; 173-74; 209; 383; 453.

"Plans for Numbering, with Especial Reference to Fiction: a Library Symposium" [Includes remarks by Dewey]. 4:38-47.

"Principles Underlying Numbering Systems—First Paper." 4:7-10.

"Principles Underlying Numbering Systems—Second Paper: a New Numbering Base." 4:75-78.

"The Schwartz Mnemonic Classification." [Comments by Dewey, Perkins and Cutter]. 4:92.

"Special Favors to Trustees or Faculty." 4:448.

1880

Library Journal:

"Alfabeting Catalog Cards." 5:176-77.

"Blank-Book Indexes." 5:318-20.

"Book Sizes Again." 5:177-79.

"Care of the Eyes." 5:175.

"Clearing-House for Duplicates." 5:216-17.

"Clippings from Periodicals." 5:146-47.

"Consulting Librarianship." 5:16-17.

"The Future of the A.L.A." 5:321.

"Incorporation of the A.L.A." 5:307-08.

"An Indexing Bureau." 5:215.

1880 (cont'd)

"Libraries in the Census." 5:318.

"More About Charging Systems: a Symposium." [Comments by Dui: pp. 74-75].
5: 72-75.

"A New Boston Idea." 5:82-83.

"Notes and Queries." 5:25; 54-55; 89; 121-22; 153-54; 189; 223-25; 291-92;
331-32.

"Past, Present, and Future of the A.L.A." 5:274-76.

"Slip-Indicator." 5:320-21.

"A Text-Book Department." 5:279.

"Useless Words." 5:321.

"Van Everen Numbers." 5:316-18.

"Washington Conference." 5:306-07.

1881

Library Journal:
"Heating Libraries." 6:31-34.
"Numbering Books." 6:53.

1882

Library Journal:
"Mr. Perkins's Classification." 7:60-62.

1883

Books, Chapters in Books:
Notes on the New Classification and Catalogues [*of Columbia College Library.*
New York: 1888-?].

Library Journal:
"School of Library Economy [Proposal for]." 8:C285-C286; C293-C294.

1884

Library Journal:

"School of Library Economy at Columbia College." 9:117-20.

1885

Books, Chapters in Books:

"[Autobiographic sketch]." *In* Jesse F. Forbes, *1874-1884: The Chronicles of '74 Since Graduation from Amherst College*. Warren, Mass.: H. M. Converse, Printer, 1885. pp. 15-18.

Decimal Classification and Relativ Index for Arranging, Cataloging and Indexing Public and Private Libraries, and for Pamflets, Clippings, Notes, Scrap Books, Index Rerums, etc. 2d ed., rev. and greatly enl. Boston: Library Bureau, 1885.

Descriptive Circular and Sample Pages of the Decimal Classification and Relativ Index. 2d ed., rev. and greatly enl. Boston: Library Bureau, 1885.

Library Abbreviations. Boston: Library Bureau [1885?]. Reprinted [1900?].

Library Journal:

"The A.L.A. Catalog." 10:73-76.

"The Cost of Cataloguing." [Comment by Dewey]. 10:323.

"Electric Lights." [Comments by Dewey]. 10:333-34; 335.

"A New Method of Size Notation, by Jacob Schwartz." [Comment by Dewey]. 10:396.

"Shelves." [Comment by Dewey]. 10:331-32.

1886

Books, Chapters in Books:

Librarianship as a Profession for College-Bred Women. An Address Delivered before the Association of Collegiate Alumnae, on March 13, 1886. Boston: Library Bureau, 1886.

Library Journal:

"Buckram and Morocco." 11:161-62.

"Close Classification vs. Bibliography." [Includes comments by Dewey]. 11:350-55.

"The Decimal Classification. A Reply to the 'Duet'." 11:100-06; 132-39.

"Eclectic Book-Numbers." 11:296-301.

"In Memoriam: Frederick Jackson." 11:478.

1886 (cont'd)

"Library Co-operation and the Index to Periodicals." 11:5-6.

"Public Libraries as Public Educators." 11:165.

Library Notes (see p. 265 for pages reprinted from v.1):

"Accession Book." 1:27-29.

"American Library Association. Milwaukee Meeting." 1:15-19.

"American Library Association. Milwaukee Meeting." 1:93-99.

"A.L.A. Publishing Section." 1:198-99.

"A.L.A. Publishing Section, First Meeting of the." 1:107.

"A.L.A. Publishing Section, Origin of the." 1:101-04.

"American vs. English Libraries." 1:192-95.

"Attractions and Opportunities of Librarianship." 1:51-53.

"Bibliothecal Museum of the A.L.A." 1:53.

"Blocks for Card Catalogs." 1:39-40.

"Book Braces, Supports or Props." 1:214-23.

"Book Plates." 1:23-25.

"British Museum Manifold System." 1:187-88.

"Building or Books." 1:[177]-79.

"Card Catalog Drawers." 1:37-39.

"Card Catalog Guards." 1:36-37.

"Card Catalogs." 1:33-34.

"Catalog Cards." 1:34-36.

"Catalog Guides." 1:40-42.

"Catalogs and Classification." 1:111.

"Catalogs and Classification." 1:212-13.

"Columbia Library School." 1:201-05.

"Condensed Rules for a Card Catalog." 1:112-31.

"Cost of Library Equipment." 1:22-23.

"Development of the Modern Library Idea, the Association, Journal, Bureau and School." 1:47-49.

"Editorial Notes." 1:3-4.

"Editor's Notes." 1:228.

"Education by Reading." 1:81-82.

"The Educational Trinity." 1:44-45.

"Embossing Stamps." 1:26-27.

1886 (cont'd)

"Experiment and Experience." 1:[79]-80.

"How Far Can a Card Catalog be Carried?" 1:189-92.

"Labor-Savers for Readers and Writers." 1:55-58.

"Librarians and Literary Labor-Savers." 1:8-9.

"The Librarian's Qualifications, Hours, and Salary." 1:91-92.

"Libraries, the True Universities for Scholars as Well as People." 1:49-50.

"Library Abbreviations." 1:206-11.

"The Library as an Educator." 1:43-44.

"Library Co-operation and the Index to Periodicals." 1:195-97.

"Library Economy." 1:132-34; 214-23.

"Library Employment vs. the Library Profession." 1:50-51.

"The Library Quartet and its Work." 1:5-7.

"Literary Methods and Labor-Savers for Readers and Writers." 1:138-43.

"Matter Wanted for the *Notes*." 1: 10.

"The Mission of the *Library Notes*." 1:7-8.

"Plan of the Labor-Saving Notes." 1:53-55.

"The Power of a Modern Book." 1:82-85.

"Progress." 1:135-37; 223-26.

"Regular Departments [17] of *Library Notes*." 1:144-45.

"School of Library Economy." 1:85-89. (Reprinted in 1933).

"School of Library Economy." 1:108-10.

"Selecting a Library System." 1:21-22.

"Shelf List." 1:29-32.

"Subject Sheets in Shelf Lists." 1:33.

"To Prospective Subscribers." 1:11.

"Why a Library Does or Does Not Succeed." 1:45-47.

"Why the Opinions of *Library Notes* are Valuable." 1:150.

"Women in Libraries: How They are Handicapped." 1:89-90.

1887

Library Journal:

"The Attendance and the Excursions [of the Thousand Islands Conference]."
12:457-58.

"The Nova Scotia Excursion [of the Thousand Islands Conference]." 12:459-60.

"Our Cheap and Effectiv Catalog of Sale Duplicates." 12:440-41.

"School of Library Economy." 12:78-80.

"Umlaut." 12:544.

Library Notes (see p. 265 for pages reprinted from v.1 and v.2):

"A.L.A. Standard Accession-Book." 2:17-27.

"American Library Association. Thousand Island [sic] Meeting." 1:260-61.

"American Library Association. Thousand Islands Meeting." 2:54-63.

"American Library Association. Thousand Island [sic] Meeting." 2:123-46.

"Card Pockets." 1:282-85.

"Children's Library Association." 1:261-63.

"Columbia Library School." 1:266-72, 2:234-42.

"Editor's Notes." 1:291-92.

"Editor's Notes." 2:68-70.

"Evolution of the Card System." 2:29-34.

"How to Keep Library Circulars." 1:285-87.

"Importance of Using Standard Sizes." 2:46-53.

"Language." 2:148-50.

"Librarians and the Eyes of the Public." 1:288-90.

"Libraries on Special Authors." 2:14-16.

"Library Economy." 2:35-43.

"Library Economy." 2:214-21.

"Library Handwriting." 1:273-82.

"Library Shelving." 2:100-22.

"Library Size, Life, Growth, and Use." 2:43-45.

"Literary Labor-Savers." 2:147; 167-68.

"Literary Methods and Labor-Savers for Readers and Writers." 2:22-24; 64-67.

"Metric System in a Card Case, The Complete." 2:224-27.

"The New Magazine 'Spelling.' " 2:151-66.

"Pictures of Library Buildings," 2:211-14.

"Shelf List System for Subject Card Catalogs." 2:28.

1887 (cont'd)

"Standard Sizes for Printed Books." 2:243-51.

"Suspension Book Cases." 2:99-100.

1888

Books, Chapters in Books:

Libraries as Related to the Educational Work of the State. [Albany, N.Y.: 1888.]
At head of title: University of the State of New York. Twenty-Sixth
Convocation, 1888. Reprinted 1889.

"Libraries as Related to the Educational Work of the State," *In* U.S. Bureau of
Education. "Report of the Commissioner of Education, 1887-88," in
U.S. Dept. of the Interior. *Report of the Secretary of the Interior;* Being
Part of the Messages and Documents Communicated to the Two Houses
of Congress at the Beginning of the Second Session of the Fiftieth Congress.
Volume 5. Washington: Government Printing Office, 1888, Chapter XX,
pp. 1031-39. (50th Congress, 2nd Session, House of Representatives,
Executive Document I, Part 5).

Rules for Author and Classed Catalogs as Used in Columbia College Library.
Boston: Library Bureau, 1888. Published later as *Library School Card
Catalog Rules.* 2nd ed. (1889).

*Tables and Index of the Decimal Classification and Relativ Index for Arranging
and Cataloging Libraries, Clippings, Notes, etc.* 3rd ed., rev. and enl.
Boston: Library Bureau, 1888. Edition 2 and later editions entitled:
Decimal Classification and Relativ Index . . .

Library Journal:

"Monthly vs. Quarterly Indexes." 13:172.

"New Library [Bureau] Headquarters." 13:236.

"Sale Duplicate Slip-Catalog." 13:284-86.

Library Notes (see p. 265 for pages reprinted from v.2):

"Columbia College Library. Facilities for Non-Resident Readers." 2:298-300.

"Columbia College Library. Paid Help Department and Facilities for Non-
Resident Readers." 2:300-04.

"Columbia Library School." 2:286-300.

"Columbia Library School. Circular Letter B." 2:304-06.

"Editor's Notes." 2:307.

"Editor's Notes." 3:354-55.

"Libraries as Related to the Educational Work of the State." 3:333-48.

"Sale Duplicate Slip Catalog." 3:350-53.

1889

Books, Chapters in Books:

"The Extension of the University of the State of New York." *In* New York
(State) University. *Proceedings of the Twenty-Seventh Annual Convocation,
Held July 9-11, 1889.* Albany: James B. Lyon, 1889.

*Library School Card Catalog Rules, With 52 Facsimiles of Sample Cards for
Author and Classed Catalogs* . . . 2d ed. Boston: 1889. Later editions
published as Part I of *Library School Rules.*

Library Journal:

"Civil Service Examinations for New York State Library." 14:118-21.

Library Notes:

"American Library Association. St. Louis Meeting." 3:474-80.

"Editor's Notes." 3:483.

Other Periodical Sources:

"On Library Progress." [Remarks at the Twelfth Annual Meeting of the Library
Association]. *The Library* 1:367-76.

1890

Books, Chapters in Books:

"Libraries as Related to the Educational Work of the State . . . " *In* New York
(State) University. *Regents' Bulletin*, No. 3. Albany: 1890. pp. [107]-25.

Library School Rules. Boston: Library Bureau, 1890.

"Statistics of Libraries in the State of New York Numbering Over 300 Volumes."
In New York (State) University. *Regents' Bulletin*, No. 3. Albany: 1890.
pp. 151-73.

Library Journal:

"The Library and the State." 15:135.

"New York Library Association." 15:267-68.

1891

Books, Chapters in Books:

Decimal Classification and Relativ Index for Libraries, Clippings, Notes, etc.
4th ed., rev. and enl. Boston: Library Bureau, 1891.

"The Relation of the Colleges to the Modern Library Movement." *In* College
Association of the Middle States and Maryland. *Proceedings of the Second
Annual Convention* . . . Held at Princeton College, N.J., Nov. 28th and
29th, 1890. [n.p.], Globe Printing House, 1891, pp. 78-83.

1891 (cont'd)

Library Journal:

"Notes on American and State Library Associations." 16:169-70.

"Pamphlets Ruined by Rolling." 16:202.

"Records of Current Public Interests [Charitable, Penal and Reformatory Subjects]." 16:328.

1892

Books, Chapters in Books:

Library School Rules. 2d ed. Boston, 1892.

Library Journal:

"Gathering Them In." 17:47.

"Library Museum in London." 17:444.

"Notes on Some Continental Libraries." 17:121-22.

"Publications of the New York State Library." 17:444.

"Too Full Name." 17:443-44.

Library Notes:

"A.L.A. Catalog. A Circular Letter from Melvil Dewey, Editor of the A.L.A. Catalog." 3:402-04.

"Editor's Notes." 3:408.

"Inter-library Loans." 3:405-07.

1893

Library Journal:

"Better Bookmaking for Libraries." 18:142.

"Bibliography in Colleges." 18:422.

"Business Skill in Library Management." 18:145.

Library Notes:

"Book Numbers." 3:419-50. (Based on "Eclectic Book-Numbers," 1886).

1894

Books, Chapters in Books:

Decimal Classification and Relativ Index for Libraries, Clippings, Notes, etc. 5th ed. Boston: Library Bureau, 1894.

Library School Rules. 3d ed. Library Bureau. 1894.

1894 (cont'd)

Library Journal:

"[Tribute to William Frederick Poole]." 19:C169-C170.

1895

Books, Chapters in Books:

Abridged Decimal Classification and Relativ Index for Libraries, Clippings, Notes, etc. Boston: Library Bureau, 1895 [C1894]. Reprinted in 1900.

American Library Association. "Papers Prepared for the World's Library Congress [Held at the Columbian Exposition, Chicago, 1893. Edited by Melvil Dewey]," *In* U.S. Bureau of Education. *Report of the Commissioner of Education for the Year, 1892-93.* Washington: Government Printing Office, 1895. v. 1, parts I and II, Chapter ix, pp. 691-1014. (U.S. Bureau of Education. Whole Number 217).

Library Notes:

"Abridged Decimal Classification and Relativ Index for Libraries, Clippings, Notes, etc." 4:1-192.

"Quotations for Inscriptions on Library Buildings or For Use in Catalogs and Finding Lists." 4:223-31.

"Summer Library School." 4:232.

Other Periodical Sources:

"Among the Libraries." Conducted by Melvil Dewey. *The Bookman* 1:203-05.

1896

Books, Chapters in Books:

"The Field of the Library Department; The Relation of the Librarian to the Teacher." [Remarks by Dewey]. *In* National Educational Association. *Journal of Proceedings and Addresses of the Thirty-Fifth Annual Meeting* Held at Buffalo, N.Y., July 3-10, 1896. Chicago: University of Chicago Press, 1896. p. 1004.

"The New Library Department of the National Education Association." *In* National Educational Association. *Journal of Proceedings and Addresses of the Thirty-Fifth Annual Meeting* Held at Buffalo, N.Y., July 3-10, 1896. Chicago: University of Chicago Press, 1896. pp. 998-1003.

Public Libraries:

"The A.L.A. Meeting for 1898." 1:174.

"Libraries as Educational Forces." 1:268-69.

"The New Library Department of the National Education Association." 1:183-85.

1896 (cont'd)

Other Periodical Sources:

"The Hon. Whitelaw Reid on Fonetik Refawrm." [Correspondence with Dewey].
The Bookman 3:410-11.

"New York State Library." *Harper's Weekly* 40: 178-81.

1897

Books, Chapters in Books:

U.S. Congress. Joint Committee on the Library. *Condition of the Library of
Congress.* [Washington: Government Printing Office, 1897]. (54th Congress,
2d Session. Senate Report no. 1573). Hearings held in 1896. [Consult
index for references to Dewey's testimony].

Library Journal:

"[Address at the Twenty-First Anniversary of the Association]." 22:117-19.

Public Libraries:

"[The Librarians' Influence]." 2:267.

"Library Department of the N.E.A. [Milwaukee Meeting]." 2:176.

"Recommendations for Library Positions." 2:493-94.

Other Periodical Sources:

"Exact Reference to Printed or Manuscript Pages." *The Bookman* 5: 174-75.

1898

Books, Chapters in Books:

"Relation of the State to the Public Library." *In* International Library Conference,
2d, London, 1897. *Transactions and Proceedings* . . . July 13-16,
1897. London: Printed for Members, 1898. pp. 19-22.

Simplified Library School Rules. Boston: Library Bureau, 1898. Reprinted in
1904 and 1912.

Library Journal:

"A.L.A. Conference Notes. Two Weeks' Work for the A.L.A." [20th General
Conference: Lakewood-on-Chautauqua]. 23:242-43.

"Comments on Dieserud's Suggested Classification." 23:609-10.

"Free Employment Registry." 23:563.

1898 (cont'd)

"The Function of the Library as a Bookstore." 23: C152.

"Library Examinations and Credentials." 23:C137. [Comment by Dewey].

"Library Postcards." 23:240-41.

"Library Schools and Training Classes: New York State Library School." 23: C59-C60.

"The New Printed Cards for Current Serials." 23:48.

Library Notes:

"Simplified Library School Rules." 4:241-315.

Public Libraries:

"American Library Association. Large Library Section, with Special Reference to Branches and Deliveries." 3:129.

"Duplicate Clearing House." 3:255-56.

"Library Notes." 3:223-25; 266.

"The New Printed Cards for Current Serials." 3:82.

"New York: To Would-Be Librarians [and] To Inquirers Regarding Positions in the New York State Library." 3:359-60.

"Waste in Trifles." 3:348.

1899

Books, Chapters in Books:

Decimal Classification and Relativ Index for Libraries, Clippings, Notes, etc. 6th ed. Boston: Library Bureau, 1899.

Library School Rules. 4th ed. Boston, Library Bureau, 1899.

Library Journal:

"Dangers of Over-Organization." 24:C159-C160.

"The Ideal Librarian." 24:14.

"Paris Library Exhibit." 24:660.

"Suitability of the Decimal Classification." [Comment by Dewey]. 24: C154.

"What a Library Should Be and What It Can Do." 24: C119-C121.

1899 (cont'd)

Public Libraries:

"[Classification] ." [Summary of Dewey's comments] . 4:265-66.

"Dangers of Over-Organization." 4:277-79.

"Letter Copying [Rapid Roller Copier] ." 4:401.

"[New York State Library] Bibliography and Library Economy Bulletins." 4:153.

"Rank of University Librarians." 4:106.

"Too Many Organizations." 4:56-57.

"What a Library Should Be and What It Can Do." 4:269-71.

Other Periodical Sources:

"Qualifications of a Librarian." *Library World* 2: 96-98.

1900

Library Journal:

"Changing Size of Catalog Cards." 25:350.

"Library Schools, Committee on: Report of." [Comment by Dewey] . 25:C112.

"Revision of the Decimal Classification." 25:684-85.

Public Libraries:

"Changing Size of Catalog Cards." 5:243.

"Does a Bindery Pay?" 5:322.

"Free Library vs. Fees." 5:430-31.

"The Paris Exhibit." 5:326.

"Trade Catalogs as Library Books." 5:425.

"Traveling A.L.A. Exhibit." 5:324.

1901

Books, Chapters in Books:

"Application for Admission to the New York State Library School." *In* New York (State) Library, Albany, *Bulletin* 66, Library School 9 (September 1901): 383-84. ("Handbook of New York State Library School Including Summer Course and Library Handwriting").

1901 (cont'd)

Traveling Libraries. Field and Future of Traveling Libraries. Albany, 1901. (University of the State of New York. Home Education Department. Bulletin 40, Traveling Libraries and Collections 2).

Library Journal:

"Cooperation Between Teachers and Librarians." [Comment by Dewey]. 26:C121.

"Libraries in the Twentieth Century. A Symposium. Development and Evolution." 26: 121-23.

"The Relationship of Publishers, Booksellers and Librarians." 26: C137-C139.

"Some Principles of Book and Picture Selection." [Comment by Dewey]. 26: C124-C125.

Public Libraries:

"A.L.A. Meeting for 1902." 6: 420.

"Illustrated Lectures on Libraries." 6: 606.

"Library Notes." 6: 161; 210-11; 401-02.

"Newspaper Print [Cause of Eye Strain]." 6: 433.

"Private Postcards." 6: 409.

"Science in Printing [Type Sizes and Reading]." 6: 110-11.

"To What Extent Should a State Library Lend Its Books to the Citizens of the State at Large?" 6: 34-35.

Other Periodical Sources:

"The Faculty Library." *The Library*, ser. 2, 2: 238-41.

"Printed Catalogue Cards from a Central Bureau." *The Library*, ser. 2, 2: 130-34.

1902

Books, Chapters in Books:

Library Editing and Printing. [Albany? N.Y., 1902].

Library Journal:

"A.L.A. Exhibit at Louisiana Purchase Exposition, Committee on: Report of." 27: C140-C142.

"Changing Catalog Rules." 27: C196; C201-C202.

"The Cheap Library Post Movement." 27: 754.

"The Function of the Trustee." 27: C217-C219.

1902 (cont'd)

"The Functions of a State Library Association." 27: C236-C238.

"Index to A.L.A. Proceedings, [Request for]." 27: 308.

"[Lectures in Libraries]." [Comment by Dewey]. 27: C165.

"Special Library Training for State Commission Library Organizers." [Comment by Dewey]. 27: C231-C233.

Public Libraries:

"Capacity of Book Stacks." 7: 28-29.

"Classification [in Decimal Classification] of Library Economy and Bibliography. [Request for suggestions, May 15, 1902]." 7: 271.

"Cost of Duplicate Card Catalog of National Library." 7: 240-41.

"Department Libraries." 7: 227.

"Library Clause in City Charters." 7: 184.

"Library Notes." 7: 70-71; 153; 191-93; 239-40; 371; 461-62.

"Library Schools of Doubtful Value." 7: 119-20.

"[New York State Library and Local Booksellers]." 7: 313-14.

"Should the Local Library Have a Museum Department?" 7:148.

"Size Versus Decoration." 7: 121.

Other Periodical Sources:

"Library Institutes [in New York State]." (Running title: "On Library Institutes") *The Library*, ser. 2, 3:103-12.

"Qualifications of a Librarian." *In* New York (State) Library. *Bulletin* 75, Library School 12 (October 1902): 91-96. (University of the State of New York, Bulletin 268).

1903

Library Journal:

"Duplicate Pay Collections of Popular Books." [Comments by Dewey]. 28: C156; C159.

"A National Headquarters for the Library Association: Some Suggestions and Opinions. Scope and Opportunities." 28: 757-59.

Public Libraries:

"Competition of Architects on Library Plans." 8: 63-64.

"The Future of the Public Librarian." 8: 327-28.

1903 (cont'd)

"Library Notes." 8: 322-23; 405-06; 460.

"[Summer Training Classes] ." [Quotations from Dewey]. 8:153.

1904

Books, Chapters in Books:

A.L.A. Catalog: 8,000 Volumes for a Popular Library, With Notes, 1904.
Prepared by the New York State Library and the Library of Congress
Under the Auspices of the American Library Association Publishing
Board. Editor: Melvil Dewey . . . Part I: Classed; Part 2: Dictionary. Washington:
Government Printing Office, 1904. 2 v. in 1.

"Libraries." *In The New International Encyclopaedia.* New York: Dodd, Mead,
1904 [c1903]. v. 12, pp. 193-206.

Authorship attributed to Prof. James Morton Paton, Mr. Charles Alexander
Nelson, Dr. Melvil Dewey, and Dr. James Hulme Canfield in "A Partial
List of the Leading Articles in Vol. XII."

Library Journal:

"A.L.A. Catalog." 29: 23-24.

"A.L.A. Exhibit at Louisiana Purchase Exposition, Committee on [Report of] ."
29: C204.

"For an American Library Academy." 29: 300.

"State Aid to Libraries." [Includes comments by Dewey]. 29: C211-C215.

"The Traveling Library School." 29: 371.

"Worcester (Mass.) F.P.L., [Management of] ." 29: 422-43.

Public Libraries:

"Accession Book, Card Shelf-List and Full Names." 9: 281-82.

"American Library Academy." 9: 238-39.

"A.L.A. Catalog." 9: 78.

"Future of the Library in the Social System [Summary] ." 9: 340.

"Indian Boys' Library." 9: 329.

"Library Conditions in America in 1904." 9: 363-65.

1904 (cont'd)

"Library Institutes." [Comment by Dewey]. 9:458.

"Library Notes." 9:84.

"National Library Institute." 9:16-18.

"[Pamphlet of 1828] To Be Given to Libraries." 9:163.

"Traveling Library Schools." 9:443-44.

1905

Books, Chapters in Books:

[Answer to] Petition to the Regents of the State of New York [for the Removal from Office of Melvil Dewey, the Present State Librarian]. Lake Placid Club, N.Y.: 1905.

Library School Rules. 5th ed. Boston: Library Bureau, 1905.

Library Journal:

"[American Library Association] Committee on A.L.A. Academy." [Report by Dewey with comments]. 30:289.

"A.L.A. Catalog, [Omissions from.]" 30:86-87.

"A.L.A. Exhibit, Report on." 30:C143-C144.

"[American Library Institute]." 30:C179.

"[Functions of the State Library and of the State Library Commission]." 30:C151, C152.

"The Ideal State Library in an Ideal Location." 30:C248-C249.

"[Library Training]." [Comment by Dewey] 30: C172-C173.

"Traveling Libraries as a First Step in Library Development." [Comments by Dewey]. 30:C158-C159; C162.

"Unity and Coöperation in Library Work." 30:C180-C184.

Public Libraries:

"A.L.A. Catalog [Errors in]." 10:94.

"A.L.A. Catalog, Omissions from." 10:118-19.

"The Future of Library Schools." 10:435-38.

"Library Notes." 10:466-67; 525-26.

"New York Library Club Dinner." 10:363.

"Relation of School Libraries to the Public Library System." 10:224-25.

1905 (cont'd)

"State Libraries in Education Work." 10:29-30.

1906

Library Journal:

"The Future of Library Commissions [Reference to]." 31: C204.

"The Ideal Relations Between Trustees and Librarian." 31: C44.

Public Libraries:

"A.L.A. Motto, Origin of." 11:55.

"Broadening of State Libraries." 11:22.

"Library Notes." 11:75-78.

"Library Pictures [Including Lantern Slides]." 11:10-11.

Other Periodical Sources:

"Field Libraries." *Dial* 40: 75-77.

1907

Books, Chapters in Books:

"American Library Association, Organized 1876, Incorporated 1879." *In*
National Educational Association, *Fiftieth Anniversary Volume, 1857-1906.*
Winona, Minn.: 1907. pp. 486-87.

Other Periodical Sources:

"Committee on Cooperation with N.E.A., Report of." [Dewey a member of
Committee.] *ALA Bulletin* 1:89.

"Man-a-Month Volunteers." *ALA Bulletin* 1:1-3.

1908

Library Journal:

"American Library Institute." 33:18.

1909

Public Libraries:

"Library Notes." 14:21-22; 261.

1911

Books, Chapters in Books:

Decimal Classification and Relativ Index for Libraries, Clippings, Notes, etc.
Ed. 7. Lake Placid Club, N.Y.: Forest Press, 1911.

Public Libraries:

"Tribute to Mr Crunden." 16:437-38.

1912

Books, Chapters in Books:

Abridged Decimal Classification and Relativ Index for Libraries, Clippings, Notes, etc.
Ed. 2. Lake Placid Club, N.Y.: Forest Press, 1912. Reprinted in 1915 and 1917.

"The Genesis of the Library School." *In* New York (State) Library School,
Albany, *The First Quarter Century of the New York State Library School,*
1887-1912. Albany: New York State Library School, 1912. pp. 12-23.

"Office Efficiency." *In* H. P. Dunham, *The Business of Insurance.* New York: Ronald
Press, 1912. v. 3, pp. 276-316.

1913

Books, Chapters in Books:

Decimal Classification and Relativ Index for Libraries, Clippings, Notes, etc.
Ed. 8. Lake Placid Club, N.Y.: Forest Press, 1913.

1914

Books, Chapters in Books:

Decimal Classification: Corrections and Additions to Editions 5, 6, and 7. Lake
Placid Club, N.Y.: Forest Press, 1914. Reprinted in 1915.

Library Journal:

"Take Books to Readers." 39:416.

Public Libraries:

"Take Books to Readers." 19:154-55.

1915

Books, Chapters in Books:

Decimal Classification and Relativ Index for Libraries, Clippings, Notes, etc.
Ed. 9, rev. Lake Placid Club, N.Y.: Forest Press, 1915.

1915 (cont'd)

Other Periodical Sources:

"[Need for A.L.A. Advisory Committee on DC]." [Comment by Dewey]
ALA Bulletin 9:256-57.

1916

Public Libraries:

"The Growth of Librarianship." 21:270.

1917

Other Periodical Sources:

"What the A.L.A. Was Intended to Be and to Do." *Wisconsin Library Bulletin*
13:41-49.

1918

Books, Chapters in Books:

Editor's Note on Agriculture Scheme for Decimal Classification. [Lake Placid,
N.Y.: 1918].

Public Libraries:

" 'No Fiction During the War.' " 23:78.

1919

Books, Chapters in Books:

Decimal Classification and Relativ Index for Libraries, Clippings, Notes, etc.
Ed. 10, rev. and enl. Lake Placid Club, N.Y.: Forest Press, 1919.

1920

Library Journal:

"Decimal Classification Beginnings." 45:151-54.
"Libraries as Book Stores." 45:493-94.

1921

Books, Chapters in Books:

*Abridged Decimal Classification and Relativ Index for Libraries, Clippings, Notes,
etc.* Ed. 3, rev. Lake Placid Club, N.Y.: Forest Press, 1921. Reprinted in 1926.

1921 (cont'd)

Outline Decimal Classification and Relativ Index for Libraries, Clippings, Notes, etc. Lake Placid Club, N.Y.: Forest Press, 1921.

Library Journal:

"May Seymour, August 31, 1857–June 14, 1921." 46:606-07.

Other Periodical Sources:

"What the Lake Placid Club Offers for Library Week." *New York Libraries* 7 (1919-21):110-11.

1922

Books, Chapters in Books:

Decimal Clasification and Relativ Index for Libraries and Personal Use, in Arranjing for Immediate Reference, Books, Pamflets, Clippings, Pictures, Manuscript Notes and Other Material. Ed. 11, rev. and enl. Lake Placid Club, N.Y.: Forest Press, 1922.

1924

Books, Chapters in Books:

Decimal Clasification and Relativ Index: Extracts 651, Offis Economy, and 658, Business Methods, Industrial Management, to Which is Prefixt 331, Labor and Laborers, Employers, Capital, from Decimal Clasification . . . [Ed. 11, rev. and enl.] Lake Placid Club, N.Y.: Forest Press, 1924.

Library Journal:

"Temporary Fads [non-use of book numbers]." 49:[38].

1925

Public Libraries:

"[A.L.A. Motto: Response to an Inquiry]." 30:79-80.

"As It Was in the Beginning [Tribute to Florence Woodworth]." 30:482-84.

"Shorthand for Librarians." 30:540-41.

1926

Library Journal:

"Adult or Home Education?" 51:185.

1926 (cont'd)

"Our Next Half-Century" [Slightly abridged] . 51:887-89.

Libraries:

"Greeting from Melvil Dewey [on 50th Anniversary of A.L.A.] ." 31:326.
"Is Adult Education the Right Name?" 31:65.

Other Periodical Sources:

"Our Next Half-Century."*ALA Bulletin* 20:309-12.
"To A L A [Fiftieth Anniversary Statement] ." *ALA Bulletin* 20:102.

1927

Books, Chapters in Books:

*Decimal Clasification and Relativ Index for Libraries and Personal Use in Arranjing
for Immediate Reference, Books, Pamflets, Clippings, Pictures, Manuscript
Notes and Other Material.* Ed. 12, rev. and enl. under direction of Dorcas
Fellows, Editor. Semi-centennial ed. Lake Placid Club, N.Y.: Forest Press,
1927.

Libraries:

"[Seventy-Fifth Birthday] Letter from Melvil Dewey." 32:66-67.

1929

Books, Chapters in Books:

*Abridged Decimal Classification and Relativ Index for Libraries and Personal
Use in Arranging for Immediate Reference, Books, Pamflets, Clippings,
Pictures, Manuscript Notes and Other Material.* Ed. 4 rev. to correspond
to the few changes in meaning of numbers in ful tables, ed. 12. Lake Placid
Club, N.Y.: Forest Press, 1929.

"Herbert Putnam." *In Essays Offered to Herbert Putnam by His Colleagues and
Friends on His Thirtieth Anniversary as Librarian of Congress, 5 April 1929.*
Edited by William Warner Bishop and Andrew Keogh. New Haven: Yale
University Press, 1929, pp. 22-23.

Library Journal:

"Cards! [Corrects error made in referring to card size as 3 x 5 in. instead of 7.5
x 12.5 cm.] ." 54:223.

1929 (cont'd)

"Duplikate Clearing Hous." 54:224.

"The Right People Needed [for the Decimal Classification Office at the Library of Congress]." 54:954.

Libraries:

"Fyrproof Branches." 34:433.

"[Tribute to John Cotton Dana]." 34:375.

Other Periodical Sources:

"[New York] Library Week, 1927: Melvil Dewey Speaks." *New York Libraries* 11 (1927-29):259.

1931

Library Journal:

"Library Colony at Lake Placid." 56:551.

Libraries:

"American Library Institute. Meeting in New Haven, Connecticut, June 23." [Letter from Dewey]. 36:348.

"Future of D.C." 36:202-03.

"An Improvement in Form of Library Reports." 36:203.

"Meeting of the All Bengal Library Association." [Letter from Dewey]. 36:266-67.

"A Notable Record [Tribute to Mary Eileen Ahern]." 36:438.

1932

Books, Chapters in Books:

Decimal Clasification and Relativ Index . . . for Libraries and Personal Use, in Arranjing for Immediate Reference, Books, Pamflets, Clippings, Pictures, Manuscript Notes and Other Material. Ed. 13, rev. and enl. by Dorkas Fellows, Editor, Myron Getchell, Associate Editor. Memorial ed. Lake Placid Club, N.Y.: Forest Press, 1932.

Library Journal:

"Outline of Library Development." [Praise from Dewey of an outline of history of the development of the American public library by Martha Connor of the Carnegie Library School of Pittsburgh]. 57:42.

REPRINTS

1896

American Library Association. *Papers Prepared for the World's Library Congress Held at the Columbian Exposition.* [1893]. Edited by Melvil Dewey. Washington: Government Printing Office, 1896, pp. 601-1014. (U.S. Bureau of Education. Whole Number 224). "Reprint of chapter IX of Part II of the Report of the Commissioner of Education for 1892-93." Published also with title: *Papers Prepared for the American Library Association for Its Annual Meeting Held at the Columbian Exposition, 1893.* Edited by Melvil Dewey. Washington: Government Printing Office, 1896.

1904

"On Libraries: For Librarians" [1903]. Being an Article Written for The New International Encyclopaedia and Reprinted from the Same in Response to Many and Urgent Requests by the Author. New York: Dodd, Mead, 1904, pp. [193]-206.

1912

"Office Efficiency" [1912]. New York: Ronald Press, 1912.

1914

"Libraries as Related to the Educational Work of the State" [1888]. *In* Arthur E. Bostwick, ed., *The Relationship Between the Library and the Public Schools.* Reprints of Papers and Addresses. White Plains, N.Y.: Wilson, 1914, pp. [63]-83. (Classics of American Librarianship, [v.1]).

1920

"The Relation of the State to the Public Library" [1898]. *In* Arthur E. Bostwick, ed., *The Library and Society.* Reprints of Papers and Addresses. New York: Wilson, 1920, pp. [185]-99. (Classics of American Librarianship, [v.3]).

"What a Library Should Be and What It Can Do" [1899]. *In Ibid,* pp. [75]-78.

1924

"American Library Association" [1877]. *In* Gertrude Gilbert Drury, ed., *The Library and Its Organization.* Reprints of Articles and Addresses. New York: Wilson, 1924, pp. [195]-99. (Classics of American Librarianship, [v.4]).

1925

"A Model Accession Catalog" [1877]. *In* Harriet Price Sawyer, ed., *The Library and Its Contents*. Reprints of Papers and Addresses. New York: Wilson, 1925, pp. [401]-10. (Classics of American Librarianship, [v.5]).

1926

" 'Tis Fifty Years Since" [1876]. *Library Journal* 51 (1926): 76. (Brief extracts from the first issue of the *American Library Journal*).

1929

"Public Documents" [1876]. *In* Katharine Twining Moody, ed., *The Library Within the Walls*. Reprints of Articles and Addresses. New York: Wilson, 1929, pp. [163]-65. (Classics of American Librarianship, [v.8]).

1933

"Apprenticeship of Librarians" [1879]. *In* Harriet Price Sawyer, ed., *The Library as a Vocation*. Reprints of Papers and Addresses. New York: Wilson, 1933, pp. [19]-22. (Classics of American Librarianship, [v. 10]).

"Book Braces, Supports or Props" [1886]. *In* Gertrude Gilbert Drury, ed., *The Library and Its Home*. Reprints of Articles and Addresses. New York: Wilson, 1933, pp. [509]-20. (Classics of American Librarianship, [v.9]).

"Card Catalogs" [1886]. *In ibid.,* pp. [501]-07.

"Electric Lights" [1885 Lake George Conference Proceedings]. *In ibid.,* pp. [431]-34.

"Heating Libraries" [Extract: 1881]. *In ibid.,* pp. [429]-30.

"School of Library Economy" [1886]. *In* Harriet Price Sawyer, ed., *The Library as a Vocation*, pp. [25]-29.

1937

Columbia University. School of Library Economy. *School of Library Economy of Columbia College, 1887-1889. Documents for a History*. [New York]: 1937.
"Apprenticeship of Librarians" [1879]. pp. 1-2.

Columbia College Library. "Excerpts from 'Second and Third Annual Reports' of the Columbia College Library, June 30, 1886." pp. 58-60.

Columbia College Library. *School of Library Economy Circular of Information, 1884*. [n.d., n.p.], pp. 17-52.

1937 (cont'd)

Columbia College Library. *School of Library Economy Circular of Information, 1886-87.* [n.d., n.p.] pp. 61-105.

Columbia College Library. School of Library Economy. "First Annual Report of the Director, June 20, 1887." pp. 203-18.

Columbia College Library. "Second Annual Report of the Director of the School of Library Economy, June 30, 1888." pp. 233-43.

Library Notes

v. 1 (October 1886): 108-10, pp. 106-08.
v. 1 (December 1886): 201-05, pp. 118-21.
v. 1 (March 1887): 266-72, pp. 109-15.
v. 2 (December 1887): 234-37, pp. 189-92; 241-42, pp. 116-17.
v. 2 (March 1888): 286-98, pp. 255-67; 304-06, "Circular Letter B."
    pp. 244-46.

"School of Library Economy [Proposal for]" [1883]. pp. 3-6.

1941

A Classification and Subject Index for Cataloguing and Arranging the Books and Pamphlets of a Library. Amherst, Mass.: 1876. New York: Brick Row Book Shop, 1941. Cover-title: An Historic Pamphlet. The Original Prospectus of the Dewey System, Amherst 1876, Reprinted from Dr. Ernest Cushing Richardson's Copy.

1951

"The Profession" [1876]. *Library Journal* 76 (1951): 457-58.

1959

"Librarianship as a Profession" [1876]. *Library Journal* 84 (1959): 25-26.
    Original title: "The Profession."

1960

"Librarianship as a Profession" [1876]. *In* John D. Marshall, comp., *Of, By, and For Librarians.* Hamden, Conn.: Shoe String Press, 1960, pp. 179-80.
    Original title: "The Profession."

1964

"Changing Catalog Rules" [1902]. *Library Journal* 89 (1964): 2296.

1967

"Herbert Putnam." *In Essays Offered to Herbert Putnam by His Colleagues and Friends on His Thirtieth Anniversary as Librarian of Congress, 5 April 1929.* [1929]. Freeport, N.Y.: Books for Libraries Press, 1967, pp. 22-23.

1968

"The Profession" [1876]. *In* Jean Key Gates, *Introduction to Librarianship.* New York: McGraw-Hill [c1968], pp. [359]-61.

1975

"The Relation of the State to the Public Library" [1898]. *In American Library Philosophy: An Anthology.* Edited by Barbara McCrimmon. Hamden, Conn.: Shoe String Press, 1975, pp. 21-23. (Contributions to Library Literature Series).

1976

A Classification and Subject Index for Cataloguing and Arranging the Books and Pamphlets of a Library. Amherst, Mass.: 1876. [Kingsport, Tenn.: Kingsport Press, 1976]. On half-title: Dewey Decimal Classification Centennial, 1876-1976. Facsimile Reprinted by Forest Press Division, Lake Placid Education Foundation.

"Preface to First Edition of Decimal Classification [*A Classification and Subject Index for Cataloguing and Arranging the Books and Pamphlets of a Library*]." Herald of Library Science 15 (1976): 235-43.

"The Profession" [1876]. *In* Jean Key Gates, *Introduction to Librarianship.* 2d ed. New York: McGraw-Hill [c1976], pp. 239-41.

_____. *In Landmarks of Library Literature, 1876-1976.* Edited by D. J. Ellsworth and N. D. Stevens. Metuchen, N.J.: Scarecrow Press, 1976, pp. 21-23.

Ahern, Mary E. "The Charges Against Mr Dewey." *Public Libraries* 10 (1905): 127-28.

_____. "The Resignation of Mr Dewey." *Public Libraries* 10 (1905): 471.

Berg, C. van den. "Vier Pioniers: 1, Melvil Dewey." *Bibliotheekleven* 48 (1963): 303-08.

Bidlack, Russell E. " 'The Coming Catalogue' or Melvil Dewey's Flying Machine: Being the Historical Background of the A.L.A. Catalog." *Library Quarterly* 27 (1957): 137-60.

Biscoe, W. S. "As It Was in the Beginning." *Public Libraries* 30 (1925): 72-78.

_____. "Melvil Dewey, 1851-1932." *New York Libraries* 13 (1932): 38-40.

Bostwick, Arthur E. "The Meaning of the Library School." *Library Journal* 51 (1925): 275-77.

Bowker, Richard R. "Melvil Dewey: Founder and Pioneer." *ALA Bulletin* 26 (1932): 93-94.

_____. "Seed Time and Harvest—The Story of the A.L.A." *Library Journal* 51 (1926): [880]-86.

_____. "[Tribute to Dewey on the 40th Anniversary of the American Library Association]." *ALA Bulletin* 10 (1916): 382-83.

Brown, James Duff. "Melvil Dewey." *Library World* 14 (1911): 161-62.

Cole, John Y. "LC and ALA, 1876-1901." *Library Journal* 98 (1973): 2965-70.

Columbia University. School of Library Service. "First Founder's Day Exercises." *Library Service News* 4 (January 1933): 17-24.

_____. "[Melvil Dewey Number]." *Library Service News* 3 (December 1931): 17-28.

_____. *School of Library Economy of Columbia College, 1887-1889. Documents for a History.* [New York] : Columbia University School of Library Service, 1937.

Comaromi, John Phillip. *The Eighteen Editions of the Dewey Decimal Classification.* Albany: Forest Press, 1976.

Datz, Harry R. "A Pioneer: the Library Bureau." *Library Journal* 51 (1926): [669]-70.

Davidson, H. E. "A Backward Look by the General Assistant." *Public Libraries* 30 (1925): 78-79.

Dawe, Grosvenor. *Melvil Dewey, Seer; Inspirier; Doer, 1851-1931.* Biografic Compilation. Club Ed. Lake Placid Club, N.Y.: Melvil Dewey Biografy, 1932.

Dewey, Adelbert M. *Life of George Dewey . . . and Dewey Family History.* Being an Authentic Historical and Genealogical Record . . . Westfield, Mass.: Dewey Publishing Co., 1898. Entry 4775: "Melvil Dewey."

Dewey, Godfrey. "Dewey, 1851-1951." *Library Journal* 76 (1951): 1964-65.

——————. ["Greetings to the American Library Association on Its Hundredth Anniversary"]. 1976. Cassette tape. (Transcribed in *American Libraries* 7 (1976): 501).

——————. "Sixty Years of Lake Placid Club." [Lake Placid Club, N.Y.: 1955?]

Dewey, Melvil. *[Answer to] Petition to the Regents of the State of New York [For the Removal from Office of Melvil Dewey, the Present State Librarian].* Lake Placid Club, N.Y.: 1905.

"Dewey, Melvil." *Dictionary of American Biography* XXI, Supplement I: (1935): 241-43. Written by H. M. Lydenberg.

"Dewey, Melvil." *Encyclopedia of Library and Information Science* VII (1972): 142-60. Written by Winifred B. Linderman.

"Dewey, Melvil [le Louis Kossuth]." *National Cyclopedia of American Biography* XXIII (1933): 14-15.

"Dewey, Melvil." *Who's Who in New York City and State.* 3d ed. New York City: L.R. Hammersly, 1907, p. 407.

"Dewey Chair at Columbia." *Library Journal* 63 (1938): 327.

"[Dewey's Retirement from the New York State Library. Editorial Comment]." *Library Journal* 31 (1906): 2.

Fellows, Dorkas. "Melvil Dewey." *Wilson Bulletin* 6 (1932): 482-84, 528.

Ferguson, Milton J. "Diamond Dewey." *DC Libraries* 22 (1951): 2-4.

Foster, William E. "Five Men of '76." *ALA Bulletin* 20 (1926): 312-23.

Friis-Hansen, J. B. "What Dewey Knew." *Libri* 26 (1976): 216-30.

Gambee, Budd L. "An 'Alien Body': Relationships between the Public Library and the Public Schools, 1876-1920." *Ball State University Library Science Lectures*, First Series (1973): 1-23.

——————. "The Great Junket: American Participation in the Conference of Librarians, London, 1877." *Journal of Library History* 2 (1967): 9-44.

——————. "The Role of American Librarians at the Second International Library Conference, London, 1897." *In Library History Seminar, Number 4,* edited by Harold Goldstein and John Goudeau. Tallahassee: Florida State University School of Library Science, 1972. pp. 52-85.

Garrison, Dee. "Tender Technicians: The Feminization of Public Librarianship, 1876-1905." *Journal of Social History* 6 (1973): 131-59.

Godard, George S. "Melvil Dewey, 1851-1931." *In Proceedings* of the National Association of State Libraries, (1931-32): 19-22.

Gray, Allison, " 'That Darned Literary Fellow Across the Lake'." *American Magazine* (1927): 56-59.

Grotzinger, Laurel A. "Melvil Dewey: the 'Sower'." *Journal of Library History* 3 (1968): 313-28.

Gunjal, S. R. "Melvil Dewey and His Achievements." *Herald of Library Science* 4 (1965): 39-45.

Gunther, Emma H. "Annie Godfrey Dewey, February 11, 1850-August 3, 1922." *Journal of Home Economics* 15 (1923): 357-67.

Harsha, David Addison. *Noted Living Albanians and State Officials.* A Series of Biographical Sketches. Albany, N.Y.: Weed, Parson, 1891. pp. 82-97: "Melvil Dewey."

Hassenforder, Jean. "Trois Pioniers des Bibliothèques Publiques: Edward Edwards, M. Dewey, Eugène Morel," *Education et Bibliothèque* no. 11 (1964): 11-40.

Hill, Frank Pierce. "Melvil Dewey: A Personal View." *ALA Bulletin* 26 (1932): 94-95.

Holley, Edward G. *Raking the Historic Coals: the A.L.A. Scrapbook of 1876.* [Urbana, Ill.] : Beta Phi Mu, 1967. (Chapbook no. 8).

"The Honorary Fiftieth Anniversary Committee . . . Melvil Dewey." *ALA Bulletin* 20 (1926): 167-69.

Horiuchi, Ikuko. "Melvil Dewey." *Library and Information Science* 12 (1974): 143-53.

Jast, Louis Stanley. "Recollections of Melvil Dewey." *Library Review* 31 (1934): 285-90.

Kennedy, R. F. "Who Was Melvil Dewey?" *Indian Librarian* 8 (June 1953): 8-13; *South African Libraries* 20 (1953): 97-100.

Kumar, P. S. G. "Dewey and Ranganathan: a Perspective." *Herald of Library Science* (1973): 163-68.

Kumar, P.S.G., ed. "Dewey Commemoration Number." *Herald of Library Science* 15 (1976) July-October Issue.

Lehnus, Donald J. *Milestones in Cataloging: Famous Catalogers and Their Writings, 1835-1969.* Littleton, Colorado: Libraries Unlimited, 1974.

"A Library Hall of Fame for the 75th Anniversary [of the American Library Association]." *Library Journal* 76 (1951): 466-72.

Linderman, Winifred B. "History of the Columbia University Libraries." Doctoral dissertation, Columbia University, 1959. Chapter 3: "Dewey the Organizer."

Maass, John. "Who Invented Dewey's Classification?" *Wilson Library Bulletin* 47 (1972): 335-41. Reprinted in William A. Katz and S. Gaherty. *Library Literature 4–The Best of 1973.* Metuchen, N.J.: Scarecrow Press, 1974. pp. 225-35. Responses are to be found in *Wilson Library Bulletin* 47(1973): 481; 734 and 48(1973): 127.

MacLeod, R. D. "Melvil Dewey and His Famous School." *Library Review* 35 (1960): 479-84.

Maddox, Lucy Jane. "Trends and Issues in American Librarianship as Reflected in the Papers and Proceedings of the American Library Association, 1876-1885." Doctoral dissertation, University of Michigan, 1958.

Magrath, Sister Gabriella. "Library Conventions of 1853, 1876, and 1877." *Journal of Library History* 8 (1973): 52-69.

Mahasai, K. M. D. R. "Melvil Dewey." *Modern Librarian* 2 (1932): 107-09.

McKinlay, John W. "025.43; or, Where Would We Be Without Melvil?" *Australian Library Journal* 25 (1976): 400-05.

"Melvil Dewey (1851-1931)." *In* John Leonard Thornton. *Mirror for Librarians.* London, Grafton, 1948. pp. 143-47.

"Melvil Dewey (1851-1931)." *In* John Leonard Thornton. *Selected Readings in the History of Librarianship.* 2d ed. London: Library Association, 1966. pp. 239-42.

"Melvil Dewey (1851-1931)." *Nature* 168 (1951): 981-82.

"Melvil Dewey Professorship of Library Service." *School & Society* 7 (1938): 532.

"Melvil Dewey [Tributes]." *Library Journal* 57 (1932): 145-58. Includes tributes from Arthur E. Bostwick, Nina E. Brown, George Watson Cole, Dorkas Fellows, Frank P. Hill, L. Stanley Jast, H. LaFontaine, Margaret Mann, *New York Times* (Editorial: Dec. 28, 1931), Herbert Putnam, Fremont Rider, and J. I. Wyer.

"Melvil Dewey." *Who's Who in New York City and State.* 5th biennial ed. New York: W. F. Brainard, 1911. p. 270.

"More Reminiscences of the 'Wellesley Half-Dozen'." *Columbia Library Columns* 3 (1954): 14-17.

"The New State Librarian." *Critic* 13 (1888): 319-20.

New York Library Association. "Library Week at Lake Placid. [Resolutions pertaining to Dewey]." *Public Libraries* 10 (1905): 485-86.

New York (State) Library School, Albany. *The First Quarter Century of the New York State Library School, 1887-1912.* [Albany]: New York State Library School, State of New York, Education Department, 1912.

New York State Library School Association. "[Letters Honoring Melvil Dewey on His 80th Birthday]." *Library School News Letter* 1 (December 1931): 6p.

_____. *New York State Library School Register, 1887-1926.* James I. Wyer Memorial Edition. New York: New York State Library Association, 1959.

O'Loughlin, Sister M. A. J. "Emergence of American Librarianship: A Study of Influence Evident in 1876." Doctoral dissertation, Columbia University, 1971.

Pollard, A. W. "Melvil Dewey." *The Library* 2:2 (1901): [337] -40.

Ranganathan, Sri R. "Melvil Dewey, the Father of Modern Librarianship." *Modern Librarian* 2 (1932): 129-30.

Rathbone, Josephine Adams. "Pioneers of the Library Profession." *Wilson Library Bulletin* 23: 775-79. "Melvil Dewey": pp. 775-76.

Rayward, W. Boyd. "Melvil Dewey and Education for Librarianship." *Journal of Library History* 3 (1968): 297-312.

Rider, Fremont. *Melvil Dewey.* Chicago: American Library Association, 1944. (American Library Pioneers, No. 6).

_____ . "Melvil Dewey, 10 December 1851-26 December 1931." In *New York State Library School Register, 1887-1926.* James I. Wyer Memorial Edition. New York: New York State Library School Association, 1959. pp. xxiii-xxviii.

Rockwood, Ruth H. "Melvil Dewey and Librarianship."*Journal of Library History* 3 (1968): 329-41.

Roseberry, Cecil R. *A History of the New York State Library.* Albany, N.Y.: New York State Library, State Education Department, University of the State of New York, 1970. pp. 53-80. At head of title: For the Government and People of This State.

Sayers, W. C. Berwick. "The Centenary of Melvil Dewey." *British Book News* 136 (1951): 749-53.

Takeuchi, Satoru. "Dewey in Florida." (Vignettes of Library History, No. 2), *Journal of Library History* 1 (1966): 127-32.

Tedder, H. R. "Mr. Melvil Dewey's Work at Columbia College." *Library Chronicle* 1 (1884): 186-91.

Thomison, Dennis. "The History and Development of the American Library Association, 1876-1947." Doctoral dissertation, University of Southern California, 1973.

Townsend, Reginald T. "A University Club in the Wilderness." *Country Life* 38 (1920): 50-53.

Trautman, Ray. *A History of the School of Library Service, Columbia University.* New York: Columbia University Press, 1954. (The Bicentennial History of Columbia University).

_____ . "Melvil Dewey and the 'Wellesley Half-Dozen'." *Columbia Library Columns* 3 (1954): 9-13.

Vann, Sarah K. *Training for Librarianship Before 1923; Education for Librarianship Prior to the Publication of Williamson's Report on Training for Library Service.* Chicago: American Library Association, 1961.

White, Carl L. *A Historical Introduction to Library Education: Problems and Progress to 1951.* Metuchen, N.J.: Scarecrow Press, 1976.

Williamson, Charles C. "Melvil Dewey, Creative Librarian." *In Fifty Years of Education for Librarianship.* Papers Presented for the Celebration of the Fiftieth Anniversary,of the University of Illinois Library School, March 2, 1943. Urbana, University of Illinois Press, 1943. pp. [1]-8.

Williamson, William L. *William Frederick Poole and the Modern Library Movement.* New York: Columbia University Press, 1963. (Columbia University Studies in Library Service, no. 13). Chapter 7: "The American Library Association."

Wyer, James I. "The New York State Library School. A Historical Sketch . . . With an Appreciation by Flora B. Ludington." *In New York State Library School Register, 1887-1926.* James I. Wyer Memorial Edition. New York: New York State Library School Association, 1959. pp. xi-xvi.

INDEX TO PART I AND PART II

Prepared by Ms. Maude Smith, Honolulu, Hawaii

Page references in italics refer to comments by the editor, both in Part I and Part II. Page references in medium type refer to writings in Part II only.